T0341193

Multi-Label Dimensionality Reduction

Chapman & Hall/CRC
Machine Learning & Pattern Recognition Series

SERIES EDITORS

Ralf Herbrich
Amazon Development Center
Berlin, Germany

Thore Graepel
Microsoft Research Ltd.
Cambridge, UK

AIMS AND SCOPE

This series reflects the latest advances and applications in machine learning and pattern recognition through the publication of a broad range of reference works, textbooks, and handbooks. The inclusion of concrete examples, applications, and methods is highly encouraged. The scope of the series includes, but is not limited to, titles in the areas of machine learning, pattern recognition, computational intelligence, robotics, computational/statistical learning theory, natural language processing, computer vision, game AI, game theory, neural networks, computational neuroscience, and other relevant topics, such as machine learning applied to bioinformatics or cognitive science, which might be proposed by potential contributors.

PUBLISHED TITLES

MACHINE LEARNING: An Algorithmic Perspective
Stephen Marsland

HANDBOOK OF NATURAL LANGUAGE PROCESSING,
Second Edition
Nitin Indurkhya and Fred J. Damerau

UTILITY-BASED LEARNING FROM DATA
Craig Friedman and Sven Sandow

A FIRST COURSE IN MACHINE LEARNING
Simon Rogers and Mark Girolami

COST-SENSITIVE MACHINE LEARNING
Balaji Krishnapuram, Shipeng Yu, and Bharat Rao

ENSEMBLE METHODS: FOUNDATIONS AND ALGORITHMS
Zhi-Hua Zhou

MULTI-LABEL DIMENSIONALITY REDUCTION
Liang Sun, Shuiwang Ji, and Jieping Ye

Chapman & Hall/CRC
Machine Learning & Pattern Recognition Series

Multi-Label Dimensionality Reduction

Liang Sun, Shuiwang Ji,
and Jieping Ye

CRC Press
Taylor & Francis Group
Boca Raton London New York

CRC Press is an imprint of the
Taylor & Francis Group, an **informa** business

A CHAPMAN & HALL BOOK

First published 2014 by Chapman and Hall/CRC Press

Published 2019 by CRC Press
Taylor & Francis Group
6000 Broken Sound Parkway NW, Suite 300
Boca Raton, FL 33487-2742

© 2014 by Taylor & Francis Group, LLC
CRC Press is an imprint of Taylor & Francis Group, an Informa business

No claim to original U.S. Government works

ISBN 13: 978-1-4398-0615-9 (hbk)

Visit the Taylor & Francis Web site at
http://www.taylorandfrancis.com

and the CRC Press Web site at
http://www.crcpress.com

Contents

Preface

Multi-label learning concerns supervised learning problems in which each instance may be associated with multiple labels simultaneously. A key difference between multi-label learning and traditional binary or multi-class learning is that the labels in multi-label learning are not mutually exclusive. Multi-label learning arises in many real-world applications. For example, in web page categorization, a web page may contain multiple topics. In gene and protein function prediction, multiple functional labels may be associated with each gene and protein, since an individual gene or protein usually performs multiple functions. In automated newswire categorization, multiple labels can be associated with a newswire story indicating its subject categories and the regional categories of reported events. Motivated by the increasing number of applications, multi-label learning has attracted significant attention in data mining and machine learning recently.

In comparison with traditional binary and multi-class classification, multi-label classification is more general and is thus more challenging to solve. One significant challenge in multi-label learning is how to effectively exploit the label structure to improve classification performance. Since the labels in multi-label learning are often correlated, how to measure and capture the correlations in the label space for improved prediction is crucial. This problem becomes particularly important when more sophisticated relations, such as hierarchical structures, exist among labels. Another challenge of multi-label learning lies in the class imbalance problem. When each label is modeled independently, the number of instances related to a specific label is much less than the number of instances that are not related to this label. In this case, it is difficult to build a highly accurate classifier for these labels without considering label correlations. The third challenge is concerned with the effectiveness and efficiency of multi-label learning for large-scale problems, especially when both the data dimensionality and the number of labels are large.

Similar to other data mining and machine learning tasks, multi-label learning also suffers from the so-called curse of dimensionality. Dimensionality reduction, which extracts a small number of features by removing irrelevant, redundant, and noisy information, is an effective way to mitigate the curse of dimensionality. Although dimensionality reduction has been well studied in the literature, we lack a unified treatment of multi-label dimensionality reduction that includes both algorithmic developments and applications. In this monograph, we give a selective treatment of dimensionality reduction for multi-label learning with emphasis on our own work. We cover a wide variety of topics, ranging from methodological developments to theoretical properties, computational algorithms, and applications. Specifically, this book focuses on the following fundamental research questions posed by multi-label dimensionality reduction: How to fully exploit label correlations for effective dimensionality reduction; How to scale dimensionality reduction algorithms to large-scale problems; How to effectively combine dimensionality reduction with classification; How to derive sparse dimensionality reduction algorithms to enhance model interpretability; How to perform multi-label dimensionality reduction effectively in practical applications. To expedite the applications of these algorithms, a MATLAB® software package that implements many popular dimensionality reduction algorithms is provided online at http://www.public.asu.edu/~jye02/Software/MLDR/. We hope that this book will appeal to both researchers and practitioners in diverse areas working on multi-label learning.

We would like to thank many people who have supported, encouraged, and inspired us during the preparation of this book. We are deeply indebted to Prof. Sudhir Kumar and his FlyExpress team, who provided support in the exploration of gene expression pattern image annotation. We would like to thank all former and current members of the machine learning research laboratory at Arizona State University, including Betul Ceran, Rita Chattopadhyay, Jianhui Chen, Pinghua Gong, Jun Liu, Yashu Liu, Zhi Nie, Qian Sun, Jie Wang, Zhen Wang, Shuo Xiang, Sen Yang, Lei Yuan, Zheng Zhao, Jiayu Zhou, and Chao Zhang. Each and every member of this dynamic group has helped us in various ways during numerous discussions and interactions. Many of our colleagues provided thoughtful reviews. We thank Jun Li, Shan Yang, Hang Zhang, and Hou Zhou for their feedback. We would like to thank anonymous reviewers for their constructive comments. We are grateful to the National Science Foundation for supporting our research on multi-label dimensionality reduction. Last but not least, we would like to thank our families for their love, understanding, and support.

Liang Sun   San Diego, California
Shuiwang Ji   Norfolk, Virginia
Jieping Ye   Tempe, Arizona

Symbol Description

x	Variable.	$\|\mathbf{A}\|_\infty$	∞-norm of matrix $\mathbf{A}$.
$\mathbf{x}$	Vector.	$\|\mathbf{A}\|_F$	Frobenius norm of matrix $\mathbf{A}$.
$\mathbf{A}$	Matrix.		
$\mathbb{R}$	The set of real numbers.	$\mathcal{N}(\boldsymbol{\mu}, \boldsymbol{\Sigma})$	Gaussian distribution with mean $\boldsymbol{\mu}$ and covariance $\boldsymbol{\Sigma}$.
$\mathbb{R}^n$	The set of real n-vectors ($n \times 1$ matrices).	$\text{diag}\,(\mathbf{v})$	Diagonal matrix with diagonal entries from $\mathbf{v}$.
$\mathbb{R}_+$	The set of nonnegative real numbers.	d	The data dimensionality.
$\mathbb{R}_{++}$	The set of positive real numbers.	n	The number of samples.
		k	The number of labels.
$\mathbb{S}^n$	The set of symmetric $n \times n$ matrices.	$\mathcal{X}$	Input instance space.
$\mathbb{S}^n_+$	The set of symmetric and positive semidefinite $n \times n$ matrices.	$\mathcal{Y}$	The label space $\{0,1\}^k$.
		$\mathfrak{L}$	The label set $\mathfrak{L} = \{C_1, \cdots, C_k\}$.
$\mathbb{S}^n_{++}$	The set of symmetric and positive definite $n \times n$ matrices.	$\mathcal{L}$	The normalized Laplacian matrix.
$\mathbf{1}$	The vector of ones.	$\mathbf{X}$	The data matrix $\mathbf{X} = [\mathbf{x}_1, \ldots, \mathbf{x}_n] \in \mathbb{R}^{d \times n}$, where $\mathbf{x}_i \in \mathbb{R}^d$ is the ith sample.
$\mathbf{0}$	The matrix or vector of all zeros.	$\mathbf{Y}$	The label matrix $\mathbf{Y} = [\mathbf{y}_1, \ldots, \mathbf{y}_n] \in \{0,1\}^{k \times n}$, where $\mathbf{y}_i \in \{0,1\}^k$ is the label information for the ith sample.
$\mathbf{I}$	The identity matrix.		
$\mathbf{A}^T$	The transpose of matrix $\mathbf{A}$.		
$\text{Tr}(\mathbf{A})$	The trace of matrix $\mathbf{A}$.		
$\mathbf{A}^\dagger$	The Moore-Penrose pseudoinverse of matrix $\mathbf{A}$.		
$\text{rank}(\mathbf{A})$	The rank of matrix $\mathbf{A}$.	$\mathbf{K}$	The kernel matrix.
$\mathcal{R}(\mathbf{A})$	The range space of matrix $\mathbf{A}$.	$\mathbf{A}_i$	The ith column of matrix $\mathbf{A}$.
		$\mathbf{A}^i$	The ith row of matrix $\mathbf{A}$.
$\mathcal{N}(\mathbf{A})$	The null space of matrix $\mathbf{A}$.	$\mathbb{E}[x]$	The expectation of variable x.
$\|\mathbf{v}\|$	A norm of vector $\mathbf{v}$.	$\mathbb{P}[e]$	The probability of event e.
$\|\mathbf{v}\|_1$	1-norm of vector $\mathbf{v}$.	$\text{std}(x)$	The standard deviation of variable x.
$\|\mathbf{v}\|_2$	2-norm of vector $\mathbf{v}$.		
$\|\mathbf{v}\|_\infty$	∞-norm of vector $\mathbf{v}$.	$\text{cov}(x,y)$	The covariance between variables x and y.
$\|\mathbf{A}\|$	A norm of matrix $\mathbf{A}$.		
$\|\mathbf{A}\|_1$	1-norm of matrix $\mathbf{A}$.	$\text{sgn}(x)$	The sign function.
$\|\mathbf{A}\|_2$	2-norm of matrix $\mathbf{A}$.	$|S|$	The cardinality of set S.

Chapter 1

Introduction

1.1 Introduction to Multi-Label Learning

Supervised learning is concerned with inferring the relations between input instances and class labels. In traditional classification tasks, each instance is associated with one class label. However, in many real-world scenarios, one instance may be associated with multiple labels. For example, in news categorization, a piece of news regarding Apple's release of a new iPhone is associated with both the label *business* and the label *technology*. In other words, each instance is associated with a set of labels instead of only one label. Multi-label learning is a machine learning field devoted to learning from multi-label data in which each instance is associated with potentially multiple labels. A major difference between multi-label learning and traditional binary or multi-class learning is that the labels in multi-label learning are not mutually exclusive, suggesting that each instance may be relevant to multiple labels. Thus, one of the key challenges of multi-label learning is how to exploit the correlations among different labels effectively.

In this book, we assume that each instance in the training set is represented as a pair of vectors, one for the input features and the other for the output labels. Multi-label learning concerns the prediction of the labels of unseen instances by building a classifier based on the training data. Formally, let $\mathcal{X}$ and $\mathcal{Y}$ denote the input instance space and the output label space, respectively. In multi-label learning, the label space $\mathcal{Y}$ is defined as $\mathcal{Y} = \{0, 1\}^k$, where k is the number of labels. That is, the jth component of the label vector is 1 if the instance is relevant to the jth label, and it is 0 otherwise. Similar to traditional classification, given a training data set, the goal of multi-label learning is to learn a classifier $f : \mathcal{X} \to \mathcal{Y}$, which predicts the labels of each instance $\mathbf{x} \in \mathcal{X}$. Specifically, the output of the classifier f for a given instance $\mathbf{x} \in \mathcal{X}$ is

$$f(\mathbf{x}) = [f_1(\mathbf{x}), f_2(\mathbf{x}), \cdots, f_k(\mathbf{x})]^T, \tag{1.1}$$

where $f_j(\mathbf{x})$ $(j = 1, \cdots, k)$ is either 1 or 0, indicating the association of $\mathbf{x}$ with the jth label. In the following, the set of labels is denoted as $\mathfrak{L} = \{C_1, \cdots, C_k\}$.

Multi-label learning finds applications in many real-world applications, such as text categorization [167, 279], image annotation [34, 126], bioinformatics [28, 279], 3D hand pose estimation [216], and biological literature classification [128]. Motivated by the increasing number of applications, multi-label learning has recently attracted significant attention, and many algorithms have been proposed [190, 235,

237]. These methods are reviewed in Section 1.4 and can be divided into two major categories:

1. *Problem transformation*: This class of methods first transforms the multi-label learning problem into a series of single-label problems, which are then solved using existing single-label learning methods.

2. *Algorithm adaptation*: This class of methods solves the multi-label problems directly by adapting existing methods for single-label learning.

Similar to other machine learning and data mining tasks, multi-label learning also suffers from the so-called *curse of dimensionality* [21]. Although there has been extensive research on dimensionality reduction in the literature, multi-label dimensionality reduction has not been well explored [8, 273, 280]. This book is devoted to the study of *multi-label dimensionality reduction*, which focuses on extracting a small number of features from multi-label data by removing the irrelevant, redundant, and noisy information while exploiting information from the label space such as the correlation among different labels. Specifically, we give a unified treatment of multi-label dimensionality reduction approaches in methodological developments, theoretical properties, computational algorithms, and applications.

In the rest of this chapter, we will briefly introduce multi-label learning and dimensionality reduction, including existing algorithms, applications, and related work. We will also highlight the main challenges of multi-label dimensionality reduction.

1.2   Applications of Multi-Label Learning

Multi-label learning has been applied successfully in many real-world applications. In this section, we present several representative examples, including scene classification, text categorization, functional genomics analysis, and gene expression pattern image annotation.

1.2.1   Scene Classification

Humans are very proficient at perceiving natural scenes and understanding their contents. In scene classification, the task is to determine the associated semantic labels, such as *mountain*, *lake*, or *party*, for given images. Scene classification finds applications in many areas, including content-based image indexing and content-sensitive image enhancement [34]. For example, many current digital library systems support content-based image retrieval, which allows the user to retrieve images that are similar to a given query image [105]. In this case, knowledge of the semantic labels of the query image can reduce the search space and improve the retrieval

(A) Scene 1   (B) Scene 2

FIGURE 1.1: Examples of multi-label scenes. The first scene (A) is associated with the labels "*lake*" and "*mountain*", and the second scene (B) is associated with the labels "*river*" and "*mountain*".

accuracy. Since a natural scene may contain multiple objects, each image can be associated with multiple labels. Hence, scene classification is naturally a multi-label learning problem. For example, Figure 1.1(A) shows an image associated with the labels "*lake*" and "*mountain*"; Figure 1.1(B) shows an image associated with the labels "*river*" and "*mountain*".

1.2.2   Text Categorization

Text Categorization (TC) is the task of classifying text documents into one or more of a set of predefined categories or subject codes [131, 208]. Originally dating back to the early 1960s, the effectiveness of text categorization has been improved significantly in the past decades mainly due to the advances of machine learning methods [131]. Text categorization has been applied in various fields, including web page categorization using hierarchical labels, detection of text genre, text (or hypertext) documents classification given a predefined label set, personalized information delivery, and content filtering [208]. Typically, the predefined labels (or categories) in text categorization are not assumed to be mutually exclusive; thus text categorization can naturally be modeled as a multi-label learning problem. For instance, consider labels *business, technology, entertainment,* and *politics* in news categorization; a news article about Apple's release of a new iPhone may be labeled with both the label *business* and the label *technology*.

When applying multi-label learning to perform text categorization, the first step is to encode documents using a suitable representation, such as the ones based on the vector space model [279] and the binary representation [140]. In the past, many multi-label learning algorithms have been proposed to perform text categorization [87, 136, 167, 206, 240, 279]. One well-known algorithm in text categorization is BoosTexter, which extends the classical boosting algorithm AdaBoost [80] to handle multi-label data. Some other algorithms include the Bayesian approach [167] using the mixture model coupled with the Expectation–Maximization (EM) algorithm, and the Maximal Figure-of-Merit (MFoM) approach [87]. We will review existing multi-label learning approaches in Section 1.4.

One widely used benchmark data set in multi-label text categorization is the Reuters-21578 data set[1]. This data set was originally collected and labeled by the Carnegie Group, Inc. and Reuters, Ltd. in the course of developing the CONSTRUE text categorization system. Reuters-21578 consists of 21,578 Reuters newswire documents that appeared in 1987. Almost all documents in the Reuters collection come with title, dateline, and text body, and the number of topics (labels) is 135. In particular, three widely used subsets of the Reuters-21578 data set have been extracted [140] by identifying the labels that suggest parent–child relationships, and the labels are organized in a hierarchical structure, as shown in Figure 1.2. Note that the roots of the three category trees are virtual categories.

Another data set that has become very popular for text categorization in recent years is the Reuters Corpus Volume 1 (RCV1) data set[2] [155]. The RCV1 data set consists of over 800,000 manually categorized newswire stories recently made available by Reuters, Ltd. for research purposes. Similar to the Reuters-21578 data set, the labels in the RCV1 data set are organized in a hierarchical structure. The original data set is referred to as RCV1-v1, and a corrected version called RCV1-v2 was generated and has become more popular in text categorization research. More details on this data set can be found in [155].

1.2.3 Functional Genomics Analysis

Functional genomics is an important field in bioinformatics. It studies gene and protein functions by conducting large-scale analysis on a vast amount of data collected by genome projects [123, 159]. For example, DNA microarrays allow researchers to simultaneously measure the expression levels of thousands of different genes, and overwhelming amounts of data are produced [161]. Recently, a large body of research has been devoted to automatic analysis of microarray data [159]. In automated gene expression analysis, the task is to predict the functions for genes. Generally, it is based on the assumption that genes with similar functions have similar expression profiles in cells [123]. Note that each gene may be associated with multiple functions in functional genomics. When the functions are considered as labels, the function prediction problem in functional genomics can be modeled as a multi-label learning problem.

A widely used benchmark data set in multi-label learning for functional genomics is the Yeast data set [38, 74]. The Yeast data set consists of microarray expression data and phylogenetic profiles from the budding yeast *Saccharomyces cerevisiae*. It contains 2417 samples, and each sample is represented as a 103-dimensional feature vector[3]. Each sample (gene) is associated with a subset of a total of 190 functional labels. The functional classes (labels) are organized in a tree structure, which is known in the literature [38, 74]. This data set is preprocessed in [74] and only the function

---

[1] http://www.research.att.com/~lewis/reuters21578.html

[2] http://www.daviddlewis.com/resources/testcollections/rcv1/

[3] http://www.csie.ntu.edu.tw/~cjlin/libsvmtools/datasets/multilabel.html#yeast

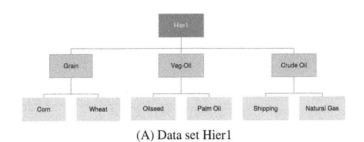

(A) Data set Hier1

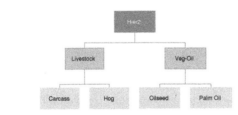

(B) Date set Hier2

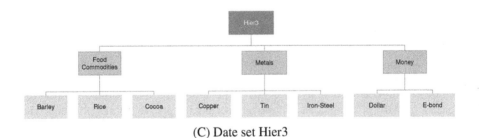

(C) Date set Hier3

FIGURE 1.2: The label structures in the Reuters-21578 data set.

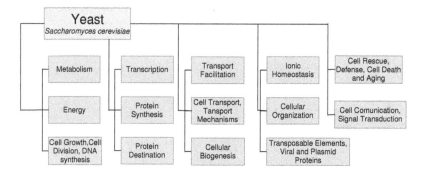

FIGURE 1.3: The labels selected in the Yeast data set.

classes in the top hierarchy are selected, resulting in a total of 14 labels, as shown in Figure 1.3.

1.2.4 Gene Expression Pattern Image Annotation

Detailed knowledge of the expression and interaction of genes is crucial to deciphering the mechanisms underlying cell-fate specification and tissue differentiation. The fruit fly *Drosophila melanogaster* is one of the model organisms in developmental biology, and its patterns of gene expression have been studied extensively [6, 42, 151, 231]. The comprehensive atlas of spatial expression patterns during *Drosophila* embryogenesis has been produced by *in situ* hybridization techniques and documented in the form of digital images [101, 108, 231, 242]. Comparative analysis of gene expression pattern images can potentially reveal new genetic interactions and yield insights into the complex regulatory networks governing embryonic development [75, 144, 183, 231].

To facilitate pattern comparison and searching, the images of *Drosophila* gene expression patterns are annotated with anatomical and developmental ontology terms from a controlled vocabulary [101, 231]. The annotation is performed not only for each terminally differentiated embryonic structure but also for the developmental intermediates that correspond to it. Four general classes of terms, called anlage *in statu nascendi*, anlage, primordium, and organ (ordered in terms of developmental time), are used in the annotation. Such an elaborate naming scheme describes a developing "path", starting from the cellular blastoderm stage until organs are formed, that documents the dynamic process of *Drosophila* embryogenesis. Due to the overwhelming complexity of this task, the images are currently annotated manually by human experts. However, the number of available images produced by high-throughput *in situ* hybridization is now rapidly increasing [103, 144, 183, 232, 272]. It is therefore tempting to design computational methods for the automated annotation of gene expression patterns.

The annotated terms from the controlled vocabulary can be considered as labels in multi-label classification. Since a variable number of terms from the controlled vocabulary can be assigned to a group of images, the problem of gene expression pattern annotation can be modeled as a multi-label learning problem. In the current image database, annotation terms are associated with a group of patterns sharing a subset of the named structures. Thus, the difficulty of this problem lies in the fact that the labels (annotation terms) are assigned to groups of patterns rather than to individual images. Figure 1.4 shows sample *Drosophila* gene expression pattern images and their corresponding annotated terms.

Stage range	BDGP terms
4–6	dorsal ectoderm anlage in statu nascendi
	mesectoderm anlage in statu nascendi
	segmentally repeated
	trunk mesoderm anlage in statu nascendi
	ventral ectoderm anlage in statu nascendi
7–8	dorsal ectoderm primordium
	hindgut anlage
	mesectoderm primordium
	procephalic ectoderm anlage
	trunk mesoderm primordium P2
	ventral ectoderm primordium P2
9–10	inclusive hindgut primordium
	mesectoderm primordium
	procephalic ectoderm primordium
	trunk mesoderm primordium
	ventral ectoderm primordium
11–12	atrium primordium
	brain primordium
	clypeo-labral primordium
	dorsal epidermis primordium
	gnathal primordium
	head epidermis primordium P1
	hindgut proper primordium
	midline primordium
	ventral epidermis primordium
	ventral nerve cord primordium

FIGURE 1.4: Sample image groups and their associated terms (class labels) in the BDGP database (http://www.fruitfly.org) for the segmentation gene *engrailed* in 4 stage ranges.

1.3 Challenges of Multi-Label Learning

In comparison with traditional binary and multi-class classification, the generality of multi-label classification makes it more challenging to solve. In the following, we describe some fundamental challenges in the successful application of multi-label learning in real-world problems.

The first challenge lies in how to effectively exploit the label structure to improve the classification performance. In multi-label learning, the labels are often correlated since they are not mutually exclusive. In this case, how to measure and capture the correlations in the label space for improved prediction is crucial. Many methods have been proposed in the literature to capture the label correlations [134, 219, 224, 237, 278]. However, how to effectively make use of the correlations in the label space still remains an open question. Furthermore, as we discussed in Section 1.2, in some applications of text categorization and bioinformatics, the labels are organized in a hierarchical structure or as a Directed Acyclic Graph (DAG). It is expected that taking advantage of such structures can lead to improved classification performance. For example, in a general-to-specific label tree structure, an instance associated with a specific label should also be associated with its parent label. How to effectively use these complex structures in specific applications also remains a challenging research question [213].

The second challenge of multi-label learning lies in the class imbalance problem. When each label is treated independently, it is often the case that most instances are irrelevant to a specific label. Since the number of positive instances for some labels is significantly less than the number of negative instances, it is difficult to build a highly accurate classifier for these labels without considering the label correlations. Thus, a fundamental research question is how to accurately classify these rare classes given their limited numbers of positive training instances. In addition, the class imbalance problem becomes worse when the number of labels is relatively large.

The third challenge is concerned with the effectiveness and efficiency of multi-label learning for large-scale problems, especially when both the data dimensionality and the number of labels are large. Multi-label learning also suffers from the curse of dimensionality, and many existing multi-label learning methods are less effective for high-dimensional data, since data points become sparse and far apart from each other in high-dimensional space. We will provide more details on learning from high-dimensional data in the context of multi-label learning in Section 1.5. In addition, the computational cost increases as the number of labels increases. For example, the Binary Relevance (BR) and Label Power-Set (LP) methods, discussed in the next subsection, are restricted to problems with a relatively small label size. Recently, some methods have been proposed [118, 226, 236] to deal with a large number of labels. For example, the dimensionality of the label space is reduced by using a random projection in [118]. Moreover, when the number of labels is large, it becomes difficult to maintain a large number of prediction models in memory [237].

1.4 State of the Art

In this section we give a brief review of the state-of-the-art multi-label learning methods in the literature. Existing methods can be divided into two major categories [237], i.e., problem transformation and algorithm adaptation. In the first approach, the multi-label learning problem is transformed into a series of single-label classification problems so that existing single-label learning algorithms can be readily applied. The second approach, i.e., algorithm adaptation, adapts existing single-label classification algorithms to handle multi-label classification directly. In [278], the methods are categorized based on the order of correlations among labels used in the algorithm. Specifically, the first-order approach only decomposes the multi-label learning problem into a sequence of independent binary classification problems; the second-order approach considers the pairwise relations between labels; the higher-order approach considers the higher-order relations among labels.

Besides classification tasks, another popular problem in multi-label learning is label ranking (LR) [37], which learns an ordering of the labels based on their relevance to a given instance. In this book we mainly focus on multi-label classification. More details on the connections between multi-label classification and label ranking can be found in [237]. In the following, we will introduce problem transformation and algorithm adaptation in detail.

1.4.1 Problem Transformation

A straightforward approach to handling multi-label classification tasks is to transform them into a series of single-label classification problems so that existing methods for single-label classification can be applied. The key idea is to eliminate the label overlapping in the original label space. Compared with the algorithm adaptation scheme, the problem transformation scheme is more flexible since any off-the-shelf single-label classifier can be applied after problem transformation. In this subsection, we will introduce three different transformation schemes, including COpy transformation (CO), BR, and LP.

1.4.1.1 Copy Transformation

CO converts the multi-label problem into a multi-class problem by performing a transformation on the data set. Specifically, for each example $(\mathbf{x}_i, \mathbf{y}_i)$ in the original multi-label problem, we replace it with a set of new examples $\{(\mathbf{x}_i, C_j) | \mathbf{y}_i(j) = 1\}$. In other words, a new example $(\mathbf{x}_i, C_j)$ is generated if $\mathbf{x}_i$ is associated with label C_j in the original multi-label problem. Some variation of this transform also adds some weight for the new instances, e.g., $1/\sum_j \mathbf{y}_i(j)$, for each new example generated from the original example $(\mathbf{x}_i, \mathbf{y}_i)$. By applying copy transformation, the original multi-label learning problem is transformed into a multi-class classification problem. The copy transformation of a toy multi-label learning problem is illustrated in Figure 1.5.

1.4.1.2 Binary Relevance

BR, or the one-against-all approach, is the most well-known and most commonly used transformation approach for multi-label learning in the literature [37,237]. It has been used widely as a baseline method to evaluate the performance of multi-label learning algorithms. Specifically, BR learns k binary classifiers for all labels in $\mathfrak{L} = \{C_1, \cdots, C_k\}$ independently. For each label C_j, it uses all instances associated with it as the positive training samples and the remaining instances as negative samples. Based on the new training data set, a classifier f_j is learned for the label C_j. After learning k classifiers $\{f_1, \cdots, f_k\}$ for all k labels, the prediction for a new instance $\mathbf{x}$ is given by $f(\mathbf{x}) = [f_1(\mathbf{x}), f_2(\mathbf{x}), \cdots, f_k(\mathbf{x})]^T$.

Binary relevance is a straightforward transformation approach and can be combined with many state-of-the-art binary classification algorithms such as Support Vector Machines (SVM) and Artificial Neural Networks (ANN). The drawback of binary relevance is that it does not consider the label correlations in the transformation as all labels are treated independently. In addition, when the number of labels is large, it may not scale to large-size data sets since a binary classifier is learned for each label. Binary relevance also suffers from the class imbalance problem, i.e., the number of positive instances is significantly less than the number of negative instances for some labels. The binary relevance transformation of a toy multi-label learning problem is illustrated in Figure 1.5.

1.4.1.3 Label Power-Set

Another popular approach in this category is the LP method [34], which treats each distinct label combination in the multi-label training data as a new label. As a result, the multi-label problem can be transformed into a series of single-label classification problems. Given a new data instance, LP will output the most probable class, i.e., a set of labels in the original problem.

Compared with the copy transformation and the binary relevance methods, label power-set transformation considers the correlations and dependencies among different labels explicitly. One drawback of label power-set transformation is that the label combinations that do not appear in the training data are not considered in making predictions. In addition, label power-set transformation is computationally expensive since the number of label combinations increases exponentially with the number of labels. In the worst case, the number of labels after LP transformation is $2^k - 1$ $(k \geq 2)$. Furthermore, many of these new labels tend to be very sparse, which leads to a very severe class imbalance problem due to the fact that many of these new labels are only associated with a limited number of instances. The label power-set transformation of a toy multi-label learning problem is illustrated in Figure 1.5.

Besides the three classical transformation approaches, some novel transformation methods that combine both binary relevance and label power-set have also been studied in the literature recently [227].

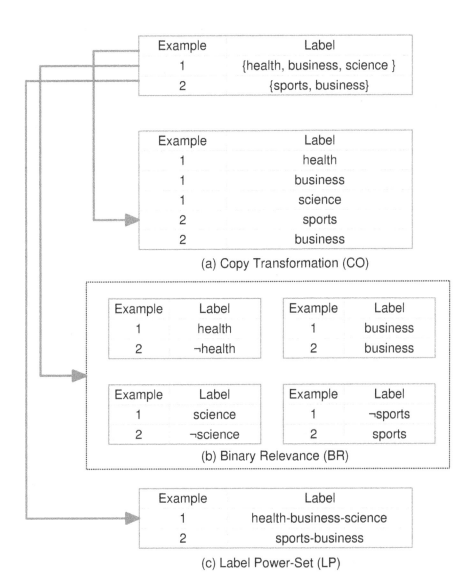

Example	Label
1	{health, business, science }
2	{sports, business}

Example	Label
1	health
1	business
1	science
2	sports
2	business

(a) Copy Transformation (CO)

Example	Label
1	health
2	¬health

Example	Label
1	business
2	business

Example	Label
1	science
2	¬science

Example	Label
1	¬sports
2	sports

(b) Binary Relevance (BR)

Example	Label
1	health-business-science
2	sports-business

(c) Label Power-Set (LP)

FIGURE 1.5: Illustration of different transformations of a toy multi-label learning problem.

1.4.1.4   Single-Label Classification after Transformation

After label transformation, some single-label classification methods can be applied to predict the final labels of new data instances. Some well-known single-label methods include SVM, decision trees, k-nearest neighbors, naive Bayes classifier, artificial neural networks, etc. [249]. The performance of different single-label classification methods after label transformation is compared in [190] and [249].

1.4.2   Algorithm Adaptation

In this subsection, we review multi-label learning methods that adapt existing single-label classification approaches. One key research question in algorithm adaptation is how to improve prediction performance by considering the correlations among different labels in the label space.

1.4.2.1   Decision Tree

In [55], the classical decision tree algorithm C4.5 is adapted to handle multi-label problems. For a given data set, the entropy is modified to consider instances associated with multiple labels. Formally, given a set of instances associated with multiple labels $\mathfrak{L} = \{C_1, \ldots, C_k\}$, the entropy is defined as

$$\text{Entropy}(\mathfrak{L}) \stackrel{\triangle}{=} -\sum_{i=1}^{k} \left(\mathbb{P}(C_i) \log \mathbb{P}(C_i) + (1 - \mathbb{P}(C_i) \log(1 - \mathbb{P}(C_i)))\right), \quad (1.2)$$

where $\mathbb{P}(C_i)$ is the probability (relative frequency) of class C_i, and $1 - \mathbb{P}(C_i)$ is the probability of not being a member of class C_i.

Following the rule of maximum information gain, defined as the difference of entropy after splitting, we can construct a decision tree to handle the multi-label data set. Note that in multi-label learning we allow the leaves of the tree to be a set of labels, i.e., the outcome of a classification of an instance can be a set of labels. In [28], the entropy is further extended to handle hierarchial multi-label classification, where the labels are organized in a hierarchical structure.

1.4.2.2   Algorithms Based on Probabilistic Framework

In [167], a Bayesian approach is proposed for multi-label classification. Specifically, a probabilistic generative model is constructed to model multiple labels associated with each document. The words in a document are generated by a mixture of word distributions, one for each topic (label). The generative model first selects a set of classes (instead of only one class) associated with this document; it then produces a set of mixture weights for these selected classes. Based on these weights we can generate each word in the document as follows: we first select a class for this document using these weights and then generate a single word based on the selected class. In classification, the Bayes rule is applied to predict the most probable class set given the document. In parameter estimation, the EM algorithm is applied to learn the distribution over mixture weights and the word distribution in each class's mixture component. Compared with single-label classification algorithms, the proposed generative model explicitly takes the label correlations into account.

Two types of generative models called Parametric Mixture Models (PMMs) are proposed in [240] for multi-label text categorization. The basic assumption of PMMs is very similar to that in [167]. That is, the words in a document belonging to a label set can be modeled as a mixture of characteristic words related to each of these labels. For example, a document that belongs to both "*sports*" and "*music*" would consist of a mixture of characteristic words mainly related to both categories. In addition, efficient learning and prediction algorithms for PMMs are proposed in [240]. Both generative models proposed in [167] and [240] are only applicable for text categorization.

1.4.2.3 Support Vector Machines

In [74], an algorithm based on SVM called RankSVM is proposed. RankSVM tries to control the model complexity while minimizing the empirical error. In fact, it shares a lot of common properties with SVM. The key idea of the RankSVM algorithm is to use a novel ranking loss function to capture the characteristics of the multi-label learning problem and then solve the resulting optimization problem accordingly.

Formally, for each label C_j, we construct a linear model

$$f_j(\mathbf{x}_i) = \text{sgn}(\mathbf{w}_j^T \mathbf{x}_i + \mathbf{b}_j).$$

Next we consider the ith sample $(\mathbf{x}_i, \mathbf{y}_i)$ in the training data set, where $\mathbf{x}_i \in \mathbb{R}^d$ and its corresponding label vector $\mathbf{y}_i \in \mathbb{R}^k$ is

$$\mathbf{y}_i = [\mathbf{y}_i(1), \mathbf{y}_i(2), \dots, \mathbf{y}_i(k)]^T,$$

where $\mathbf{y}_i(j)$ is either 1 or 0, indicating the association of $\mathbf{x}_i$ with the jth label. Let $\mathbf{Y}_i = \{j | \mathbf{y}_i(j) = 1\}$ and $\bar{\mathbf{Y}}_i = \{j | \mathbf{y}_i(j) = 0\}$, i.e., $\mathbf{Y}_i$ contains the label indices associated with $\mathbf{x}_i$, and $\bar{\mathbf{Y}}_i$ contains the label indices not associated with $\mathbf{x}_i$. Let the output of the k linear models be $f(\mathbf{x}_i) = [f_1(\mathbf{x}_i)), f_2(\mathbf{x}_i), \dots, f_k(\mathbf{x}_i)]^T$. The ranking loss function over $(\mathbf{x}_i, \mathbf{y}_i)$ is defined as

$$RL(f, \mathbf{x}_i, \mathbf{y}_i) = \sum_{i=1}^{n} \frac{1}{|\mathbf{Y}_i||\bar{\mathbf{Y}}_i|} \left| (q, l) \in (\mathbf{Y}_i \times \bar{\mathbf{Y}}_i) \text{ s.t. } f_q(\mathbf{x}_i) \le f_l(\mathbf{x}_i) \right|. \quad (1.3)$$

Note that in Eq. (1.3) we use the index q to denote the label index associated with $\mathbf{x}_i$ and use the index l to denote the label index not associated with $\mathbf{x}_i$. Also note that there are $|\mathbf{Y}_i||\bar{\mathbf{Y}}_i|$ pairs of labels with one associated with $\mathbf{x}_i$ and the other not associated with $\mathbf{x}_i$; thus we use $\frac{1}{|\mathbf{Y}_i||\bar{\mathbf{Y}}_i|}$ to normalize the error. As a result, $RL(f, \mathbf{x}_i, \mathbf{y}_i)$ measures the average fraction of pairs which are not ordered correctly.

The basic idea of RankSVM is to find a series of linear models

$$\{f_1(\mathbf{x}), f_2(\mathbf{x}), \cdots, f_k(\mathbf{x})\}$$

such that the ranking loss function is minimized while a large margin is also achieved. In multi-label learning, the margin of $(\mathbf{x}_i, \mathbf{y}_i)$ is defined as

$$\min_{q \in \mathbf{Y}_i, l \in \bar{\mathbf{Y}}_i} \frac{(\mathbf{w}_q - \mathbf{w}_l)^T \mathbf{x}_i + \mathbf{b}_q - \mathbf{b}_l}{\|\mathbf{w}_q - \mathbf{w}_l\|_2}. \tag{1.4}$$

In fact, this is the signed ℓ_2 distance of $\mathbf{x}_i$ to the decision boundary. Similar to SVM, an optimization problem can be formulated and solved. In the above discussion, we focus on linear models. These linear models can be extended to the kernel-induced feature space by applying the kernel trick [207].

In [93], two methods for enhancing existing discriminative classifiers for multi-label classification are proposed. Specifically, the first one exploits label correlations by combining text features and information about relationships between classes in constructing a new kernel for SVMs with heterogeneous features. The second one improves the margin of SVMs for more accurate multi-label classification.

1.4.2.4 Artificial Neural Networks

In [279], a neural network algorithm known as BackPropagation for Multi-Label Learning (BP-MLL) is proposed. It extends the backpropagation algorithm by defining a novel error function that captures the characteristics of multi-label learning. Based on the proposed error function, the resulting minimization problem can be solved by gradient descent combined with the error backpropagation strategy [200]. Specifically, given the training data set $\{(\mathbf{x}_1, \mathbf{y}_1), (\mathbf{x}_2, \mathbf{y}_2), \ldots, (\mathbf{x}_n, \mathbf{y}_n)\}$, let the output of the neural network be $\{f(\mathbf{x}_1), f(\mathbf{x}_2), \ldots, f(\mathbf{x}_n)\}$ where $\mathbf{y}_i = [\mathbf{y}_i(1), \mathbf{y}_i(2), \ldots, \mathbf{y}_i(k)]^T$, $f(\mathbf{x}_i) = [f_1(\mathbf{x}_i)), f_2(\mathbf{x}_i), \cdots, f_k(\mathbf{x}_i)]^T$, and $\mathbf{y}_i(j)$ is either 1 or 0. Then the novel error function for multi-label learning in [279] is defined as

$$E_z \overset{\triangle}{=} \sum_{i=1}^{n} E(\mathbf{x}_i), \tag{1.5}$$

where $E(\mathbf{x}_i)$ is defined as

$$E(\mathbf{x}_i) \overset{\triangle}{=} \sum_{i=1}^{n} \frac{1}{|\mathbf{Y}_i||\bar{\mathbf{Y}}_i|} \sum_{q \in \in \mathbf{Y}_i, l \in \bar{\mathbf{Y}}_i} \exp\left(-(f_q(\mathbf{x}_i) - f_l(\mathbf{x}_i))\right). \tag{1.6}$$

In Eq. (1.6), $\mathbf{Y}_i = \{j | \mathbf{y}_i(j) = 1\}$ and $\bar{\mathbf{Y}}_i = \{j | \mathbf{y}_i(j) = 0\}$, i.e., $\mathbf{Y}_i$ contains the label indices associated with $\mathbf{x}_i$ and $\bar{\mathbf{Y}}_i$ contains the label indices not associated with $\mathbf{x}_i$. In Eq. (1.6) we also use the index q to denote the label index associated with $\mathbf{x}_i$ and the index l to denote the label index not associated with $\mathbf{x}_i$. As a result, $f_q(\mathbf{x}_i) - f_l(\mathbf{x}_i)$ measures the difference between the outputs of the network on one label belonging to $\mathbf{x}_i$ and the other label not belonging to it. Clearly, a larger difference between $f_q(\mathbf{x}_i)$ and $f_l(\mathbf{x}_i)$ leads to better classification performance. In Eq. (1.6) the exponential function is employed to penalize the difference if $f_q(\mathbf{x}_i)$ is much smaller than $f_l(\mathbf{x}_i)$ and make the error function smooth. Similar to Eq. (1.3), we use $\frac{1}{|\mathbf{Y}_i||\overline{\mathbf{Y}_i}|}$ to normalize the loss. Similar to RankSVM, the intuitive idea behind this error function is that the labels associated with an instance should be ranked higher than those not associated with that instance.

1.4.2.5 k-Nearest Neighbor

In [276], a lazy learning algorithm called Multi-Label k-Nearest Neighbor (ML-kNN) is proposed by extending the k-Nearest Neighbor (kNN) to handle multi-label data. The basic idea of ML-kNN is very similar to the traditional kNN. Specifically, the k nearest neighbors of an unseen instance are identified first in ML-kNN. Based on the statistical information gained from the label sets of these neighboring instances, the maximum a posterior is applied to predict the label set for the unseen instance. Compared with traditional kNN, one advantage of ML-kNN is that the prior probabilities can be incorporated into the estimation. In [253], a novel class balanced kNN approach for multi-label classification is proposed by emphasizing a balanced usage of data from all classes.

In [50], a multi-label learning algorithm that unifies the kNN and logistic regression is proposed. A key idea of this approach is that the labels of neighboring instances are considered as new features for a new query instance.

1.4.2.6 Ensemble Learning

Ensemble learning methods, such as the boosting algorithm, have been extended to handle multi-label data. The basic idea of boosting is to combine many simple and less accurate classifiers called weak classifiers into a single highly accurate classifier. Generally, the weak classifiers are trained sequentially so that the classifiers built at later stages concentrate more on the instances misclassified by earlier classifiers. The AdaBoost is the simplest version of boosting for single-label classification. This method maintains a set of importance weights over training examples so that the weak classifiers can concentrate on those examples that are difficult to classify.

BoosTexter [206] extends the AdaBoost algorithm [80] to multi-label learning. BoosTexter maintains a set of weights over both training examples and labels to handle multiple labels. In the boosting process, training examples and their corresponding labels that are difficult to classify get incrementally higher weights while examples and labels that are easy to classify get lower weights. In other words, we force the weak learning algorithm to focus on the combination of examples and labels that are difficult to predict and thus improve the overall performance of the ensemble method. Specifically, two different extensions of AdaBoost have been proposed [206]. The first extension, AdaBoost.MH, focuses on the correct prediction of labels while the second one, AdaBoost.MR, focuses on consistency in label ranking.

As discussed in Section 1.4.1.3, the label power-set transformation explicitly considers the label correlations. Unfortunately, it suffers from the huge number of new labels and the majority of them are associated with very few positive samples. To overcome the limitations of the label power-set transformation, the RAndom k-labELsets (RAKEL) algorithm [238] based on the ensemble method was proposed recently. Given the label set $\mathfrak{L} = \{C_1, C_2, \ldots, C_k\}$, a set $S \subseteq \mathfrak{L}$ with $|S| = q$

is called a q-labelset. The set of all distinct q-labelsets on $\mathfrak{L}$ is denoted as $\mathfrak{L}^q$. The RAKEL algorithm iteratively constructs a single-label weak learner from $\mathcal{X}$ to the selected q-labelset. Specifically, in the pth iteration of RAKEL, a q-labelset S_p is selected randomly from $\mathfrak{L}^q$ without replacement. Then the weak learner constructs a single-label classifier $h_p : \mathcal{X} \rightarrow S_p$. Two parameters are specified by the user, i.e., the size of label set q and the number of iterations in RAKEL. It has been shown in [238] that RAKEL can model label correlations effectively by using small q and an adequate number of iterations. For the prediction of a new instance $\mathbf{x}$, we first apply all weak learners to obtain the binary decisions for all q-labelsets. Then RAKEL computes a ranking of all original labels by averaging the predictions of all weak learners. The final positive decision for a specific original label is made if the average is greater than a user-specified threshold. Although RAKEL explicitly considers the label correlations, one disadvantage is its inefficiency. In the current RAKEL algorithm, random selection is used to speed up the computation. Hence, parameter selection is also an open research question.

In [268], a multi-label learning algorithm called Model-Shared Subspace Boosting (MSSBoost) is proposed to reduce the information redundancy in the learning process. Specifically, it learns a number of base models across multiple labels, and each model is based on a random feature subspace and bootstrap data samples. By combining these shared subspace models, the decision function for each label can be jointly estimated. Recently, ensemble learning has also been applied in hierarchical multi-label learning [76].

1.4.2.7 Other Algorithms

There have also been a number of other multi-label learning methods in the literature, and several selected methods are discussed below. Note that the literature on multi-label learning is vast and continuously expanding, and the discussions below are not intended to be comprehensive.

In [134], an algorithm called Correlated Label Propagation (CLP) is proposed to model the interactions between labels explicitly. CLP propagates multiple labels from training data points to test data points simultaneously. CLP is formulated as an optimization problem, and an efficient algorithm based on the properties of submodular functions is developed to compute its optimal solution.

In [87], a multi-label classification algorithm for text categorization is proposed. It generalizes the Maximal Figure-of-Merit (MFoM) [86] approach from binary classification to the multi-label setting. In particular, all MFoM classifiers are trained simultaneously. Compared with binary MFoM classifiers, which are trained independently, the resulting models are more robust, especially for labels with a very small number of positive training examples.

In [91], two models based on the Conditional Random Field (CRF) that directly parameterize label co-occurrences in multi-label classification are proposed. The conditional probability models for classification offer a rich framework for parameterizing relationships between class labels and features. Compared with other models, they can naturally model arbitrary dependencies between features and labels, as well as among multiple labels. Specifically, two multi-label graphical models are proposed for multi-label classification; the first model learns parameters for each pair of labels, while the second one learns parameters for feature-label-label triples and captures the impact that an individual feature has on the co-occurrence probability of a pair of labels.

In [118], an algorithm is proposed to make use of the sparsity in the label space, i.e., the majority of the data instances are only associated with a limited number of labels. The basic idea is to project the label vector onto a lower-dimensional space using some random matrix. Then the multi-label classification problem is transformed into a series of regression problems. In particular, it has been shown that the number of regression problems is only logarithmic in the total number of possible labels. Following established theories and tools in compressed sensing [43, 67], the prediction in the regression model can be converted to the label vector in the original label space.

Although the binary relevance scheme treats all labels independently and ignores the label correlations, its computational complexity is low compared to other multi-label learning algorithms. In [191], a Classifier Chain (CC) method is proposed to model label correlations while maintaining acceptable computational complexity. Specifically, each classifier in the chain is responsible for learning and predicting the binary association of the label C_i given the feature space, augmented by all prior binary relevance predictions in the chain $C_1, C_2, \ldots, C_{i-1}$. In addition, its ensemble variant (ECC) [191] and probabilistic variant (PCC) [64] have also been proposed to further improve its performance.

Ranking by Pairwise Comparison (RPC) [122] approaches multi-label learning using pairwise preference ranking and learns a mapping from instances to rankings over a finite number of labels. Specifically, it first induces a binary preference relation from suitable training data using a natural extension of pairwise classification. A ranking is then derived from the preference relation using a ranking procedure. Note that the sample imbalance problem is mitigated in the training data set, but the number of binary classifiers is $k(k-1)/2$ since each pair of labels is considered. Related methods include multi-label pairwise perceptron [163] and calibrated label ranking [84].

Recently, multi-label learning has been studied in the context of multi-instance learning [49, 65, 165], where each object is described by a number of instances. Specifically, in multi-instance learning, the label of the object is determined by the labels of its corresponding instances. If all instances are negative, then the label of the object is negative. If there exists at least one positive instance, then the corresponding object is labeled as positive. The task of multi-instance learning is to learn a function that can predict the label for an unseen object given its relevant instances. In [110, 277, 285], the multi-instance multi-label problem is studied. Specifically, in [285], each object is associated with not only multiple instances but also multiple labels. Two new algorithms known as MIMLBOOST and MIMLSVM are proposed to solve multi-instance multi-label problems. The relationship between multi-instance multi-label learning, multi-class learning, multi-instance learning, and multi-label learning is also studied in [285].

In [224], a multi-label learning algorithm is proposed to solve the weak label problem, which is similar to multi-instance learning. In the weak label problem, the appearance of a label means that the instance is associated with this label, while the absence of a label does not imply that this label is not relevant to this instance. In other words, the label information for a given instance in the training set is "partial". In the algorithm proposed in [224], a convex optimization problem is formulated to make sure that the classification boundary for each label goes across low density regions. The novelty of the proposed algorithm is that different similarities between instances are used for different labels. In addition, it is assumed that these similarities can be derived from a group of low-rank base similarities.

1.5   Dimensionality Reduction for Multi-Label Learning

In this section, we discuss dimensionality reduction in the context of multi-label learning.

1.5.1   Introduction to Dimensionality Reduction

Recent technological innovations have allowed us to collect massive amounts of data with a large number of features, such as gene expression pattern images [231], microarray gene expression data [95], protein/gene sequences [171], text documents [257], and neuroimages [2]. The proliferation of such data has facilitated knowledge discovery and pattern prediction/analysis using computational approaches [89, 95, 144, 166]. A common characteristic of such data is that the number of features is much larger than the sample size. High-dimensional data analysis has recently attracted increasing attention, as Donoho noted in [66]: *"The trend today is towards more observations but even more so, to radically larger numbers of variables .... Classical methods are simply not designed to cope with this kind of explosive growth of dimensionality of the observation vector. We can say with complete confidence that in the coming century, high-dimensional data analysis will be a very significant activity."*

One of the key issues in high-dimensional data analysis is the so-called *curse of dimensionality* [21]. This term was coined by Bellman [21] to show that the number of samples required to estimate a function with a given level of accuracy grows exponentially with dimensions that it comprises. In other words, the curse of dimensionality means that for a given sample size, there is a maximum number of features above which the performance of an algorithm will degrade rather than improve. In fact, many data mining algorithms fail when the dimensionality is high [66, 109], since data points become sparse and far apart from each other.

Dimensionality reduction, which extracts a small number of features by removing the irrelevant, redundant, and noisy information, is an effective way to mitigate the curse of dimensionality. Basically, dimensionality reduction transforms the high-dimensional data into a meaningful representation with a reduced dimensionality. Dimensionality reduction has been widely used in many domains for data compression, noise removal, etc. It leads to a significant reduction of the size of the data while some important properties of the original data set are preserved.

Data visualization is another important application of dimensionality reduction. It is the study of the visual representation of data through graphical representations and is effective in exploratory data analysis [17, 135, 245, 246]. In data visualization, the data in the original high-dimensional space are represented as data points in a 2- or 3-dimensional space. The task of data visualization is to construct the new representation in a 2- or 3-dimensional space in such a way that the essential properties or information in the original data space are preserved [245]. By applying dimensionality reduction, the data can be embedded into 2- or 3-dimensional space so that analysts can explore the data in an intuitive manner [135]. For example, nonlinear dimensionality reduction has been applied successfully in the visualization of gene expression compendia for retrieving relevant experiments [135].

Dimensionality reduction has been studied extensively in many areas (reviewed in [39, 45, 153, 205]). These dimensionality reduction algorithms can be divided into different categories based on different criteria, e.g., supervised and unsupervised dimensionality reduction algorithms, linear and nonlinear dimensionality reduction algorithms, etc. In linear dimensionality reduction algorithms, the data are projected onto a lower-dimensional space through a linear mapping or transformation, e.g., Principal Component Analysis (PCA) [133] and Linear Discriminant Analysis (LDA) [78, 82]. Recently, some nonlinear dimensionality reduction algorithms have been proposed to reduce the data dimensionality in a nonlinear fashion [153, 241]. For example, in manifold learning, the goal is to find a low-dimensional nonlinear manifold embedded in the original high-dimensional space, which preserves certain properties of the data distribution. In supervised dimensionality reduction the label information is used so that the label discriminatory information can be preserved after projection, e.g., LDA [78, 82], Canonical Correlation Analysis (CCA) [117], and Partial Least Squares (PLS) [196, 255, 261, 264]. In unsupervised dimensionality reduction, no label information is used and the goal is to preserve some properties of the data, e.g., the variance in PCA [133], the global geometric properties in Isomap [15], and the local geometric properties in Locally Linear Embedding (LLE) [199]. Commonly used unsupervised dimensionality reduction methods also include Latent Semantic Indexing (LSI) [62], Nonnegative Matrix Factorization (NMF) [152, 215], Latent Dirichlet Allocation [27], and Independent Component Analysis (ICA) [11, 150]. Other popular dimensionality reduction algorithms include Multi-Dimensional Scaling (MDS) [56], LLE [199], Isomap [15], Laplacian Eigenmaps [20], Hessian Eigenmaps [69], Maximum Variance Unfolding (MVU) [217, 256], Local Tangent Space Alignment (LTSA) [281], and kernel methods [207], as well as their extensions [72, 73, 187, 209, 233, 244, 274]. Multi-layer neural networks can also be used to reduce data dimensionality [113].

CCA [117] and PLS [196, 255, 261, 264] are classical techniques for modeling relations between multiple sets of observed variables. One popular use of CCA and PLS is for multi-label classification, in which one set of variables is derived from the data and the other set is derived from the class labels. This book is devoted to the study of dimensionality reduction in the context of multi-label learning. Hence, we will focus on supervised dimensionality reduction methods.

1.5.2   Linear and Nonlinear Dimensionality Reduction

Formally, dimensionality reduction studies the following problem: given a d-dimensional variable $\mathbf{x} = [x_1, \ldots, x_d]^T \in \mathbb{R}^d$, the goal is to find a lower-dimensional representation of $\mathbf{x}$, i.e., $\mathbf{s} = [s_1, \ldots, s_p]^T \in \mathbb{R}^p$ where $p \ll d$ is the reduced dimensionality, to preserve the information and structure of the original data based on a certain criterion. In this book, we mainly focus on linear dimensionality reduction. Specifically, in linear dimensionality reduction, each new feature is a linear combination of all the input features, i.e.,

$$\mathbf{s} = \mathbf{W}^T \mathbf{x}, \tag{1.7}$$

where $\mathbf{W} \in \mathbb{R}^{d \times p}$ is the so-called projection (transformation) matrix. By optimizing different criteria, we can obtain different $\mathbf{W}$'s.

In this book we mainly focus on supervised linear dimensionality reduction, i.e., dimensionality reduction in the feature space with the aid of the associated label information. Note that dimensionality reduction in the label space was also considered recently in the literature [118, 226], but we focus on the feature space in this book. A typical example of supervised linear dimensionality reduction is linear discriminate analysis [78, 82], one of the most popular dimensionality reduction algorithms. Specifically, LDA attempts to minimize the within-class variance while maximizing the between-class variance after the linear projection. As a result, the data points belonging to the same class tend to be close while those belonging to different classes tend to be far away in the projected space. Note that in LDA we assume that the classes are mutually exclusive. Consequently, LDA cannot be directly applied to perform multi-label dimensionality reduction.

To reduce the dimensionality of a complex data set, it is necessary to employ nonlinear dimensionality reduction techniques [153]. These nonlinear algorithms are designed to deal with more complex patterns, especially data that intrinsically lies in more complex lower-dimensional spaces, e.g., a lower-dimensional manifold [15]. For example, a set of images produced by the rotation of a face through different angles can be considered as data points lying along a continuous 1-dimensional curve. These nonlinear dimensionality reduction algorithms outperform traditional linear algorithms on artificial data sets, e.g., the Swiss role data set, which consists of a set of data points lying on a spiral-like 2-dimensional manifold within a 3-dimensional space. The effectiveness of nonlinear dimensionality reduction algorithms on real-world data sets critically depends on the characteristics of the data [241].

1.5.3   Multi-Label Dimensionality Reduction

Similar to many other machine learning and data mining tasks, multi-label learning also suffers from the curse of dimensionality. In addition, data visualization is an important tool to provide insights into the data in many applications of multi-label learning such as text processing [119]. Although numerous studies have been devoted to dimensionality reduction, most of them focus on either the unsupervised or the multi-class setting. On the other hand, many real-world applications can be cast as multi-label classification problems due to its generality. Some well-known examples include scene classification, text categorization, functional genomics, and gene expression pattern image annotation, as discussed in Section 1.2. Multi-label classification also finds applications in many other fields, including music retrieval and annotation [234] and chemical informatics [186]. In comparison with the traditional binary or multi-class classification that assumes mutually exclusive class membership, multi-label classification allows different classes to overlap each other. Therefore, a key challenge of multi-label dimensionality reduction is how to exploit the label correlations.

We use dimensionality reduction in text processing as a motivating example [119, 269]. In text categorization and visualization, the documents are first transformed into some feature representations for learning algorithms. A popular representation is the vector space model [164] in which each document is represented as a vector of length $|T|$ where $|T|$ is the size of the dictionary. Since the size of the dictionary is usually very large, $|T|$ may be very high and the resulting high-dimensional space using the vector space model is inherently sparse, which are the major challenges for text processing [269]. In this case, it is necessary to reduce the dimensionality of the feature vectors.

However, existing dimensionality reduction algorithms are less effective for multi-label learning. For example, the unsupervised dimensionality reduction algorithms, e.g., PCA, ignore the label information; the supervised dimensionality reduction algorithms, e.g., LDA, typically assume mutually exclusive labels. One possible solution is to use the problem transformation approaches discussed in Section 1.4.1 so that the traditional supervised dimensionality reduction algorithms can be applied after transformation. A drawback of this approach is that the label correlations are often ignored in the transformation and meanwhile the computational cost increases dramatically. For example, dimensionality reduction algorithms have been proposed for text categorization and visualization in the literature [269], such as term selection methods based on document frequency, information gain, etc. However, the overlapping between labels in the label space is not considered in existing algorithms.

As we discussed in Section 1.3, a fundamental challenge in multi-label learning is how to effectively exploit the label structure for improved classification performance. This is also the case for dimensionality reduction, since we expect that the label discriminative information is preserved after projection. Also note that dimensionality reduction is a preprocessing step for classification. A natural question is whether we can combine dimensionality reduction algorithms with some classification algorithms for improved performance. In traditional linear dimensionality reduction, the new features are linear combinations of all the original features; thus it is often difficult to interpret the resulting model. Hence, another challenge is how to build interpretable models for dimensionality reduction. To this end, it is desirable to achieve dimensionality reduction by reducing the number of explicitly used original features. Recently, some sparse feature selection algorithms have been proposed [230, 288, 289] via ℓ_1-norm minimization. It is of great interest to explore the sparse formulations in multi-label dimensionality reduction. Finally, the scalability of dimensionality reduction algorithms is also an important consideration, especially for large-scale problems.

1.5.4   Related Work

Recently, several dimensionality reduction algorithms have been proposed for multi-label learning [8, 179, 253, 273, 280]. In [273], an algorithm called Multi-label informed Latent Semantic Indexing (MLSI) that preserves the information of data and meanwhile captures the correlations between multiple labels is proposed. Note that LSI is a purely unsupervised dimensionality reduction algorithm. In order to incorporate the discriminative information encoded in the labels, a projection is computed for both the data X and the corresponding label Y. The difference between MLSI and CCA is that in CCA two different projections are computed simultaneously for X and Y while in MLSI the same projection is computed for both X and Y. As a result, MLSI obtains a new feature space, which captures the information of both the original feature space and the label space.

In [8], the sparse kernel orthonormalized partial least squares is proposed to handle multi-label data by imposing sparsity constraints on kernel orthonormalized partial least squares for feature extraction. When partial least squares is applied for supervised learning, one view corresponds to the data X while the other view corresponds to the associated label Y. It has been shown that orthonormalized PLS is competitive with various PLS variants [8]. The proposed algorithm in [8] is claimed to be applicable for multi-label learning, although no empirical result is reported.

In [280], a dimensionality reduction algorithm called Multi-label Dimensionality reduction via Dependence Maximization (MDDM) is proposed. In MDDM, the goal is to find a projection such that the dependence between the feature (data) and the corresponding label is maximized after projection. In particular, the Hilbert–Schmidt independence criterion [100] is adopted to measure the dependence between the features and the corresponding labels due to its simplicity and elegant theoretical properties. Furthermore, it is shown in [280] that a closed-form solution can be obtained for the resulting optimization problem in MDDM, leading to efficient implementations of the proposed algorithm.

In [253], a dimensionality reduction technique called class balanced linear discriminant analysis is proposed. The key idea of this method is to define a within-class scatter matrix and a between-class scatter matrix for multi-label learning. Since each instance may be associated with multiple labels, the traditional definition of within-class and between-class scatter matrices cannot be applied. In fact, it can be shown that the proposed class balanced LDA is equivalent to the traditional LDA performed on the data set after applying copy transformation.

Specifically, in [253] the multi-label within-class scatter matrix $\mathbf{S}_w$ is defined as:

$$\mathbf{S}_w = \sum_{j=1}^{k} \mathbf{S}_w^{(j)}, \text{ where } \mathbf{S}_w^{(j)} = \sum_{i=1}^{n} \mathbf{y}_i(j)(\mathbf{x}_i - \mathbf{m}_j), \tag{1.8}$$

and $\mathbf{m}_j$ is the mean of label j defined as

$$\mathbf{m}_j = \frac{\sum_{i=1}^{n} \mathbf{y}_i(j)\mathbf{x}_i}{\sum_{i=1}^{n} \mathbf{y}_i(j)}. \tag{1.9}$$

In other words, all instances relevant to label j are counted in the computation of the label mean $\mathbf{m}_j$. The multi-label between-class scatter matrix $\mathbf{S}_b$ is defined as

$$\mathbf{S}_b = \sum_{j=1}^{k} \mathbf{S}_b^{(j)}, \text{ where } \mathbf{S}_b^{(j)} = \left(\sum_{i=1}^{n} \mathbf{y}_i(j)\right)(\mathbf{m}_j - \mathbf{m})(\mathbf{m}_j - \mathbf{m})^T, \tag{1.10}$$

and $\mathbf{m}$ is the global mean of the data set for multi-label learning defined as

$$\mathbf{m} = \frac{\sum_{j=1}^{k} \sum_{i=1}^{n} \mathbf{y}_i(j)\mathbf{x}_i}{\sum_{j=1}^{k} \sum_{i=1}^{n} \mathbf{y}_i(j)}. \tag{1.11}$$

Note that the definition of the global mean $\mathbf{m}$ also considers the multiple counts for instances belonging to multiple labels; thus it is different from the global mean in the standard LDA in the multi-class setting.

Based on the modified definitions of the within-class and between-class scatter matrices for multi-label learning, the transformation matrix $\mathbf{W}$ can be computed readily as in the standard LDA algorithm. Namely, $\mathbf{W} \in \mathbb{R}^{d \times r}$ consists of the top r eigenvectors of the matrix $\mathbf{S}_w^{\dagger}\mathbf{S}_b$, where r is the reduced dimensionality. LDA is also extended for multi-label learning in [179] by applying copy transformation.

1.6 Overview of the Book

This book focuses on *multi-label dimensionality reduction*. Specifically, this book is concerned with the following fundamental research questions: (1) How to fully exploit the label correlations for effective dimensionality reduction in multi-label learning; (2) How to scale dimensionality reduction algorithms to large-scale data sets; (3) How to derive sparse dimensionality reduction algorithms to enhance model interpretability; (4) How to effectively combine dimensionality reduction with classification; and (5) How to perform multi-label dimensionality reduction effectively in practical applications. This book can be divided into the following three major parts:

- The design and analysis of dimensionality reduction algorithms for multi-label learning;

- Efficient implementations of dimensionality reduction algorithms, including both classical and recently proposed approaches;

- The application of multi-label dimensionality reduction methods to the automated annotation of *Drosophila* gene expression pattern images.

In the remainder of this section, we will discuss each part in more detail.

1.6.1   Design and Analysis of Algorithms

We start by discussing partial least squares [261], a classical tool to model the relationships between two sets of variables in statistics and data analysis. PLS has been shown to be effective even for data with massive collinearity among the variables [175, 189]. In this book, we introduce the basic concepts of PLS and present many popular variants of PLS including PLS Mode A, PLS1, PLS2, PLS-SB, SIM-PLS and Orthonormalized PLS (OPLS). In particular, we focus on PLS regression and classification, including the shrinkage properties of PLS regression.

Canonical correlation analysis [117] is a well-known technique for finding the correlations between two sets of multi-dimensional variables. CCA can be applied as a multi-label dimensionality reduction tool in which the two sets of variables are derived from the data and the class labels, respectively. By maximizing the correlation between the data and the associated label information, the data can be projected onto a lower-dimensional space directed by the label information. In this book, we introduce CCA and reveal its key properties. In particular, we show that the CCA projection for one set of variables is independent of the regularization on the other set of multi-dimensional variables, providing new insights on the effect of regularization on CCA [222, 223]. The relationship between CCA and PLS is also discussed in this book [223].

We next present Hypergraph Spectral Learning (HSL) for multi-label dimensionality reduction. HSL exploits correlations among different labels using a hypergraph [219]. A hypergraph [1, 23, 24] is a generalization of the traditional graph in which the edges, called hyperedges, are arbitrary nonempty subsets of the vertex set. In comparison with the traditional graph, the hyperedge can contain more than two vertices. As the discrete analog of the Laplace–Beltrami operator on compact Riemannian manifolds [54], the Laplacian matrix can be defined on the hypergraph [1]. Specifically, one can either define a hypergraph Laplacian directly using the analogies from a traditional 2-graph or expand it into a 2-graph.

In order to model multi-label learning problems using the hypergraph, a hyperedge is constructed in HSL for each label and all data points relevant to this label are included in the hyperedge to capture the correlation among labels. Based on the Laplacian of the constructed hypergraph, we present the hypergraph spectral learning framework for learning a lower-dimensional embedding through a linear transformation by solving an optimization problem. Specifically, the objective function in the optimization problem attempts to preserve the inherent relationship among data points captured by the hypergraph Laplacian. Intuitively, data points that share many common labels tend to be close to each other in the embedded space. HSL is a rather general dimensionality reduction method, since different definitions of the hypergraph Laplacian can be used in HSL. For example, it can be shown that CCA is a special case of HSL with a specific Laplacian matrix.

We further discuss a general framework for extracting shared structures in multi-label classification. In this framework, the correlation among multiple labels is captured by a lower-dimensional subspace shared among all labels. When the squared loss is used in classification, the shared structure can be computed by solving a generalized eigenvalue problem. To reduce the computational cost, we present an efficient algorithm for high-dimensional problems. This formulation includes several well-known formulations as special cases.

In order to better integrate dimensionality reduction with classification, we present a joint learning framework in which we perform dimensionality reduction and multi-label classification simultaneously. In particular, we show that when the squared loss is used in classification, this joint learning decouples into two separate components, i.e., a separate dimensionality reduction step followed by multi-label classification. This partially justifies the current practice of a separate application of dimensionality reduction for classification problems. Other loss functions, including hinge loss and squared hinge loss, are also studied in this joint framework. One appealing feature of these joint learning formulations is that they can be extended naturally to cases where the input data for different labels may differ, overcoming the limitation of traditional dimensionality reduction algorithms.

In some applications it is desirable to apply nonlinear dimensionality reduction algorithms due to the complex nature of the problems. Kernel methods [207, 210] map the data from the original space to a high-dimensional Hilbert space (or feature space) where linear models can be applied. One advantage of kernel methods is that they can handle different types of data which are not in the form of vectors or matrices. In this book, we introduce the kernel extensions of many popular dimensionality reduction algorithms. In addition, we present the equivalence relationship between kernel least squares and a class of kernel dimensionality reduction algorithms.

1.6.2 Scalable Implementations

Both HSL and CCA can be formulated as a generalized eigenvalue problem. In addition, many popular dimensionality reduction algorithms can also be cast as the same type of generalized eigenvalue problem, such as orthonormalized PLS, and LDA. It is well-known that solving large-scale generalized eigenvalue problems is much more challenging than the standard eigenvalue problems [201, 254]. In practical applications, scalability becomes a major concern when the size of data increases.

In this book, we introduce a direct least squares formulation to efficiently solve a class of dimensionality reduction algorithms, including HSL, CCA, OPLS, and LDA as special cases [220, 221]. Specifically, we show that under a mild condition, the generalized eigenvalue problem involved in a class of dimensionality reduction algorithms can be formulated as an equivalent least squares problem with a specific target matrix. Based on the equivalent least squares formulation, we extend these dimensionality reduction algorithms by incorporating different regularization terms into the least squares formulation. For example, sparse dimensionality reduction algorithms can be obtained by incorporating the ℓ_1-norm penalty. After transforming it into the least squares formulation, we can then apply the iterative conjugate gradient algorithm to solve it efficiently.

One limitation of the direct least squares approach is that the equivalence relationship only holds when the data points are linearly independent, which may not be the case for lower-dimensional data. Furthermore, the equivalence relationship between the least squares formulation and the original generalized eigenvalue problem fails when regularization is considered. To overcome these limitations, we further introduce a scalable two-stage approach for the same class of dimensionality reduction algorithms. One appealing feature of the two-stage approach is that it can be applied in the regularization setting without the independence assumption [218].

1.6.3 Applications

To demonstrate the application of multi-label dimensionality reduction, we apply kernel hypergraph spectral learning to annotate the *Drosophila* gene expression pattern images, as described in Section 1.2.4. Note that in this application the labels are anatomical and developmental ontology terms from a controlled vocabulary. In the current high-throughput database, annotation terms are assigned to groups of patterns rather than to individual images. We first extract invariant features from images, and construct pyramid match kernels to measure the similarity between sets of patterns. To exploit the complementary information conveyed by different features and incorporate the correlation among patterns sharing common structures, we apply efficient convex formulations to integrate the kernels derived from various features. Based on the learned kernel, hypergraph spectral learning is applied to predict annotated terms. The framework is evaluated by comparing its annotation with that of human curators, and promising performance has been observed. We present more details on this application in Chapter 8.

1.7 Notations

Throughout the book, all matrices are boldface uppercase, and vectors are boldface lowercase. n is the number of samples in the training data set, d is the data dimensionality, and k is the number of classes (or labels). The ith sample in the training data set is denoted as $\mathbf{x}_i \in \mathbb{R}^d$, and its corresponding label is denoted as $\mathbf{y}_i \in \mathbb{R}^k$, where $\mathbf{y}_i(j) = 1$ if $\mathbf{x}_i$ belongs to class j and $\mathbf{y}_i(j) = 0$ otherwise. The label set is denoted as $\mathfrak{L} = \{C_1, C_2, \ldots, C_k\}$. $\mathbf{X} = [\mathbf{x}_1, \mathbf{x}_2, \cdots, \mathbf{x}_n] \in \mathbb{R}^{d \times n}$ represents the data matrix, and $\mathbf{Y} = [\mathbf{y}_1, \mathbf{y}_2, \cdots, \mathbf{y}_n] \in \mathbb{R}^{k \times n}$ is the matrix representation for the label information. The training data set with n multi-label examples is denoted as $\mathcal{D} = \{(\mathbf{x}_1, \mathbf{y}_1), \ldots, (\mathbf{x}_n, \mathbf{y}_n)\}$. $\mathbf{I}_p$ is the p-by-p identity matrix, and $\mathbf{1}_p \in \mathbb{R}^p$ is the vector of all ones. Note that the subscript p may be omitted when the size is clear from the context.

1.8   Organization

The rest of the book is organized as follows:

- Chapter 2 introduces partial least squares, including some popular variants and its applications in both regression and classification.

- Chapter 3 provides an in-depth study of canonical correlation analysis, including various sparse CCA algorithms and the relationship between CCA and PLS.

- Chapter 4 presents hypergraph spectral learning for multi-label dimensionality reduction. The equivalent least squares formulation for a class of dimensionality reduction algorithms, including HSL, CCA, OPLS, and LDA, is also discussed. An efficient algorithm based on the equivalent least squares formulation is presented in this chapter.

- Chapter 5 discusses an efficient two-stage approach for the same class of dimensionality reduction algorithms discussed in Chapter 4.

- Chapter 6 present a general framework for extracting shared structures (subspace) in multi-label classification.

- Chapter 7 introduces a joint learning framework in which we perform dimensionality reduction and multi-label classification simultaneously.

- Chapter 8 presents nonlinear dimensionality reduction algorithms using the kernel trick. The application of multi-label dimensionality reduction algorithms to *Drosophila* gene expression pattern image annotation is also discussed in detail.

Chapter 2

Partial Least Squares

Partial Least Squares (PLS) is a family of methods for modeling the relationships between two sets of variables [33, 261, 263, 264]. In comparison with Principal Component Analysis (PCA) which maximizes the variance of the input data, PLS extracts latent features from data by maximizing the covariance between two blocks of variables. PLS is a popular tool for regression, classification, and dimensionality reduction [16, 142, 196], especially in the field of chemometrics. Recently, PLS has gained a lot of attention in the analysis of high-dimensional data in many fields [7, 32, 120, 202], such as medical diagnosis and bioinformatics [31, 44, 51, 52, 102, 185]. This is because PLS is resistant to overfitting and has been shown to be effective even for data with massive collinearity among the variables [175, 189]. PLS can be applied to classification problems by encoding the class membership in an appropriate indicator matrix. There is a close relationship between PLS and linear discriminant analysis [16] in classification. PLS can also be applied as a dimensionality reduction tool. After relevant latent vectors are extracted, an appropriate classifier, such as support vector machines [207], can be applied for classification [198]. PLS can be extended to regression problems by treating each of the predictor and response variables as a block of variables. Furthermore, similar to principal component regression and ridge regression, PLS regression yields a shrinkage estimator [142] which produces smaller minimum square error.

2.1 Basic Models of Partial Least Squares

Partial least squares models the relationship between two data sets, or two blocks of variables. The basic assumption in PLS is that high multi-collinearity exists among the variables, and this can be deduced by dimensionality reduction via latent variables. PLS computes orthogonal score vectors (also called latent vectors) by maximizing the covariance between different sets of variables. This is commonly done through an iterative procedure or by solving an eigenvalue problem. Given the latent variables, the data sets are then transformed so that information contained in the latent variables is subtracted. This process is often referred to as "deflation" in PLS.

Formally, we denote the two data sets as $\mathbf{X} \in \mathbb{R}^{d \times n}$ and $\mathbf{Y} \in \mathbb{R}^{k \times n}$, where n is the number of samples, and d and k are the dimensionality of $\mathbf{X}$ and $\mathbf{Y}$, respectively. Without loss of generality, we assume that both $\mathbf{X}$ and $\mathbf{Y}$ have been centered, i.e.,

---

Algorithm 2.1 The NIPALS Algorithm

Input: X, Y
Output: t, u, p, q
Initialize u
repeat
  $\mathbf{w} = \mathbf{X}\mathbf{u}$
  $\mathbf{w} = \frac{\mathbf{w}}{\|\mathbf{w}\|_2}$
  $\mathbf{t} = \mathbf{X}^T\mathbf{w}$
  $\mathbf{c} = \mathbf{Y}\mathbf{t}$
  $\mathbf{c} = \frac{\mathbf{c}}{\|\mathbf{c}\|_2}$
  $\mathbf{u} = \mathbf{Y}^T\mathbf{c}$
until convergence
$\mathbf{p} = \frac{\mathbf{X}\mathbf{t}}{\mathbf{t}^T\mathbf{t}}, \mathbf{q} = \frac{\mathbf{Y}\mathbf{u}}{\mathbf{u}^T\mathbf{u}}$

$\mathbf{X}\mathbf{1} = \mathbf{0}$, and $\mathbf{Y}\mathbf{1} = \mathbf{0}$, where $\mathbf{1}$ is the vector of all ones, and $\mathbf{0}$ is the vector of all zeros. In the general model of PLS, we assume that $\mathbf{X}$ and $\mathbf{Y}$ can be decomposed into the following form:

$$\mathbf{X} = \mathbf{P}\mathbf{T}^T + \mathbf{E} \tag{2.1}$$
$$\mathbf{Y} = \mathbf{Q}\mathbf{U}^T + \mathbf{F}, \tag{2.2}$$

where $\mathbf{T} = [\mathbf{t}_1, \mathbf{t}_2, \ldots, \mathbf{t}_p] \in \mathbb{R}^{n \times p}$ and $\mathbf{U} = [\mathbf{u}_1, \mathbf{u}_2, \ldots, \mathbf{u}_p] \in \mathbb{R}^{n \times p}$ denote the score vectors, or latent vectors of $\mathbf{X}$ and $\mathbf{Y}$, respectively; $\mathbf{P} = [\mathbf{p}_1, \mathbf{p}_2, \ldots, \mathbf{p}_p] \in \mathbb{R}^{d \times p}$ and $\mathbf{Q} = [\mathbf{q}_1, \mathbf{q}_2, \ldots, \mathbf{q}_p] \in \mathbb{R}^{k \times p}$ are called loadings for $\mathbf{X}$ and $\mathbf{Y}$, respectively; $\mathbf{E} \in \mathbb{R}^{d \times n}$ and $\mathbf{F} \in \mathbb{R}^{k \times n}$ are called residuals. The assumption in PLS is that the latent variables $\mathbf{T}$ and $\mathbf{U}$ capture the underlying information of the original blocks $\mathbf{X}$ and $\mathbf{Y}$. The difference between PLS and PCA is that the latent scores $\mathbf{T}$ and $\mathbf{U}$ are extracted by considering the two blocks $\mathbf{X}$ and $\mathbf{Y}$ simultaneously in PLS whereas only one block is considered in PCA.

In the past several decades, various PLS variants have been proposed [196, 255]. In the following, we discuss the classical formulation, known as Nonlinear Iterative Partial Least Squares (NIPALS) [262].

2.1.1 The NIPALS Algorithm

The nonlinear iterative partial least squares algorithm [262] is a classical PLS formulation, and it is considered the basis of other PLS variants. The NIPALS algorithm is described in Algorithm 2.1. Note that in this framework, only one pair of $(\mathbf{t}, \mathbf{p})$ and $(\mathbf{u}, \mathbf{q})$ is computed. In order to compute a sequence of the pairs, the deflation scheme can be applied to update $\mathbf{X}$ and $\mathbf{Y}$ so that different pairs can be obtained by applying the NIPALS algorithm repeatedly.

NIPALS tries to maximize the covariance between the latent vectors t and u where $t = X^T w$ and $u = Y^T c$ and $w \in \mathbb{R}^d$ and $c \in \mathbb{R}^k$ are weight vectors:

$$\max_{t,u} \text{cov}(t, u) = \max_{w,c} \text{cov}(X^T w, Y^T c) = \max_{w,c} w^T X Y^T c.$$

Thus, in the NIPALS algorithm, we update c as $c = Y X^T w$ and update w as $w = X Y^T c$. Based on w and c, the score vectors t and u can be updated accordingly. After the convergence of t and u, p and q can be obtained by regressing X on t and Y on u, respectively.

One important consequence of the NIPALS algorithm is that the solution of the NIPALS algorithm can be computed directly by solving some eigenvalue problems. It follows from the procedure of NIPALS in Algorithm 2.1 that

$$w \propto Xu \propto XY^T c \propto XY^T Yt \propto XY^T YX^T w.$$

Thus, w corresponds to the eigenvector of the following eigenvalue problem:

$$XY^T YX^T w = \lambda w. \tag{2.3}$$

Note that $t = X^T w$, which implies that t corresponds to the eigenvector of the following eigenvalue problem:

$$X^T XY^T Yt = \lambda t. \tag{2.4}$$

Similarly, we can show that c corresponds to the eigenvector of the following eigenvalue problem:

$$YX^T XY^T c = \lambda c, \tag{2.5}$$

and u corresponds to the eigenvector of the following eigenvalue problem:

$$Y^T YX^T Xu = \lambda u. \tag{2.6}$$

Following Eqs. (2.3) and (2.5), w and c are left and right singular vectors of the matrix XY^T associated with the singular value $\sqrt{\lambda}$, respectively.

2.2 Partial Least Squares Variants

PLS involves an iterative process. After the first pair of score vectors (t, u) is obtained, the next step is to compute the next pair of score vectors. Various deflation schemes have been proposed to compute the score vector pairs sequentially [196, 255, 264], resulting in different variants of PLS. In addition, many new variants of PLS have been proposed recently, such as kernel PLS [7, 143, 170, 197, 198, 228] and sparse PLS [7, 44, 52, 170]. In this section, we focus on popular variants of PLS, including PLS Mode A [262], PLS1 [88], PLS2 [116], PLS-SB [203], SIMPLS [60], and orthonormalized PLS [265].

2.2.1 PLS Mode A

The key of PLS Mode A is to deflate $\mathbf{X}$ and $\mathbf{Y}$ by subtracting the rank-one approximation using the corresponding score and loading vectors. Specifically, the loading vectors $\mathbf{p}$ and $\mathbf{q}$, which form the columns of $\mathbf{P}$ and $\mathbf{Q}$, respectively, are computed as the coefficients of regressing $\mathbf{X}$ on $\mathbf{t}$ and $\mathbf{Y}$ on $\mathbf{u}$, respectively:

$$\begin{aligned} \mathbf{p} &= \mathbf{X}\mathbf{t}/(\mathbf{t}^T\mathbf{t}), \\ \mathbf{q} &= \mathbf{Y}\mathbf{u}/(\mathbf{u}^T\mathbf{u}). \end{aligned}$$

At each iteration of PLS Mode A, we update $\mathbf{X}$ and $\mathbf{Y}$ as follows:

$$\begin{aligned} \mathbf{X} &\leftarrow \mathbf{X} - \mathbf{p}\mathbf{t}^T, \\ \mathbf{Y} &\leftarrow \mathbf{Y} - \mathbf{q}\mathbf{u}^T. \end{aligned}$$

The full procedure of PLS Mode A is described in Algorithm 2.2, where p is the number of extracted pairs of score vectors.

An important property of PLS Mode A is that the extracted score vectors $\{\mathbf{t}_i\}_{i=1}^{p}$ and $\{\mathbf{u}_i\}_{i=1}^{p}$ are mutually orthogonal, which is summarized in the following theorem:

Theorem 2.1 *For $i \neq j$, the score vectors obtained at the ith and the jth steps of PLS Mode A are mutually orthogonal, that is,*

$$\mathbf{t}_i^T\mathbf{t}_j = 0, \ \ \mathbf{u}_i^T\mathbf{u}_j = 0.$$

The full proof of Theorem 2.1 is given in Appendix A.1.

2.2.2 PLS2

PLS2 is one of the most popular PLS formulations for regression [116], especially in chemometrics [255]. Unlike PLS Mode A, the relationship between $\mathbf{X}$ and $\mathbf{Y}$ in PLS2 is asymmetric, and the extracted latent vectors of $\mathbf{X}$ are assumed to be good predictors of $\mathbf{Y}$. In particular, a linear relationship between the score vectors $\mathbf{T}$ and $\mathbf{U}$ is assumed as

$$\mathbf{U} = \mathbf{T}\mathbf{D} + \mathbf{H}, \tag{2.7}$$

where $\mathbf{D}$ is a $p \times p$ diagonal matrix and $\mathbf{H}$ denotes the matrix of residuals. As a result, we can deflate $\mathbf{Y}$ using $\mathbf{t}$ directly instead of $\mathbf{u}$. Specifically, at each iteration, the following deflation scheme is applied on $\mathbf{X}$ and $\mathbf{Y}$:

$$\begin{aligned} \mathbf{X} &\leftarrow \mathbf{X} - \mathbf{p}\mathbf{t}^T = \mathbf{X} - \frac{\mathbf{X}\mathbf{t}}{\mathbf{t}^T\mathbf{t}}\mathbf{t}^T, \\ \mathbf{Y} &\leftarrow \mathbf{Y} - \frac{\mathbf{Y}\mathbf{t}}{\mathbf{t}^T\mathbf{t}}\mathbf{t}^T. \end{aligned}$$

Similar to PLS Mode A, this deflation scheme guarantees the mutual orthogonality of the extracted score vectors $\{\mathbf{t}_i\}_{i=1}^{k}$.

Algorithm 2.2 PLS Mode A

Input: $\mathbf{X}$, $\mathbf{Y}$, p.
Output: $\mathbf{T}$, $\mathbf{U}$, $\mathbf{P}$, $\mathbf{Q}$.
Initialize $\mathbf{T}$, $\mathbf{U}$, $\mathbf{P}$, and $\mathbf{Q}$:

$$\mathbf{T} = [\,], \mathbf{U} = [\,], \mathbf{P} = [\,], \mathbf{Q} = [\,].$$

for $i = 1$ to p **do**

Compute the first pair of singular vectors of $\mathbf{X}\mathbf{Y}^T$ corresponding to the largest singular value: $(\mathbf{w}, \mathbf{c})$.
Compute the score vectors as:

$$\mathbf{t} = \mathbf{X}^T\mathbf{w}, \mathbf{u} = \mathbf{Y}^T\mathbf{c}.$$

Regress $\mathbf{X}$ on $\mathbf{t}$ and $\mathbf{Y}$ on $\mathbf{u}$:

$$\mathbf{p} = \frac{\mathbf{X}\mathbf{t}}{\mathbf{t}^T\mathbf{t}}, \mathbf{q} = \frac{\mathbf{Y}\mathbf{u}}{\mathbf{u}^T\mathbf{u}}.$$

Subtract the rank-one approximation to deflate $\mathbf{X}$ and $\mathbf{Y}$:

$$\mathbf{X} \leftarrow \mathbf{X} - \mathbf{p}\mathbf{t}^T, \mathbf{Y} \leftarrow \mathbf{Y} - \mathbf{q}\mathbf{u}^T.$$

Update $\mathbf{T}$, $\mathbf{U}$, $\mathbf{P}$, and $\mathbf{Q}$ as:

$$\mathbf{T} \leftarrow [\mathbf{T}, \mathbf{t}], \mathbf{U} \leftarrow [\mathbf{U}, \mathbf{u}], \mathbf{P} \leftarrow [\mathbf{P}, \mathbf{p}], \mathbf{Q} \leftarrow [\mathbf{Q}, \mathbf{q}].$$

if $\mathbf{X} = 0$ or $\mathbf{Y} = 0$ **then**
   break;
end if
end for

2.2.3 PLS1

PLS1 [79, 88, 111] is a special case of PLS2 in which one of the blocks contains only a single variable. Without loss of generality, we assume that $\mathbf{Y} \in \mathbb{R}^{1 \times n}$, i.e., $k = 1$. In fact, PLS1 can be considered as a regularization technique similar to ridge regression and principal component regression [255], which will be discussed in detail in Section 2.3. In particular, the deflation of $\mathbf{Y}$ is not necessary, since $\text{rank}(\mathbf{Y}) = 1$. In PLS1, the mutual orthogonality of $\{\mathbf{t}_i\}_{i=1}^p$ is preserved, and PLS1 essentially finds a direction in the space of regression coefficients that is orthogonal to all previous coefficients.

2.2.4   PLS-SB

PLS-SB was introduced in behavioral teratology by Sampson et al. [203] (S denotes Sampson and B denotes Bookstein, who proposed this PLS variant). The overall procedure of PLS-SB is similar to that of PLS Mode A. The major difference between PLS-SB and PLS Mode A is that in PLS-SB, $\mathbf{X}$ and $\mathbf{Y}$ are not updated at each iteration. Instead, we update the covariance matrix $\mathbf{XY}^T$ at each iteration. Unlike PLS Mode A, all singular vectors of the covariance matrix $\mathbf{XY}^T$ are computed at once in PLS-SB, whereas only the singular vectors corresponding to the largest singular value are computed at each iteration in PLS Mode A. In contrast to PLS2 and PLS Mode A, the extracted score vectors $\{\mathbf{t}_i\}_{i=1}^{p}$ are in general not mutually orthogonal, since $\mathbf{t}_i = \mathbf{Xw}_i$, where $\{\mathbf{w}_i\}_{i=1}^{p}$ are left singular vectors of $\mathbf{XY}^T$, and are mutually orthogonal. Similarly, the orthogonality property does not hold for the score vectors $\{\mathbf{u}\}_{i=1}^{p}$ for the other block $\mathbf{Y}$.

2.2.5   SIMPLS

SIMPLS [60] was proposed to avoid the deflation steps at each iteration of PLS2 by directly computing the weight vectors $\{\mathbf{w}_i\}_{i=1}^{p}$ such that $\mathbf{t} = \mathbf{X}^T\mathbf{w}$. Since no deflation is performed, $\mathbf{w}$ is applied to the original matrix $\mathbf{X}$ before deflation directly. At each iteration of SIMPLS, the Singular Value Decomposition (SVD) of the sample covariance $\mathbf{XY}^T$ is computed under some constraint such that the mutual orthogonality of score vectors $\{\mathbf{t}_i\}_{i=1}^{p}$ is preserved. It has been shown that SIMPLS is equivalent to PLS1 when $\mathbf{Y}$ contains only a single variable but differs from PLS2 when applied to a multi-dimensional matrix $\mathbf{Y}$ [60].

2.2.6   Orthonormalized PLS

Recall that the objective function in the NIPALS algorithm can be expressed as

$$\mathrm{cov}\left(\mathbf{X}^T\mathbf{w}, \mathbf{Y}^T\mathbf{c}\right)^2 = \mathrm{var}(\mathbf{X}^T\mathbf{w})\,\mathrm{corr}\left(\mathbf{X}^T\mathbf{w}, \mathbf{Y}^T\mathbf{c}\right)^2 \mathrm{var}(\mathbf{Y}^T\mathbf{c}). \qquad (2.8)$$

This can be considered as a penalized version of Canonical Correlation Analysis (CCA) in which only the correlation term is maximized. Formally, Orthonormalized PLS (OPLS) [265] solves the following optimization problem by removing the penalty term $\mathrm{var}\left(\mathbf{X}^T\mathbf{w}\right)$:

$$
\begin{aligned}
(\mathbf{w}^*, \mathbf{c}^*) &= \underset{\|\mathbf{w}\|_2 = \|\mathbf{c}\|_2 = 1}{\arg\max}\ \mathrm{var}\left(\mathbf{Y}^T\mathbf{c}\right)\mathrm{corr}\left(\mathbf{X}^T\mathbf{w}, \mathbf{Y}^T\mathbf{c}\right)^2 \\
&= \underset{\|\mathbf{w}\|_2 = \|\mathbf{c}\|_2 = 1}{\arg\max}\ \frac{\mathrm{cov}\left(\mathbf{X}^T\mathbf{w}, \mathbf{Y}^T\mathbf{c}\right)^2}{\mathrm{var}\left(\mathbf{X}^T\mathbf{w}\right)}.
\end{aligned}
\qquad (2.9)
$$

Since the objective function is invariant to the scaling of $\mathbf{w}$, OPLS can be formulated equivalently as the following optimization problem:

$$\max_{\mathbf{w},\mathbf{c}} \quad \mathbf{w}^T\mathbf{X}\mathbf{Y}^T\mathbf{c}$$

$$\text{s.t.} \quad \mathbf{w}^T\mathbf{X}\mathbf{X}^T\mathbf{w} = 1 \tag{2.10}$$

$$\mathbf{c}^T\mathbf{c} = 1.$$

Based on this constrained optimization problem, we can construct the Lagrangian function

$$L(\mathbf{w},\mathbf{c},\lambda_x,\lambda_y) = \mathbf{w}^T\mathbf{X}\mathbf{Y}^T\mathbf{c} - \frac{\lambda_x}{2}\left(\mathbf{w}^T\mathbf{X}\mathbf{X}^T\mathbf{w} - 1\right) - \frac{\lambda_y}{2}\left(\mathbf{c}^T\mathbf{c} - 1\right),$$

where λ_x and λ_y are Lagrange multipliers. Taking the derivatives of L with respect to $\mathbf{w}$ and $\mathbf{c}$, and setting them to zero, we obtain the following equations:

$$\mathbf{X}\mathbf{Y}^T\mathbf{c} - \lambda_x\mathbf{X}\mathbf{X}^T\mathbf{w} = 0 \tag{2.11}$$

$$\mathbf{Y}\mathbf{X}^T\mathbf{w} - \lambda_y\mathbf{c} = 0. \tag{2.12}$$

Hence, we have

$$\begin{aligned}
\lambda_x &= \lambda_x\left(\mathbf{w}^T\mathbf{X}\mathbf{X}^T\mathbf{w}\right) \\
&= \mathbf{w}^T\left(\lambda_x\mathbf{X}\mathbf{X}^T\mathbf{w}\right) \\
&= \mathbf{w}^T\mathbf{X}\mathbf{Y}^T\mathbf{c} \\
&= \mathbf{c}^T\mathbf{Y}\mathbf{X}^T\mathbf{w} \\
&= \mathbf{c}^T\left(\lambda_y\mathbf{c}\right) \\
&= \lambda_y,
\end{aligned}$$

where we make use of Eqs. (2.11) and (2.12). In the following discussion, we use λ to denote both λ_x and λ_y as they are identical.

In supervised learning, $\mathbf{X}$ typically corresponds to the data while $\mathbf{Y}$ corresponds to the label. As a result, the weight vectors for $\mathbf{X}$ are of more interest. Next we derive an optimization problem involving only the weight vector $\mathbf{w}$. It follows from Eq. (2.12) that

$$\mathbf{c} = \frac{1}{\lambda}\mathbf{Y}\mathbf{X}^T\mathbf{w}. \tag{2.13}$$

Substituting this into Eq. (2.11), we obtain the following generalized eigenvalue problem:

$$\mathbf{X}\mathbf{Y}^T\mathbf{Y}\mathbf{X}^T\mathbf{w} = \lambda^2\mathbf{X}\mathbf{X}^T\mathbf{w}. \tag{2.14}$$

We can substitute Eq. (2.13) into the original problem in Eq. (2.10), resulting in the following optimization problem:

$$\max_{\mathbf{w}} \quad \mathbf{w}^T\mathbf{X}\mathbf{Y}^T\mathbf{Y}\mathbf{X}^T\mathbf{w} \tag{2.15}$$

$$\text{s.t.} \quad \mathbf{w}^T\mathbf{X}\mathbf{X}^T\mathbf{w} = 1.$$

Multiple weight vectors $\{\mathbf{w}_i\}_{i=1}^p$ for $\mathbf{X}$ in OPLS can be computed simultaneously by solving the following optimization problem [8]:

$$\max_{\mathbf{W}} \quad \mathrm{Tr}\left(\mathbf{W}^T\mathbf{X}\mathbf{Y}^T\mathbf{Y}\mathbf{X}^T\mathbf{W}\right)$$

$$\text{s. t.} \quad \mathbf{W}^T\mathbf{X}\mathbf{X}^T\mathbf{W} = \mathbf{I}_p, \tag{2.16}$$

where $\mathbf{W} = [\mathbf{w}_1,\ldots,\mathbf{w}_p] \in \mathbb{R}^{d\times p}$ is the weight matrix and $\mathbf{I}_p \in \mathbb{R}^{p\times p}$ is the identity matrix.

OPLS can be used for multivariate regression problems when $\mathbf{X}$ contains the input data and $\mathbf{Y}$ contains the response variables. Similar to other PLS variants discussed above, OPLS can also be used for dimensionality reduction in supervised classification problems when $\mathbf{Y}$ encodes the class membership information. OPLS has been shown to be competitive with other PLS variants [8].

2.2.7   Relationship between OPLS and Other PLS Models

OPLS is closely related to several other PLS variants discussed above. It has been shown that PLS2 maximizes the same objective function as SIMPLS, but with different (and less intuitive) constraints [229]. Let $\mathbf{W}^{(i-1)} = [\mathbf{w}_1,\ldots,\mathbf{w}_{i-1}]$. Then the ith weight vector $\mathbf{w}_i$ in PLS2 and SIMPLS can be computed by solving the following optimization problem:

$$\max_{\mathbf{w}} \quad \mathbf{w}^T\mathbf{X}\mathbf{Y}^T\mathbf{Y}\mathbf{X}^T\mathbf{w} \tag{2.17}$$

$$\text{s. t.} \quad \mathbf{w}^T\mathbf{X}\mathbf{X}^T\mathbf{w}_j = 0, \text{ for } j = 1,\ldots,i-1,$$

$$\mathbf{w}^T\mathbf{L}\mathbf{w} = 1,$$

for some matrix $\mathbf{L}$. The difference between PLS2 and SIMPLS lies in the use of different matrix $\mathbf{L}$. In particular,

$$\mathbf{L} = \mathbf{I}_d - \mathbf{W}^{(i-1)}\left(\mathbf{W}^{(i-1)}\right)^\dagger \text{ and } \mathbf{L} = \mathbf{I}_d$$

are used in PLS2 and SIMPLS, respectively, where $(\mathbf{W}^{(i-1)})^\dagger$ denotes the Moore–Penrose pseudoinverse of $\mathbf{W}^{(i-1)}$. By comparing the optimization problem in Eq. (2.16) and the one in Eq. (2.17), we can observe that OPLS is also a special case of the optimization problem in Eq. (2.17) by setting

$$\mathbf{L} = \mathbf{X}\mathbf{X}^T.$$

In summary, OPLS optimizes the same objective function as PLS2 and SIMPLS, and the orthogonality property, i.e.,

$$\mathbf{w}_i^T\mathbf{X}\mathbf{X}^T\mathbf{w}_j = 0, \text{ for } i \neq j,$$

is enforced in all of the three PLS formulations. The difference lies in how the length, denoted as

$$\|\mathbf{w}\|_{\mathbf{L}} = \sqrt{\mathbf{w}^T\mathbf{L}\mathbf{w}},$$

of each weight vector is measured based on the different choices of $\mathbf{L}$.

2.3 PLS Regression

PLS has been used as a popular tool for regression in many fields, especially in chemometrics [184]. In this section, we discuss the variant PLS1 in the regression setting, where the response $\mathbf{Y} \in \mathbb{R}^{1 \times n}$ consists of a single variable and the deflation is not performed on $\mathbf{Y}$. Similar to principal component regression and ridge regression, PLS regression yields a shrinkage estimator. However, PLS regression extracts components from the data $\mathbf{X}$ that have a high covariance with the response $\mathbf{Y}$. As a result, the estimator computed by PLS regression depends on the response $\mathbf{Y}$ nonlinearly and it is not straightforward to obtain the shrinkage factors for PLS. In this section, we give an overview of the shrinkage properties of PLS regression in comparison with several popular regression algorithms including ordinary least squares, principal component regression, and ridge regression.

2.3.1 Basics of PLS Regression

In PLS regression, the latent variables of $\mathbf{X}$ are assumed to be predictive of $\mathbf{Y}$. In addition, we assume that there is a linear relationship between the latent scores $\mathbf{t}$ and $\mathbf{u}$. This linear relationship leads to a deflation scheme for both $\mathbf{X}$ and $\mathbf{Y}$. Specifically, we assume that

$$\mathbf{U} = \mathbf{TD} + \mathbf{H}. \tag{2.18}$$

Substituting Eq. (2.18) into Eq. (2.2), we obtain

$$\mathbf{Y} = \mathbf{QD}^T\mathbf{T}^T + \left(\mathbf{QH}^T + \mathbf{F}\right). \tag{2.19}$$

As a result, we can assume a linear relationship between $\mathbf{Y}$ and $\mathbf{T}$, and $\mathbf{QH}^T + \mathbf{F}$ can be considered as the residual. In the following discussion, we primarily focus on the PLS1 regression. As we discuss in Section 2.2.3, PLS1 is a special case of PLS2 when $\mathbf{Y} \in \mathbb{R}^{1 \times n}$ contains a single variable. Thus, there is no need to perform deflation for $\mathbf{Y}$; otherwise the algorithm will terminate in one step. We give the detailed procedure of PLS1 for regression in Algorithm 2.3. Note that in Algorithm 2.3, p is the number of components extracted by PLS1. At the ith iteration, we denote the latent vectors $\mathbf{T}^{(i)}$ and weight vectors $\mathbf{W}^{(i)}$ as

$$\mathbf{T}^{(i)} = \left[\mathbf{t}^{(1)}, \ldots, \mathbf{t}^{(i)}\right], \quad \mathbf{W}^{(i)} = \left[\mathbf{w}^{(1)}, \ldots, \mathbf{w}^{(i)}\right]. \tag{2.20}$$

The weight vectors $\mathbf{W}^{(i)}$ will be used extensively in the discussion of the shrinkage properties of PLS regression. Let the compact SVD of $\mathbf{X}$ be

$$\mathbf{X} = \mathbf{U}_1 \mathbf{\Sigma} \mathbf{V}_1^T, \tag{2.21}$$

where $\mathbf{U}_1 = [\mathbf{u}_1, \ldots, \mathbf{u}_r] \in \mathbb{R}^{d \times r}$, $\mathbf{V}_1 = [\mathbf{v}_1, \ldots, \mathbf{v}_r] \in \mathbb{R}^{n \times r}$ are matrices with orthonormal columns, $\mathbf{\Sigma} = \mathrm{diag}\,(\sigma_1, \ldots, \sigma_r)$, $\sigma_1 \geq \sigma_2 \geq \ldots \geq \sigma_r > 0$, and $r = \mathrm{rank}(\mathbf{X})$. Given $\mathbf{U}_1 = [\mathbf{u}_1, \ldots, \mathbf{u}_r] \in \mathbb{R}^{d \times r}$, there exists a matrix

---

Algorithm 2.3 The PLS1 Algorithm for Regression

Input: X, Y, p
Output: β
$\mathbf{T} = []$
for $i = 0$ to p **do**
$\quad \mathbf{w} = \mathbf{XY}^T$
$\quad \mathbf{t} = \mathbf{X}^T \mathbf{w}$
$\quad \mathbf{X} = \mathbf{X} - \frac{\mathbf{Xtt}^T}{\mathbf{t}^T \mathbf{t}}$
$\quad \mathbf{T} = [\mathbf{T}, \mathbf{t}]$
end for

$\mathbf{U}_1^\perp \in \mathbb{R}^{d \times (d-r)}$ with orthonormal columns such that $[\mathbf{U}_1, \mathbf{U}_1^\perp]$ is an orthogonal matrix [94], i.e., $\mathbf{U}_1 \mathbf{U}_1^T + \mathbf{U}_1^\perp {\mathbf{U}_1^\perp}^T = \mathbf{I}_d$ and ${\mathbf{U}_1^\perp}^T \mathbf{U}_1^\perp = \mathbf{I}_{d-r}$. We denote $\mathbf{U}_1^\perp$ as $\mathbf{U}_1^\perp = [\mathbf{u}_{r+1}, \ldots, \mathbf{u}_d]$ in the following discussion.

2.3.2 Shrinkage in Regression

Shrinkage regression methods are particularly effective when there is multi-collinearity among the regressors. We assume that $\theta \in \mathbb{R}^d$ is the parameter to be estimated and our estimator is $\hat{\theta} = [\hat{\theta}_1, \ldots, \hat{\theta}_d]$. We can compute the expectation error $\hat{\theta} - \theta$ at each point and average over all feasible points, leading to the Mean Squared Error (MSE) for the estimation $\hat{\theta}$:

$$
\begin{aligned}
&\mathrm{MSE}(\hat{\boldsymbol{\theta}}) \\
&= \mathbb{E}\left[\left\| \hat{\boldsymbol{\theta}} - \boldsymbol{\theta} \right\|_2^2 \right] \\
&= \mathbb{E}\left[\left\| \hat{\boldsymbol{\theta}} - \mathbb{E}[\hat{\boldsymbol{\theta}}] + \mathbb{E}[\hat{\boldsymbol{\theta}}] - \boldsymbol{\theta} \right\|_2^2 \right] \\
&= \mathbb{E}\left[\left\| \hat{\boldsymbol{\theta}} - \mathbb{E}[\hat{\boldsymbol{\theta}}] \right\|_2^2 + \left\| \mathbb{E}[\hat{\boldsymbol{\theta}}] - \boldsymbol{\theta} \right\|_2^2 + 2(\hat{\boldsymbol{\theta}} - \mathbb{E}[\hat{\boldsymbol{\theta}}])^T (\mathbb{E}[\hat{\boldsymbol{\theta}}] - \boldsymbol{\theta}) \right] \\
&= \mathbb{E}\left[\left\| \hat{\boldsymbol{\theta}} - \mathbb{E}[\hat{\boldsymbol{\theta}}] \right\|_2^2 \right] + \mathbb{E}\left[\left\| \mathbb{E}[\hat{\boldsymbol{\theta}}] - \boldsymbol{\theta} \right\|_2^2 \right] + \mathbb{E}\left[2(\hat{\boldsymbol{\theta}} - \mathbb{E}[\hat{\boldsymbol{\theta}}])^T (\mathbb{E}[\hat{\boldsymbol{\theta}}] - \boldsymbol{\theta}) \right] \\
&= \mathbb{E}\left[\left\| \hat{\boldsymbol{\theta}} - \mathbb{E}[\hat{\boldsymbol{\theta}}] \right\|_2^2 \right] + \left\| \mathbb{E}[\hat{\boldsymbol{\theta}}] - \boldsymbol{\theta} \right\|_2^2 + 2\mathbb{E}\left[\hat{\boldsymbol{\theta}} - \mathbb{E}[\hat{\boldsymbol{\theta}}] \right]^T (\mathbb{E}[\hat{\boldsymbol{\theta}}] - \boldsymbol{\theta}) \\
&= \mathbb{E}\left[\left\| \hat{\boldsymbol{\theta}} - \mathbb{E}[\hat{\boldsymbol{\theta}}] \right\|_2^2 \right] + \left\| \mathbb{E}[\hat{\boldsymbol{\theta}}] - \boldsymbol{\theta} \right\|_2^2 \\
&= \mathrm{Tr}(\mathrm{var}(\hat{\boldsymbol{\theta}})) + \mathrm{bias}^2(\hat{\boldsymbol{\theta}}), \quad\quad\quad\quad\quad\quad\quad\quad\quad (2.22)
\end{aligned}
$$

where

$$
\begin{aligned}
\operatorname{Tr}(\operatorname{var}(\hat{\boldsymbol{\theta}})) &= \mathbb{E}\left[\left\|\hat{\boldsymbol{\theta}} - \mathbb{E}[\hat{\boldsymbol{\theta}}]\right\|_2^2\right] = \sum_{i=1}^d \mathbb{E}[(\hat{\theta}_i - \mathbb{E}[\hat{\theta}_i])^2] = \sum_{i=1}^d \operatorname{var}(\hat{\theta}_i), \\
\operatorname{bias}^2(\hat{\boldsymbol{\theta}}) &= \left\|\mathbb{E}[\hat{\boldsymbol{\theta}}] - \boldsymbol{\theta}\right\|_2^2.
\end{aligned}
$$

Note that in the derivation we use the property that $\mathbb{E}[\hat{\boldsymbol{\theta}} - \mathbb{E}[\hat{\boldsymbol{\theta}}]] = \mathbb{E}[\hat{\boldsymbol{\theta}}] - \mathbb{E}[\hat{\boldsymbol{\theta}}] = \mathbf{0}$.

This decomposition of MSE is called the bias-variance decomposition [109], in which the MSE is decomposed into two components: variance and squared bias. Following this decomposition, an estimator $\hat{\boldsymbol{\theta}}$ is called unbiased if $\operatorname{bias}(\hat{\boldsymbol{\theta}}) = 0$ and biased otherwise.

It is well-known that Ordinary Least Squares (OLS) produces the minimum variance among all linear unbiased estimators in regression [109]. It follows from the bias-variance decomposition that there may exist some biased estimators with small variance, which results in a smaller MSE compared to OLS. In other words, we hope to decrease $\operatorname{Tr}(\operatorname{var}(\hat{\boldsymbol{\theta}}))$ even at the price of increasing $\operatorname{bias}(\hat{\boldsymbol{\theta}})$. Biased estimators are very popular in statistics and machine learning [26, 109].

In linear regression, we are given the regressors $\mathbf{X} \in \mathbb{R}^{d \times n}$ and the response $\mathbf{Y} \in \mathbb{R}^{1 \times n}$. We assume there is a linear relationship between $\mathbf{X}$ and $\mathbf{Y}$:

$$
\mathbf{Y} = \boldsymbol{\beta}^T \mathbf{X} + \boldsymbol{\epsilon}, \tag{2.23}
$$

where $\boldsymbol{\beta} \in \mathbb{R}^d$ and $\boldsymbol{\epsilon} = [\epsilon_1, \ldots, \epsilon_n] \in \mathbb{R}^{1 \times n}$ is the error term with $\mathbb{E}[\epsilon_i] = 0$ and $\operatorname{var}(\epsilon_i) = \sigma^2$ for $i = 1, \ldots, n$.

We next investigate a linear estimator $\hat{\boldsymbol{\theta}} = \mathbf{S}\mathbf{Y}^T$ for some $\mathbf{S}$. Note that throughout the discussion, we assume that $\mathbf{X}$ is fixed and the focus is on $\mathbf{Y}$. Assume that $\mathbf{S}$ is independent of $\mathbf{Y}$; then the expectation and the variance of $\hat{\boldsymbol{\theta}}$ can be computed as follows:

$$
\begin{aligned}
\mathbb{E}[\hat{\boldsymbol{\theta}}] &= \mathbb{E}[\mathbf{S}\mathbf{Y}^T] \\
&= \mathbf{S}\mathbb{E}[\mathbf{Y}^T] \\
&= \mathbf{S}\mathbf{X}^T\boldsymbol{\beta}, \tag{2.24} \\
\operatorname{Tr}(\operatorname{var}(\hat{\boldsymbol{\theta}})) &= \mathbb{E}\left[(\hat{\boldsymbol{\theta}} - \mathbb{E}[\hat{\boldsymbol{\theta}}])^T(\hat{\boldsymbol{\theta}} - \mathbb{E}[\hat{\boldsymbol{\theta}}])\right] \\
&= \mathbb{E}\left[(\mathbf{S}\mathbf{Y}^T - \mathbf{S}\mathbf{X}^T\boldsymbol{\beta})^T(\mathbf{S}\mathbf{Y}^T - \mathbf{S}\mathbf{X}^T\boldsymbol{\beta})\right] \\
&= \mathbb{E}\left[(\mathbf{S}\boldsymbol{\epsilon}^T)^T(\mathbf{S}\boldsymbol{\epsilon}^T)\right] \\
&= \sigma^2 \operatorname{Tr}(\mathbf{S}\mathbf{S}^T). \tag{2.25}
\end{aligned}
$$

In OLS, the estimator $\hat{\boldsymbol{\beta}}_{OLS}$ is given by

$$
\hat{\boldsymbol{\beta}}_{OLS} = \left(\mathbf{X}\mathbf{X}^T\right)^\dagger \mathbf{X}\mathbf{Y}^T = \mathbf{U}_1 \boldsymbol{\Sigma}^{-1} \mathbf{V}_1^T \mathbf{Y}^T = \sum_{i=1}^r \frac{1}{\sigma_i} \mathbf{u}_i (\mathbf{v}_i^T \mathbf{Y}^T) = \sum_{i=1}^r \mathbf{b}_i,
$$

$$
\tag{2.26}
$$

where $\mathbf{b}_i = \frac{1}{\sigma_i}\mathbf{u}_i(\mathbf{v}_i^T\mathbf{Y}^T) \in \mathbb{R}^d$. Defining $\mathbf{S}_{OLS} = (\mathbf{X}\mathbf{X}^T)^\dagger\mathbf{X}$ and using Eqs. (2.24) and (2.25), we obtain that

$$\mathbb{E}[\hat{\boldsymbol{\beta}}_{OLS}] = \mathbf{S}_{OLS}\mathbf{X}^T\boldsymbol{\beta} = (\mathbf{X}\mathbf{X}^T)^\dagger\mathbf{X}\mathbf{X}^T\boldsymbol{\beta} = \mathbf{U}_1\mathbf{U}_1^T\boldsymbol{\beta}, \quad (2.27)$$

$$\begin{aligned}
\mathrm{Tr}(\mathrm{var}(\hat{\boldsymbol{\beta}}_{OLS})) &= \sigma^2\,\mathrm{Tr}(\mathbf{S}_{OLS}\mathbf{S}_{OLS}^T) \\
&= \sigma^2\,\mathrm{Tr}\left((\mathbf{X}\mathbf{X}^T)^\dagger\mathbf{X}\left((\mathbf{X}\mathbf{X}^T)^\dagger\mathbf{X}\right)^T\right) \\
&= \sigma^2\,\mathrm{Tr}(\mathbf{U}_1\boldsymbol{\Sigma}^{-2}\mathbf{U}_1^T) \\
&= \sigma^2\sum_{i=1}^{r}\frac{1}{\sigma_i^2}. \quad (2.28)
\end{aligned}$$

Note that when $\boldsymbol{\beta} \in \mathcal{R}(\mathbf{X}) = \mathcal{R}(\mathbf{U}_1)$, $\mathbb{E}[\hat{\boldsymbol{\beta}}_{OLS}] = \mathbf{U}_1\mathbf{U}_1^T\boldsymbol{\beta} = \boldsymbol{\beta}$, which implies that OLS produces an unbiased estimator $\hat{\boldsymbol{\beta}}_{OLS}$.

One consequence of Eq. (2.28) is that small singular values of $\mathbf{X}$ may lead to high variance of the estimator $\hat{\boldsymbol{\beta}}_{OLS}$. In order to investigate the MSE of the general shrinkage estimator, we consider the shrinkage estimator $\hat{\boldsymbol{\beta}}_s$ in the following form:

$$\hat{\boldsymbol{\beta}}_s = \sum_{i=1}^{r} f(\sigma_i)\mathbf{b}_i, \quad (2.29)$$

where $\mathbf{b}_i = \frac{1}{\sigma_i}\mathbf{u}_i(\mathbf{v}_i^T\mathbf{Y}^T) \in \mathbb{R}^d$ and $f(\sigma_i)$ $(i = 1,\ldots,r)$ are called shrinkage factors. Then the shrinkage estimator $\hat{\boldsymbol{\beta}}_s$ can be represented in the following matrix form:

$$\hat{\boldsymbol{\beta}}_s = \mathbf{U}_1\boldsymbol{\Sigma}^{-1}\mathbf{G}\mathbf{V}_1^T\mathbf{Y}^T, \quad (2.30)$$

where $\mathbf{G} = \mathrm{diag}\,(f(\sigma_1),\ldots,f(\sigma_r)) \in \mathbb{R}^{r\times r}$. Thus, we define $\mathbf{S}_s$ as follows:

$$\mathbf{S}_s = \mathbf{U}_1\boldsymbol{\Sigma}^{-1}\mathbf{G}\mathbf{V}_1^T = \mathbf{U}_1\mathbf{G}\boldsymbol{\Sigma}^{-1}\mathbf{V}_1^T. \quad (2.31)$$

Based on the above discussion, we can estimate the MSEs of estimators $\hat{\boldsymbol{\beta}}_s = \mathbf{S}_s\mathbf{Y}^T$ and $\hat{\mathbf{Y}}_s = \hat{\boldsymbol{\beta}}_s^T\mathbf{X} = \mathbf{Y}\mathbf{S}^T\mathbf{X}$, as summarized in the following theorem [142]:

Theorem 2.2 *Given the shrinkage estimator $\hat{\boldsymbol{\beta}}_s$ defined in Eq. (2.29), the MSEs of $\hat{\boldsymbol{\beta}}_s$ and $\hat{\mathbf{Y}}_s$ are given as:*

$$\mathrm{MSE}(\hat{\boldsymbol{\beta}}_s) = \sigma^2\sum_{i=1}^{r}\frac{f(\sigma_i)^2}{\sigma_i^2} + \sum_{i=1}^{r}(f(\sigma_i)-1)^2(\mathbf{u}_i^T\boldsymbol{\beta})^2 + \sum_{i=r+1}^{d}(\mathbf{u}_i^T\boldsymbol{\beta})^2, \quad (2.32)$$

$$\mathrm{MSE}(\hat{\mathbf{Y}}_s) = \sigma^2\sum_{i=1}^{r}f(\sigma_i)^2 + \sum_{i=1}^{r}\sigma_i^2(f(\sigma_i)-1)^2(\mathbf{u}_i^T\boldsymbol{\beta})^2. \quad (2.33)$$

The full proof of Theorem 2.2 is given in Appendix A.1.

Theorem 2.2 shows that when $f(\sigma_i) = 1$ for all i, then the bias is minimized. Note that $|f(\sigma_i) < 1|$ decreases the variance while $|f(\sigma_i) > 1|$ increases the variance. As a result, we typically set $|f(\sigma_i) < 1|$ to decrease the MSE of the estimator.

2.3.3 Principal Component Regression

Both Principal Component Regression (PCR) and PLS regression involve selecting a subspace onto which the response vector $\mathbf{Y}$ is projected. The major difference is that the subspace in PLS regression is determined by both $\mathbf{X}$ and $\mathbf{Y}$, while in PCR the first p components are used to approximate the data $\mathbf{X}$. Recall that in PLS1 regression in Algorithm 2.3, we select $\mathbf{w}$ that achieves the maximum covariance between $\mathbf{X}$ and $\mathbf{Y}$ at each step. In PCR, when $p \leq r = \text{rank}(\mathbf{X})$, the approximation of $\mathbf{X}$ using the first p principal components is:

$$\tilde{\mathbf{X}} = \mathbf{U}_1(:, 1:p)\mathbf{\Sigma}(1:p, 1:p)\mathbf{V}_1(:, 1:p)^T = \sum_{i=1}^{p} \sigma_i \mathbf{u}_i \mathbf{v}_i^T, \tag{2.34}$$

where $\mathbf{U}_1(:, 1:p)$ and $\mathbf{V}_1(:, 1:p)$ contain the first p columns of $\mathbf{U}_1$ and $\mathbf{V}_1$, respectively, $\mathbf{\Sigma}(1:p, 1:p)$ contains the first p rows and the first p columns of $\mathbf{\Sigma}$, i.e., $\mathbf{\Sigma}(1:p, 1:p) = \text{diag}(\sigma_1, \ldots, \sigma_p)$.

Based on the approximate formulation $\tilde{\mathbf{X}}$, we perform OLS by regressing $\tilde{\mathbf{X}}$ on $\mathbf{Y}$, leading to the following estimator $\hat{\boldsymbol{\beta}}_{PCR}$:

$$
\begin{aligned}
\hat{\boldsymbol{\beta}}_{PCR} &= \left(\tilde{\mathbf{X}}\tilde{\mathbf{X}}^T\right)^{\dagger} \tilde{\mathbf{X}}\mathbf{Y}^T \\
&= \mathbf{U}_1(:, 1:p)\mathbf{\Sigma}(1:p, 1:p)^{-1}\mathbf{V}_1(:, 1:p)^T\mathbf{Y}^T \\
&= \sum_{i=1}^{p} \frac{1}{\sigma_i}\mathbf{u}_i \mathbf{v}_i^T \mathbf{Y}^T \\
&= \sum_{i=1}^{p} \mathbf{b}_i.
\end{aligned}
\tag{2.35}
$$

It follows from Eq. (2.35) that the estimator $\hat{\boldsymbol{\beta}}_{PCR}$ can be expressed equivalently in the following form:

$$\hat{\boldsymbol{\beta}}_{PCR} = \sum_{i=1}^{r} f(\sigma_i)\mathbf{b}_i, \tag{2.36}$$

where the shrinkage factors $f(\sigma_i)$ $(i = 1, \ldots, r)$ in PCR are defined as

$$f(\sigma_i) = \begin{cases} 1, & \text{if } i \leq p \\ 0, & \text{otherwise}, \end{cases} \tag{2.37}$$

where $p \leq \text{rank}(\mathbf{X})$ is the number of selected principal components. Compared with OLS, the $\mathbf{b}_i$'s associated with small singular values are removed in PCR. Thus, the variance of the estimator $\hat{\boldsymbol{\beta}}_{PCR}$ is reduced at the cost of an increased bias.

2.3.4 Ridge Regression

In ridge regression, the regression coefficients are shrunk by imposing a penalty on the ℓ_2-norm of the regression coefficients. Specifically, ridge regression minimizes the following loss function:

$$\hat{\boldsymbol{\beta}}_{RR} = \arg\min_{\boldsymbol{\beta}} \|\boldsymbol{\beta}^T \mathbf{X} - \mathbf{Y}\|_2^2 + \lambda \|\boldsymbol{\beta}\|_2^2, \tag{2.38}$$

where $\lambda > 0$ is called the regularization parameter, or complexity parameter, which controls the shrinkage of $\hat{\boldsymbol{\beta}}_{RR}$. It is clear that $\lambda = 0$ corresponds to the OLS. It has been shown that the optimization problem in Eq. (2.38) is equivalent to the following problem [26, 109]:

$$\min_{\boldsymbol{\beta}} \quad \|\boldsymbol{\beta}^T \mathbf{X} - \mathbf{Y}\|_2$$
$$\text{s. t.} \quad \|\boldsymbol{\beta}\|_2 \le t, \tag{2.39}$$

for some parameter $t > 0$ which depends on λ. It has also been shown that there is a one-to-one correspondence between the complexity parameter λ in Eq. (2.38) and t in the problem in Eq. (2.39) [26].

Note that the loss function in ridge regression can be expressed as

$$
\begin{aligned}
L(\boldsymbol{\beta}) &= \|\boldsymbol{\beta}^T \mathbf{X} - \mathbf{Y}\|_2^2 + \lambda \|\boldsymbol{\beta}\|_2^2 \\
&= \boldsymbol{\beta}^T \mathbf{X} \mathbf{X}^T \boldsymbol{\beta} - 2\boldsymbol{\beta}^T \mathbf{X} \mathbf{Y}^T + \mathbf{Y} \mathbf{Y}^T + \lambda \boldsymbol{\beta}^T \boldsymbol{\beta}.
\end{aligned}
$$

Taking the derivative with respect to $\boldsymbol{\beta}$ and setting it to zero, we have

$$\left(\mathbf{X}\mathbf{X}^T + \lambda \mathbf{I}\right) \boldsymbol{\beta} = \mathbf{X}\mathbf{Y}^T. \tag{2.40}$$

Then the solution of ridge regression can be represented as

$$
\begin{aligned}
\hat{\boldsymbol{\beta}}_{RR} &= (\mathbf{X}\mathbf{X}^T + \lambda \mathbf{I})^{-1} \mathbf{X} \mathbf{Y}^T \\
&= \mathbf{U}_1 (\boldsymbol{\Sigma}^2 + \lambda \mathbf{I})^{-1} \boldsymbol{\Sigma} \mathbf{V}_1^T \mathbf{Y}^T \\
&= \sum_{i=1}^{r} \frac{\sigma_i}{\sigma_i^2 + \lambda} \mathbf{u}_i (\mathbf{v}_i^T \mathbf{Y}^T) \\
&= \sum_{i=1}^{r} f(\sigma_i) \mathbf{b}_i,
\end{aligned}
$$

where the shrinkage factors $f(\sigma_i)$ $(i = 1, \dots, r)$ are defined as

$$f(\sigma_i) = \frac{\sigma_i^2}{\sigma_i^2 + \lambda}. \tag{2.41}$$

In comparison with OLS, the shrinkage factor $f(\sigma_i)$ is shrunk toward zero. In addition, larger σ_i leads to larger $f(\sigma_i)$, which implies that a greater amount of shrinkage is applied to $\mathbf{b}_i$'s with small singular values. Similarly, the variance of the estimator $\hat{\boldsymbol{\beta}}_{RR}$ is reduced at the cost of an increased bias.

2.3.5 Shrinkage Properties of PLS Regression

The shrinkage properties of PLS regression have been studied extensively in the literature [61, 79, 142, 158, 184]. In particular, the connection between PLS, the Lanczos algorithm, and the conjugate gradient algorithm [142, 143, 184] provides some insights into the shrinkage properties of PLS regression. In fact, PLS is identical to a common implementation of the conjugate gradient algorithm for solving the normal equation [142]. In this subsection, we briefly present the most important shrinkage properties of PLS regression via its connection with the Lanczos algorithm.

In the following, the PLS estimator after the ith step is denoted as $\hat{\beta}_{PLS}^{(i)}$. Similar to OLS and ridge regression, in PLS regression the estimator $\hat{\beta}_{PLS}^{(i)}$ can also be represented in the following form:

$$\hat{\beta}_{PLS}^{(i)} = \mathbf{S}_{PLS}^{(i)} \mathbf{Y}^T.$$

However, $\mathbf{S}_{PLS}^{(i)}$ depends on $\mathbf{Y}$ in a complicated, nonlinear way. As a result, Theorem 2.2 does not hold since its assumption is violated.

Next we consider the PLS regression estimator $\hat{\beta}_{PLS}^{(i)}$ from the perspective of the Lanczos algorithm and the conjugate gradient algorithm. Consider the matrix $\mathbf{K}^{(i)}$ that consists of the Krylov sequence of $\mathbf{X}\mathbf{X}^T \in \mathbb{R}^{d \times d}$ and $\mathbf{b} = \mathbf{X}\mathbf{Y}^T \in \mathbb{R}^d$:

$$\mathbf{K}^{(i)} \triangleq \left[(\mathbf{X}\mathbf{X}^T)^0 \mathbf{b}, (\mathbf{X}\mathbf{X}^T)^1 \mathbf{b}, \ldots, (\mathbf{X}\mathbf{X}^T)^{i-1} \mathbf{b} \right] \in \mathbb{R}^{d \times i}. \qquad (2.42)$$

We denote the space spanned by the columns of $\mathbf{K}^{(i)}$ by $\mathcal{K}^{(i)}$, i.e., $\mathcal{K}^{(i)} = \mathcal{R}(\mathbf{K}^{(i)})$.

Using the Krylov sequence $\mathbf{K}^{(i)}$, it can be shown that the estimator $\beta_{PLS}^{(i)}$ after the ith step of PLS can be expressed in the following form [111]:

Theorem 2.3 *The PLS estimator after the ith step can be expressed in the following form:*

$$\beta_{PLS}^{(i)} = \mathbf{K}^{(i)} \left[\left(\mathbf{K}^{(i)} \right)^T \mathbf{X}\mathbf{X}^T \mathbf{K}^{(i)} \right]^\dagger \left(\mathbf{K}^{(i)} \right)^T \mathbf{X}\mathbf{Y}^T. \qquad (2.43)$$

The proof of this theorem is rather involved, and thus it is skipped. The full proof can be found in [111].

Note that any matrix $\mathbf{M}$ can be used in place of $\mathbf{K}^{(i)}$ as long as $\mathbf{M}$ forms a basis for the Krylov space $\mathcal{K}^{(i)}$ [184]. Due to the equivalence between the space spanned by the columns of $\mathbf{W}^{(i)} = \left[\mathbf{w}^{(1)}, \ldots, \mathbf{w}^{(i)} \right]$ and the Krylov space $\mathcal{K}^{(i)}$ [111, 184], $\mathbf{W}^{(i)}$ can be considered as a basis of $\mathcal{K}^{(i)}$. Based on $\mathbf{W}^{(i)}$, we define $\mathbf{D}^{(i)}$ as

$$\mathbf{D}^{(i)} \triangleq \mathbf{W}^{(i)T} \mathbf{X}\mathbf{X}^T \mathbf{W}^{(i)} \in \mathbb{R}^{i \times i}. \qquad (2.44)$$

$\mathbf{D}^{(i)}$ is symmetric and positive semidefinite and it also possesses many appealing properties, as summarized in [142]. In particular, the eigenvalues of $\mathbf{D}^{(i)}$ play important roles in investigating the shrinkage properties of PLS regression. Formally, we denote the eigenvalues of $\mathbf{D}^{(i)}$ by

$$\mu_1^{(i)} \geq \mu_2^{(i)} \geq \ldots \mu_i^{(i)} \geq 0. \qquad (2.45)$$

It turns out that the shrinkage factors of PLS can be represented using the eigenvalues of the matrix $\mathbf{D}^{(i)}$ and the result is summarized in the following theorem [142, 184]:

Theorem 2.4 *If* $\dim(\mathbf{K}^{(i)}) = i$, *then the PLS estimator after the ith step can be represented in the following form:*

$$\hat{\beta}_{PLS}^{(i)} = \sum_{j=1}^{r} f^{(i)}(\sigma_j^2)\mathbf{b}_j, \qquad (2.46)$$

where $\sigma_1 \geq \sigma_2 \geq \ldots \geq \sigma_r > 0$ *are singular values of* $\mathbf{X}$ *and* $f^{(i)}$ *is defined as:*

$$f^{(i)}(\lambda) \triangleq 1 - \prod_{j=1}^{i} \left(1 - \frac{\lambda}{\mu_j^{(i)}}\right). \qquad (2.47)$$

The proof of this theorem is skipped since it is quite involved. The full proof can be found in [142]. It follows from Theorem 2.4 that the shrinkage factor for $\mathbf{b}_j$ in PLS regression is $f^{(i)}(\sigma_j^2)$. By comparing the PLS regression estimator $\hat{\beta}_{PLS}$ with the estimators obtained by OLS, PCR, and ridge regression, we can observe that the main difference lies in the definitions of the shrinkage factors. Note that all shrinkage factors in OLS, PCR, and ridge regression are not greater than 1. However, this is not true for PLS regression, and some counterexamples are given in [40, 142]. Furthermore, unlike OLS, PCR, and ridge regression, the shrinkage factors in PLS regression also depend on the response $\mathbf{Y}$ nonlinearly. When $\mathbf{S}_s$ is independent of $\mathbf{Y}$, Theorem 2.2 implies that it is desirable to impose the constraint that $|f(\sigma_i)| < 1$ to decrease the overall MSE. However, it is not clear how to control the shrinkage factors in PLS regression, since $\mathbf{S}_s$ depends on $\mathbf{Y}$. The authors [79] and [142] propose to upper bound the absolute value of shrinkage factors by 1 in PLS regression. As reported in [142], bounding the absolute value of the PLS shrinkage factors by 1 seems to yield a lower MSE empirically.

2.4   Partial Least Squares Classification

In this section we discuss the application of PLS for classification where $\mathbf{X}$ is the data matrix while $\mathbf{Y}$ is called the indicator matrix that encodes the class membership for the corresponding data in $\mathbf{X}$. Although PLS is not inherently designed for classification, it is also widely used in many applications as a classification tool [16, 162]. Some typical applications of PLS in classification include Alzheimer's disease discrimination [96], classification between Arabica and Robusta coffee beans [36], water pollution classification [214], separation between active and inactive compounds in a quantitative structure-activity relationship study [25], hard red wheat classification [63], microarray classification [31], and other applications in a variety of other areas [124, 176, 225, 250].

Linear Discriminant Analysis (LDA) [82] is a popular discriminative tool, and it is well-known that CCA is equivalent to LDA under certain circumstances, which was first recognized in 1938 by Bartlett [18]. Note that CCA and PLS share many common features. In the following, we consider the use of PLS for multi-class classification and in particular we discuss the connections between PLS and LDA in classification.

We denote the ith class as C_i, the sample size of the ith class as $n_i = |C_i|$, the mean of the ith class as $\bar{\mathbf{x}}_i = \frac{1}{n_i} \sum_{j \in C_i} \mathbf{x}_j$, and the mean of all samples as $\bar{\mathbf{x}} = \frac{1}{n} \mathbf{X} \mathbf{1}$. Since we assume $\mathbf{X}$ are centered, $\bar{\mathbf{x}} = \mathbf{0}$. Without loss of generality, we assume that the data matrix $\mathbf{X}$ is organized according to k classes as $\mathbf{X} = [\mathbf{X}_1, \ldots, \mathbf{X}_k]$, where $\mathbf{X}_i \in \mathbb{R}^{d \times n_i}$ contains all samples belonging to the ith class.

In LDA, the between-class covariance matrix $\mathbf{S}_b$ and the within-class covariance matrix $\mathbf{S}_w$ are defined as follows:

$$\mathbf{S}_b = \sum_{i=1}^{k} n_i (\bar{\mathbf{x}}_i - \bar{\mathbf{x}})(\bar{\mathbf{x}}_i - \bar{\mathbf{x}})^T, \tag{2.48}$$

$$\mathbf{S}_w = \sum_{i=1}^{k} \sum_{j \in C_i} (\mathbf{x}_j - \bar{\mathbf{x}}_i)(\mathbf{x}_j - \bar{\mathbf{x}}_i)^T. \tag{2.49}$$

The total covariance matrix $\mathbf{S}_t$, which is defined below, can be decomposed as the sum of $\mathbf{S}_b$ and $\mathbf{S}_w$:

$$\mathbf{S}_t = \sum_{i=1}^{n} (\mathbf{x}_i - \bar{\mathbf{x}})(\mathbf{x}_i - \bar{\mathbf{x}})^T = \mathbf{S}_b + \mathbf{S}_w. \tag{2.50}$$

The objective of LDA is to maximize the distance between instances belonging to different classes while minimizing the distance between instances belonging to the same class after projection. Formally, LDA solves the following optimization problem:

$$\max J(\mathbf{w}) = \frac{\mathbf{w}^T \mathbf{S}_b \mathbf{w}}{\mathbf{w}^T \mathbf{S}_w \mathbf{w}}, \tag{2.51}$$

where $\mathbf{w} \in \mathbb{R}^d$ is the linear projection. It has been shown that LDA reduces to computing the eigenvectors corresponding to the largest nonzero eigenvalues of the matrix $\mathbf{S}_w^{\dagger} \mathbf{S}_b$ [82].

When PLS is applied for classification, one block of variables corresponds to the data matrix $\mathbf{X}$ while the other block encodes the class membership information. The commonly used scheme to encode the class membership information in multi-class classification is the 1-of-k binary coding scheme [26]:

$$\mathbf{Y}_0 = \begin{bmatrix} \mathbf{1}_{n_1} & \mathbf{0} & \cdots & \mathbf{0} \\ \mathbf{0} & \mathbf{1}_{n_2} & \cdots & \mathbf{0} \\ \vdots & \vdots & \ddots & \vdots \\ \mathbf{0} & \mathbf{0} & \cdots & \mathbf{1}_{n_k} \end{bmatrix}^T \in \mathbb{R}^{k \times n}. \tag{2.52}$$

Note that in our discussion of PLS, we typically assume the columns of $\mathbf{Y}$ are centered, i.e., $\mathbf{Y}\mathbf{1}_n = 0$. It is equivalent to performing the centering operation on the matrix $\mathbf{Y}_0$ as

$$\mathbf{Y} = \mathbf{Y}_0\mathbf{C}, \qquad (2.53)$$

where $\mathbf{C} = \mathbf{I} - \frac{1}{n}\mathbf{1}\mathbf{1}^T$ is called the centering matrix. Note that $\mathbf{C} = \mathbf{C}^T$ and $\mathbf{C}^2 = \mathbf{C}$, which implies that $\mathbf{C}$ is an orthogonal projection [94].

An alternative form of the indicator matrix as proposed in [16] is defined as follows:

$$\mathbf{Z}_0 = \begin{bmatrix} \mathbf{1}_{n_1} & \mathbf{0} & \cdots & \mathbf{0} \\ \mathbf{0} & \mathbf{1}_{n_2} & \cdots \mathbf{0} \\ \vdots & \vdots & \ddots & \vdots \\ \mathbf{0} & \mathbf{0} & \cdots & \mathbf{1}_{n_{k-1}} \\ \mathbf{0} & \mathbf{0} & \cdots & \mathbf{0} \end{bmatrix}^T \in \mathbb{R}^{(k-1)\times n}. \qquad (2.54)$$

The difference between $\mathbf{Z}_0$ and $\mathbf{Y}_0$ is that the last row in $\mathbf{Y}_0$ is deleted in $\mathbf{Z}_0$. Note that in this section we focus on multi-class classification, where the classes are mutually exclusive. As a result, $\mathbf{Z}_0$ still conveys the full membership information by deleting the last row in $\mathbf{Y}_0$. Similarly, we also perform the centering operation for $\mathbf{Z}_0$:

$$\mathbf{Z} = \mathbf{Z}_0\mathbf{C}. \qquad (2.55)$$

Note that for the sample covariance matrix $\mathbf{S}_y = \mathbf{Y}\mathbf{Y}^T \in \mathbb{R}^{k\times k}$, where the indicator matrix $\mathbf{Y}$ is given in Eq. (2.53), we have $\text{rank}(\mathbf{S}_y) = k - 1$ in multi-class classification and $\text{rank}(\mathbf{S}_y) = k$ in multi-label classification. For multi-class classification, we have $\mathbf{S}_z = \mathbf{Z}\mathbf{Z}^T \in \mathbb{R}^{(k-1)\times(k-1)}$ and $\text{rank}(\mathbf{S}_z) = k - 1$. As discussed in Section 2.1.1, the weight vector $\mathbf{w}$ is the eigenvector of the matrix $\mathbf{X}\mathbf{Y}^T\mathbf{Y}\mathbf{X}^T$, and $\mathbf{c}$ is the eigenvector of $\mathbf{Y}\mathbf{X}^T\mathbf{X}\mathbf{Y}^T$. In classification, we are more interested in the projection for the data matrix $\mathbf{X}$. The following results, established in [16], elucidate the connection between PLS and LDA.

Theorem 2.5 *Given the data matrix* $\mathbf{X}$, *and indicator matrices* $\mathbf{Y}$ *and* $\mathbf{Z}$ *as defined in Eqs. (2.53) and (2.55), and assume that* $\mathbf{X}$, $\mathbf{Y}$, *and* $\mathbf{Z}$ *are all centered. Then we have*

$$\mathbf{X}\mathbf{Y}^T\mathbf{Y}\mathbf{X}^T = \mathbf{H}^*, \text{ where } \mathbf{H}^* = \sum_{i=1}^{k} n_i^2(\bar{\mathbf{x}}_i - \bar{\mathbf{x}})(\bar{\mathbf{x}}_i - \bar{\mathbf{x}})^T, \qquad (2.56)$$

$$\mathbf{X}\mathbf{Z}^T\mathbf{Z}\mathbf{X}^T = \mathbf{H}^{**}, \text{ where } \mathbf{H}^{**} = \sum_{i=1}^{k-1} n_i^2(\bar{\mathbf{x}}_i - \bar{\mathbf{x}})(\bar{\mathbf{x}}_i - \bar{\mathbf{x}})^T. \qquad (2.57)$$

Proof Since $\mathbf{X}$ has already been centered, we have $\mathbf{XC} = \mathbf{X}$. It follows that

$$
\begin{aligned}
\mathbf{XY}^T\mathbf{YX}^T &= \mathbf{X}(\mathbf{Y}_0\mathbf{C})^T(\mathbf{Y}_0\mathbf{C})\mathbf{X}^T \\
&= \mathbf{XC}^T\mathbf{Y}_0^T\mathbf{Y}_0\mathbf{C}\mathbf{X}^T \\
&= (\mathbf{XC})\,\mathbf{Y}_0^T\mathbf{Y}_0\,(\mathbf{XC})^T \\
&= \mathbf{XY}_0^T\mathbf{Y}_0\mathbf{X} \\
&= [\mathbf{X}_1, \mathbf{X}_2, \ldots, \mathbf{X}_k]
\begin{bmatrix}
\mathbf{1}_{n_1}\mathbf{1}_{n_1}^T & \mathbf{0} & \cdots & \mathbf{0} \\
\mathbf{0} & \mathbf{1}_{n_2}\mathbf{1}_{n_2}^T & \cdots & \mathbf{0} \\
\vdots & \vdots & \ddots & \vdots \\
\mathbf{0} & \mathbf{0} & \cdots & \mathbf{1}_{n_k}\mathbf{1}_{n_k}^T
\end{bmatrix}
\begin{bmatrix}
\mathbf{X}_1^T \\
\mathbf{X}_2^T \\
\vdots \\
\mathbf{X}_k^T
\end{bmatrix} \\
&= \sum_{i=1}^{k} \mathbf{X}_i\mathbf{1}_{n_i}\mathbf{1}_{n_i}^T\mathbf{X}_i^T \\
&= \sum_{i=1}^{k} (n_i\bar{\mathbf{x}}_i)(n_i\bar{\mathbf{x}}_i)^T \\
&= \sum_{i=1}^{k} n_i^2\bar{\mathbf{x}}_i(\bar{\mathbf{x}}_i)^T \\
&= \sum_{i=1}^{k} n_i^2(\bar{\mathbf{x}}_i - \bar{\mathbf{x}})(\bar{\mathbf{x}}_i - \bar{\mathbf{x}})^T \\
&= \mathbf{H}^*.
\end{aligned}
$$

In the above derivation we use the fact that $\mathbf{x}_i = \frac{1}{n_i}\mathbf{X}_i\mathbf{1}_{n_i}$ and $\bar{\mathbf{x}} = \mathbf{0}$ as $\mathbf{X}$ has been centered. Similarly, we can show that

$$
\mathbf{XZ}^T\mathbf{ZX}^T = \sum_{i=1}^{k-1} n_i^2(\bar{\mathbf{x}}_i - \bar{\mathbf{x}})(\bar{\mathbf{x}}_i - \bar{\mathbf{x}})^T = \mathbf{H}^{**}.
$$

This completes the proof of this theorem. ∎

Theorem 2.5 shows that the projection vector for $\mathbf{X}$, i.e., $\mathbf{w}$, is the eigenvector of $\mathbf{H}^*$ if the indicator matrix is defined in Eq. (2.53). Note that $\mathbf{H}^*$ is similar to the between-class covariance matrix $\mathbf{S}_b$, while the weights are different. This connection to LDA reveals the success of PLS in classification. The argument also holds for $\mathbf{H}^{**}$ if the indicator matrix is defined in Eq. (2.55). Although the eigenstructures of $\mathbf{H}^*$ and $\mathbf{H}^{**}$ are computed in PLS, they are still different from the between-class covariance matrix $\mathbf{S}_b$. However, we can show that the between-class covariance matrix $\mathbf{S}_b$ equals the matrix $\mathbf{XZ}^T(\mathbf{ZZ}^T)^{-1}\mathbf{ZX}^T$ when the class indicator matrix $\mathbf{Z}$ is used.

Theorem 2.6 *Given the data matrix $\mathbf{X}$, and the class indicator matrix $\mathbf{Z}$ as defined in Eq. (2.55), and assume that $\mathbf{X}$ and $\mathbf{Z}$ are centered. Then we have*

$$
\mathbf{XZ}^T(\mathbf{ZZ}^T)^{-1}\mathbf{ZX}^T = \mathbf{S}_b = \sum_{i=1}^{k} n_i(\bar{\mathbf{x}}_i - \bar{\mathbf{x}})(\bar{\mathbf{x}}_i - \bar{\mathbf{x}})^T. \tag{2.58}
$$

The proof of Theorem 2.6 is given in Appendix A.1.

Recall that in PLS we try to maximize the covariance between two blocks of variables after projection. In contrast, CCA tries to maximize the correlation. Note the the objective function of PLS in Eq. (2.8) can be considered a penalized version of CCA, with PCA on $\mathbf{X}$ and $\mathbf{Y}$ simultaneously. In classification tasks, it is not necessary to analyze the variance of the indicator matrix $\mathbf{Y}$. Thus, we consider the following objective function:

$$\frac{\text{cov}\left(\mathbf{X}^T\mathbf{w}, \mathbf{Y}^T\mathbf{c}\right)^2}{\text{var}\left(\mathbf{Y}^T\mathbf{c}\right)} = \text{var}\left(\mathbf{X}^T\mathbf{w}\right)\text{corr}\left(\mathbf{X}^T\mathbf{w}, \mathbf{Y}^T\mathbf{c}\right)^2. \qquad (2.59)$$

The optimal weight vector $\mathbf{w}^*$ can be obtained by solving the following optimization problem:

$$\max_{\mathbf{w},\mathbf{c}} \quad \mathbf{w}^T\mathbf{X}\mathbf{Y}^T\mathbf{c} \qquad (2.60)$$

$$\text{s.t.} \quad \mathbf{w}^T\mathbf{w} = 1$$
$$\mathbf{c}^T\mathbf{Y}\mathbf{Y}^T\mathbf{c} = 1.$$

Using the Lagrange dual function in optimization theory, it can be shown that $\mathbf{w}^*$ is the eigenvector corresponding to the largest eigenvalue of the following eigenvalue problem:

$$\mathbf{X}\mathbf{Y}^T\left(\mathbf{Y}\mathbf{Y}^T\right)^{-1}\mathbf{Y}\mathbf{X}^T\mathbf{w} = \lambda\mathbf{w}. \qquad (2.61)$$

It can also be shown that multiple weight vectors $\{\mathbf{w}_i\}_{i=1}^{\ell}(\ell < k)$ under the orthogonality constraint $\mathbf{w}_i^T\mathbf{w}_j = \delta_{ij}$ can be obtained by computing eigenvectors corresponding to the largest ℓ eigenvalues of $\mathbf{X}\mathbf{Y}^T\left(\mathbf{Y}\mathbf{Y}^T\right)^{-1}\mathbf{Y}\mathbf{X}^T$, where $\delta_{ij} = 0$ if $i \neq j$ and $\delta_{ij} = 1$ otherwise.

Using the modified objective function in Eq. (2.59) and the new indicator matrix in Eq. (2.55), we can show that the revised PLS amounts to solving the eigenvector of the between-class covariance matrix $\mathbf{S}_b$ in LDA. The main results are summarized in the following theorem:

Theorem 2.7 *If the modified objective function given in Eq. (2.59) is used in PLS classification, and the indicator matrix is defined as $\mathbf{Z}_0$ in Eq. (2.55), then the weight vector for $\mathbf{X}$ is the eigenvector of the between-class covariance matrix $\mathbf{S}_b$ associated with the largest eigenvalue.*

Proof   As discussed above, the weight vector $\mathbf{w}$ for $\mathbf{X}$ is the eigenvector of the following eigenvalue problem associated with the largest eigenvalue:

$$\mathbf{X}\mathbf{Z}^T\left(\mathbf{Z}\mathbf{Z}^T\right)^{-1}\mathbf{Z}\mathbf{X}^T\mathbf{w} = \lambda\mathbf{w}, \qquad (2.62)$$

where $\mathbf{Z} = \mathbf{Z}_0\mathbf{C}$. It follows from Theorem 2.6 that $\mathbf{X}\mathbf{Z}^T\left(\mathbf{Z}\mathbf{Z}^T\right)^{-1}\mathbf{Z}\mathbf{X}^T = \mathbf{S}_b$. This completes the proof of this theorem.   ∎

Chapter 3

Canonical Correlation Analysis

Canonical Correlation Analysis (CCA) is a classical technique for finding the correlations between two sets of multi-dimensional variables [132]. CCA makes use of two views of the same set of objects and projects them onto lower-dimensional spaces in which they are maximally correlated. It has become a powerful tool to analyze so-called paired data $(\mathbf{X}, \mathbf{Y})$, where $\mathbf{X}$ and $\mathbf{Y}$ are two different representations of the same set of objects [210]. Such a scenario arises in many real-world applications. For example, in parallel corpus [139], there are texts in two languages that are similar in content, which can be considered as the paired data sets. In content-based image retrieval [105], the image and the associated texts can be considered as two different views of the same semantic representation.

Canonical correlation analysis and its extensions have been used widely in a variety of areas, such as machine learning [105, 220], biomedical informatics [149, 181, 247, 251, 252, 259, 260], and natural language processing [157]. For example, in [105, 107] CCA is applied to integrate image and text data to enable the retrieval of images from a text query without reference to the label information associated with images, and promising results have been achieved. In particular, CCA is widely used in genomic data analysis since it is an ideal tool to analyze multiple types of genomic data simultaneously. Sparse CCA formulations have also been used to identify genes whose expression is correlated with other data [251, 252, 259].

3.1 Classical Canonical Correlation Analysis

3.1.1 Linear Correlation Coefficient

The linear correlation coefficient between two variables x and y ($x, y \in \mathbb{R}$) is defined as the covariance of the two variables divided by the product of their standard deviations:

$$\rho = \frac{\text{cov}(x, y)}{\text{std}(x)\,\text{std}(y)} = \frac{\mathbb{E}[(x - \overline{x})(y - \overline{y})]}{\text{std}(x)\,\text{std}(y)}, \tag{3.1}$$

where $\mathbb{E}[z]$ denotes the expectation of variable z, $\text{std}(x)$ and $\text{std}(y)$ are the standard deviations of x and y, and $\overline{x}$ and $\overline{y}$ are the means of x and y, respectively. Given the samples $\{x_i\}_{i=1}^n$ and $\{y_i\}_{i=1}^n$, the sample correlation coefficient, or the Pearson product-moment correlation coefficient between x and y, is defined as

$$\rho = \frac{\sum_{i=1}^{n}(x_i - \bar{x})(y_i - \bar{y})}{\sqrt{\sum_{i=1}^{n}(x_i - \bar{x})^2}\sqrt{\sum_{i=1}^{n}(y_i - \bar{y})^2}}. \tag{3.2}$$

Note that when $\bar{x} = \bar{y} = 0$, the sample correlation coefficient can be simplified as:

$$\rho = \frac{\sum_{i=1}^{n} x_i y_i}{\sqrt{\sum_{i=1}^{n} x_i^2}\sqrt{\sum_{i=1}^{n} y_i^2}}, \tag{3.3}$$

which can be expressed in the following vector form:

$$\rho = \frac{\mathbf{x}^T \mathbf{y}}{\|\mathbf{x}\|_2 \|\mathbf{y}\|_2}, \tag{3.4}$$

where $\mathbf{x} = [x_1, \ldots, x_n]^T$ and $\mathbf{y} = [y_1, \ldots, y_n]^T$.

The linear correlation coefficient measures the strength of the linear association between two variables x and y. In fact, the sample correlation coefficient is the standardized version of the sample covariance. It can be verified easily that the correlation coefficient is between -1 and $+1$ using Eq. (3.4). The sign of ρ shows the direction of the association. A negative value of ρ indicates a negative correlation while a positive value of ρ implies a positive association between x and y. In particular, the value of -1 implies a perfect negative correlation while the value of $+1$ shows a perfect positive correlation. The value of 0 indicates a lack of linear association. Figure 3.1 gives some sample distributions and the corresponding linear correlation coefficients.

Intuitively, the correlation coefficient measures the extent to which the two variables can be fitted by a straight line. The line is called the regression line or the least squares line, since the sum of squared distances from all data points to the line is minimized. This definition of the correlation coefficient also reveals some interesting connections between the correlation coefficient and linear regression. In Figure 3.1(A), the data points are distributed along a straight line, which leads to a large correlation coefficient close to 1. In contrast, in Figure 3.1 (C) the correlation coefficient is close to 0 since there is no linear relationship between x and y. Note that the correlation coefficient can only capture the linear association between two variables. Thus, nonlinear association cannot be revealed by the correlation coefficient.

3.1.2 The Maximum Correlation Formulation of CCA

The motivation of CCA is that the linear relationship between variables may not be obvious in the original space, even though they are highly correlated. In order to capture the underlying linear association, CCA tries to find basis vectors for the two sets of variables such that they are maximally correlated after they are projected onto the basis vectors.

Let $\mathbf{X} = [\mathbf{x}_1, \ldots, \mathbf{x}_n] \in \mathbb{R}^{d \times n}$ and $\mathbf{Y} = [\mathbf{y}_1, \ldots, \mathbf{y}_n] \in \mathbb{R}^{k \times n}$ be the matrix representations for two different sets of variables, where $\mathbf{x}_i$ and $\mathbf{y}_i$ correspond to the

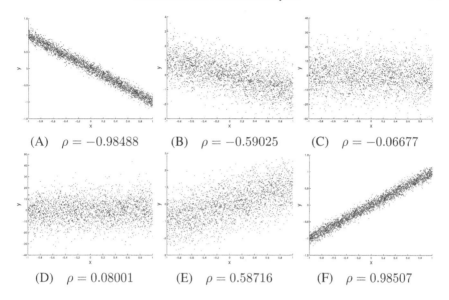

(A)　$\rho = -0.98488$　　　(B)　$\rho = -0.59025$　　　(C)　$\rho = -0.06677$

(D)　$\rho = 0.08001$　　　(E)　$\rho = 0.58716$　　　(F)　$\rho = 0.98507$

FIGURE 3.1: Illustration of the linear correlation coefficient.

ith sample. Assume that both $\{\mathbf{x}_i\}_{i=1}^n$ and $\{\mathbf{y}_i\}_{i=1}^n$ are centered. CCA computes two projection vectors, $\mathbf{w}_x \in \mathbb{R}^d$ and $\mathbf{w}_y \in \mathbb{R}^k$, such that the correlation coefficient

$$\rho = \frac{\mathbf{w}_x^T \mathbf{X}\mathbf{Y}^T \mathbf{w}_y}{\|\mathbf{w}_x^T \mathbf{X}\|_2 \|\mathbf{w}_y^T \mathbf{Y}\|_2} \tag{3.5}$$

is maximized. Here we apply Eq. (3.4) to compute the correlation coefficient between $\mathbf{w}_x^T \mathbf{X}$ and $\mathbf{w}_y^T \mathbf{Y}$. Note that $(\mathbf{w}_x^T \mathbf{X}, \mathbf{w}_y^T \mathbf{Y})$ is often called the pair of canonical variables, or canonical variate pair [132].

Since ρ is invariant to the scaling of $\mathbf{w}_x$ and $\mathbf{w}_y$, CCA can be formulated equivalently as the following optimization problem:

$$\max_{\mathbf{w}_x, \mathbf{w}_y} \quad \mathbf{w}_x^T \mathbf{X}\mathbf{Y}^T \mathbf{w}_y \tag{3.6}$$

$$\text{s.t.} \quad \mathbf{w}_x^T \mathbf{X}\mathbf{X}^T \mathbf{w}_x = 1,$$

$$\mathbf{w}_y^T \mathbf{Y}\mathbf{Y}^T \mathbf{w}_y = 1.$$

The Lagrangian L associated with the problem in Eq. (3.6) is

$$L(\mathbf{w}_x, \mathbf{w}_y, \lambda_x, \lambda_y) = \mathbf{w}_x^T \mathbf{X}\mathbf{Y}^T \mathbf{w}_y - \frac{\lambda_x}{2}(\mathbf{w}_x^T \mathbf{X}\mathbf{X}^T \mathbf{w}_x - 1) - \frac{\lambda_y}{2}(\mathbf{w}_y^T \mathbf{Y}\mathbf{Y}^T \mathbf{w}_y - 1). \tag{3.7}$$

We compute the derivatives of L with respect to $\mathbf{w}_x$ and $\mathbf{w}_y$ and set them to zero. This leads to the following equations:

$$\mathbf{X}\mathbf{Y}^T \mathbf{w}_y - \lambda_x \mathbf{X}\mathbf{X}^T \mathbf{w}_x = 0, \tag{3.8}$$

$$\mathbf{Y}\mathbf{X}^T \mathbf{w}_x - \lambda_y \mathbf{Y}\mathbf{Y}^T \mathbf{w}_y = 0. \tag{3.9}$$

As a result, we have

$$
\begin{aligned}
\lambda_x &= \lambda_x \mathbf{w}_x^T \mathbf{X} \mathbf{X}^T \mathbf{w}_x \\
&= \mathbf{w}_x^T (\lambda_x \mathbf{X} \mathbf{X}^T \mathbf{w}_x) \\
&= \mathbf{w}_x^T \mathbf{X} \mathbf{Y}^T \mathbf{w}_y \\
&= \mathbf{w}_y^T \mathbf{Y} \mathbf{X}^T \mathbf{w}_x \\
&= \mathbf{w}_y^T (\lambda_y \mathbf{Y} \mathbf{Y}^T \mathbf{w}_y) \\
&= \lambda_y (\mathbf{w}_y^T \mathbf{Y} \mathbf{Y}^T \mathbf{w}_y) \\
&= \lambda_y.
\end{aligned}
$$

In the following discussion, we use λ to denote both λ_x and λ_y as they are always identical. The equalities in Eqs. (3.8) and (3.9) can be formulated equivalently in the following form:

$$
\begin{bmatrix} \mathbf{X} \mathbf{X}^T & \mathbf{X} \mathbf{Y}^T \\ \mathbf{Y} \mathbf{X}^T & \mathbf{Y} \mathbf{Y}^T \end{bmatrix} \begin{bmatrix} \mathbf{w}_x \\ \mathbf{w}_y \end{bmatrix} = (\lambda + 1) \begin{bmatrix} \mathbf{X} \mathbf{X}^T & 0 \\ 0 & \mathbf{Y} \mathbf{Y}^T \end{bmatrix} \begin{bmatrix} \mathbf{w}_x \\ \mathbf{w}_y \end{bmatrix}. \tag{3.10}
$$

Thus, the projections $\mathbf{w}_x$ and $\mathbf{w}_y$ can be computed simultaneously by solving the generalized eigenvalue problem in Eq. (3.10). This formulation also suggests the generalization of CCA to multiple sets of variables, which will be discussed in detail in Section 3.1.5.

In multi-label learning, $\mathbf{X}$ corresponds to the data and $\mathbf{Y}$ corresponds to the associated label information. Thus, the projection of $\mathbf{X}$ is of more interest. Assume that $\mathbf{Y} \mathbf{Y}^T$ is nonsingular. It follows from Eq. (3.9) that

$$
\mathbf{w}_y = \frac{1}{\lambda} \left(\mathbf{Y} \mathbf{Y}^T \right)^{-1} \mathbf{Y} \mathbf{X}^T \mathbf{w}_x. \tag{3.11}
$$

Substituting Eq. (3.11) into Eq. (3.8), we obtain the following generalized eigenvalue problem:

$$
\mathbf{X} \mathbf{Y}^T \left(\mathbf{Y} \mathbf{Y}^T \right)^{-1} \mathbf{Y} \mathbf{X}^T \mathbf{w}_x = \lambda^2 \mathbf{X} \mathbf{X}^T \mathbf{w}_x. \tag{3.12}
$$

Using the Lagrange multiplier technique, $\mathbf{w}$ corresponding to the largest eigenvalue in Eq. (3.12) can also be obtained by solving the following optimization problem:

$$
\max_{\mathbf{w}_x} \quad \mathbf{w}_x^T \mathbf{X} \mathbf{Y}^T \left(\mathbf{Y} \mathbf{Y}^T \right)^{-1} \mathbf{Y} \mathbf{X}^T \mathbf{w}_x \tag{3.13}
$$

$$
\text{s.t.} \quad \mathbf{w}_x^T \mathbf{X} \mathbf{X}^T \mathbf{w}_x = 1.
$$

After determining the first pair of $(\mathbf{w}_x, \mathbf{w}_y)$, we next focus on the second pair. We denote the ith pair of projection vectors as $(\mathbf{w}_x^{(i)}, \mathbf{w}_y^{(i)})$. We impose the constraint that the ith pair of canonical variables, $({\mathbf{w}_x^{(i)}}^T \mathbf{X}, {\mathbf{w}_y^{(i)}}^T \mathbf{Y})$, is the pair of linear combinations having unit variance. Also we maximize the correlation among all choices that are uncorrelated with the previous $i - 1$ pairs of canonical variables. Formally, we solve the following optimization problem in order to obtain the second pair of projection vectors $(\mathbf{w}_x^{(2)}, \mathbf{w}_y^{(2)})$:

$$\max_{\mathbf{w}_x, \mathbf{w}_y} \quad \mathbf{w}_x^{(2)^T} \mathbf{X}\mathbf{Y}^T \mathbf{w}_y^{(2)} \tag{3.14}$$

$$\text{s. t.} \quad \mathbf{w}_x^{(2)^T} \mathbf{X}\mathbf{X}^T \mathbf{w}_x^{(2)} = 1,$$

$$\mathbf{w}_y^{(2)^T} \mathbf{Y}\mathbf{Y}^T \mathbf{w}_y^{(2)} = 1,$$

$$\mathbf{w}_x^{(2)^T} \mathbf{X}\mathbf{X}^T \mathbf{w}_x^{(1)} = 0,$$

$$\mathbf{w}_y^{(2)^T} \mathbf{Y}\mathbf{Y}^T \mathbf{w}_y^{(1)} = 0.$$

Similarly, we can construct the Lagrangian:

$$L(\mathbf{w}_x^{(2)}, \mathbf{w}_y^{(2)}, \lambda_x, \lambda_y, \alpha_x, \alpha_y)$$

$$= \mathbf{w}_x^{(2)^T} \mathbf{X}\mathbf{Y}^T \mathbf{w}_y^{(2)} - \frac{\lambda_x}{2}(\mathbf{w}_x^{(2)^T} \mathbf{X}\mathbf{X}^T \mathbf{w}_x^{(2)} - 1) - \frac{\lambda_y}{2}(\mathbf{w}_y^{(2)^T} \mathbf{Y}\mathbf{Y}^T \mathbf{w}_y^{(2)} - 1)$$

$$- \alpha_x \mathbf{w}_x^{(2)^T} \mathbf{X}\mathbf{X}^T \mathbf{w}_x^{(1)} - \alpha_y \mathbf{w}_y^{(2)^T} \mathbf{Y}\mathbf{Y}^T \mathbf{w}_y^{(1)}.$$

Taking the derivatives of L with respect to $\mathbf{w}_x^{(2)}$ and $\mathbf{w}_y^{(2)}$ and setting them to zero, we have

$$\mathbf{X}\mathbf{Y}^T \mathbf{w}_y^{(2)} - \lambda_x \mathbf{X}\mathbf{X}^T \mathbf{w}_x^{(2)} - \alpha_x \mathbf{X}\mathbf{X}^T \mathbf{w}_x^{(1)} = 0 \tag{3.15}$$

$$\mathbf{Y}\mathbf{X}^T \mathbf{w}_x^{(2)} - \lambda_y \mathbf{Y}\mathbf{Y}^T \mathbf{w}_y^{(2)} - \alpha_y \mathbf{Y}\mathbf{Y}^T \mathbf{w}_y^{(1)} = 0. \tag{3.16}$$

It follows from Eq. (3.15) that

$$\begin{aligned} \lambda_x &= \lambda_x \mathbf{w}_x^{(2)^T} \mathbf{X}\mathbf{X}^T \mathbf{w}_x^{(2)} \\ &= \mathbf{w}_x^{(2)^T} \left(\mathbf{X}\mathbf{Y}^T \mathbf{w}_y^{(2)} - \alpha_x \mathbf{X}\mathbf{X}^T \mathbf{w}_x^{(1)} \right) \\ &= \mathbf{w}_x^{(2)^T} \mathbf{X}\mathbf{Y}^T \mathbf{w}_y^{(2)} - \alpha_x \mathbf{w}_x^{(2)^T} \mathbf{X}\mathbf{X}^T \mathbf{w}_x^{(1)} \\ &= \mathbf{w}_x^{(2)^T} \mathbf{X}\mathbf{Y}^T \mathbf{w}_y^{(2)}, \end{aligned}$$

and

$$\begin{aligned} \alpha_x &= \alpha_x \mathbf{w}_x^{(1)^T} \mathbf{X}\mathbf{X}^T \mathbf{w}_x^{(1)} \\ &= \mathbf{w}_x^{(1)^T} \left(\mathbf{X}\mathbf{Y}^T \mathbf{w}_y^{(2)} - \lambda_x \mathbf{X}\mathbf{X}^T \mathbf{w}_x^{(2)} \right) \\ &= \mathbf{w}_x^{(1)^T} \mathbf{X}\mathbf{Y}^T \mathbf{w}_y^{(2)} \\ &= \lambda \mathbf{w}_y^{(1)^T} \mathbf{Y}\mathbf{Y}^T \mathbf{w}_y^{(2)} \\ &= 0. \end{aligned}$$

In the above derivation we use the fact that $\mathbf{w}_x^{(1)^T} \mathbf{X}\mathbf{Y}^T = \lambda \mathbf{w}_y^{(1)^T} \mathbf{Y}\mathbf{Y}^T$ based on Eq. (3.9). Similarly, it follows from Eq. (3.16) that

$$\lambda_y = \mathbf{w}_y^{(2)^T} \mathbf{Y}\mathbf{X}^T \mathbf{w}_x^{(2)}, \text{ and } \alpha_y = 0.$$

Thus, we have $\lambda_x = \lambda_y$ and denote it as λ as before. Using similar arguments as in the discussion of the first pair of projection vectors, we can show that $[\mathbf{w}_x^{(2)}; \mathbf{w}_y^{(2)}]$ is the second eigenvector of the generalized eigenvalue problem in Eq. (3.10), and $\mathbf{w}_x^{(2)}$ is the second eigenvector of the generalized eigenvalue problem in Eq. (3.12).

Generally, multiple projection vectors $\mathbf{W}_x = [\mathbf{w}_x^{(1)}, \mathbf{w}_x^{(2)}, \dots, \mathbf{w}_x^{(\ell)}] \in \mathbb{R}^{d \times \ell}$ for $\mathbf{X}$ and $\mathbf{W}_y = [\mathbf{w}_y^{(1)}, \mathbf{w}_y^{(2)}, \dots, \mathbf{w}_y^{(\ell)}] \in \mathbb{R}^{k \times \ell}$ for $\mathbf{Y}$ under the orthonormality constraints can be computed by solving the following optimization problem:

$$\min_{\mathbf{W}_x, \mathbf{W}_y} \quad \text{Tr}\left(\mathbf{W}_x^T \mathbf{X} \mathbf{Y}^T \mathbf{W}_y\right) \tag{3.17}$$

$$\text{s.t.} \quad \mathbf{W}_x^T \mathbf{X} \mathbf{X}^T \mathbf{W}_x = \mathbf{I}_\ell,$$
$$\mathbf{W}_y^T \mathbf{Y} \mathbf{Y}^T \mathbf{W}_y = \mathbf{I}_\ell,$$

where ℓ is the number of projection vectors and $\mathbf{I}_\ell$ is the identity matrix. Following the previous discussions, $\mathbf{W}_x$ and $\mathbf{W}_y$ consist of the first ℓ eigenvectors of the generalized eigenvalue problem in Eq. (3.10). In multi-label learning, the projection for $\mathbf{X}$ is of more interest. Similarly, it can be shown that $\mathbf{W}_x$ consists of the first ℓ eigenvectors of the generalized eigenvalue problem in Eq. (3.12), which can also be obtained by solving the following optimization problem [107]:

$$\max_{\mathbf{W}_x \in \mathbb{R}^{d \times \ell}} \quad \text{Tr}(\mathbf{W}_x^T \mathbf{X} \mathbf{Y}^T (\mathbf{Y} \mathbf{Y}^T)^{-1} \mathbf{Y} \mathbf{X}^T \mathbf{W}_x) \tag{3.18}$$

$$\text{s.t.} \quad \mathbf{W}_x^T \mathbf{X} \mathbf{X}^T \mathbf{W}_x = \mathbf{I}_\ell.$$

3.1.3 The Distance Minimization Formulation of CCA

The optimization problem in Eq. (3.6) can be expressed as the following distance minimization problem, where we try to minimize the distance between two views $\mathbf{X}$ and $\mathbf{Y}$ after they are projected onto the lower-dimensional spaces:

$$\min_{\mathbf{w}_x, \mathbf{w}_y} \quad \|\mathbf{w}_x^T \mathbf{X} - \mathbf{w}_y^T \mathbf{Y}\|_2 \tag{3.19}$$

$$\text{s.t.} \quad \mathbf{w}_x^T \mathbf{X} \mathbf{X}^T \mathbf{w}_x = 1,$$
$$\mathbf{w}_y^T \mathbf{Y} \mathbf{Y}^T \mathbf{w}_y = 1.$$

The equivalence relationship between the optimization problems in Eqs. (3.6) and (3.19) can be verified as follows:

$$\begin{aligned}
\|\mathbf{w}_x^T \mathbf{X} - \mathbf{w}_y^T \mathbf{Y}\|_2^2 &= \mathbf{w}_x^T \mathbf{X} \mathbf{X}^T \mathbf{w}_x + \mathbf{w}_y^T \mathbf{Y} \mathbf{Y}^T \mathbf{w}_y - 2\mathbf{w}_x^T \mathbf{X} \mathbf{Y}^T \mathbf{w}_y \\
&= 2 - 2\mathbf{w}_x^T \mathbf{X} \mathbf{Y}^T \mathbf{w}_y,
\end{aligned}$$

where we use the constraints that $\mathbf{w}_x^T \mathbf{X} \mathbf{X}^T \mathbf{w}_x = \mathbf{w}_y^T \mathbf{X} \mathbf{X}^T \mathbf{w}_y = 1$. Thus, maximizing $\mathbf{w}_x^T \mathbf{X} \mathbf{Y}^T \mathbf{w}_y$ is equivalent to minimizing $\|\mathbf{w}_x^T \mathbf{X} - \mathbf{w}_y^T \mathbf{Y}\|_2^2$ or $\|\mathbf{w}_x^T \mathbf{X} - \mathbf{w}_y^T \mathbf{Y}\|_2$.

When multiple projection vectors are required, it can be shown that the optimization problem in Eq. (3.17) can also be formulated as the following distance minimization problem in which the Frobenius norm is used instead:

$$\min_{\mathbf{W}_x, \mathbf{W}_y} \quad \|\mathbf{W}_x^T \mathbf{X} - \mathbf{W}_y^T \mathbf{Y}\|_F \tag{3.20}$$

$$\text{s.t.} \quad \mathbf{W}_x^T \mathbf{X} \mathbf{X}^T \mathbf{W}_x = \mathbf{I},$$

$$\mathbf{W}_y^T \mathbf{Y} \mathbf{Y}^T \mathbf{W}_y = \mathbf{I}.$$

Similarly, we can verify the equivalence relationship between the distance minimization formulation and the original optimization problem in Eq. (3.17) as follows:

$$
\begin{aligned}
& \|\mathbf{W}_x^T \mathbf{X} - \mathbf{W}_y^T \mathbf{Y}\|_F^2 \\
= \ & \text{Tr}\left((\mathbf{W}_x^T \mathbf{X} - \mathbf{W}_y^T \mathbf{Y})(\mathbf{W}_x^T \mathbf{X} - \mathbf{W}_y^T \mathbf{Y})^T\right) \\
= \ & \text{Tr}(\mathbf{W}_x^T \mathbf{X} \mathbf{X}^T \mathbf{W}_x) + \text{Tr}(\mathbf{W}_y^T \mathbf{Y} \mathbf{Y}^T \mathbf{W}_y) - 2\,\text{Tr}(\mathbf{W}_x^T \mathbf{X} \mathbf{Y}^T \mathbf{W}^T) \\
= \ & 2\,\text{Tr}(\mathbf{I}) - 2\,\text{Tr}(\mathbf{W}_x^T \mathbf{X} \mathbf{Y}^T \mathbf{W}^T).
\end{aligned}
$$

The distance minimization formulation possesses a number of appealing properties connecting CCA to other classical problems, such as linear regression. Thus, different variants of CCA can be obtained by incorporating some penalty terms into the corresponding linear regression [252], including ℓ_2-norm regularization, ℓ_1-norm regularization [230], and elastic net regularization [288].

3.1.4 Regularized CCA

In practice, the performance of CCA critically depends on regularization, especially when the sample size is relatively small as compared to the data dimensionality. Note that the generalized eigenvalue problem in Eq. (3.12) can be transformed into an eigenvalue problem by multiplying $(\mathbf{X}\mathbf{X}^T)^{-1}$ on both sides, where $\mathbf{X}\mathbf{X}^T$ is the sample covariance matrix. The solution to the eigenvalue problem may not be reliable if $\mathbf{X}\mathbf{X}^T$ is close to being singular. To improve robustness and reduce overfitting, one common approach is to add a scaled identity matrix to the sample covariance matrices $\mathbf{X}\mathbf{X}^T$ and $\mathbf{Y}\mathbf{Y}^T$ [11, 58], resulting in the following generalized eigenvalue problem in regularized CCA (rCCA):

$$\mathbf{X}\mathbf{Y}^T(\mathbf{Y}\mathbf{Y}^T + \gamma_y \mathbf{I})^{-1}\mathbf{Y}\mathbf{X}^T\mathbf{w}_x = \lambda^2(\mathbf{X}\mathbf{X}^T + \gamma_x \mathbf{I})\mathbf{w}_x, \tag{3.21}$$

where $\gamma_x > 0$ and $\gamma_y > 0$ are regularization parameters. The regularization employed in CCA can also be interpreted from the Bayesian perspective [12].

In the above discussions, regularization terms on both $\mathbf{X}$ and $\mathbf{Y}$ are considered. In fact, only regularization on $\mathbf{X}$ affects the computation of $\mathbf{W}_x$. We will discuss the effects of regularization on $\mathbf{X}$ and $\mathbf{Y}$ in detail in Section 3.3.

3.1.5 CCA for Multiple Sets of Variables

In traditional CCA, only two sets of variables are considered. In fact, CCA can be generalized to deal with problems with more than two sets of variables. The CCA formulation for multiple sets of variables aims to compute linear projections for multiple sets of variables simultaneously [137]. We will discuss CCA for multiple sets of variables based on the minimum distance formulation in the following.

Let $\mathbf{X}^{(i)} \in \mathbb{R}^{d_i \times n}$ be the ith view, for $i = 1, \ldots, K$, where K is the number of views. CCA for multiple sets of variables involves the following optimization problem [92, 137]:

$$\min_{\mathbf{W}^{(1)}, \ldots, \mathbf{W}^{(K)}} \sum_{i,j=1, i \neq j}^{K} \| \mathbf{W}^{(i)^T} \mathbf{X}^{(i)} - \mathbf{W}^{(j)^T} \mathbf{X}^{(j)} \|_F \qquad (3.22)$$

$$\text{s.t.} \quad \mathbf{W}^{(i)^T} \mathbf{X}^{(i)} \mathbf{X}^{(i)^T} \mathbf{W}^{(i)} = \mathbf{I}, \quad i = 1, \ldots, K,$$

where $\mathbf{W}^{(i)}$ is the projection matrix for the ith view $\mathbf{X}^{(i)}$. The main idea of generalized CCA for multiple sets of variables is that the sum of all pairwise distances between different views in the projected subspaces is minimized. Similar to traditional CCA discussed above, it can be shown that the optimization problem in Eq. (3.22) reduces to the following generalized eigenvalue problem [210]:

$$\begin{bmatrix} \mathbf{C}_{11} & \mathbf{C}_{12} & \cdots & \mathbf{C}_{1K} \\ \mathbf{C}_{21} & \mathbf{C}_{22} & \cdots & \mathbf{C}_{2K} \\ \vdots & \vdots & \ddots & \vdots \\ \mathbf{C}_{K1} & \mathbf{C}_{K2} & \cdots & \mathbf{C}_{KK} \end{bmatrix} \begin{bmatrix} \mathbf{w}^{(1)} \\ \mathbf{w}^{(2)} \\ \vdots \\ \mathbf{w}^{(K)} \end{bmatrix} = (\lambda + 1) \begin{bmatrix} \mathbf{C}_{11} & 0 & \cdots & 0 \\ 0 & \mathbf{C}_{22} & \cdots & 0 \\ \vdots & \vdots & \ddots & \vdots \\ 0 & 0 & \cdots & \mathbf{C}_{KK} \end{bmatrix} \begin{bmatrix} \mathbf{w}^{(1)} \\ \mathbf{w}^{(2)} \\ \vdots \\ \mathbf{w}^{(K)} \end{bmatrix},$$

where $\mathbf{C}_{ij} = \mathbf{X}^{(i)} \mathbf{X}^{(j)^T}$ is the sample covariance matrix between the ith set of variables and the jth set of variables. It reduces to the generalized eigenvalue problem in Eq. (3.10) for traditional CCA when $K = 2$.

3.2 Sparse CCA

Recently, many extensions of CCA have been proposed as new problems arise in various applications. For example, as multiple assays on the same set of patients become popular, it requires effective tools to integrate the data and select important features in genomic data analysis [260]. One challenge of genomic data analysis is that the dimensionality is much larger than the sample size. To circumvent this problem, various sparse CCA formulations have been proposed.

Sparsity has attracted a lot of attention in statistics and machine learning recently [68, 109, 230]. Sparsity often leads to easy interpretation, and it has been incorporated into many formulations such as multivariate linear regression [230], principal component analysis [289], and CCA [85, 106, 149, 181, 188, 220, 251, 252, 258–260]. Sparse CCA computes pairs of linear projections such that the maximal correlation is achieved in the reduced subspace with a small number of variables being involved in each projection. Indeed, it has been shown that a significant proportion of the correlations can be captured using a relatively small number of variables [258].

The existing sparse CCA algorithms can be roughly categorized into three classes:

- The first approach formulates CCA as an equivalent least squares problem and then applies ℓ_1-norm regularization [230] to the resulting least squares formulation.

- The second approach employs the iterative greedy scheme to compute the projection vectors sequentially.

- The third approach extends the CCA formulation based on the probabilistic interpretation of CCA from the Bayesian perspective.

3.2.1 Sparse CCA via Linear Regression

It has been shown in [220] that CCA is equivalent to the least squares formulation for the following the target matrix:

$$\tilde{\mathbf{T}} = \mathbf{Y}^T (\mathbf{Y}\mathbf{Y}^T)^{-\frac{1}{2}} \in \mathbb{R}^{n \times k}. \tag{3.23}$$

The detailed proof of this equivalence relationship, which is summarized in Theorem 4.2, is given in Chapter 4. Based on the equivalence relationship, sparsity in CCA can be achieved by applying an appropriate regularization to the least squares formulation. It is well-known that ℓ_1-norm regularization can induce sparse solutions [68, 230], and it has been introduced into the least squares formulation, resulting in the so-called lasso [230]. Based on the equivalence relationship between CCA and least squares, ℓ_1-norm regularized least squares CCA formulation, called "LS-CCA$_1$", has been developed, which minimizes the following objective function:

$$L_1(\mathbf{W}, \lambda) = \|\mathbf{W}^T \mathbf{X} - \tilde{\mathbf{T}}\|_F^2 + \lambda \sum_{j=1}^{k} \|\mathbf{w}_j\|_1, \tag{3.24}$$

where $\mathbf{W} = [\mathbf{w}_1, \ldots, \mathbf{w}_k] \in \mathbb{R}^{d \times k}$ are projection vectors for $\mathbf{X}$. LS-CCA$_1$ can be solved efficiently using existing solvers for ℓ_1-norm regularized linear regression [81, 104, 160].

3.2.2 Sparse CCA via Iterative Greedy Algorithms

The second approach employs greedy schemes to compute sparse projections iteratively [106, 149, 181, 251, 258–260]. The overall structure of this type of algorithm is summarized in Algorithm 3.1, where ℓ is the number of pairs of projection vectors $(\mathbf{w}_x, \mathbf{w}_y)$. This approach computes the projection vectors in a sequential fashion, and at each step the projection pair $(\mathbf{w}_x, \mathbf{w}_y)$ is computed using a greedy algorithm. The

---

Algorithm 3.1 The Greedy Iterative Sparse CCA Algorithm

Input: X, Y, ℓ, and other control parameters.
Output: $\mathbf{W}_x$, $\mathbf{W}_y$.
for $i = 1$ to ℓ **do**
  Compute $\mathbf{w}_x^{(i)}$ and $\mathbf{w}_y^{(i)}$ using the greedy algorithm.
  Update **X** and **Y** using $\mathbf{w}_x^{(i)}$ and $\mathbf{w}_y^{(i)}$.
end for
Set $\mathbf{W}_x = [\mathbf{w}_x^{(1)}, \ldots, \mathbf{w}_x^{(\ell)}]$ and $\mathbf{W}_y = [\mathbf{w}_y^{(1)}, \ldots, \mathbf{w}_y^{(\ell)}]$.

---

major difference among different sparse CCA algorithms lies in the different greedy algorithms used to compute $(\mathbf{w}_x, \mathbf{w}_y)$.

In [258], the greedy algorithm selects pairs of features from **X** and **Y** such that the correlation between **X** and **Y** after projection is maximized. At each stage, this greedy algorithm selects two index sets I and J using a forward and stepwise subset selection method, where I and J correspond to the selected indices in **X** and **Y**, respectively. Initially, I and J are both set to be an empty set. At each iteration, the algorithm selects one index from **X** or **Y** such that the resulting correlation after projection is maximized. The procedure is terminated when the required number of features have been selected at each stage.

In [106, 251, 252], the projection vectors $(\mathbf{w}_x, \mathbf{w}_y)$ are computed based on the distance minimization formulation of CCA using an alternating algorithm. At each iteration, one of $\mathbf{w}_x$ and $\mathbf{w}_y$ is fixed while the other one is optimized. Note that in this case, the distance minimization formulation reduces to a least squares problem. Sparse solutions can be obtained by incorporating ℓ_1-norm regularization. This procedure is repeated until convergence, resulting in the projection pair $(\mathbf{w}_x, \mathbf{w}_y)$ at that stage.

In [181, 259, 260], an iterative sparse algorithm is developed by estimating the singular vectors of $\mathbf{X}\mathbf{Y}^T$. At each step, the singular vectors of $\mathbf{X}\mathbf{Y}^T$ are estimated using soft-thresholding. In [260], the sparse CCA is further extended to analyze multiple data sets simultaneously, and a technique called sparse supervised CCA is proposed to integrate different views as well as some label information. Note that many other extensions of CCA can be derived based on Algorithm 3.1. For example, nonnegative CCA algorithms have been proposed by imposing the nonnegativity constraint in the greedy framework to compute the projection pairs $(\mathbf{w}_x, \mathbf{w}_y)$ [212, 260].

3.2.3 Sparse CCA via Bayesian Learning

The third approach is based on the probabilistic interpretation of CCA [12, 85, 188]. Following the probabilistic interpretation of CCA [12], a nonparametric, fully Bayesian framework is proposed to capture the sparsity underlying the projections [188]. The sparse CCA framework proposed in [188] can automatically select the number of correlation components using the Indian Buffet Process (IBP) [90]. In

TABLE 3.1: A list of algorithms derived from different combinations of γ_x and γ_y in the unified framework for CCA and PLS.

Algorithm	γ_x	γ_y
Canonical Correlation Analysis	0	0
Regularized CCA	$\frac{\lambda}{1+\lambda}$	0
Orthonormalized PLS	0	1
Regularized OPLS	$\frac{\lambda}{1+\lambda}$	1
Partial Least Squares	1	1

addition, this framework can be applied for semi-supervised dimensionality reduction by making use of partial labels.

3.3 Relationship between CCA and Partial Least Squares

CCA and Partial Least Squares (PLS) share many common features. They both model the relationship between two blocks of variables by seeking the optimal projections. However, CCA finds the optimal projections by maximizing the correlation coefficient after the projection while PLS maximizes the covariance after the projection. CCA reduces to a generalized eigenvalue problem while PLS involves an iterative procedure. At each iteration of PLS, it also reduces to eigenvalue problems in Eqs. (2.3) and (2.6). However, different deflation schemes are applied in PLS, resulting in different variants of PLS.

In this section we first discuss the relationship between PLS and CCA by establishing a unified framework using canonical ridge analysis [248]. Next we focus on orthonormalized PLS and present the equivalence relationship between CCA and orthonormalized PLS. Based on the equivalence relationship, regularization effects on CCA are also discussed.

3.3.1 A Unified Framework for PLS and CCA

The similarities between PLS and CCA have been observed in the past [30, 196, 255]. For example, a unified framework for Principal Component Analysis (PCA), PLS, CCA, and multiple linear regression is proposed in [30], where each technique can be obtained by selecting a different parameter value. In this subsection, we focus on the unified framework established in [248] using canonical ridge analysis, which considers the following optimization problem:

$$\max_{|\mathbf{w}_x|=|\mathbf{w}_y|=1} \frac{\text{cov}(\mathbf{w}_x^T \mathbf{X}, \mathbf{w}_y^T \mathbf{Y})}{\sqrt{\left([1-\gamma_x]\,\text{var}(\mathbf{w}_x^T \mathbf{X}) + \gamma_x\right)\left([1-\gamma_y]\,\text{var}(\mathbf{w}_y^T \mathbf{Y}) + \gamma_y\right)}}, \quad (3.25)$$

where $0 \leq \gamma_x,\ \gamma_y \leq 1$ are regularization parameters, and $\mathbf{w}_x \in \mathbb{R}^d$, $\mathbf{w}_y \in \mathbb{R}^k$ are projection vectors (or weight vectors) for $\mathbf{X}$ and $\mathbf{Y}$, respectively. It can be verified that the projection vector $\mathbf{w}_x$ can be computed by solving the following eigenvalue problem:

$$\left([1-\gamma_x]\mathbf{XX}^T + \gamma_x\mathbf{I}\right)^{-1}\mathbf{XY}^T\left([1-\gamma_x]\mathbf{YY}^T + \gamma_y\mathbf{I}\right)^{-1}\mathbf{YX}^T\mathbf{w}_x = \lambda\mathbf{w}_x. \quad (3.26)$$

By choosing different values for γ_x and γ_y, the unified framework encompasses PLS, Orthonormalized PLS (OPLS), and CCA, as summarized in Table 3.1. From the unified framework, PLS can be considered a special case of "regularized OPLS" when $\lambda \to +\infty$.

3.3.2 The Equivalence without Regularization

CCA is closely related to orthonormalized partial least squares. In this subsection, we show that the difference between the CCA solution and the OPLS solution is a mere orthogonal transformation. Unlike the discussions in [16], which focus on discrimination only, the analysis here can be applied to regression and dimensionality reduction as well. We further extend the equivalence relationship to the case in which regularization is applied for both sets of variables in the next subsection.

In the following discussion, we use the subscripts *cca* and *pls* to distinguish the variables associated with CCA and OPLS, respectively. We assume that $\mathbf{Y}$ has full row rank, i.e., $\text{rank}(\mathbf{Y}) = k$. Thus, $(\mathbf{YY}^T)^{-\frac{1}{2}}$ is well-defined. We first define two key matrices as follows:

$$\begin{aligned}\mathbf{H}_{cca} &= \mathbf{Y}^T(\mathbf{YY}^T)^{-\frac{1}{2}} \in \mathbb{R}^{n \times k}, &(3.27)\\ \mathbf{H}_{pls} &= \mathbf{Y}^T \in \mathbb{R}^{n \times k}. &(3.28)\end{aligned}$$

It follows from Section 2.1 and Section 3.1 that the solutions to both CCA and OPLS can be expressed as the eigenvectors corresponding to the top eigenvalues of the following matrix:

$$(\mathbf{XX}^T)^{\dagger}(\mathbf{XHH}^T\mathbf{X}^T), \quad (3.29)$$

where $\mathbf{H} = \mathbf{H}_{cca}$ for CCA and $\mathbf{H} = \mathbf{H}_{pls}$ for OPLS.

Next we derive the principal eigenvectors of the generalized eigenvalue problem in Eq. (3.29). Let the Singular Value Decomposition (SVD) of $\mathbf{X}$ be

$$\mathbf{X} = \mathbf{U\Sigma V}^T = \mathbf{U}_1\mathbf{\Sigma}_1\mathbf{V}_1^T, \quad (3.30)$$

where $\mathbf{U} \in \mathbb{R}^{d \times d}$ and $\mathbf{V} \in \mathbb{R}^{n \times n}$ are orthogonal, $\mathbf{U}_1 \in \mathbb{R}^{d \times r}$ and $\mathbf{V}_1 \in \mathbb{R}^{n \times r}$ have orthonormal columns, $\mathbf{\Sigma} \in \mathbb{R}^{d \times n}$ and $\mathbf{\Sigma}_1 \in \mathbb{R}^{r \times r}$ are diagonal, and $r = \text{rank}(\mathbf{X})$. Denote

$$\mathbf{A} = \mathbf{\Sigma}_1^{-1}\mathbf{U}_1^T\mathbf{XH} = \mathbf{\Sigma}_1^{-1}\mathbf{U}_1^T\mathbf{U}_1\mathbf{\Sigma}_1\mathbf{V}_1^T\mathbf{H} = \mathbf{V}_1^T\mathbf{H} \in \mathbb{R}^{r \times k}, \quad (3.31)$$

and let the SVD of $\mathbf{A}$ be $\mathbf{A} = \mathbf{P\Sigma}_A\mathbf{Q}^T$, where $\mathbf{P} \in \mathbb{R}^{r \times r}$ and $\mathbf{Q} \in \mathbb{R}^{k \times k}$ are orthogonal and $\mathbf{\Sigma}_A \in \mathbb{R}^{r \times k}$ is diagonal. Then we have

$$\mathbf{AA}^T = \mathbf{P\Sigma}_A\mathbf{\Sigma}_A^T\mathbf{P}^T. \quad (3.32)$$

Lemma 3.1 *The eigenvectors of* $(\mathbf{X}\mathbf{X}^T)^\dagger(\mathbf{X}\mathbf{H}\mathbf{H}^T\mathbf{X}^T)$ *corresponding to the top* ℓ *eigenvalues are given by*

$$\mathbf{W} = \mathbf{U}_1\boldsymbol{\Sigma}_1^{-1}\mathbf{P}_\ell, \tag{3.33}$$

where $\mathbf{P}_\ell$ *consists of the first* ℓ $(\ell \leq rank(\mathbf{A}))$ *columns of* $\mathbf{P}$.

It follows from Lemma 3.1 that $\mathbf{U}_1$ and $\boldsymbol{\Sigma}_1$ are determined by $\mathbf{X}$. Thus, the only difference between the projections computed by CCA and OPLS lies in $\mathbf{P}_\ell$. The following lemma reveals the property of $\mathbf{P}_\ell$:

Lemma 3.2 *Let* $\mathbf{H}_{cca}$ *and* $\mathbf{H}_{pls}$ *be defined in Eqs. (3.27) and (3.28). Let* $\mathbf{A}_{cca} = \mathbf{V}_1^T\mathbf{H}_{cca}$ *and* $\mathbf{A}_{pls} = \mathbf{V}_1^T\mathbf{H}_{pls}$ *be the matrix* $\mathbf{A}$ *defined in Eq. (3.31) for CCA and OPLS, respectively. Then the range spaces of* $\mathbf{A}_{cca}$ *and* $\mathbf{A}_{pls}$ *are the same, i.e.,* $\mathcal{R}(\mathbf{A}_{cca}) = \mathcal{R}(\mathbf{A}_{pls})$.

The full proofs of Lemmas 3.1 and 3.2 are given in Appendix A.2. With these two lemmas, we can explicate the relationship between the projections computed by CCA and OPLS, as summarized in the following theorem:

Theorem 3.1 *Let the SVD of* $\mathbf{A}_{cca}$ *and* $\mathbf{A}_{pls}$ *be*

$$\mathbf{A}_{cca} = \mathbf{P}_{cca}\boldsymbol{\Sigma}_{\mathbf{A}_{cca}}\mathbf{Q}_{cca}^T,$$
$$\mathbf{A}_{pls} = \mathbf{P}_{pls}\boldsymbol{\Sigma}_{\mathbf{A}_{pls}}\mathbf{Q}_{pls}^T,$$

where $\mathbf{P}_{cca}, \mathbf{P}_{pls} \in \mathbb{R}^{r \times r_A}$, *and* $r_A = \mathrm{rank}(\mathbf{A}_{cca}) = \mathrm{rank}(\mathbf{A}_{pls})$. *Then there exists an orthogonal matrix* $\mathbf{R} \in \mathbb{R}^{r_A \times r_A}$ *such that* $\mathbf{P}_{cca} = \mathbf{P}_{pls}\mathbf{R}$.

Proof Note that $\mathbf{P}_{cca}\mathbf{P}_{cca}^T$ and $\mathbf{P}_{pls}\mathbf{P}_{pls}^T$ are orthogonal projections onto the range spaces of $\mathbf{A}_{cca}$ and $\mathbf{A}_{pls}$, respectively. It follows from Lemma 3.2 that both $\mathbf{P}_{cca}\mathbf{P}_{cca}^T$ and $\mathbf{P}_{pls}\mathbf{P}_{pls}^T$ are orthogonal projections onto the same subspace. Since the orthogonal projection onto a subspace is unique [94], then we have

$$\mathbf{P}_{cca}\mathbf{P}_{cca}^T = \mathbf{P}_{pls}\mathbf{P}_{pls}^T. \tag{3.34}$$

Therefore,

$$\mathbf{P}_{cca} = \mathbf{P}_{cca}\mathbf{P}_{cca}^T\mathbf{P}_{cca} = \mathbf{P}_{pls}\mathbf{P}_{pls}^T\mathbf{P}_{cca} = \mathbf{P}_{pls}\mathbf{R},$$

where $\mathbf{R} = \mathbf{P}_{pls}^T\mathbf{P}_{cca} \in \mathbb{R}^{r_A \times r_A}$. It is easy to verify that $\mathbf{R}$ is orthogonal. ∎

If we retain all the eigenvectors corresponding to the nonzero eigenvalues, i.e., $\ell = r_A$, the difference between CCA and OPLS lies in the orthogonal transformation $\mathbf{R} \in \mathbb{R}^{r_A \times r_A}$. In this case, CCA and OPLS are essentially equivalent, since an orthogonal transformation preserves all pairwise distances.

3.3.3 The Equivalence with Regularization

The equivalence relationship still holds when regularization is employed. We consider regularization on $\mathbf{X}$ and $\mathbf{Y}$ separately.

3.3.3.1   Regularization on X

With regularization on $\mathbf{X}$, we consider the principal eigenvectors of the following matrix for both regularized CCA and regularized OPLS:

$$(\mathbf{X}\mathbf{X}^T + \gamma\mathbf{I})^{-1}(\mathbf{X}\mathbf{H}\mathbf{H}^T\mathbf{X}^T). \tag{3.35}$$

The eigendecomposition of this matrix is derived and summarized in Lemma 3.3. The full proof of this lemma is also provided in Appendix A.2.

Lemma 3.3 *Define the matrix $\mathbf{B} \in \mathbb{R}^{r \times k}$ as*

$$\mathbf{B} = (\boldsymbol{\Sigma}_1^2 + \gamma\mathbf{I})^{-1/2}\boldsymbol{\Sigma}_1\mathbf{V}_1^T\mathbf{H} \tag{3.36}$$

and denote its SVD as $\mathbf{B} = \mathbf{P}_B\boldsymbol{\Sigma}_B\mathbf{Q}_B^T$, where $\mathbf{P}_B \in \mathbb{R}^{r \times r}$ and $\mathbf{Q}_B \in \mathbb{R}^{k \times k}$ are orthogonal, and $\boldsymbol{\Sigma}_B \in \mathbb{R}^{r \times k}$ is diagonal. Then the eigenvectors corresponding to the top ℓ eigenvalues of the matrix $(\mathbf{X}\mathbf{X}^T + \gamma\mathbf{I})^{-1}(\mathbf{X}\mathbf{H}\mathbf{H}^T\mathbf{X}^T)$ are given by

$$\mathbf{W} = \mathbf{U}_1(\boldsymbol{\Sigma}_1^2 + \gamma\mathbf{I})^{-1/2}\mathbf{P}_{B\ell}, \tag{3.37}$$

where $\mathbf{P}_{B\ell}$ consists of the first ℓ ($\ell \leq rank(\mathbf{B})$) columns of $\mathbf{P}_B$.

Using Lemma 3.3 we can show that the equivalence relationship between CCA and OPLS still holds when regularization on $\mathbf{X}$ is applied. The main results are summarized in Lemma 3.4 and Theorem 3.2 below (proofs are similar to the ones in Lemma 3.2 and Theorem 3.1 and are omitted).

Lemma 3.4 *Let $\mathbf{B}_{cca}$ and $\mathbf{B}_{pls}$ be defined as follows:*

$$\begin{aligned}
\mathbf{B}_{cca} &= (\boldsymbol{\Sigma}_1^2 + \gamma\mathbf{I})^{-1/2}\boldsymbol{\Sigma}_1\mathbf{V}_1^T\mathbf{H}_{cca} \\
\mathbf{B}_{pls} &= (\boldsymbol{\Sigma}_1^2 + \gamma\mathbf{I})^{-1/2}\boldsymbol{\Sigma}_1\mathbf{V}_1^T\mathbf{H}_{pls}.
\end{aligned}$$

Then the range spaces of $\mathbf{B}_{cca}$ and $\mathbf{B}_{pls}$ are the same, i.e., $\mathcal{R}(\mathbf{B}_{cca}) = \mathcal{R}(\mathbf{B}_{pls})$.

Theorem 3.2 *Let the SVD of $\mathbf{B}_{cca}$ and $\mathbf{B}_{pls}$ be*

$$\begin{aligned}
\mathbf{B}_{cca} &= \mathbf{P}_{cca}^B\boldsymbol{\Sigma}_{cca}^B(\mathbf{Q}_{cca}^B)^T, \\
\mathbf{B}_{pls} &= \mathbf{P}_{pls}^B\boldsymbol{\Sigma}_{pls}^B(\mathbf{Q}_{Bpls}^B)^T,
\end{aligned}$$

where $\mathbf{P}_{cca}^B, \mathbf{P}_{pls}^B \in \mathbb{R}^{r \times r_B}$, and $r_B = \mathrm{rank}(\mathbf{B}_{cca}) = \mathrm{rank}(\mathbf{B}_{pls})$. Then there exists an orthogonal matrix $\mathbf{R}^B \in \mathbb{R}^{r_B \times r_B}$ such that $\mathbf{P}_{cca}^B = \mathbf{P}_{pls}^B\mathbf{R}^B$.

3.3.3.2   Regularization on Y

With regularization applied on $\mathbf{Y}$, we consider the eigendecomposition of following matrix:

$$(\mathbf{X}\mathbf{X}^T)^\dagger\mathbf{X}\mathbf{Y}^T(\mathbf{Y}\mathbf{Y}^T + \gamma\mathbf{I})^{-1}\mathbf{Y}\mathbf{X}^T. \tag{3.38}$$

The above formulation corresponds to a new matrix $\mathbf{H}_{rcca}$ for regularized CCA:

$$\mathbf{H}_{rcca} = \mathbf{Y}^T(\mathbf{Y}\mathbf{Y}^T + \gamma\mathbf{I})^{-1/2}. \tag{3.39}$$

We establish the equivalence relationship between CCA and OPLS when regularization is applied on $\mathbf{Y}$.

Lemma 3.5 *Let* $\mathbf{H}_{cca}, \mathbf{H}_{pls}$, *and* $\mathbf{H}_{rcca}$ *be defined as in Eqs. (3.27), (3.28), and (3.39), respectively. Then the range spaces of* $\mathbf{H}_{cca}$, $\mathbf{H}_{pls}$, *and* $\mathbf{H}_{rcca}$ *are the same.*

Proof   The proof follows directly from the definitions.   ∎

Lemma 3.5 shows that regularization on $\mathbf{Y}$ does not change the range space of $\mathbf{A}_{cca}$. Thus, the equivalence relationship between CCA and OPLS still holds.

Similarly, regularization on $\mathbf{Y}$ does not change the range space of $\mathbf{B}_{cca}$ when regularization on $\mathbf{X}$ is applied. Therefore, the established equivalence relationship holds when regularization is applied on both $\mathbf{X}$ and $\mathbf{Y}$.

3.3.4   Analysis of Regularization on CCA

Regularization is commonly employed to control the complexity of a learning model and it has been applied in various machine learning algorithms such as support vector machines [207]. In particular, regularization is crucial to kernel CCA [107] in order to avoid the trivial solution. Moreover, the use of regularization in CCA has natural statistical interpretations [11].

The established equivalence relationship between CCA and OPLS provides novel insights into the effect of regularization in CCA. In addition, it leads to a significant reduction in the computations involved in CCA. Regularization is commonly applied on both views in CCA [107, 210], since it is commonly believed that the CCA solution is dependent on both regularization terms. It follows from Lemma 3.5 that the range space of $\mathbf{H}_{rcca}$ is independent of the regularization parameter γ_y. Thus, the range spaces of $\mathbf{A}_{cca}$ and $\mathbf{A}_{pls}$ are the same and the projection for $\mathbf{X}$ computed by rCCA is independent of γ_y. Similarly, we can show that the projection for $\mathbf{Y}$ is independent of regularization on $\mathbf{X}$. Therefore, an important consequence from the equivalence relationship between CCA and OPLS is that the projection of CCA for one view is independent of regularization on the other view.

Recall that the CCA formulation reduces to a generalized eigenvalue problem. In this formulation, we need to compute the inverse of the matrix $\mathbf{Y}\mathbf{Y}^T \in \mathbb{R}^{k \times k}$, which may cause numerical problems. Moreover, the dimensionality k of the data in $\mathbf{Y}$ may be large, and thus computing the inverse can be computationally expensive. For example, in content-based image retrieval [105], the two views correspond to text and image data that are both of high dimensionality. Another important consequence of the established equivalence relationship between CCA and OPLS is that if only the projection for one view is required and the other view is only used to guide the projection on this view, then the inverse of a possibly large matrix can be effectively avoided.

3.4   The Generalized Eigenvalue Problem

Recall that CCA reduces to a generalized eigenvalue problem as in Eq. (3.12). In fact, several other dimensionality reduction algorithms can also be formulated as generalized eigenvalue problems [58], including linear discriminant analysis and partial least squares. In this section, we investigate a class of generalized eigenvalue problems encompassing these algorithms. In addition, we discuss its relationship to the generalized Rayleigh quotient cost function.

Formally, we are interested in the following generalized eigenvalue problem:

$$\mathbf{A}\mathbf{w} = \lambda \mathbf{B}\mathbf{w}, \tag{3.40}$$

where $\mathbf{A} \in \mathbb{S}^d$ and $\mathbf{B} \in \mathbb{S}^d$, i.e., both $\mathbf{A}$ and $\mathbf{B}$ are symmetric $d \times d$ matrices. The generalized eigenvalue problem arises in many scenarios [254], and many algorithms have been proposed to solve it in the literature [94, 254]. For example, we have $\mathbf{A} = \mathbf{X}\mathbf{Y}^T(\mathbf{Y}\mathbf{Y}^T)^{-1}\mathbf{Y}\mathbf{X}^T$ and $\mathbf{B} = \mathbf{X}\mathbf{X}^T$ for computing the projection for $\mathbf{X}$ in CCA.

3.4.1   The Generalized Rayleigh Quotient Cost Function

An important family of cost functions in machine learning and pattern recognition is the so-called generalized Rayleigh quotient [58]:

$$f(\mathbf{w}) = \frac{\mathbf{w}^T \mathbf{A} \mathbf{w}}{\mathbf{w}^T \mathbf{B} \mathbf{w}}. \tag{3.41}$$

For example, the objective function in linear discriminant analysis [82] is in the form of the generalized Rayleigh quotient. It turns out that the generalized eigenvalue problem in Eq. (3.40) provide an efficient way to optimize the generalized Rayleigh quotient cost function.

In the following, we analyze the connection between the generalized eigenvalue problem in Eq. (3.40) and the cost function $f(\mathbf{w})$ in Eq. (3.41). Note that the scaling of $\mathbf{w}$ does not affect the objective function $f(\mathbf{w})$. Hence, maximizing the generalized Rayleigh quotient function $f(\mathbf{w})$ is equivalent to solving the following optimization problem:

$$\max_{\mathbf{w}} \quad \mathbf{w}^T \mathbf{A} \mathbf{w} \tag{3.42}$$
$$\text{s.t.} \quad \mathbf{w}^T \mathbf{B} \mathbf{w} = 1.$$

Applying the Lagrange multiplier technique gives rise to

$$L = \mathbf{w}^T \mathbf{A} \mathbf{w} - \frac{\lambda}{2}(\mathbf{w}^T \mathbf{B} \mathbf{w} - 1).$$

Taking the derivative with respect to $\mathbf{w}$ and setting it to zero, we obtain

$$\mathbf{A}\mathbf{w} - \lambda \mathbf{B}\mathbf{w} = 0$$
$$\Leftrightarrow \quad \mathbf{A}\mathbf{w} = \lambda \mathbf{B}\mathbf{w}.$$

Note that the maximum value of the generalized Rayleigh quotient function $f(\mathbf{w})$ is the largest eigenvalue λ in the generalized eigenvalue problem in Eq. (3.40).

The discussion above can be extended to the more general case when more than one eigenpairs of the generalized eigenvalue problem in Eq. (3.40) are of interest. In this case, these eigenpairs correspond to maximizing the following cost function:

$$f(\mathbf{W}) = \frac{\mathrm{Tr}(\mathbf{W}^T \mathbf{A} \mathbf{W})}{\mathrm{Tr}(\mathbf{W}^T \mathbf{B} \mathbf{W})}, \tag{3.43}$$

where each column of $\mathbf{W}$ corresponds to an eigenvector of the generalized eigenvalue problem in Eq. (3.40).

3.4.2 Properties of the Generalized Eigenvalue Problem

It is well-known that the eigenvalues of the symmetric real eigenvalue problem $\mathbf{A}\mathbf{w} = \lambda\mathbf{w}$ are real, and the resulting eigenvectors are real and orthogonal. However, the orthogonality of eigenvectors generally does not hold for the generalized eigenvalue problem in Eq. (3.40) even when both $\mathbf{A}$ and $\mathbf{B}$ are real and symmetric. Interestingly, the so-called generalized orthogonality properties hold, which are summarized in the following theorem:

Theorem 3.3 *Let the ith eigenpair of the generalized eigenvalue problem $\mathbf{A}\mathbf{w} = \lambda\mathbf{B}\mathbf{w}$ be $(\lambda_i, \mathbf{w}_i)$. If $\mathbf{A} \in \mathbb{S}^d$ and $\mathbf{B} \in \mathbb{S}^d_{++}$, i.e., $\mathbf{A} \in \mathbb{R}^{d \times d}$ is symmetric and $\mathbf{B} \in \mathbb{R}^{d \times d}$ is symmetric and positive definite, then the following generalized orthogonality properties hold:*

$$\mathbf{w}_i^T \mathbf{A} \mathbf{w}_j = \delta_{ij} \lambda_i \tag{3.44}$$

$$\mathbf{w}_i^T \mathbf{B} \mathbf{w}_j = \delta_{ij}, \tag{3.45}$$

where $\delta_{ij} = 1$ if $i = j$ and 0 otherwise.

Proof Since $\mathbf{B} \in \mathbb{R}^{d \times d}$ is symmetric and positive definite, $\mathbf{B}^{1/2}$ is well-defined and nonsingular. Define $\mathbf{u} = \mathbf{B}^{1/2}\mathbf{w}$; then the generalized eigenvalue problem $\mathbf{A}\mathbf{w} = \lambda\mathbf{B}\mathbf{w}$ can be transformed into a symmetric eigenvalue problem:

$$\mathbf{B}^{-1/2} \mathbf{A} \mathbf{B}^{-1/2} \mathbf{u} = \lambda \mathbf{u}.$$

Note that the ith eigenpair of this symmetric eigenvalue problem can be denoted as $(\lambda_i, \mathbf{u}_i)$ where $\mathbf{u}_i = \mathbf{B}^{1/2}\mathbf{w}_i$. It follows from the properties of the symmetric eigenvalue problem that

$$\mathbf{u}_i^T \mathbf{u}_j = \delta_{ij}.$$

Therefore, for $i \neq j$, we have

$$0 = \mathbf{u}_i^T \mathbf{u}_j = \mathbf{w}_i^T \mathbf{B}^{1/2} \mathbf{B}^{1/2} \mathbf{w}_j = \mathbf{w}_i^T \mathbf{B} \mathbf{w}_j = \frac{1}{\lambda_j} \mathbf{w}_i^T \mathbf{A} \mathbf{w}_j.$$

Next we consider the case that $i = j$:

$$\lambda_i = \lambda_i \mathbf{u}_i^T \mathbf{u}_i = \lambda_i \mathbf{w}_i^T \mathbf{B}^{1/2} \mathbf{B}^{1/2} \mathbf{w}_i = \lambda_i \mathbf{w}_i^T \mathbf{B} \mathbf{w}_i = \mathbf{w}_i^T \mathbf{A} \mathbf{w}_i.$$

This completes the proof.   ∎

In the case that $\mathbf{B}$ is singular, an alternative formulation used frequently in machine learning is

$$\mathbf{B}^\dagger \mathbf{A} \mathbf{w} = \lambda \mathbf{w}, \tag{3.46}$$

where $\mathbf{B}^\dagger$ is the Moore–Penrose pseudoinverse of $\mathbf{B}$. The connection between the eigenvalue problem in Eq. (3.46) and the generalized eigenvalue problem $\mathbf{A}\mathbf{w} = \lambda \mathbf{B}\mathbf{w}$ is summarized in the following theorem, and the full proof is given in Appendix A.2.

Theorem 3.4 *Let $\mathbf{A} \in \mathbb{S}^{d \times d}$ and $\mathbf{B} \in \mathbb{S}^{d \times d}$, and assume that $\mathcal{R}(\mathbf{A}) \subseteq \mathcal{R}(\mathbf{B})$, where $\mathcal{R}(\mathbf{A})$ and $\mathcal{R}(\mathbf{B})$ are range spaces of $\mathbf{A}$ and $\mathbf{B}$, respectively. If $(\lambda, \mathbf{w})$ $(\lambda \neq 0)$ is an eigenpair of the eigenvalue problem in Eq. (3.46), then $(\lambda, \mathbf{w})$ is also the eigenpair of the generalized eigenvalue problem $\mathbf{A}\mathbf{w} = \lambda \mathbf{B}\mathbf{w}$. Conversely, if $(\lambda, \mathbf{w})$ $(\lambda \neq 0)$ is an eigenpair of the generalized eigenvalue problem $\mathbf{A}\mathbf{w} = \lambda \mathbf{B}\mathbf{w}$ and $\mathbf{B}\mathbf{B}^\dagger \mathbf{w} \neq 0$, then $(\lambda, \mathbf{B}\mathbf{B}^\dagger \mathbf{w})$ is also the eigenpair of the eigenvalue problem in Eq. (3.46).*

3.4.3   Algorithms for the Generalized Eigenvalue Problem

Many algorithms have been developed to solve the generalized eigenvalue problem in Eq. (3.40) [182]. A natural method to solve the generalized eigenvalue problem when $\mathbf{B}$ is nonsingular is to transform it into the following eigenvalue problem:

$$\mathbf{B}^{-1} \mathbf{A} \mathbf{w} = \lambda \mathbf{w}. \tag{3.47}$$

However, this approach suffers from several limitations. First, the eigenvalues computed by Eq. (3.47) could deviate from true eigenvalues significantly when $\mathbf{B}^{-1}\mathbf{A}$ is ill-conditioned. Second, $\mathbf{B}^{-1}\mathbf{A}$ is usually not symmetric; thus many efficient algorithms for symmetric eigenvalue problems cannot be applied [94]. In addition, when $\mathbf{A}$ and $\mathbf{B}$ are sparse, such sparsity is not preserved in $\mathbf{B}^{-1}\mathbf{A}$, since the inverse of a sparse matrix may not be sparse.

In numerical linear algebra, the Cholesky decomposition is commonly applied to solve the symmetric generalized eigenvalue problem by transforming it into a symmetric eigenvalue problem [182, 254]. Assume that both $\mathbf{A}$ and $\mathbf{B}$ are symmetric and $\mathbf{B}$ is positive definite. In this case, the pair $(\mathbf{A}, \mathbf{B})$ is called a symmetric pair. As a result, we can obtain the Cholesky decomposition of $\mathbf{B}$ as

$$\mathbf{B} = \mathbf{L}\mathbf{L}^T, \tag{3.48}$$

where $\mathbf{L}$ is a lower triangular matrix and all its diagonal entries are positive. Denote $\mathbf{v} = \mathbf{L}^T \mathbf{w}$. Then $\mathbf{w} = \mathbf{L}^{-T} \mathbf{v}$. The generalized eigenvalue problem can be transformed into the following eigenvalue problem:

$$\mathbf{A}\mathbf{w} = \lambda \mathbf{B}\mathbf{w} \Leftrightarrow \mathbf{A}\mathbf{L}^{-T}\mathbf{v} = \lambda \mathbf{L}\mathbf{v} \Leftrightarrow \mathbf{L}^{-1}\mathbf{A}\mathbf{L}^{-T}\mathbf{v} = \lambda \mathbf{v}. \tag{3.49}$$

One benefit of the Cholesky decomposition is that the resulting eigenvalue problem in Eq. (3.49) is symmetric. Thus, efficient algorithms for symmetric eigenvalue problems, such as the Lanczos method [94, 182], can be applied. Also the transformation to the symmetric eigenvalue problem via Cholesky decomposition suggests that the eigenvalues of the original generalized eigenvalue problem are real. However, the eigenvalues may not be real when $\mathbf{B}$ is not positive definite [254].

In order to further improve efficiency, some algorithms based on the incomplete Cholesky decomposition have been proposed to solve CCA and kernel CCA recently [11, 107]. The key idea of the incomplete Cholesky decomposition is to find a lower triangular matrix $\tilde{\mathbf{L}} \in \mathbb{R}^{d \times \tilde{d}} (\tilde{d} < d)$ for a small $\tilde{d}$ such that

$$\mathbf{B} \approx \tilde{\mathbf{L}}\tilde{\mathbf{L}}^T. \tag{3.50}$$

In other words, the difference $\mathbf{B} - \tilde{\mathbf{L}}\tilde{\mathbf{L}}^T$ measured in a certain norm is less than some threshold. In terms of implementation, the pivots below a certain threshold are skipped in comparison with the standard Cholesky decomposition.

Although the incomplete Cholesky decomposition provides an efficient way of solving the generalized eigenvalue problem, it does not scale to large-size data sets and only an approximate solution is obtained. It has been shown that a class of dimensionality reduction techniques, including CCA, in the form of the generalized eigenvalue problem in Eq. (3.40), can be transformed into an equivalent least squares problem [220, 221]. As a result, efficient algorithms for solving the least squares problem, such as the conjugate gradient algorithm [94], can be applied. We will discuss the equivalence relationship and the resulting efficient implementations in Chapters 4 and 5.

Chapter 4

Hypergraph Spectral Learning

One of the challenges in multi-label learning is how to effectively capture and utilize the correlation among different labels in classification. In this chapter, we present Hypergraph Spectral Learning (HSL), which employs a hypergraph [1] to capture the correlation among different labels for improved classification performance. A hypergraph is a generalization of the traditional graph in which the edges are arbitrary nonempty subsets of the vertex set. It has been applied for domains where higher-order relations such as co-authorship exist [1, 283]. In HSL, a hyperedge is constructed for each label and all instances annotated with a common label are included in one hyperedge. Following spectral graph embedding theory [54], HSL computes the lower-dimensional embedding through a linear transformation, which preserves the instance-label relations captured by the hypergraph. Thus, the projection is guided by the label information encoded in the hypergraph which captures the label correlations.

4.1 Hypergraph Basics

We review the basics of hypergraphs in this section. In particular, we discuss three different approaches to defining the Laplacian for a hypergraph, including clique expansion, star expansion, and a direct definition.

A hypergraph [1, 23, 24] is a generalization of the traditional graph in which the edges, called hyperedges, are arbitrary nonempty subsets of the vertex set. In a hypergraph $G = (V, E)$, V is the vertex set and E is the edge set, where each $e \in E$ is a subset of V. A hyperedge e is said to be incident with a vertex v when $v \in e$. The degree of a hyperedge e, denoted as $\delta(e)$, is the number of vertices in e, i.e.,

$$\delta(e) = |e|. \tag{4.1}$$

The degree of every edge in a traditional graph is 2, and it is therefore called a "2-graph". The degree of a vertex $v \in V$, $d(v)$, is defined as

$$d(v) = \sum_{v \in e, e \in E} w(e), \tag{4.2}$$

where $w(e)$ is the weight associated with the hyperedge $e \in E$. The diagonal matrix forms for $\delta(e)$, $d(v)$, $w(e)$ are denoted as $\mathbf{D}_e$, $\mathbf{D}_v$, $\mathbf{W}_H$, respectively. The vertex-edge incidence matrix $\mathbf{J} \in \mathbb{R}^{|V| \times |E|}$ is defined as

$$\mathbf{J}(v, e) = \begin{cases} 1 & \text{if } v \in e \\ 0 & \text{otherwise.} \end{cases} \tag{4.3}$$

Based on the above definitions, the following equations can be verified:

$$d(v) = \sum_{e \in E} w(e)\mathbf{J}(v, e), \tag{4.4}$$

$$\delta(e) = \sum_{v \in V} \mathbf{J}(v, e). \tag{4.5}$$

The adjacency matrix $\mathbf{A} \in \mathbb{R}^{|V| \times |V|}$ is defined as

$$\mathbf{A}_{ij} = \begin{cases} \sum_{e \in E} w(e)\mathbf{J}(v_i, e)\mathbf{J}(v_j, e) & \text{if } i \neq j \\ 0 & \text{otherwise.} \end{cases} \tag{4.6}$$

In fact, the adjacency matrix $\mathbf{A}$ can be represented in matrix form:

$$\mathbf{A} = \mathbf{J}\mathbf{W}_H\mathbf{J}^T - \mathbf{D}_v. \tag{4.7}$$

As the discrete analog of the Laplace–Beltrami operator on compact Riemannian manifolds [54], the graph Laplacian is extensively used in machine learning and data mining, especially in semi-supervised learning [48] and spectral clustering [174, 211]. Since the graph Laplacian matrix plays an important role in learning, a key issue is how to define the graph Laplacian matrix for a hypergraph.

The graph Laplacian has already been extended to higher-order structures [53]. Similar to traditional 2-graphs, the Laplacian can be defined for a hypergraph using analogies from the Laplace–Beltrami operator on Riemannian manifolds. Formally, a function is called a p-chain if it is defined for p-simplices, i.e., simplices with size p. For example, in the traditional 2-graph, a vertex is a 0-simplex and an edge is a 1-simplex. Thus, in a 2-graph $f : V \to \mathbb{R}$ is a 0-chain, and $f : E \to \mathbb{R}$ is a 1-chain. The general definition of the pth Laplacian operator on p-chains in a hypergraph can be given as:

$$L_p = \partial_{p+1}\partial_{p+1}^T + \partial_p^T\partial_p, \tag{4.8}$$

where ∂_p is the boundary operator that maps p-chains to $(p-1)$-chains, and ∂_p^T is the co-boundary operator that maps $(p-1)$-chains to p-chains. Similar to the Laplacian defined for a 2-graph, L_p can measure the variation in p-chains with respect to the hypergraph. In fact, the structure of L_p depends on the incidence relations between $p-1$, p, and $p+1$ simplices. Note that this definition is the same as the Laplace operator on p-forms on a Riemannian manifold [195]. When $p = 0$, the second term $\partial_0^T\partial_0$ in Eq. (4.8) is omitted since there is no simplex with size -1. Therefore, the Laplacian defined in Eq. (4.8) reduces to the commonly used Laplacian matrix in machine learning [48] when $p = 0$.

One drawback of the definition in Eq. (4.8) is that it does not capture useful information in the learning process. In machine learning one fundamental goal is the learning of the vertex function, i.e., 0-chain. For example, in classification we are interested in the class label for each vertex, which is a 0-chain. However, it follows from the definition in Eq. (4.8) that L_0 considers the 0-chain and only the incidence relations between 0-simplices and 1-simplices and $L_p(p \geq 1)$ does not consider the 0-chain. Note that in a hypergraph 1-simplices correspond to hyperedges consisting of 2 vertices. As a result, the definition of L_p in Eq. (4.8) does not provide useful information for studying vertex functions from a hypergraph.

In order to capture the underlying information from a hypergraph for learning 0-chains, many hypergraph Laplacian matrices have been proposed [1]. Specifically, one can either define the hypergraph Laplacian directly using analogies from traditional 2-graphs or expand the hypergraph into a 2-graph. It has been shown that the Laplacians defined in both ways are similar [1]. In addition, the eigenvectors of these Laplacians have been shown to be useful for learning higher-order relations, and that there is a close relationship between their hypergraph Laplacians. In this section, we discuss two commonly used expansions as well as a popular direct definition of the hypergraph Laplacian.

4.1.1 Clique Expansion

In graph theory, a clique in an undirected 2-graph G is a set of vertices C such that for every two vertices in C there exists an edge connecting the two. This is equivalent to saying that the subgraph induced by C is a complete graph. In clique expansion, each hyperedge is expanded into a clique. Denote by $G_c = (V_c, E_c)$ the 2-graph expanded from a hypergraph $G = (V, E)$ using the clique expansion. We have $V_c = V$ and $E_c = \{(u, v) : u \in e, v \in e, e \in E\}$. The edge weight $w_c(u, v)$ of G_c is given by

$$w_c(u, v) = \sum_{u, v \in e, e \in E} w(e). \tag{4.9}$$

Assume that $w_c(u, u)$ is also given by Eq. (4.9); then the adjacency matrix $\mathbf{A}_c \in \mathbb{R}^{|V| \times |V|}$ in the clique expansion can be written in the following matrix form:

$$\mathbf{A}_c = \mathbf{J} \mathbf{W}_H \mathbf{J}^T. \tag{4.10}$$

The vertex degree in the expanded 2-graph $G_c = (V_c, E_c)$ can be expressed as

$$d_c(u) = \sum_{v \in V} w_c(u, v). \tag{4.11}$$

Let $\mathbf{D}_c$ be the diagonal matrix form for $d_c(u)$. Then the normalized Laplacian of G_c is given by

$$\mathcal{L}_c = \mathbf{D}_c^{-1/2}(\mathbf{D}_c - \mathbf{A}_c)\mathbf{D}_c^{-1/2} = \mathbf{I} - \mathbf{S}_c,$$

where $\mathbf{S}_c$ is defined as

$$\mathbf{S}_c = \mathbf{D}_c^{-1/2} \mathbf{A}_c \mathbf{D}_c^{-1/2}. \tag{4.12}$$

Note that in hypergraph spectral learning, we construct a hyperedge for each label and include all relevant vertices (instances) in the hyperedge. Intuitively, the similarity between two instances in clique expansion is proportional to the sum of weights of common labels, thus capturing the instance-label relations.

4.1.2 Star Expansion

In star expansion, a new vertex is introduced for each hyperedge and this new vertex is connected to each vertex in this hyperedge. Specifically, for a hypergraph $G = (V, E)$, the vertex and edge sets of the star-expanded 2-graph, denoted as V_* and E_*, are defined as $V_* = V \cup E$ and $E_* = \{(u, e) : u \in e, e \in E\}$, respectively. Thus, each hyperedge in G is expanded into a star in G_*, which is a bipartite graph.

The weight $w_*(u, e)$ of edge (u, e) in G_* is defined as

$$w_*(u, e) \overset{\triangle}{=} \begin{cases} \dfrac{w(e)}{\delta(e)} & \text{if } u \in e \\ 0 & \text{otherwise,} \end{cases} \tag{4.13}$$

where $w(e)$ and $\delta(e)$ are the weight and degree of hyperedge e, respectively. Since $V_* = V \cup E$, we can assume that in V_*, all $v \in V$ are ordered before $v \in E$. Then the adjacency matrix $\mathbf{A}_* \in \mathbb{R}^{(|V|+|E|) \times (|V|+|E|)}$ can be represented as

$$\mathbf{A}_* = \begin{bmatrix} \mathbf{0} & \mathbf{M} \\ \mathbf{M}^T & \mathbf{0} \end{bmatrix}, \tag{4.14}$$

where $\mathbf{M} \in \mathbb{R}^{|V| \times |E|}$ and its (u, e) entry are given as follows:

$$\mathbf{M}(u, e) \overset{\triangle}{=} \frac{\mathbf{J}(u, e)w(e)}{\delta(e)}. \tag{4.15}$$

The degree of each vertex in the star-expanded graph G_* can be computed as follows:

$$d_*(u) = \sum_{e \in E} \frac{\mathbf{J}(u, e)w(e)}{\delta(e)}, \quad \text{if} \quad u \in V, \tag{4.16}$$

$$d_*(e) = \sum_{u \in e} \frac{w(e)}{\delta(e)} = w(e), \quad \text{if} \quad e \in E. \tag{4.17}$$

We use $\mathbf{D}_{*v}$ and $\mathbf{D}_{*e}$ to denote the diagonal matrices of vertex degrees for vertices in V and E, respectively. Thus, the normalized Laplacian for G_* can be expressed as follows:

$$\mathcal{L}_* = \mathbf{I} - \begin{bmatrix} \mathbf{D}_{*v} & \mathbf{0} \\ \mathbf{0} & \mathbf{D}_{*e} \end{bmatrix}^{-\frac{1}{2}} \mathbf{A}_* \begin{bmatrix} \mathbf{D}_{*v} & \mathbf{0} \\ \mathbf{0} & \mathbf{D}_{*e} \end{bmatrix}^{-\frac{1}{2}}. \tag{4.18}$$

By substituting Eq. (4.14) into Eq. (4.18), it can be shown that $\mathcal{L}_*$ can be simplified as

$$\mathcal{L}_* = \begin{bmatrix} \mathbf{I} & -\mathbf{B} \\ -\mathbf{B}^T & \mathbf{I} \end{bmatrix}, \tag{4.19}$$

where $\mathbf{B} = \mathbf{D}_{*v}^{-1/2}\mathbf{M}\mathbf{D}_{*e}^{-1/2}$, or its (u, e)th entry is

$$\mathbf{B}(u, e) = \frac{\mathbf{M}(u, e)}{\sqrt{d_*(u)}\sqrt{d_*(e)}} = \frac{\mathbf{J}(u, e)w(e)}{\sqrt{d_*(u)}\sqrt{d_*(e)}\delta(e)}. \qquad (4.20)$$

Suppose $\mathbf{x}^T = [\mathbf{x}_v^T, \mathbf{x}_e^T]$ is an eigenvector of the normalized Laplacian $\mathcal{L}_*$ for the star-expanded graph with corresponding eigenvalue γ; then we have

$$\begin{bmatrix} \mathbf{I} & -\mathbf{B} \\ -\mathbf{B}^T & \mathbf{I} \end{bmatrix} \begin{bmatrix} \mathbf{x}_v \\ \mathbf{x}_e \end{bmatrix} = \gamma \begin{bmatrix} \mathbf{x}_v \\ \mathbf{x}_e \end{bmatrix}.$$

This eigenvalue problem can be simplified as follows:

$$\begin{aligned} &\mathbf{x}_v - \mathbf{B}\mathbf{x}_e = \gamma\mathbf{x}_v, \; -\mathbf{B}^T\mathbf{x}_v + \mathbf{x}_e = \gamma x_e \\ \Leftrightarrow \quad &\mathbf{B}\mathbf{x}_e = (1 - \gamma)\mathbf{x}_v, \; \mathbf{B}^T\mathbf{x}_v = (1 - \gamma)\mathbf{x}_e \\ \Rightarrow \quad &\mathbf{B}\mathbf{B}^T\mathbf{x}_v = (\gamma - 1)^2\mathbf{x}_v. \end{aligned} \qquad (4.21)$$

In spectral learning, the eigenpair of the Laplacian $\mathcal{L}_*$ is essential for learning. Recall that only $\mathbf{x}_v$ corresponds to the real vertices in the original hypergraph while $\mathbf{x}_e$ corresponds to the artificially constructed vertices; thus $\mathbf{x}_v$ and its corresponding eigenvalue are more important for learning. It follows from Eq. (4.21) that we can obtain the eigenpair $(\mathbf{x}_v, \gamma)$ from $\mathbf{B}\mathbf{B}^T$, which simplifies the computation. We denote $\mathbf{S}_* = \mathbf{B}\mathbf{B}^T$ in the following discussion, and the equivalent matrix form is

$$\mathbf{S}_* = \mathbf{D}_{*v}^{-1/2}\mathbf{M}\mathbf{D}_{*e}^{-1}\mathbf{M}^T\mathbf{D}_{*v}^{-1/2}. \qquad (4.22)$$

Intuitively, when the star expansion is applied in hypergraph spectral learning, the constructed vertices connect to the vertices (instances) from the corresponding label, capturing the interaction between the instances and the labels. Thus, the relationship among different labels can be captured by their interactions with the data points. More details can be found in [1, 287].

A hypergraph example, including its table representation, graph representation, as well as the corresponding clique expansion and star expansion, is demonstrated in Figure 4.1.

4.1.3 Hypergraph Laplacian

Several other definitions of a hypergraph Laplacian have been proposed using analogies from the graph Laplacian for traditional 2-graphs, such as Bolla's Laplacian [29], Rodriguez's Laplacian [193, 194], and Zhou's Laplacian [283]. In the following, we discuss Zhou's Laplacian due to its popularity and good performance [282, 283].

Following the random walk model, Zhou et al. [283] proposed the following normalized hypergraph Laplacian $\mathcal{L}_z$:

$$\mathcal{L}_z = \mathbf{I} - \mathbf{S}_z, \qquad (4.23)$$

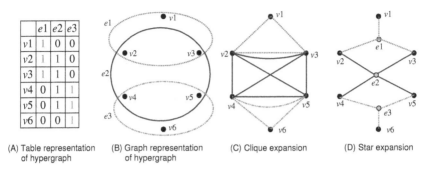

	e1	e2	e3
v1	1	0	0
v2	1	1	0
v3	1	1	0
v4	0	1	1
v5	0	1	1
v6	0	0	1

(A) Table representation   (B) Graph representation   (C) Clique expansion   (D) Star expansion
of hypergraph   of hypergraph

FIGURE 4.1: Illustration of a hypergraph and two hypergraph extensions (clique and star).

where

$$\mathbf{S}_z = \mathbf{D}_v^{-\frac{1}{2}} \mathbf{J} \mathbf{W}_H \mathbf{D}_e^{-1} \mathbf{J}^T \mathbf{D}_v^{-\frac{1}{2}}.$$

In the random walk model, given the current position $u \in V$, the walker first chooses a hyperedge e over all hyperedges incident with u with the probability proportional to $w(e)$, and then chooses a vertex $v \in e$ uniformly at random. Note that each label corresponds to a hyperedge in the random walk model. The transition probability between the nodes associated with two labels captures their similarity. More details can be found in [283].

4.2 Multi-Label Learning with a Hypergraph

In this section, we present the hypergraph spectral learning formulation for multi-label learning. HSL exploits the spectral property of the hypergraph that encodes the correlation information among labels. To capture the correlation among labels, it creates a hyperedge for each label and includes all instances relevant to this label in the hyperedge. Based on the Laplacian of the constructed hypergraph, it learns a lower-dimensional embedding through a linear transformation $\mathbf{W} \in \mathbb{R}^{d \times k}$ by solving the following optimization problem:

$$\min_{\mathbf{W}} \quad \text{Tr}(\mathbf{W}^T \mathbf{X} \mathcal{L} \mathbf{X}^T \mathbf{W}) \tag{4.24}$$

$$\text{s.t.} \quad \mathbf{W}^T \mathbf{X} \mathbf{X}^T \mathbf{W} = \mathbf{I}_k,$$

where $\mathcal{L}$ is the normalized Laplacian of the hypergraph. In this formulation, the objective function in Eq. (4.24) attempts to preserve the inherent relationship among data points captured by the Laplacian [19]. It follows from traditional spectral graph embedding theory [54] that instances sharing many common labels tend to be close to each other in the embedded space.

Define the matrix $\mathbf{S}$ as

$$\mathbf{S} = \mathbf{I} - \mathcal{L}. \tag{4.25}$$

Based on the properties of the normalized Laplacian $\mathcal{L}$ [48], $\mathbf{S} \in \mathbb{R}^{n \times n}$ reflects the normalized similarities between different instances (or vertices). Hence, the original optimization problem in Eq. (4.24) can be reformulated equivalently into the following form:

$$\max_{\mathbf{W}} \quad \mathrm{Tr}(\mathbf{W}^T \mathbf{X} \mathbf{S} \mathbf{X}^T \mathbf{W}) \tag{4.26}$$

$$\text{s.t.} \quad \mathbf{W}^T \mathbf{X} \mathbf{X}^T \mathbf{W} = \mathbf{I}_k.$$

It can be verified that the optimal $\mathbf{W}^*$ to Eq. (4.26) consists of the eigenvectors corresponding to the largest eigenvalues of the following generalized eigenvalue problem:

$$\mathbf{X} \mathbf{S} \mathbf{X}^T \mathbf{w} = \lambda \mathbf{X} \mathbf{X}^T \mathbf{w}, \tag{4.27}$$

where $\lambda \in \mathbb{R}$ denotes the eigenvalue.

To avoid singularity of $\mathbf{X} \mathbf{X}^T$, a regularization term $\gamma \mathbf{I}$ with $\gamma > 0$ is commonly added. This leads to the following regularized hypergraph spectral learning formulation:

$$\left((\mathbf{X} \mathbf{X}^T + \gamma \mathbf{I})^{-1} (\mathbf{X} \mathbf{S} \mathbf{X}^T) \right) \mathbf{w} = \lambda \mathbf{w}. \tag{4.28}$$

Recall from Section 4.1 that different Laplacians can be constructed from the hypergraph that encodes the label information, resulting in different spectral learning algorithms.

4.3 A Class of Generalized Eigenvalue Problems

We have investigated the generalized eigenvalue problem in Chapter 3. Note that hypergraph spectral learning can also be formulated as a generalized eigenvalue problem in Eq. (4.27). In this section, we focus on a particular class of generalized eigenvalue problems which includes hypergraph spectral learning as a special case in the following form:

$$\mathbf{X} \mathbf{S} \mathbf{X}^T \mathbf{w} = \lambda \mathbf{X} \mathbf{X}^T \mathbf{w}, \tag{4.29}$$

where $\mathbf{S} \in \mathbb{R}^{n \times n}$ is a symmetric and positive semi-definite matrix. In general, we are interested in the principal eigenvectors corresponding to nonzero eigenvalues. The generalized eigenvalue problem in Eq. (4.29) is often reformulated as the following eigenvalue problem:

$$(\mathbf{X} \mathbf{X}^T)^{\dagger} \mathbf{X} \mathbf{S} \mathbf{X}^T \mathbf{w} = \lambda \mathbf{w}, \tag{4.30}$$

where $(\mathbf{X}\mathbf{X}^T)^\dagger$ is the Moore–Penrose pseudoinverse of $\mathbf{X}\mathbf{X}^T$. As discussed in Section 3.4, we can formulate the generalized eigenvalue problem in Eq. (4.29) equivalently as an optimization problem:

$$\max_{\mathbf{W}} \quad \mathrm{Tr}(\mathbf{W}^T\mathbf{X}\mathbf{S}\mathbf{X}^T\mathbf{W}) \tag{4.31}$$

$$\mathrm{s.\,t.} \quad \mathbf{W}^T\mathbf{X}\mathbf{X}^T\mathbf{W} = \mathbf{I}.$$

In the following derivation, we generally use the formulation in Eq.(4.30).

In order to avoid singularity of $\mathbf{X}\mathbf{X}^T$, a regularization term $\gamma\mathbf{I}_d$ with $\gamma > 0$ is often added to $\mathbf{X}\mathbf{X}^T$ in Eq. (4.29), leading to the following generalized eigenvalue problem:

$$\mathbf{X}\mathbf{S}\mathbf{X}^T\mathbf{w} = \lambda(\mathbf{X}\mathbf{X}^T + \gamma\mathbf{I}_d)\mathbf{w}. \tag{4.32}$$

Many existing dimensionality reduction algorithms exhibit the form in Eqs. (4.29) or (4.30). In particular, the matrix $\mathbf{S}$ can be represented in the following form in supervised learning:

$$\mathbf{S} = \mathbf{H}\mathbf{H}^T, \tag{4.33}$$

where $\mathbf{H} \in \mathbb{R}^{n\times k}$ is often constructed from the label information for the data.

In the following, we discuss several dimensionality reduction algorithms involving the generalized eigenvalue problem in the form of Eq. (4.29). Specifically, they include canonical correlation analysis, orthonormalized partial least squares, hypergraph spectral learning, and linear discriminant analysis. For supervised learning methods, the label information is encoded in the matrix $\mathbf{Y} = [\mathbf{y}_1, \mathbf{y}_2, \cdots, \mathbf{y}_n] \in \mathbb{R}^{k\times n}$, where $\mathbf{y}_i(j) = 1$ if $\mathbf{x}_i$ belongs to class (or label) j and $\mathbf{y}_i(j) = 0$ otherwise.

4.3.1   Canonical Correlation Analysis

Assume that $\mathbf{Y}\mathbf{Y}^T$ is nonsingular in Canonical Correlation Analysis (CCA). As discussed in Eq. (3.12) in Chapter 3, the projection vector $\mathbf{w}_x$ for $\mathbf{X}$ is the first principal eigenvector of the following generalized eigenvalue problem:

$$\mathbf{X}\mathbf{Y}^T(\mathbf{Y}\mathbf{Y}^T)^{-1}\mathbf{Y}\mathbf{X}^T\mathbf{w}_x = \lambda\mathbf{X}\mathbf{X}^T\mathbf{w}_x. \tag{4.34}$$

Multiple projection vectors can be obtained simultaneously by computing the first ℓ principal eigenvectors of the generalized eigenvalue problem in Eq. (4.34). It can be observed that CCA is in the form of the generalized eigenvalue problem in Eq. (4.29), and the matrices $\mathbf{S}$ and $\mathbf{H}$ are defined as

$$\mathbf{S} = \mathbf{Y}^T(\mathbf{Y}\mathbf{Y}^T)^{-1}\mathbf{Y}, \tag{4.35}$$

$$\mathbf{H} = \mathbf{Y}^T(\mathbf{Y}\mathbf{Y}^T)^{-1/2}. \tag{4.36}$$

4.3.2   Orthonormalized Partial Least Squares

As shown in Eq. (2.14) in Chapter 2, Orthonormalized Partial Least Squares (OPLS) involves the following generalized eigenvalue problem:

$$\mathbf{X}\mathbf{Y}^T\mathbf{Y}\mathbf{X}^T\mathbf{w} = \lambda\mathbf{X}\mathbf{X}^T\mathbf{w}. \tag{4.37}$$

It follows from Eq. (4.37) that orthonormalized PLS involves a generalized eigenvalue problem in the form of Eq. (4.29), and the matrices $\mathbf{S}$ and $\mathbf{H}$ are defined as

$$\mathbf{S} = \mathbf{Y}^T\mathbf{Y}, \tag{4.38}$$

$$\mathbf{H} = \mathbf{Y}^T. \tag{4.39}$$

4.3.3 Hypergraph Spectral Learning

Given the normalized Laplacian $\mathcal{L}$ for the constructed hypergraph, HSL solves the following generalized eigenvalue problem:

$$\mathbf{X}\mathbf{S}\mathbf{X}^T\mathbf{w} = \lambda(\mathbf{X}\mathbf{X}^T)\mathbf{w}, \text{ where } \mathbf{S} = \mathbf{I} - \mathcal{L}. \tag{4.40}$$

Based on the definitions of $\mathbf{S}$ in Section 4.1 for clique expansion, star expansion, and Zhou's Laplacian, the matrix $\mathbf{S}$ is always symmetric and positive semi-definite and can be further represented as $\mathbf{S} = \mathbf{H}\mathbf{H}^T$, where $\mathbf{H} \in \mathbb{R}^{n \times k}$. Specifically, the definitions of $\mathbf{H}$ for clique expansion, star expansion, and Zhou's Laplacian are given as follows:

$$\mathbf{H}_c = \mathbf{D}_c^{-1/2}\mathbf{J}\mathbf{W}_H^{1/2}, \tag{4.41}$$

$$\mathbf{H}_* = \mathbf{D}_{*v}^{-1/2}\mathbf{M}\mathbf{D}_{*e}^{-1/2}, \tag{4.42}$$

$$\mathbf{H}_z = \mathbf{D}_v^{-\frac{1}{2}}\mathbf{J}\mathbf{W}_H^{1/2}\mathbf{D}_e^{-1/2}. \tag{4.43}$$

In all cases, the matrix $\mathbf{H}$ is constructed from the label information $\mathbf{Y}$ explicitly without using matrix decomposition.

4.3.4 Linear Discriminant Analysis

As a supervised dimensionality reduction algorithm, Linear Discriminant Analysis (LDA) attempts to minimize the within-class variance while maximizing the between-class variance after linear projection. It has been shown that the optimal linear projection consists of the top eigenvectors of $\mathbf{S}_t^\dagger\mathbf{S}_b$ corresponding to nonzero eigenvalues [82], where $\mathbf{S}_t$ is the total covariance matrix and $\mathbf{S}_b$ is the between-class covariance matrix. Assuming that $\mathbf{X}$ is centered, i.e., $\sum_{i=1}^n \mathbf{x}_i = 0$, the matrices $\mathbf{S}_t$ and $\mathbf{S}_b$ are defined as follows:

$$\mathbf{S}_t = \frac{1}{n}\mathbf{X}\mathbf{X}^T, \tag{4.44}$$

$$\mathbf{S}_b = \frac{1}{n}\sum_{j=1}^k n_j\bar{\mathbf{x}}_j\bar{\mathbf{x}}_j^T, \tag{4.45}$$

where $\bar{\mathbf{x}}_j$ is the centroid of the jth class. We also assume that the data matrix $\mathbf{X}$ is partitioned into k classes as $\mathbf{X} = [\mathbf{X}_1, \cdots, \mathbf{X}_k]$, where $\mathbf{X}_j \in \mathbb{R}^{d \times n_j}$ corresponds to the data points from the jth class, n_j is the size of the jth class, and $\sum_{j=1}^k n_j = n$.

Note that $\bar{\mathbf{x}}_j = \frac{1}{n_j}\mathbf{X}_j\mathbf{1}_j$, where $\mathbf{1}_j$ is a vector of all ones with length n_j. Thus, we have

$$
\begin{aligned}
n\mathbf{S}_b &= \sum_{j=1}^{k} \frac{1}{n_j}\mathbf{X}_j\mathbf{1}_j\mathbf{1}_j^T\mathbf{X}_j^T \\
&= \sum_{j=1}^{k} \mathbf{X}_j\left(\frac{1}{n_j}\mathbf{1}_j\mathbf{1}_j^T\right)\mathbf{X}_j^T \\
&= \sum_{j=1}^{k} \mathbf{X}_j\mathbf{S}_j\mathbf{X}_j^T = \mathbf{X}\mathbf{S}\mathbf{X}^T,
\end{aligned}
$$

where $\mathbf{S}_j = \frac{1}{n_j}\mathbf{1}_j\mathbf{1}_j^T$, and $\mathbf{S}$ is defined as $\mathrm{diag}\,(\mathbf{S}_1, \mathbf{S}_2, \cdots, \mathbf{S}_k)$ for LDA. Therefore, $\mathbf{S}_t^\dagger\mathbf{S}_b$ can also be expressed in the following form:

$$
\mathbf{S}_t^\dagger\mathbf{S}_b = (\mathbf{X}\mathbf{X}^T)^\dagger(\mathbf{X}\mathbf{S}\mathbf{X}^T). \tag{4.46}
$$

It can be verified that $\mathbf{S} = \mathbf{H}\mathbf{H}^T$, where

$$
\mathbf{H} = \mathrm{diag}\left(\frac{1}{\sqrt{n_1}}\mathbf{1}_1, \frac{1}{\sqrt{n_2}}\mathbf{1}_2, \cdots, \frac{1}{\sqrt{n_k}}\mathbf{1}_k\right) \in \mathbb{R}^{n \times k}. \tag{4.47}
$$

4.4 The Generalized Eigenvalue Problem versus the Least Squares Problem

In this section, we study the relationship between the generalized eigenvalue problem in Eq. (4.29) or its equivalent formulation in Eq. (4.30) and the least squares formulation. In particular, we show that under a mild condition[1], the eigenvalue problem in Eq. (4.30) can be formulated equivalently as a least squares problem with a specific target matrix. Before presenting the equivalence relationship, we review multivariate linear regression and least squares first.

4.4.1 Multivariate Linear Regression and Least Squares

We have discussed regression techniques in Chapter 2, including Ordinary Least Squares (OLS), Principal Component Regression (PCR), ridge regression, and PLS regression. In this subsection, we review ordinary least squares, which is a classical technique for both regression and classification [26].

Given a set of observations $\mathbf{x}_i \in \mathbb{R}^d$ $(1 \leq i \leq n)$ and their corresponding targets

---

[1]It states that $\{\mathbf{x}_i\}_{i=1}^n$ are linearly independent before centering, i.e., $\mathrm{rank}(\mathbf{X}) = n - 1$ after the data is centered (of zero mean).

$t_i \in \mathbb{R}^k$ $(1 \le i \le n)$, the goal is to fit a linear model

$$t = W^T x + b$$

to the data, where $b \in \mathbb{R}^k$ is the bias vector, and $W \in \mathbb{R}^{d \times k}$ is the weight matrix. Assuming that both the observations $\{x_i\}_{i=1}^n$ and the targets $\{t_i\}_{i=1}^n$ are centered, the bias term becomes zero and can be ignored. The optimal W can be computed by minimizing the following sum-of-squares loss function:

$$\sum_{i=1}^{n} \|W^T x_i - t_i\|_2^2 = \|W^T X - T\|_F^2, \tag{4.48}$$

where $T = [t_1, \dots, t_n] \in \mathbb{R}^{k \times n}$. The optimal matrix W is given by

$$W_{ls} = (XX^T)^\dagger X T^T. \tag{4.49}$$

When least squares is applied for classification, T is known as the class indicator matrix. Typically the 1-of-k binary coding scheme is applied: $t_j(i) = 1$ if t_j is associated with the ith class or label; otherwise $t_j(i) = 0$.

The least squares problem can be solved efficiently using existing techniques, which is very attractive for large-scale data analysis. Many iterative algorithms, including the conjugate gradient method, have been proposed in the literature [94, 178]. Compared with direct methods, these iterative algorithms converge very fast for large and sparse problems.

4.4.2 Matrix Orthonormality Property

In this subsection we present some preliminary results. To simplify the discussion of the eigenvalue problem in Eq. (4.30), we define matrices C_X and C_S as follows:

$$C_X = XX^T \in \mathbb{R}^{d \times d}, \tag{4.50}$$
$$C_S = XSX^T \in \mathbb{R}^{d \times d}. \tag{4.51}$$

The eigenvalue problem in Eq. (4.30) can then be expressed as

$$C_X^\dagger C_S w = \lambda w. \tag{4.52}$$

Recall that S is symmetric and positive semi-definite; thus it can be decomposed as

$$S = HH^T, \tag{4.53}$$

where $H \in \mathbb{R}^{n \times s}$, and $s \le n$. For all dimensionality reduction algorithms discussed in Section 4.3, the closed form of H can be obtained and $s = k \ll n$.

Since X is centered, i.e., $X1 = 0$, we have $XC = X$, where $C = I - \frac{1}{n}11^T$ is the centering matrix satisfying $C^T = C$ and $C1 = 0$. It follows that

$$
\begin{aligned}
C_S &= XSX^T \\
&= (XC)S(XC)^T \\
&= X(CSC^T)X^T \\
&= X(C^TSC)X^T \\
&= X\tilde{S}X^T, \tag{4.54}
\end{aligned}
$$

where $\tilde{\mathbf{S}} = \mathbf{C}^T \mathbf{S} \mathbf{C}$. Note that

$$\mathbf{1}^T \tilde{\mathbf{S}} \mathbf{1} = \mathbf{1}^T \mathbf{C}^T \mathbf{S} \mathbf{C} \mathbf{1} = 0. \tag{4.55}$$

Thus, we can assume that $\mathbf{1}^T \mathbf{S} \mathbf{1} = 0$, that is, both columns and rows of $\mathbf{S}$ are centered.

In order to prove the main results, we need the following lemmas. The full proofs of these two lemmas are given in Appendix A.3.

Lemma 4.1 *Assume that $\mathbf{1}^T \mathbf{S} \mathbf{1} = 0$. Let $\mathbf{H}$ be defined in Eq. (4.53). Let $\mathbf{H}\mathbf{P} = \mathbf{Q}\mathbf{R}$ be the QR decomposition of $\mathbf{H}$ with column pivoting, where $\mathbf{Q} \in \mathbb{R}^{n \times r}$ has orthonormal columns, $\mathbf{R} \in \mathbb{R}^{r \times k}$ is upper triangular, $r = \mathrm{rank}(\mathbf{H}) \leq k$, and $\mathbf{P} \in \mathbb{R}^{k \times k}$ is a permutation matrix. Then we have $\mathbf{Q}^T \mathbf{1} = \mathbf{0}$.*

Lemma 4.2 *Let $\mathbf{A} \in \mathbb{R}^{m \times (m-1)}$ and $\mathbf{B} \in \mathbb{R}^{m \times p}$ $(p \leq m)$ be two matrices satisfying $\mathbf{A}^T \mathbf{1} = \mathbf{0}$, $\mathbf{A}^T \mathbf{A} = \mathbf{I}_{m-1}$, $\mathbf{B}^T \mathbf{B} = \mathbf{I}_p$, and $\mathbf{B}^T \mathbf{1} = \mathbf{0}$. Let $\mathbf{F} = \mathbf{A}^T \mathbf{B}$. Then $\mathbf{F}^T \mathbf{F} = \mathbf{I}_p$.*

Let $\mathbf{R} = \mathbf{U}_R \mathbf{\Sigma}_R \mathbf{V}_R^T$ be the thin Singular Value Decomposition (SVD) of $\mathbf{R} \in \mathbb{R}^{r \times k}$, where $\mathbf{U}_R \in \mathbb{R}^{r \times r}$ is orthogonal, $\mathbf{V}_R \in \mathbb{R}^{k \times r}$ has orthonormal columns, and $\mathbf{\Sigma}_R \in \mathbb{R}^{r \times r}$ is diagonal. Note that $(\mathbf{Q}\mathbf{U}_R)^T (\mathbf{Q}\mathbf{U}_R) = \mathbf{I}_r$, and then the SVD of $\mathbf{S}$ can be derived as follows:

$$
\begin{aligned}
\mathbf{S} &= \mathbf{H}\mathbf{H}^T \\
&= \mathbf{Q}\mathbf{R}\mathbf{R}^T \mathbf{Q}^T \\
&= \mathbf{Q}\mathbf{U}_R \mathbf{\Sigma}_R^2 \mathbf{U}_R^T \mathbf{Q}^T \\
&= (\mathbf{Q}\mathbf{U}_R) \mathbf{\Sigma}_R^2 (\mathbf{Q}\mathbf{U}_R)^T .
\end{aligned}
\tag{4.56}
$$

Assume that the columns of $\mathbf{X}$ are centered, i.e., $\mathbf{X}\mathbf{1} = \mathbf{0}$, and $\mathrm{rank}(\mathbf{X}) = n - 1$. Let the SVD of $\mathbf{X}$ be

$$\mathbf{X} = \mathbf{U}\mathbf{\Sigma}\mathbf{V}^T = \mathbf{U}_1 \mathbf{\Sigma}_1 \mathbf{V}_1^T,$$

where $\mathbf{U}$ and $\mathbf{V}$ are orthogonal, $\mathbf{\Sigma} \in \mathbb{R}^{d \times n}$ is diagonal, $\mathbf{U}_1 \mathbf{\Sigma}_1 \mathbf{V}_1^T$ is the compact SVD of $\mathbf{X}$, $\mathbf{U}_1 \in \mathbb{R}^{d \times (n-1)}$, $\mathbf{V}_1 \in \mathbb{R}^{n \times (n-1)}$, and $\mathbf{\Sigma}_1 \in \mathbb{R}^{(n-1) \times (n-1)}$ is diagonal. Define $\mathbf{M}_1$ as

$$\mathbf{M}_1 = \mathbf{V}_1^T (\mathbf{Q}\mathbf{U}_R) \in \mathbb{R}^{(n-1) \times r}. \tag{4.57}$$

It can be shown that the columns of $\mathbf{M}_1$ are orthonormal, as summarized in the following lemma:

Lemma 4.3 *Let $\mathbf{M}_1$ be defined as above. Then $\mathbf{M}_1^T \mathbf{M}_1 = \mathbf{I}_r$.*

Proof Since $\mathbf{X}\mathbf{1} = \mathbf{0}$, we have $\mathbf{V}_1^T \mathbf{1} = \mathbf{0}$. Also note that $\mathbf{V}_1^T \mathbf{V}_1 = \mathbf{I}_{n-1}$ and $(\mathbf{Q}\mathbf{U}_R)^T (\mathbf{Q}\mathbf{U}_R) = \mathbf{I}_r$. It follows from Lemma 4.1 that

$$(\mathbf{Q}\mathbf{U}_R)^T \mathbf{1} = \mathbf{U}_R^T \mathbf{Q}^T \mathbf{1} = \mathbf{0}.$$

Then we have from Lemma 4.2 that $\mathbf{M}_1^T \mathbf{M}_1 = \mathbf{I}_r$. ∎

4.4.3 The Equivalence Relationship

We first derive the solution to the eigenvalue problem in Eq. (4.30) in the following theorem:

Theorem 4.1 *Let* $\mathbf{U}_1$, $\mathbf{\Sigma}_1$, $\mathbf{V}_1$, $\mathbf{Q}$, $\mathbf{\Sigma}_R$, *and* $\mathbf{U}_R$ *be defined as above. Assume that the columns of* $\mathbf{X}$ *are centered, i.e.,* $\mathbf{X}\mathbf{1} = \mathbf{0}$, *and* $\text{rank}(\mathbf{X}) = n - 1$. *Then the nonzero eigenvalues of the eigenvalue problem in Eq. (4.30) are* $\text{diag}(\mathbf{\Sigma}_R^2)$, *and the corresponding eigenvectors are* $\mathbf{W}_{eig} = \mathbf{U}_1 \mathbf{\Sigma}_1^{-1} \mathbf{V}_1^T \mathbf{Q} \mathbf{U}_R$.

Proof It follows from Lemma 4.3 that the columns of $\mathbf{M}_1 \in \mathbb{R}^{(n-1) \times r}$ are orthonormal. Hence, there exists $\mathbf{M}_2 \in \mathbb{R}^{(n-1) \times (n-1-r)}$ such that $\mathbf{M} = [\mathbf{M}_1, \mathbf{M}_2] \in \mathbb{R}^{(n-1) \times (n-1)}$ is orthogonal [94]. Then we can derive the eigendecomposition of the matrix $\mathbf{C}_X^\dagger \mathbf{C}_S$ as follows:

$$
\begin{aligned}
& \mathbf{C}_X^\dagger \mathbf{C}_S \\
= \; & (\mathbf{X}\mathbf{X}^T)^\dagger \, \mathbf{X}\mathbf{S}\mathbf{X}^T \\
= \; & (\mathbf{U}_1 \mathbf{\Sigma}_1^{-2} \mathbf{U}_1^T) \mathbf{U}_1 \mathbf{\Sigma}_1 \mathbf{V}_1^T \, (\mathbf{Q}\mathbf{U}_R) \, \mathbf{\Sigma}_R^2 \, (\mathbf{Q}\mathbf{U}_R)^T \, \mathbf{V}_1 \mathbf{\Sigma}_1 \mathbf{U}_1^T \\
= \; & \mathbf{U}_1 \mathbf{\Sigma}_1^{-1} \mathbf{V}_1^T \, (\mathbf{Q}\mathbf{U}_R) \, \mathbf{\Sigma}_R^2 \, (\mathbf{Q}\mathbf{U}_R)^T \, \mathbf{V}_1 \mathbf{\Sigma}_1 \mathbf{U}_1^T \\
= \; & \mathbf{U}_1 \mathbf{\Sigma}_1^{-1} \mathbf{M}_1 \mathbf{\Sigma}_R^2 \mathbf{M}_1^T \mathbf{\Sigma}_1 \mathbf{U}_1^T \\
= \; & \mathbf{U} \begin{bmatrix} \mathbf{I}_{n-1} \\ \mathbf{0} \end{bmatrix} \mathbf{\Sigma}_1^{-1} \begin{bmatrix} \mathbf{M}_1 & \mathbf{M}_2 \end{bmatrix} \begin{bmatrix} \mathbf{\Sigma}_R^2 & \mathbf{0} \\ \mathbf{0} & \mathbf{0}_{n-1-r} \end{bmatrix} \begin{bmatrix} \mathbf{M}_1^T \\ \mathbf{M}_2^T \end{bmatrix} \mathbf{\Sigma}_1 [\mathbf{I}_{n-1}, \mathbf{0}] \mathbf{U}^T \\
= \; & \mathbf{U} \begin{bmatrix} \mathbf{I}_{n-1} \\ \mathbf{0} \end{bmatrix} \mathbf{\Sigma}_1^{-1} \mathbf{M} \begin{bmatrix} \mathbf{\Sigma}_R^2 & \mathbf{0} \\ \mathbf{0} & \mathbf{0}_{n-1-r} \end{bmatrix} \mathbf{M}^T \mathbf{\Sigma}_1 [\mathbf{I}_{n-1}, \mathbf{0}] \mathbf{U}^T \\
= \; & \mathbf{U} \begin{bmatrix} \mathbf{\Sigma}_1^{-1}\mathbf{M} & \mathbf{0} \\ \mathbf{0} & 1 \end{bmatrix} \begin{bmatrix} \mathbf{\Sigma}_R^2 & \mathbf{0} \\ \mathbf{0} & \mathbf{0}_{n-r} \end{bmatrix} \begin{bmatrix} \mathbf{M}^T \mathbf{\Sigma}_1 & \mathbf{0} \\ \mathbf{0} & 1 \end{bmatrix} \mathbf{U}^T.
\end{aligned} \tag{4.58}
$$

There are r nonzero eigenvalues, which are $\text{diag}(\mathbf{\Sigma}_R^2)$, and the corresponding eigenvectors are

$$
\mathbf{W}_{eig} = \mathbf{U}_1 \mathbf{\Sigma}_1^{-1} \mathbf{M}_1 = \mathbf{U}_1 \mathbf{\Sigma}_1^{-1} \mathbf{V}_1^T \mathbf{Q} \mathbf{U}_R. \tag{4.59}
$$

This completes the proof of the theorem. ∎

We summarize the main result of this section in the following theorem:

Theorem 4.2 *Assume that the class indicator matrix* $\mathbf{T}$ *for the least squares classification is defined as*

$$
\mathbf{T} = \mathbf{U}_R^T \mathbf{Q}^T \in \mathbb{R}^{r \times n}. \tag{4.60}
$$

Then the solution to the least squares formulation in Eq. (4.48) is given by

$$
\mathbf{W}_{ls} = \mathbf{U}_1 \mathbf{\Sigma}_1^{-1} \mathbf{V}_1^T \mathbf{Q} \mathbf{U}_R. \tag{4.61}
$$

Thus, the eigenvalue problem and the least squares problem are equivalent.

Proof When $\mathbf{T}$ is used as the class indicator matrix, the solution to the least squares problem is

$$
\begin{aligned}
\mathbf{W}_{ls} &= (\mathbf{X}\mathbf{X}^T)^\dagger \mathbf{X}\mathbf{T}^T \\
&= (\mathbf{X}\mathbf{X}^T)^\dagger \mathbf{X}\mathbf{Q}\mathbf{U}_R \\
&= \mathbf{U}_1\boldsymbol{\Sigma}_1^{-2}\mathbf{U}_1^T\mathbf{U}_1\boldsymbol{\Sigma}_1\mathbf{V}_1^T\mathbf{Q}\mathbf{U}_R \\
&= \mathbf{U}_1\boldsymbol{\Sigma}_1^{-1}\mathbf{V}_1^T\mathbf{Q}\mathbf{U}_R.
\end{aligned}
$$

It follows from Eq. (4.59) that $\mathbf{W}_{ls} = \mathbf{W}_{eig}$. This completes the proof of the theorem. ∎

Remark 4.1 *The analysis in [220, 271] is based on a key assumption that the $\mathbf{H}$ matrix in $\mathbf{S} = \mathbf{H}\mathbf{H}^T$ as defined in Eq. (4.53) has orthonormal columns, which is the case for LDA and CCA. However, this is in general not true, e.g., the $\mathbf{H}$ matrix in OPLS and HSL. The equivalence result presented in this chapter significantly improves previous work by relaxing this assumption.*

The weight matrix $\mathbf{W}_{ls}$ in least squares can also be used for dimensionality reduction. If $\mathbf{T} = \mathbf{Q}^T$ is used as the class indicator matrix, the weight matrix becomes $\tilde{\mathbf{W}}_{ls} = \mathbf{U}_1\boldsymbol{\Sigma}_1^{-1}\mathbf{V}_1^T\mathbf{Q}$. Thus, the difference between $\mathbf{W}_{eig}$ and $\tilde{\mathbf{W}}_{ls}$ is the orthogonal matrix $\mathbf{U}_R$. Note that the Euclidean distance is invariant to any orthogonal transformation. If a classifier, such as k-Nearest-Neighbor (kNN) or linear support vector machines [207] based on the Euclidean distance, is applied on the dimensionality-reduced data via $\mathbf{W}_{eig}$ and $\tilde{\mathbf{W}}_{ls}$, they will achieve the same classification performance.

In some cases, the number of nonzero eigenvalues, i.e., r, is large (comparable to n). It is common to use the top eigenvectors corresponding to the largest $\ell < r$ eigenvalues as in Principal Component Analysis (PCA). From Theorems 4.1 and 4.2, if we keep the top ℓ singular vectors of $\mathbf{S}$ as the class indicator matrix, the equivalence relationship between the generalized eigenvalue problem and the least squares problem holds, as summarized below:

Corollary 4.1 *The top $\ell < r$ eigenvectors in Eq. (4.30) can be computed by solving a least squares problem with the top ℓ singular vectors of $\mathbf{S}$ employed as the class indicator matrix.*

4.4.4 Regularized Least Squares

Based on the equivalence relationship presented in Section 4.4, the original generalized eigenvalue problem in Eq. (4.29) can be extended using the regularization technique. As we discussed in Chapter 2, ridge regression [109] minimizes the penalized sum-of-squares loss function by incorporating ℓ_2-norm regularization. By using the target matrix $\mathbf{T}$ in Eq. (4.60), we obtain the ℓ_2-norm regularized least squares formulation by minimizing the following objective function:

$$
L_2(\mathbf{W}, \gamma) = \|\mathbf{W}^T\mathbf{X} - \mathbf{T}\|_F^2 + \gamma \sum_{j=1}^{k} \|\mathbf{w}_j\|_2^2, \tag{4.62}
$$

where $\mathbf{W} = [\mathbf{w}_1, \ldots, \mathbf{w}_k]$ and $\gamma > 0$ is the regularization parameter. We can then apply the LSQR algorithm, a conjugate gradient method proposed in [178] for solving large-scale sparse least squares problems. Complexity analysis is discussed in detail in the next section.

It is well-known that model sparsity can often be achieved by applying ℓ_1-norm regularization [68, 230]. This has been introduced into the least squares formulation and the resulting model is called the lasso [230]. Based on the equivalence relationship, we derive ℓ_1-norm regularized least squares formulation by minimizing the following objective function:

$$L_1 = \|\mathbf{W}^T\mathbf{X} - \mathbf{T}\|_F^2 + \gamma \sum_{j=1}^{k} \|\mathbf{w}_j\|_1, \tag{4.63}$$

for some tuning parameter $\gamma > 0$ [230]. The lasso can be solved efficiently using state-of-the-art algorithms [81, 104, 160]. In addition, the entire solution path for all values of γ can be obtained by applying the least angle regression algorithm [71].

In the following discussion, the equivalent least squares formulation for all dimensionality reduction algorithms is named using a prefix "LS" such as "LS-Star" for hypergraph spectral learning using the star expansion. And the resulting ℓ_1-norm and ℓ_2-norm regularized formulations are named by adding subscripts 1 and 2, respectively, e.g., "LS-Star$_1$" and "LS-Star$_2$". For the original eigenvalue problem with regularization in Eq. (4.28), we name it using a prefix "r" before the corresponding method, e.g., "rStar".

4.4.5 Efficient Implementation via LSQR

Recall that we deal with the generalized eigenvalue problem in Eq. (4.29), although an equivalent eigenvalue problem in Eq. (4.30) is used in our theoretical derivation. Large-scale generalized eigenvalue problems are known to be much more difficult to solve than regular eigenvalue problems [201]. There are two options to transform the problem in Eq. (4.29) into a standard eigenvalue problem [201]: (1) factor $\mathbf{X}\mathbf{X}^T$; or (2) employ the standard Lanczos algorithm [94] for the matrix $(\mathbf{X}\mathbf{X}^T)^{-1}\mathbf{X}\mathbf{S}\mathbf{X}^T$ using the $\mathbf{X}\mathbf{X}^T$ inner product. The second option has its own issue on singular matrices, which is the case for high-dimensional problems with a small regularization. Thus, we factor $\mathbf{X}\mathbf{X}^T$ and solve a symmetric eigenvalue problem using the Lanczos algorithm.

The equivalent least squares formulation leads to an efficient implementation. The pseudo-code of the algorithm is given in Algorithm 4.1. Next we analyze the time complexity of Algorithm 4.1. The complexity of the QR decomposition in the first step is $O(nk^2)$. Note that k is the number of classes (or labels), and $k \ll n$. The SVD of $\mathbf{R}$ costs $O(k^3)$. In the last step, we solve k least squares problems using the LSQR algorithm proposed in [178], which is a conjugate gradient method for solving large-scale least squares problems. In practice, the original data matrix $\mathbf{X} \in \mathbb{R}^{d \times n}$ may be sparse in many applications such as text document modeling. Note that the centering of $\mathbf{X}$ is necessary in some techniques such as CCA. However,

---

Algorithm 4.1 Implementation of the Generalized Eigenvalue Problem via LSQR

Input: X, H.
Output: W.
Compute the QR decomposition of $\mathbf{H}$: $\mathbf{HP} = \mathbf{QR}$.
Compute the SVD of $\mathbf{R}$: $\mathbf{R} = \mathbf{U}_R \mathbf{\Sigma}_R \mathbf{V}_R^T$.
Compute the class indicator matrix $\mathbf{T} = \mathbf{U}_R^T \mathbf{Q}^T$.
Compute $\mathbf{W}$ by regressing $\mathbf{X}$ on $\mathbf{T}$ using LSQR.

$\mathbf{X}$ is no longer sparse after centering. In order to keep the sparsity of $\mathbf{X}$, we follow the method proposed in [41] to augment the vector $\mathbf{x}_i$ by an additional component as $\tilde{\mathbf{x}}_i^T = [1, \mathbf{x}_i^T]$, and the extended data matrix $\mathbf{X}$ is denoted as $\tilde{\mathbf{X}} \in \mathbb{R}^{(d+1) \times n}$. This new component acts as the bias for least squares. The revised least squares problem is formulated as

$$\min_{\tilde{\mathbf{W}}} \| \tilde{\mathbf{W}}^T \tilde{\mathbf{X}} - \mathbf{T} \|_F^2, \tag{4.64}$$

where $\tilde{\mathbf{W}} \in \mathbb{R}^{(d+1) \times k}$. For a new data point $\mathbf{x} \in \mathbb{R}^d$, its projection is given by $\tilde{\mathbf{W}}^T [1; \mathbf{x}]$.

For the dense data matrix, the overall computational cost of each iteration of LSQR is $O(3n + 5d + 2dn)$ [178]. Since the least squares problem is solved k times, the overall cost of LSQR is $O(Nk(3n + 5d + 2dn))$, where N is the total number of iterations. When the matrix $\tilde{\mathbf{X}}$ is sparse, the cost is significantly reduced. Let the number of nonzero elements in $\tilde{\mathbf{X}}$ be z; then the overall cost of LSQR is reduced to $O(Nk(3n + 5d + 2z))$. In summary, the total time complexity for solving the least squares formulation via LSQR is $O(nk^2 + Nk(3n + 5d + 2z))$.

4.5   Empirical Evaluation

In this section, we empirically evaluate the effectiveness and efficiency of hypergraph spectral learning. We also report experimental results that validate the equivalence relationship for all dimensionality reduction algorithms exhibiting the form of the generalized eigenvalue problem in Eq. (4.29). The scalability of the least squares extensions is also demonstrated.

4.5.1   Empirical Evaluation Setup

The dimensionality reduction algorithms discussed in Section 4.3 can be divided into two categories: (1) CCA, PLS, and HSL for multi-label learning and (2) LDA for multi-class learning. We use both multi-label and multi-class data sets in the experiments, including the Scene data set [34], the Yeast data set [74], the USPS data set [121], and two high-dimensional document data sets [136, 240]. All data

TABLE 4.1: Statistics of the data sets.

Data Set	n	d	k
Scene	2407	294	6
Yeast	2417	103	14
USPS	9298	256	10
Yahoo\Arts&Humanities	3712	23146	26
Yahoo\Computers&Internet	6270	34096	33

sets are available online[2,3]. For all data sets, the labels that contain less than 50 instances are removed. We follow the feature selection methods studied in [269] for text documents and extract different numbers of terms to study the performance of algorithms. The statistics of these data sets are summarized in Table 4.1, where n is number of data points, d is the dimensionality, and k is the number of labels or classes.

For each data set, a transformation matrix $\mathbf{W}$ is learned from the training set, and it is then used to project the test data onto a lower-dimensional space. Linear Support Vector Machine (SVM) is applied for each label separately for classification. The mean Area Under the Receiver Operating Characteristic Curve (AUC) over all labels and classification accuracy are used to evaluate the performance of multi-label and multi-class tasks, respectively. Ten random partitions of the data sets into training and test sets are generated in the experiments, and the mean performance over all labels and all partitions is reported.

4.5.2 Performance of Hypergraph Spectral Learning

In this section we present the performance of hypergraph spectral learning on multi-label data sets. Three different Laplacian matrices of the constructed hypergraph are studied, including clique expansion, star expansion, and Zhou's Laplacian matrix. The performance of HSL is compared with CCA and RankSVM [74]. We also apply SVM to each label independently and our results show that it is less effective than RankSVM and is thus omitted in the table. For all algorithms with regularization, 3-fold cross-validation is applied to select the optimal value of the regularization parameter. All the features of the Scene and Yeast data sets are used while the most frequent 2000 terms of the Arts and Computers data sets are used. We report the mean AUC score over all labels and all partitions for each algorithm in Table 4.2.

Note that for all data sets and the training/test partitions, the assumption that $\text{rank}(\mathbf{X}) = n - 1$ is not satisfied; thus the equivalence relationship between the generalized eigenvalue formulation in Eq. (4.29) and the corresponding least squares formulation does not hold. We can observe from Table 4.2 that hypergraph spectral learning formulations and the corresponding least squares formulations achieve different performance results, although the difference is very small in all cases. More-

---

[2]http://www.csie.ntu.edu.tw/~cjlin/libsvmtools/datasets
[3]http://www.kecl.ntt.co.jp/as/members/ueda/yahoo.tar.gz

TABLE 4.2: Summary of mean AUC scores over all labels of HSL, CCA, and RankSVM.

Algorithm	Scene	Yeast	Arts	Computers
Training size	900	900	2000	2000
Clique	0.8548	0.6460	0.5215	0.5369
rClique	0.9216	0.6496	0.8106	0.7968
LS-Clique	0.8598	0.6493	0.5213	0.5375
LS-Clique$_2$	**0.9255**	0.6523	**0.8130**	0.7996
Star	0.8546	0.6529	0.5209	0.5384
rStar	0.9216	0.6558	0.8051	0.7970
LS-Star	0.8597	0.6540	0.5209	0.5381
LS-Star$_2$	**0.9255**	0.6565	0.8067	0.7999
Zhou	0.8547	0.6518	0.5206	0.5389
rZhou	0.9216	0.6521	0.8074	0.7991
LS-Zhou	0.8597	0.6537	0.5205	0.5389
LS-Zhou$_2$	0.9254	0.6559	0.8087	**0.8025**
CCA	0.8538	0.6547	0.5213	0.5341
rCCA	0.9215	0.6555	0.8015	0.7917
LS-CCA	0.8586	0.6561	0.5215	0.5340
LS-CCA$_2$	**0.9255**	**0.6568**	0.8036	0.7952
RankSVM	0.9001	0.6294	0.8073	0.7893

over, regularized algorithms always outperform those without regularization, which justifies the use of regularization. The results in Table 4.2 show that the methods with regularization perform better than the RankSVM algorithm. Results also show that three different Laplacian matrices lead to similar performance, which is consistent with the theoretical analysis in [1].

4.5.3   Evaluation of the Equivalence Relationship

In this experiment, we evaluate the equivalence relationship between the generalized eigenvalue problem and its corresponding least squares formulation for all dimensionality reduction algorithms discussed in Section 4.3, i.e., CCA, OPLS, HSL, and LDA. We observe that for all data sets, when the data dimensionality d is larger than the sample size n, $\text{rank}(\mathbf{X}) = n - 1$ is likely to hold after centering $\mathbf{X}$. We also observe that the generalized eigenvalue problem and its corresponding least squares formulation achieve the same performance when $\text{rank}(\mathbf{X}) = n - 1$ holds. These are consistent with the theoretical results in Theorems 4.1 and 4.2.

We compare the performance of the generalized eigenvalue problem and the corresponding least squares formulation when the assumption in Theorems 4.1 and 4.2 is violated. Figure 4.2 shows the mean AUC score over all labels of different formulations when the size of the training set varies from 100 to 900 with a step size about 100 on the Yeast data set. The performance of CCA, OPLS, and two variants of HSL is summarized in Figure 4.2. We can observe from the figure that when n is small, the assumption in Theorem 4.1 holds and the two formulations achieve the

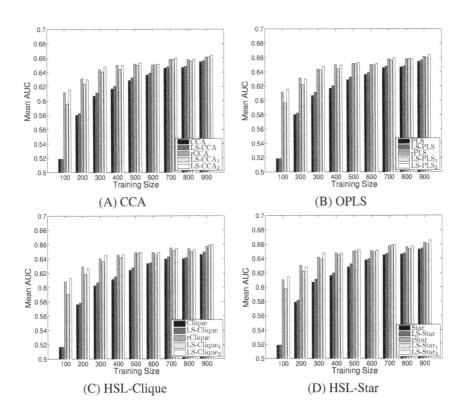

FIGURE 4.2: Comparison of different formulations in terms of AUC scores for different algorithms on the Yeast data set. CCA, OPLS, and HSL are applied on the Yeast data set. For regularized algorithms, the optimal value of γ is estimated from $\{1e-6, 1e-4, 1e-2, 1, 10, 100, 1000\}$ using cross-validation.

same performance; when n is large, the assumption in Theorem 4.1 does not hold and the two formulations achieve different performance, although the difference is always very small in the experiment. We can also observe from Figure 4.2 that regularized methods outperform unregularized ones, which validates the effectiveness of regularization.

A similar experiment is performed for LDA on the multi-class USPS data, and its performance is summarized in Figure 4.3, from which we obtain similar observations.

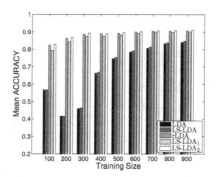

FIGURE 4.3: Comparison of different LDA formulations in terms of accuracies on the USPS data set. For regularized algorithms, the optimal value of γ is estimated from $\{1e-6, 1e-4, 1e-2, 1, 10, 100, 1000\}$ using cross-validation.

4.5.4 Evaluation of Scalability

In this experiment, we compare the scalability of the original generalized eigenvalue problem and the equivalent least squares formulation. Since regularization is commonly employed in practice, we compare the generalized eigenvalue problem with regularization and ℓ_2-norm regularized least squares formulation. The least squares problem is solved by the LSQR algorithm [178]. We solve the original generalized eigenvalue problem by factoring $\mathbf{X}\mathbf{X}^T$ and solving a symmetric eigenvalue problem using the Lanczos method [201].

The computation time of the two formulations on the high-dimensional multi-label Yahoo! data set is shown in Figure 4.4, where the data dimensionality increases and the training sample size is fixed at 1000. CCA, OPLS, and HSL, which are applicable for multi-label data, are tested. It can be observed that the computation time for both algorithms increases steadily as the data dimensionality increases. However, the computation time of the least squares formulation is substantially less than that of the original generalized eigenvalue problem.

We also evaluate the scalability of the two formulations in terms of the training sample size. Figure 4.5 shows the computation time of the two formulations on the Yahoo! data set as the training sample size increases with the data dimensionality

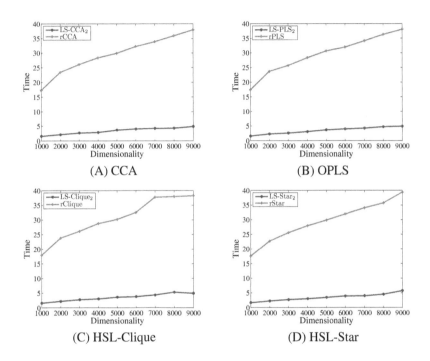

FIGURE 4.4: Computation time (in seconds) of the generalized eigenvalue problem and the corresponding least squares formulation on the Yahoo\Arts&Humanities data set as the data dimensionality increases. The x-axis represents the data dimensionality and the y-axis represents the computation time.

fixed at 5000. We can also observe that the least squares formulation is much more scalable than the original one.

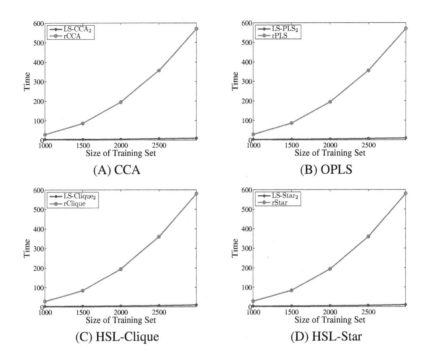

(A) CCA

(B) OPLS

(C) HSL-Clique

(D) HSL-Star

FIGURE 4.5: Computation time (in seconds) of the generalized eigenvalue problem and the corresponding least squares formulation on the Yahoo\Arts&Humanities data set as the training sample size increases. The x-axis represents the training sample size and the y-axis represents the computation time.

Chapter 5

A Scalable Two-Stage Approach for Dimensionality Reduction

In Chapter 4, we transform several dimensionality reduction algorithms that exhibit the form of a specific type of generalized eigenvalue problem into an equivalent least squares formulation, which can be solved efficiently using existing algorithms such as the iterative conjugate gradient algorithm [94, 178]. However, it suffers from several drawbacks. First, the equivalent transformation relies on a key assumption that all the data points are linearly independent. This assumption tends to hold for high-dimensional data, but it is likely to fail for (relatively) lower-dimensional data. Second, the equivalence relationship between the least squares formulation and the original formulation does not hold when regularization is applied in the generalized eigenvalue problem.

In this chapter, we present an efficient two-stage approach [218] to solve the class of dimensionality reduction algorithms discussed in Section 4.3, which includes CCA, orthonormalized PLS, HSL, and LDA. In the first stage we solve a least squares problem using the iterative conjugate gradient algorithm [94, 178]. The distinct property of this stage is its low time complexity. In the second stage, the original data is projected onto a lower-dimensional space, and then we solve a generalized eigenvalue problem with a significantly reduced size. The two-stage approach scales linearly in terms of both the sample size and the data dimensionality and is thus applicable for large-scale problems. Compared with the one-stage approach in Chapter 4, the two-stage approach does not require any assumption. Also, it can be further extended to the regularization setting.

5.1 The Two-Stage Approach without Regularization

In this section, we present the two-stage approach and show that this approach is equivalent to the direct approach, which solves the generalized eigenvalue problem in Eq. (4.29) directly.

Algorithm 5.1 The Two-Stage Approach without Regularization

Input: X, H.
Output: W.
Stage 1: Solve the following least squares problem:

$$\min_{\mathbf{W}_1} \| \mathbf{W}_1^T \mathbf{X} - \mathbf{H}^T \|_F^2. \tag{5.1}$$

Stage 2: Compute $\tilde{\mathbf{X}} = \mathbf{W}_1^T \mathbf{X}$, and solve the following optimization problem:

$$\max_{\mathbf{W}_2} \quad \mathrm{Tr}(\mathbf{W}_2^T \tilde{\mathbf{X}} \mathbf{H} \mathbf{H}^T \tilde{\mathbf{X}}^T \mathbf{W}_2) \tag{5.2}$$

$$\mathrm{s.\,t.} \quad \mathbf{W}_2^T \tilde{\mathbf{X}} \tilde{\mathbf{X}}^T \mathbf{W}_2 = \mathbf{I}_\ell.$$

Compute $\mathbf{W} = \mathbf{W}_1 \mathbf{W}_2$ as the final solution.

5.1.1 The Algorithm

In the two-stage approach, we first solve a least squares problem by regressing $\mathbf{X}$ on $\mathbf{H}^T$, where the definition of $\mathbf{H}$ for different dimensionality reduction algorithms is given in Section 4.3. In other words, $\mathbf{H}^T$ can be considered as the "latent target" encoded by label information $\mathbf{Y}$. Using the solution of least squares as the projection matrix, we project the data matrix $\mathbf{X}$ onto a lower-dimensional subspace. Then we solve a generalized eigenvalue problem by replacing the data matrix in Eq. (4.29) with the projected data matrix. Note that the data dimensionality is reduced dramatically after the projection; thus the resulting generalized eigenvalue problem in the second step can be solved efficiently. The two-stage approach is summarized in Algorithm 5.1.

5.1.2 Time Complexity Analysis

As in Chapter 4, we apply the LSQR algorithm [178], a conjugate gradient method to solve least squares problem in the first stage. Previous studies have shown that LSQR is reliable even for ill-conditioned problems [178]. In addition, when the data matrix $\mathbf{X}$ is sparse, the least squares can be solved very efficiently using LSQR. Note that $\mathbf{H} \in \mathbb{R}^{n \times k}$ where n is the number of samples and k is the number of labels. Thus, k least squares problems are solved in the first stage of Algorithm 5.1. As a result, the total computational cost of the first stage is $O(Nk(3n + 5d + 2dn))$ using LSQR when $\mathbf{X}$ is dense, where N is the total number of iterations and d is the data dimensionality. When the data matrix $\mathbf{X}$ is sparse, the cost of LSQR is reduced to $O(Nk(3n + 5d + 2z))$, where z is the number of nonzero entries in $\mathbf{X}$.

In the second stage, the cost of computing $\tilde{\mathbf{X}}$ is $O(ndk)$ when $\mathbf{X}$ is dense or $O(kz)$ when $\mathbf{X}$ is sparse. Since the size of $\tilde{\mathbf{X}}$ is significantly reduced, the cost of solving the optimization problem is $O(nk^2)$. The cost of combining $\mathbf{W}_1$ and $\mathbf{W}_2$

is $O(nk\ell)$, where ℓ ($\ell \leq k$) is the number of final projection vectors. Therefore, the total computational cost is $O(Nk(3n + 5d + 2z) + kz)$ when $\mathbf{X}$ is sparse.

5.1.3 The Equivalence Relationship

Next we show the equivalence relationship between the two-stage approach and the direct approach, which solves the original eigenvalue problem in Eq. (4.30). It follows from standard techniques in linear algebra that the solution to the least squares problem in Eq. (5.1) is given by

$$\mathbf{W}_1 = (\mathbf{X}\mathbf{X}^T)^\dagger \mathbf{X}\mathbf{H} \in \mathbb{R}^{d \times k}. \tag{5.3}$$

Let the Singular Value Decomposition (SVD) of $\mathbf{X}$ be

$$\mathbf{X} = \mathbf{U}\mathbf{\Sigma}\mathbf{V}^T = \mathbf{U}_1\mathbf{\Sigma}_1\mathbf{V}_1^T, \tag{5.4}$$

where $\mathbf{U} \in \mathbb{R}^{d \times d}$ and $\mathbf{V} \in \mathbb{R}^{n \times n}$ are orthogonal matrices, $\mathbf{U}_1 \in \mathbb{R}^{d \times r}$ and $\mathbf{V}_1 \in \mathbb{R}^{n \times r}$ have orthonormal columns, $\mathbf{\Sigma} \in \mathbb{R}^{d \times n}$ and $\mathbf{\Sigma}_1 \in \mathbb{R}^{r \times r}$ are diagonal matrices, and $r = \text{rank}(\mathbf{X})$. Then $\mathbf{W}_1$ can be represented as

$$\mathbf{W}_1 = \mathbf{U}_1\mathbf{\Sigma}_1^{-1}\mathbf{V}_1^T\mathbf{H}. \tag{5.5}$$

It follows that $\tilde{\mathbf{X}}$ can be expressed as

$$\tilde{\mathbf{X}} = \mathbf{W}_1^T\mathbf{X} = \mathbf{H}^T\mathbf{V}_1\mathbf{\Sigma}_1^{-1}\mathbf{U}_1^T\mathbf{U}_1\mathbf{\Sigma}_1\mathbf{V}_1^T = \mathbf{H}^T\mathbf{V}_1\mathbf{V}_1^T, \tag{5.6}$$

and

$$\tilde{\mathbf{X}}\tilde{\mathbf{X}}^T = \mathbf{H}^T\mathbf{V}_1\mathbf{V}_1^T\mathbf{V}_1\mathbf{V}_1^T\mathbf{H} = \mathbf{H}^T\mathbf{V}_1\mathbf{V}_1^T\mathbf{H}.$$

Thus, the optimization problem in Eq. (5.2) can be simplified into the following form:

$$\max_{\mathbf{W}_2} \quad \text{Tr}(\mathbf{W}_2^T\mathbf{H}^T\mathbf{V}_1\mathbf{V}_1^T\mathbf{H}\mathbf{H}^T\mathbf{V}_1\mathbf{V}_1^T\mathbf{H}\mathbf{W}_2)$$

$$\text{s.t.} \quad \mathbf{W}_2^T\mathbf{H}^T\mathbf{V}_1\mathbf{V}_1^T\mathbf{H}\mathbf{W}_2 = \mathbf{I}_\ell.$$

Denote

$$\mathbf{A} = \mathbf{H}^T\mathbf{V}_1 \in \mathbb{R}^{k \times r}. \tag{5.7}$$

Then the optimization problem in the second stage can be reformulated as follows:

$$\max_{\mathbf{W}_2} \quad \text{Tr}(\mathbf{W}_2^T\mathbf{A}\mathbf{A}^T\mathbf{A}\mathbf{A}^T\mathbf{W}_2) \tag{5.8}$$

$$\text{s.t.} \quad \mathbf{W}_2^T\mathbf{A}\mathbf{A}^T\mathbf{W}_2 = \mathbf{I}_\ell,$$

Let the compact SVD of $\mathbf{A}$ be

$$\mathbf{A} = \mathbf{U}_A\mathbf{\Sigma}_A\mathbf{V}_A^T, \tag{5.9}$$

where $\mathbf{U}_A \in \mathbb{R}^{k \times t}$, $\mathbf{\Sigma}_A \in \mathbb{R}^{t \times t}$, $\mathbf{V}_A \in \mathbb{R}^{r \times t}$, and $t = \text{rank}(\mathbf{A})$. Based on the SVD of $\mathbf{A}$, the optimization problem in Eq. (5.8) can be reformulated as follows:

$$\max_{\mathbf{G}} \quad \text{Tr}(\mathbf{G}^T \mathbf{\Sigma}_A^2 \mathbf{G}) \tag{5.10}$$

$$\text{s. t.} \quad \mathbf{G}^T \mathbf{G} = \mathbf{I}_\ell$$

where $\mathbf{G} = \mathbf{\Sigma}_A \mathbf{U}_A^T \mathbf{W}_2 \in \mathbb{R}^{t \times \ell}$. It follows from Ky Fan's theorem [115] that the maximum of $\text{Tr}(\mathbf{G}^T \mathbf{\Sigma}_A^2 \mathbf{G})$ under the constraint $\mathbf{G}^T \mathbf{G} = \mathbf{I}_\ell$ is the sum of the largest ℓ eigenvalues of $\mathbf{\Sigma}_A^2$, and the optimal $\mathbf{G}^*$ is given by $\mathbf{G}^* = \mathbf{P}\mathbf{Q}$ where $\mathbf{P}$ contains the eigenvectors of $\mathbf{\Sigma}_A^2$ corresponding to the largest ℓ eigenvalues and $\mathbf{Q}$ is an arbitrary orthogonal matrix of size ℓ by ℓ. Let $\mathbf{P} = [\mathbf{I}_\ell, \mathbf{0}]^T$ and $\mathbf{Q} = \mathbf{I}_\ell$; then we have

$$\mathbf{\Sigma}_A \mathbf{U}_A^T \mathbf{W}_2 = \begin{bmatrix} \mathbf{I}_\ell \\ \mathbf{0} \end{bmatrix}$$

$$\Leftrightarrow \quad \mathbf{W}_2 = (\mathbf{U}_A \mathbf{\Sigma}_A^{-1})_\ell, \tag{5.11}$$

where $\ell \leq \text{rank}(\mathbf{A})$ and $(\mathbf{U}_A \mathbf{\Sigma}_A^{-1})_\ell$ consists of the first ℓ columns of $(\mathbf{U}_A \mathbf{\Sigma}_A^{-1})$. Combining Eqs. (5.5) and (5.11), we have

$$\mathbf{W} = \mathbf{W}_1 \mathbf{W}_2 = \mathbf{U}_1 \mathbf{\Sigma}_1^{-1} \mathbf{A}^T (\mathbf{U}_A \mathbf{\Sigma}_A^{-1})_\ell = \mathbf{U}_1 \mathbf{\Sigma}_1^{-1} \mathbf{V}_{A\ell},$$

where $\mathbf{V}_{A\ell}$ contains the first ℓ columns of $\mathbf{V}_A$. When $\ell = \text{rank}(\mathbf{A})$, we have $\mathbf{V}_{A\ell} = \mathbf{V}_A$ and $\mathbf{W} = \mathbf{U}_1 \mathbf{\Sigma}_1^{-1} \mathbf{V}_A$.

We summarize these results in the following theorem:

Theorem 5.1 *The optimal solution to Eq. (5.2) is given by*

$$\mathbf{W}_2 = (\mathbf{U}_A \mathbf{\Sigma}_A^{-1})_\ell, \tag{5.12}$$

where $\ell \leq \text{rank}(\mathbf{A})$ and $(\mathbf{U}_A \mathbf{\Sigma}_A^{-1})_\ell$ consists of the first ℓ columns of $(\mathbf{U}_A \mathbf{\Sigma}_A^{-1})$. Thus, the projection vectors computed by the two-stage approach are

$$\mathbf{W} = \mathbf{W}_1 \mathbf{W}_2 = \mathbf{U}_1 \mathbf{\Sigma}_1^{-1} \mathbf{V}_{A\ell}. \tag{5.13}$$

When $\ell = \text{rank}(\mathbf{A})$, $\mathbf{W}$ can be simplified as

$$\mathbf{W} = \mathbf{U}_1 \mathbf{\Sigma}_1^{-1} \mathbf{V}_A. \tag{5.14}$$

Note that the solution to the generalized eigenvalue problem in Eq. (4.29) consists of the principal eigenvectors of matrix $(\mathbf{X}\mathbf{X}^T)^\dagger (\mathbf{X}\mathbf{H}\mathbf{H}^T\mathbf{X}^T)$. We follow [220] to derive the eigendecomposition of $(\mathbf{X}\mathbf{X}^T)^\dagger (\mathbf{X}\mathbf{H}\mathbf{H}^T\mathbf{X}^T)$ and show the equivalence relationship between the two-stage approach and the direct approach. The results are summarized in the following theorem:

Theorem 5.2 *The eigenvectors corresponding to the top ℓ ($\ell \leq \text{rank}(\mathbf{A})$) eigenvalues of $(\mathbf{X}\mathbf{X}^T)^\dagger (\mathbf{X}\mathbf{H}\mathbf{H}^T\mathbf{X}^T)$ are given by*

$$\mathbf{W}_0 = \mathbf{U}_1 \mathbf{\Sigma}_1^{-1} \mathbf{V}_{A\ell}, \tag{5.15}$$

where $\mathbf{V}_{A\ell}$ consists of the first ℓ columns of $\mathbf{V}_A$. Thus, the two-stage approach produces the same solution as the direct approach, which solves the original generalized eigenvalue problem directly.

Proof Given $\mathbf{V}_A \in \mathbb{R}^{r \times t}$ with orthonormal columns, there exists $\mathbf{V}_A^{\perp} \in \mathbb{R}^{r \times (r-t)}$ such that $[\mathbf{V}_A, \mathbf{V}_A^{\perp}] \in \mathbb{R}^{r \times r}$ is an orthogonal matrix [94]. Hereafter, we denote $[\mathbf{V}_A, \mathbf{V}_A^{\perp}] = \mathbf{V}_A^s$.

We can decompose $(\mathbf{X}\mathbf{X}^T)^{\dagger}(\mathbf{X}\mathbf{H}\mathbf{H}^T\mathbf{X}^T)$ as follows:

$$
\begin{aligned}
& (\mathbf{X}\mathbf{X}^T)^{\dagger}(\mathbf{X}\mathbf{H}\mathbf{H}^T\mathbf{X}^T) \\
= {}& \mathbf{U}_1\boldsymbol{\Sigma}_1^{-2}\mathbf{U}_1^T\mathbf{X}\mathbf{H}\mathbf{H}^T\mathbf{X}^T \\
= {}& \mathbf{U}_1\boldsymbol{\Sigma}_1^{-2}\mathbf{U}_1^T\mathbf{U}_1\boldsymbol{\Sigma}_1\mathbf{V}_1^T\mathbf{H}\mathbf{H}^T\mathbf{V}_1\boldsymbol{\Sigma}_1\mathbf{U}_1^T \\
= {}& \mathbf{U}_1\boldsymbol{\Sigma}_1^{-1}\mathbf{A}^T\mathbf{A}\boldsymbol{\Sigma}_1\mathbf{U}_1^T \\
= {}& \mathbf{U}\begin{bmatrix}\mathbf{I}_r \\ \mathbf{0}\end{bmatrix}\boldsymbol{\Sigma}_1^{-1}\mathbf{A}^T\mathbf{A}\boldsymbol{\Sigma}_1\begin{bmatrix}\mathbf{I}_r & \mathbf{0}\end{bmatrix}\mathbf{U}^T \\
= {}& \mathbf{U}\begin{bmatrix}\boldsymbol{\Sigma}_1^{-1}\mathbf{A}^T\mathbf{A}\boldsymbol{\Sigma}_1 & \mathbf{0} \\ \mathbf{0} & \mathbf{0}\end{bmatrix}\mathbf{U}^T \\
= {}& \mathbf{U}\begin{bmatrix}\boldsymbol{\Sigma}_1^{-1}\mathbf{V}_A^s & \mathbf{0} \\ \mathbf{0} & \mathbf{I}\end{bmatrix}\begin{bmatrix}\boldsymbol{\Sigma}_A^2 & \mathbf{0} \\ \mathbf{0} & \mathbf{0}\end{bmatrix}\begin{bmatrix}\mathbf{V}_A^{s\,T}\boldsymbol{\Sigma}_1 & \mathbf{0} \\ \mathbf{0} & \mathbf{I}\end{bmatrix}\mathbf{U}^T.
\end{aligned}
$$

Thus, the eigenvectors corresponding to the top ℓ eigenvalues of $(\mathbf{X}\mathbf{X}^T)^{\dagger}(\mathbf{X}\mathbf{H}\mathbf{H}^T\mathbf{X}^T)$ are given by

$$
\mathbf{W}_0 = \mathbf{U}_1\boldsymbol{\Sigma}_1^{-1}\mathbf{V}_{A\ell}.
$$

The equivalence relationship follows from Eqs. (5.13) and (5.15). This completes the proof of the theorem. ∎

A consequence of Theorem 5.1 is that solving the optimization problem in Eq. (5.2) in the second stage amounts to computing the SVD of matrix $\mathbf{A}$. Note that $\mathbf{A} \in \mathbb{R}^{k \times r}$, where $r = \text{rank}(\mathbf{X}) \leq \min\{d, n\}$; thus the computational cost of the SVD of $\mathbf{A}$ is quite low. In practice we can perform SVD on $\mathbf{A}$ directly instead of solving the optimization problem in Eq. (5.2).

Remark 5.1 *In Chapter 4 we discussed an equivalent least squares formulation for the same class of dimensionality reduction algorithms, which has the same computational cost as the two-stage approach discussed in this chapter. However, the analysis in Chapter 4 assumes that the data matrix $\mathbf{X}$ is of full rank (before centering). This tends to fail for (relatively) lower-dimensional data. In particular, when the number of data points is larger than the number of dimensions, this assumption is likely to be violated. The two-stage algorithm presented in this chapter significantly improves previous work by relaxing this assumption.*

5.2 The Two-Stage Approach with Regularization

Regularization is commonly employed to control model complexity and mitigate overfitting. In this section we present the two-stage approach with regularization.

Algorithm 5.2 The Two-Stage Approach with Regularization

Input: X, H, γ.
Output: W.
Stage 1: Solve the following least squares problem:

$$\min_{\mathbf{W}_1} \|\mathbf{W}_1^T\mathbf{X} - \mathbf{H}^T\|_F^2 + \gamma\|\mathbf{W}_1\|_F^2. \tag{5.16}$$

Stage 2: Compute $\tilde{\mathbf{X}} = \mathbf{W}_1^T\mathbf{X}$ and $\mathbf{D} = \tilde{\mathbf{X}}\mathbf{H}$. Compute the compact SVD of
$\mathbf{D} = \mathbf{U}_D\boldsymbol{\Sigma}_D\mathbf{U}_D^T$ and set $\mathbf{W}_2 = \mathbf{U}_D\boldsymbol{\Sigma}_D^{-1/2}$.
Compute $\mathbf{W} = \mathbf{W}_1\mathbf{W}_2$ as the final solution.

We show the equivalence relationship between the two-stage approach and the direct approach, which solves the generalized eigenvalue problem with regularization in Eq. (4.32).

5.2.1   The Algorithm

To handle regularization in the generalized eigenvalue problem in Eq. (4.32), we solve a penalized least squares problem, or ridge regression [109], in the first step. Note that the "latent target" is the same as the one used in Algorithm 5.1, and the difference is the regularization term included in the least squares problem. After projecting the data matrix $\mathbf{X}$ onto the subspace, we compute an auxiliary matrix $\mathbf{D} \in \mathbb{R}^{k \times k}$ and its SVD. Intuitively, the SVD computation of $\mathbf{D}$ amounts to solving the original optimization problem by replacing $\mathbf{X}$ with $\tilde{\mathbf{X}}$. Note that the size of $\mathbf{D}$ is very small, and thus the cost of computing the SVD of $\mathbf{D}$ is relatively low. The algorithm is summarized in Algorithm 5.2.

5.2.2   Time Complexity Analysis

Similar to Algorithm 5.1, the least squares problem in the first stage is solved using the LSQR algorithm [178] with the same cost. In the second stage, since $k \ll d$, the most expensive part is the computation of $\tilde{\mathbf{X}}$ with a cost of $O(kdn)$ if $\mathbf{X}$ is dense or $O(kz)$ if $\mathbf{X}$ is sparse, where z is the number of nonzero entries in the data matrix $\mathbf{X}$. Therefore, the total computational cost is $O(Nk(3n + 5d + 2z) + kz)$ if $\mathbf{X}$ is sparse where N is the total number of iterations in LSQR.

5.2.3   The Equivalence Relationship

Next we show that the two-stage approach with regularization yields the same solution as the direct approach, which solves the generalized eigenvalue problem with regularization in Eq. (4.32). Following standard techniques in linear algebra, the solution to the least squares problem with regularization in Eq. (5.16) is given by

$$\mathbf{W}_1 = (\mathbf{X}\mathbf{X}^T + \gamma\mathbf{I})^\dagger \mathbf{X}\mathbf{H} = \mathbf{U}_1 \left(\mathbf{\Sigma}_1^2 + \gamma\mathbf{I}\right)^{-1}\mathbf{\Sigma}_1\mathbf{V}_1^T\mathbf{H}. \qquad (5.17)$$

Then $\tilde{\mathbf{X}}$ can be expressed as

$$\tilde{\mathbf{X}} = \mathbf{W}_1^T\mathbf{X} = \mathbf{H}^T\mathbf{V}_1\mathbf{\Sigma}_1 \left(\mathbf{\Sigma}_1^2 + \gamma\mathbf{I}\right)^{-1}\mathbf{\Sigma}_1\mathbf{V}_1^T, \qquad (5.18)$$

and the matrix $\mathbf{D} \in \mathbb{R}^{k \times k}$ can be represented as

$$\mathbf{D} = \tilde{\mathbf{X}}\mathbf{H} = \mathbf{H}^T\mathbf{V}_1\mathbf{\Sigma}_1 \left(\mathbf{\Sigma}_1^2 + \gamma\mathbf{I}\right)^{-1}\mathbf{\Sigma}_1\mathbf{V}_1^T\mathbf{H} = \mathbf{B}\mathbf{B}^T, \qquad (5.19)$$

where $\mathbf{B} \in \mathbb{R}^{k \times r}$ is defined as

$$\mathbf{B} = \mathbf{H}^T\mathbf{V}_1\mathbf{\Sigma}_1 \left(\mathbf{\Sigma}_1^2 + \gamma\mathbf{I}\right)^{-1/2}. \qquad (5.20)$$

Let the compact SVD of $\mathbf{B}$ be

$$\mathbf{B} = \mathbf{U}_B\mathbf{\Sigma}_B\mathbf{V}_B^T, \qquad (5.21)$$

where $\mathbf{U}_B \in \mathbb{R}^{k \times q}$, $\mathbf{\Sigma}_B \in \mathbb{R}^{q \times q}$, $\mathbf{V}_B \in \mathbb{R}^{r \times q}$, and $q = \text{rank}(\mathbf{B})$. Note that $\mathbf{D} = \mathbf{B}\mathbf{B}^T$. The SVD of $\mathbf{D}$ can be obtained based on the SVD of $\mathbf{B}$ as follows:

$$\mathbf{D} = \mathbf{U}_B\mathbf{\Sigma}_B^2\mathbf{U}_B^T = \mathbf{U}_D\mathbf{\Sigma}_D\mathbf{U}_D^T. \qquad (5.22)$$

It follows from Algorithm 5.2 that

$$\mathbf{W}_2 = \mathbf{U}_B\mathbf{\Sigma}_B^{-1}.$$

Recall that $\mathbf{W}_1$ can also be represented using $\mathbf{B}$ as

$$\mathbf{W}_1 = \mathbf{U}_1 \left(\mathbf{\Sigma}_1^2 + \gamma\mathbf{I}\right)^{-1}\mathbf{\Sigma}_1\mathbf{V}_1^T\mathbf{H} = \mathbf{U}_1 \left(\mathbf{\Sigma}_1^2 + \gamma\mathbf{I}\right)^{-1/2}\mathbf{B}^T.$$

We can thus derive $\mathbf{W}$ as follows:

$$
\begin{aligned}
\mathbf{W} &= \mathbf{W}_1\mathbf{W}_2 \\
&= \mathbf{U}_1 \left(\mathbf{\Sigma}_1^2 + \gamma\mathbf{I}\right)^{-1/2}\mathbf{B}^T\mathbf{U}_B\mathbf{\Sigma}_B^{-1} \\
&= \mathbf{U}_1 \left(\mathbf{\Sigma}_1^2 + \gamma\mathbf{I}\right)^{-1/2}\mathbf{V}_B\mathbf{\Sigma}_B\mathbf{U}_B^T\mathbf{U}_B\mathbf{\Sigma}_B^{-1} \\
&= \mathbf{U}_1 \left(\mathbf{\Sigma}_1^2 + \gamma\mathbf{I}\right)^{-1/2}\mathbf{V}_B.
\end{aligned}
$$

If only the first ℓ projection vectors are required, then the resulting $\mathbf{W}$ is given by

$$\mathbf{W} = \mathbf{U}_1(\mathbf{\Sigma}_1^2 + \gamma\mathbf{I})^{-1/2}\mathbf{V}_{B\ell},$$

where $\mathbf{V}_{B\ell}$ consists of the first ℓ columns of $\mathbf{V}_B$.

Formally, the solution to the two-stage approach in Algorithm 5.2 is summarized in Theorem 5.3.

Theorem 5.3 *The top ℓ ($\ell \leq \mathrm{rank}(\mathbf{B})$) projection vectors computed by Algorithm 5.2 are given by*

$$\mathbf{W} = \mathbf{W}_1 \mathbf{W}_2 = \mathbf{U}_1 (\boldsymbol{\Sigma}_1^2 + \gamma \mathbf{I})^{-1/2} \mathbf{V}_{B\ell}, \tag{5.23}$$

where

$$\mathbf{W}_2 = (\mathbf{U}_B \boldsymbol{\Sigma}_B^{-1})_\ell, \tag{5.24}$$

$\mathbf{V}_{B\ell}$ *consists of the first ℓ columns of $\mathbf{V}_B$, and $(\mathbf{U}_B \boldsymbol{\Sigma}_B^{-1})_\ell$ consists of the first ℓ columns of $\mathbf{U}_B \boldsymbol{\Sigma}_B^{-1}$. When $\ell = \mathrm{rank}(\mathbf{B})$, $\mathbf{W}$ can be simplified as*

$$\mathbf{W} = \mathbf{U}_1 (\boldsymbol{\Sigma}_1^2 + \gamma \mathbf{I})^{-1/2} \mathbf{V}_B. \tag{5.25}$$

We follow [223] for the eigendecomposition of the matrix $(\mathbf{X}\mathbf{X}^T + \gamma \mathbf{I})^{-1} (\mathbf{X}\mathbf{H}\mathbf{H}^T\mathbf{X}^T)$. The eigendecomposition is summarized in the following theorem, based on which we also obtain the equivalence relationship between the two-stage approach and the direct approach in the regularization setting.

Theorem 5.4 *The eigenvectors corresponding to the top ℓ ($\ell \leq \mathrm{rank}(\mathbf{B})$) eigenvalues of the matrix $(\mathbf{X}\mathbf{X}^T + \gamma \mathbf{I})^{-1}(\mathbf{X}\mathbf{H}\mathbf{H}^T\mathbf{X}^T)$ are given by*

$$\mathbf{W}_0 = \mathbf{U}_1 (\boldsymbol{\Sigma}_1^2 + \gamma \mathbf{I})^{-1/2} \mathbf{V}_{B\ell}, \tag{5.26}$$

where $\mathbf{V}_{B\ell}$ consists of the first ℓ columns of $\mathbf{V}_B$. Thus, the two-stage approach in Algorithm 5.2 is equivalent to the direct approach, which solves the generalized eigenvalue problem with regularization directly.

Proof Given $\mathbf{V}_B \in \mathbb{R}^{r \times q}$ with orthonormal columns, there exists $\mathbf{V}_B^\perp \in \mathbb{R}^{r \times (r-q)}$ such that $[\mathbf{V}_B, \mathbf{V}_B^\perp] \in \mathbb{R}^{r \times r}$ is an orthogonal matrix. Hereafter, we denote $[\mathbf{V}_B, \mathbf{V}_B^\perp] = \mathbf{V}_B^s$. We can diagonalize $(\mathbf{X}\mathbf{X}^T + \gamma \mathbf{I})^{-1}(\mathbf{X}\mathbf{H}\mathbf{H}^T\mathbf{X}^T)$ as follows:

$$
\begin{aligned}
& (\mathbf{X}\mathbf{X}^T + \gamma \mathbf{I})^{-1}(\mathbf{X}\mathbf{H}\mathbf{H}^T\mathbf{X}^T) \\
= \; & \mathbf{U}_1 (\boldsymbol{\Sigma}_1^2 + \gamma \mathbf{I})^{-1} \boldsymbol{\Sigma}_1 \mathbf{V}_1^T \mathbf{H}\mathbf{H}^T \mathbf{V}_1 \boldsymbol{\Sigma}_1 \mathbf{U}_1^T \\
= \; & \mathbf{U}_1 (\boldsymbol{\Sigma}_1^2 + \gamma \mathbf{I})^{-1/2} (\boldsymbol{\Sigma}_1^2 + \gamma \mathbf{I})^{-1/2} \boldsymbol{\Sigma}_1 \mathbf{V}_1^T \mathbf{H}\mathbf{H}^T \\
& \mathbf{V}_1 \boldsymbol{\Sigma}_1 (\boldsymbol{\Sigma}_1^2 + \gamma \mathbf{I})^{-1/2} (\boldsymbol{\Sigma}_1^2 + \gamma \mathbf{I})^{1/2} \mathbf{U}_1^T \\
= \; & \mathbf{U}_1 (\boldsymbol{\Sigma}_1^2 + \gamma \mathbf{I})^{-1/2} \mathbf{B}^T \mathbf{B} (\boldsymbol{\Sigma}_1^2 + \gamma \mathbf{I})^{1/2} \mathbf{U}_1^T \\
= \; & \mathbf{U} \begin{bmatrix} \mathbf{I}_r \\ \mathbf{0} \end{bmatrix} (\boldsymbol{\Sigma}_1^2 + \gamma \mathbf{I})^{-1/2} \mathbf{B}^T \mathbf{B} (\boldsymbol{\Sigma}_1^2 + \lambda \mathbf{I})^{1/2} \begin{bmatrix} \mathbf{I}_r & \mathbf{0} \end{bmatrix} \mathbf{U}^T \\
= \; & \mathbf{U} \begin{bmatrix} (\boldsymbol{\Sigma}_1^2 + \gamma \mathbf{I})^{-1/2} \mathbf{B}^T \mathbf{B} (\boldsymbol{\Sigma}_1^2 + \gamma \mathbf{I})^{1/2} & \mathbf{0} \\ \mathbf{0} & \mathbf{0} \end{bmatrix} \mathbf{U}^T \\
= \; & \mathbf{U} \begin{bmatrix} (\boldsymbol{\Sigma}_1^2 + \lambda \mathbf{I})^{-1/2} \mathbf{V}_B^s & \mathbf{0} \\ \mathbf{0} & \mathbf{I} \end{bmatrix} \begin{bmatrix} \boldsymbol{\Sigma}_B^2 & \mathbf{0} \\ \mathbf{0} & \mathbf{0} \end{bmatrix} \begin{bmatrix} \mathbf{V}_B^{s\,T} (\boldsymbol{\Sigma}_1^2 + \gamma \mathbf{I})^{1/2} & \mathbf{0} \\ \mathbf{0} & \mathbf{I} \end{bmatrix} \mathbf{U}^T.
\end{aligned}
$$

Thus, the eigenvectors corresponding to the top ℓ eigenvalues of $(\mathbf{X}\mathbf{X}^T + \gamma \mathbf{I})^{-1}(\mathbf{X}\mathbf{H}\mathbf{H}^T\mathbf{X}^T)$ are given by $\mathbf{U}_1 (\boldsymbol{\Sigma}_1^2 + \gamma \mathbf{I})^{-1/2} \mathbf{V}_{B\ell}$. The equivalence between the two-stage approach and the direct approach follows from Eqs. (5.23) and (5.26). This completes the proof of the theorem. ■

Remark 5.2 *The least squares algorithm discussed in Chapter 4 only works for dimensionality reduction algorithms without regularization. This drawback limits its applicability in practice, since regularized algorithms are more effective in practice due to their better generalization performance. The two-stage algorithm presented in this chapter significantly improves previous work by extending the equivalence to the regularization setting.*

Remark 5.3 *Kernel dimensionality reduction algorithms will be discussed in Chapter 8. Note that the two-stage approach can be extended to the kernel-induced feature space by following the trick in [58]. The equivalence relationship still holds for all dimensionality reduction algorithms discussed above with and without regularization.*

5.3 Empirical Evaluation

In this section we present extensive experiments to verify the equivalence relationship and demonstrate the scalability of the two-stage approach.

5.3.1 Empirical Evaluation Setup

The dimensionality reduction algorithms discussed in this chapter can be divided into two categories: 1) LDA for multi-class classification; 2) HSL, CCA, and OPLS for multi-label classification. We use both multi-class and multi-label data sets, including synthetic and real-world data sets, in the experiments. Two synthetic data sets for multi-class classification as well as two synthetic data sets for multi-label classification are generated. In the synthetic data sets, each entry of the data matrix $\mathbf{X}$ is generated independently from the standard Gaussian distribution $\mathcal{N}(0, 1)$. We generate the label matrix $\mathbf{Y}$ as follows: in multi-class data sets Syn1 and Syn2, we randomly select a label for each instance; in multi-label data sets Syn3 and Syn4, for each label we randomly select $1.2 * n/k$ instances and assign the label to these selected instances. Five real-world data sets from the UCI machine learning repository [13] and two benchmark multi-label data sets [34, 74] are tested in our experiments. To investigate the scalability of the two-stage approach, two large-scale data sets including news20 [147] and RCV1-v2 [155] are used. The statistics of all data sets are summarized in Table 5.1, where n is the number of samples, d is the data dimensionality, and k is the number of labels (classes).

To distinguish different algorithms tested in the experiments, we name regularized ones using a prefix "r" before the corresponding algorithm, e.g., "rCCA". The two-stage approach version is named using a prefix "2S" ("2S" means two stage) such as "2SCCA" and "2SrCCA", which are the two-stage approach implementations of CCA and regularized CCA, respectively.

TABLE 5.1:   Statistics of the data sets.

Data Set	Type	n	d	k
Syn1	Multi-class	1000	100	5
Syn2	Multi-class	1000	5000	5
Syn3	Multi-label	1000	100	5
Syn4	Multi-label	1000	5000	5
Ionosphere	Multi-class	351	34	2
Optical digits	Multi-class	5620	64	10
Satimage	Multi-class	6435	36	6
USPS	Multi-class	9298	256	10
Wine	Multi-class	178	13	3
Scene	Multi-label	2407	294	6
Yeast	Multi-label	2417	103	14
News20	Multi-class	15935	62061	20
RCV1-v2	Multi-label	3000	47236	101

Note: n is the number of samples, d is the data dimensionality, and k is the number of labels (classes).

5.3.2   Performance Comparison

In this experiment, we compare the performance of different approaches for all dimensionality reduction algorithms using both synthetic and real-world data sets. Denote $\mathbf{W}_0$ as the solution of the generalized eigenvalue problem in Eq. (4.32) obtained directly, and $\mathbf{W}$ as the solution of Eq. (4.32) obtained by using the two-stage approach.

To verify whether both approaches produce equivalent projections, we compute $\|\mathbf{W}_0\mathbf{W}_0^T - \mathbf{W}\mathbf{W}^T\|_2$ under different values of the regularization parameter γ. We vary the value of γ from 1e-6 to 1e6. It follows from [223] that $\|\mathbf{W}_0\mathbf{W}_0^T - \mathbf{W}\mathbf{W}^T\|_2 = 0$ if and only if $\mathbf{W}_0 = \mathbf{W}\mathbf{R}$, where $\mathbf{R}$ is an orthogonal matrix. Thus, both $\mathbf{W}$ and $\mathbf{W}_0$ project the original data onto the same lower-dimensional space. Note that a direct comparison between $\mathbf{W}$ and $\mathbf{W}_0$ is possible only when the generalized eigenvalue problem in Eq. (4.32) admits a unique solution. This is not always the case, e.g., when two eigenvalues coincide.

The values of $\|\mathbf{W}_0\mathbf{W}_0^T - \mathbf{W}\mathbf{W}^T\|_2$ for all data sets are summarized in Table 5.2. In Table 5.2, each row corresponds to a specific dimensionality reduction algorithm and each column corresponds to a specific value of the regularization parameter γ. Note that we test two different variants of HSL which compute the Laplacian using different expansion schemes, i.e., HSL-Clique and HSL-Star. It can be observed from Table 5.2 that for all values of the regularization parameter γ, $\|\mathbf{W}_0\mathbf{W}_0^T - \mathbf{W}\mathbf{W}^T\|_2$ is always very small, which confirms the equivalence relationship between $\mathbf{W}$ and $\mathbf{W}_0$ for projection.

Next, we investigate the classification performance of different dimensionality reduction algorithms. We compare the performance of different approaches on the multi-label data set Yeast [74]. The data set is randomly partitioned into a training set and a test data set with equal size. After the projection matrix is learned from

TABLE 5.2: The value of $\| \mathbf{W}\mathbf{W}^T - \mathbf{W}_0\mathbf{W}_0^T \|_2$ under different values of the regularization parameter γ on the synthetic and real-world data sets.

Data	Algorithm	0	1.0e-6	1.0e-4	1.0e-2	1.0e+0	1.0e+2	1.0e+4	1.0e+6
Syn1	LDA	2.9e-18	3.6e-18	3.4e-18	3.1e-18	2.6e-18	2.5e-18	3.1e-19	3.0e-21
Syn2	LDA	5.8e-19	1.4e-18	1.2e-18	8.9e-19	1.2e-18	9.9e-19	2.3e-19	2.9e-21
Syn3	CCA	4.9e-18	8.4e-18	7.0e-18	6.5e-18	9.5e-18	6.0e-18	5.1e-19	7.2e-21
	OPLS	4.6e-18	5.0e-18	8.7e-18	5.0e-18	6.6e-18	6.1e-18	5.4e-19	5.0e-21
	HSL-Clique	1.0e-17	1.8e-17	1.2e-17	1.2e-17	1.5e-17	1.4e-17	2.9e-18	2.5e-20
	HSL-Star	1.4e-17	2.4e-17	9.3e-18	2.6e-17	2.1e-17	5.0e-17	9.8e-18	1.3e-20
Syn4	CCA	1.3e-18	5.2e-18	3.2e-18	1.8e-18	1.3e-18	1.8e-18	4.2e-19	5.9e-21
	OPLS	1.0e-18	1.1e-18	1.3e-18	1.5e-18	1.3e-18	1.3e-18	2.9e-19	5.9e-21
	HSL-Clique	2.7e-18	2.9e-18	2.7e-18	5.0e-18	3.2e-18	2.7e-18	8.9e-19	1.4e-20
	HSL-Star	2.5e-18	3.7e-18	2.9e-18	5.7e-18	4.1e-18	2.9e-18	1.1e-18	3.1e-20
Scene	CCA	2.4e-15	2.1e-15	6.1e-15	3.7e-15	1.2e-15	1.8e-16	6.0e-18	9.0e-20
	OPLS	2.0e-15	3.4e-15	3.8e-15	2.5e-15	1.1e-15	2.3e-16	1.1e-17	1.4e-19
	HSL-Clique	4.5e-15	9.1e-15	2.6e-14	1.2e-14	3.6e-15	1.3e-15	5.9e-17	1.0e-18
	HSL-Star	4.6e-15	3.3e-14	2.1e-14	7.7e-15	1.1e-14	2.5e-16	1.0e-16	6.5e-19
Yeast	CCA	1.6e-12	1.5e-11	1.2e-12	1.4e-15	6.9e-16	5.9e-17	1.7e-18	1.4e-20
	OPLS	4.1e-12	1.6e-12	3.7e-12	1.2e-14	1.5e-15	3.7e-16	3.2e-18	2.9e-20
	HSL-Clique	1.5e-12	1.4e-11	3.7e-12	3.9e-15	1.6e-15	2.7e-16	5.1e-18	2.5e-20
	HSL-Star	2.1e-12	1.0e-11	2.4e-12	1.1e-14	9.4e-15	1.1e-15	1.5e-17	4.4e-19
Wine	LDA	5.9e-17	2.1e-16	2.3e-16	2.1e-16	3.2e-17	2.2e-18	1.3e-20	2.0e-20
Satimage	LDA	4.6e-16	2.2e-15	8.4e-16	7.3e-16	7.7e-16	8.1e-17	3.9e-17	6.2e-19
Ionosphere	LDA	8.5e-18	1.0e-17	4.3e-18	2.1e-17	6.8e-18	6.6e-18	6.6e-20	1.1e-21
Optical	LDA	6.2e-18	7.2e-18	6.7e-18	5.7e-18	1.9e-18	1.5e-19	5.9e-20	5.6e-21
USPS	LDA	7.0e-15	3.0e-14	2.6e-14	6.6e-15	1.1e-16	3.0e-18	4.1e-19	6.6e-21

Note: $\mathbf{W}_0$ is the solution of the generalized eigenvalue problem in Eq. (4.32) by solving it directly, and $\mathbf{W}$ is the solution of Eq. (4.32) by solving it using the two-stage approach. Each row corresponds to a specific dimensionality reduction algorithm and each column corresponds to a specific value of the regularization parameter γ.

the training set, the test data set is projected onto the lower-dimensional space. In our experiments, the linear Support Vector Machine (SVM) is applied for classification. The mean AUC score, namely, the Area Under the ROC Curve, over all labels is summarized in Figure 5.1 for all multi-label dimensionality reduction algorithms. The regularization parameter γ varies from 1e-6 to 1e6. From Figure 5.1, we conclude that the two-stage approach always produces the same classification results as the direct approach in all cases.

A similar experiment is performed on the multi-class data set Wine [13] for LDA. The classification accuracies of LDA under different values of γ are summarized in Figure 5.2, and similar observations can be made.

5.3.3 Scalability Comparison

In this experiment, we study the scalability of the two-stage approach in comparison with the direct approach. Since regularization is commonly used in practice, we compare the scalability of different algorithms with regularization. In terms of implementation, the least squares problem in the first stage of the two-stage approach is solved using the LSQR algorithm [178]. For the direct approach which solves the generalized eigenvalue problem directly, we apply the method discussed in Section 4.4.5.

The computation time (in log scale) of different multi-label dimensionality reduction algorithms on the large-scale data set RCV1-v2 is shown in Figures 5.3 and

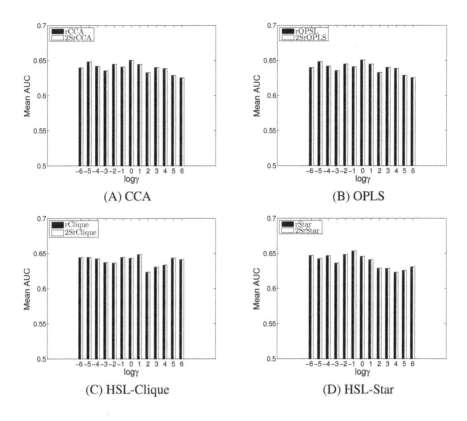

FIGURE 5.1: Comparison of different approaches in terms of mean Area Under the ROC Curve (AUC) for different dimensionality reduction algorithms on the Yeast data set as the regularization parameter γ varies.

5.4. In Figure 5.3, we increase the sample size from 500 to 3000 with a step size of 500, and the dimensionality is fixed at 5000. The computation time of both approaches increases as the sample size increases. However, it can be observed that the computation time of the two-stage approach is significantly less than that of the direct approach. In Figure 5.4 we fix the sample size at 3000 and increase the dimensionality from 500 to 5000 with a step size of 500. Similar observations can be made from Figure 5.4.

A similar experiment is performed on the News20 data set for LDA (multi-class classification). The experimental results are summarized in Figure 5.5. In Figure 5.5 (left), we fix the dimensionality at 5000 and increase the sample size from 500 to 3000 with a step size of 500. In Figure 5.5 (right), the dimensionality is increased from 500 to 3000 with a step size of 500 while the sample size is fixed at 5000. It can be observed from these figures that the two-stage approach is much more efficient than the direct approach.

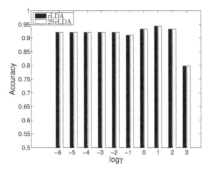

FIGURE 5.2: Comparison of different LDA approaches in terms of classification accuracy on the Wine data set as the regularization parameter γ varies.

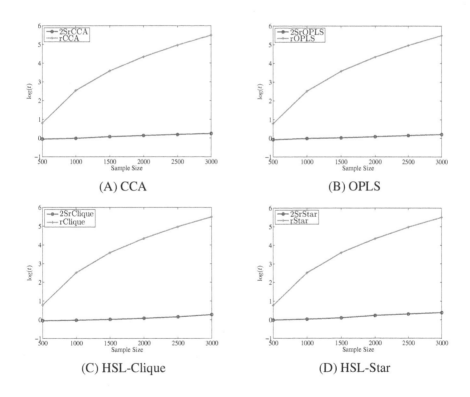

(A) CCA

(B) OPLS

(C) HSL-Clique

(D) HSL-Star

FIGURE 5.3: Scalability comparison on the RCV1-v2 data set as the sample size increases. The horizontal axis is the sample size, and the vertical axis is $\log(t)$, where t is the computation time (in seconds).

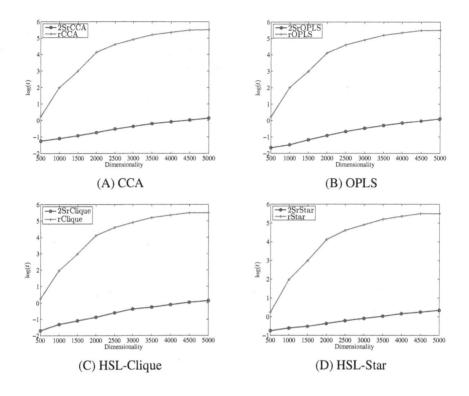

FIGURE 5.4: Scalability comparison on the RCV1-v2 data set as the dimensionality increases. The horizontal axis is the dimensionality, and the vertical axis is $\log(t)$, where t is the computation time (in seconds).

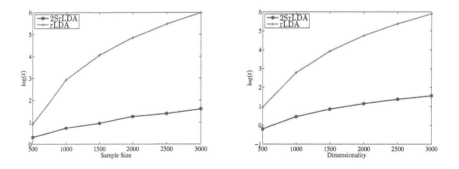

FIGURE 5.5: Scalability comparison on the News20 data set as the sample size (left) and dimensionality (right) increase. The horizontal axis is the sample size (left) or the dimensionality (right), and the vertical axis is $\log(t)$, where t is the computation time (in seconds).

Chapter 6

A Shared-Subspace Learning Framework

A central question in multi-label learning is how to share information among related labels. In this chapter, a general framework for extracting shared structures (subspace) in multi-label classification is presented. In this framework, a binary classifier is constructed for each label to discriminate this label from the rest of them. However, unlike binary relevance, which builds binary classifiers independently for all labels, a lower-dimensional subspace is assumed to be shared among multiple labels. The predictive functions in this formulation consist of two parts: the first part is contributed from the representations in the original data space, and the second one is contributed from the embedding in the shared subspace.

6.1 The Framework

We are given a set of input data $\{\mathbf{x}_i\}_{i=1}^n \in \mathbb{R}^d$ and the class label indicator matrix $\mathbf{Y} \in \mathbb{R}^{k \times n}$ that encodes the label information, where k and n are the number of labels and the number of instances, respectively. In multi-label classification, we learn k functions $\{f_j\}_{j=1}^k$ from the data that minimize the following regularized empirical risk:

$$R(\{f_j\}_{j=1}^k) = \sum_{j=1}^k \left(\frac{1}{n} \sum_{i=1}^n L(f_j(\mathbf{x}_i), \mathbf{y}_i(j)) + \mu \Omega(f_j) \right), \qquad (6.1)$$

where $\mathbf{y}_i(j)$ indicates the association of $\mathbf{x}_i$ to the label C_j, L is a prescribed loss function, $\Omega(f)$ is a regularization functional measuring the smoothness of f, and $\mu > 0$ is the regularization parameter.

6.1.1 Problem Formulation

In the shared-subspace learning framework, a lower-dimensional subspace is shared by all labels. The predictive functions in this framework consist of two parts: one part is contributed from the original data space, and the other part is derived from the shared subspace as follows:

$$f_j(\mathbf{x}) = \mathbf{w}_j^T \mathbf{x} + \mathbf{v}_j^T \mathbf{\Theta}^T \mathbf{x}, \qquad (6.2)$$

105

where $\mathbf{w}_j \in \mathbb{R}^d$ and $\mathbf{v}_j \in \mathbb{R}^r$ are the weight vectors, $\Theta \in \mathbb{R}^{d \times r}$ is the linear transformation used to parameterize the shared lower-dimensional subspace, and r is the dimensionality of the shared subspace. The transformation Θ is common for all labels, and it has orthonormal columns, that is, $\Theta^T \Theta = \mathbf{I}$. In this formulation, the input data are projected onto a lower-dimensional subspace by Θ, and this lower-dimensional projection is combined with the original representation to produce the final prediction. Note that a similar formulation has been proposed in [5] to capture the shared predictive structures in multi-task learning, but they differ in several key aspects (see Section 6.3 for a comparison).

Following the regularization formulation in Eq. (6.1), the parameters $\{\mathbf{w}_j, \mathbf{v}_j\}_{j=1}^k$ and Θ are estimated by minimizing the following regularized empirical risk:

$$\sum_{j=1}^{k} \left(\frac{1}{n} \sum_{i=1}^{n} L((\mathbf{w}_j + \Theta \mathbf{v}_j)^T \mathbf{x}_i, \mathbf{y}_i(j)) + \alpha \|\mathbf{w}_j\|_2^2 + \beta \|\mathbf{w}_j + \Theta \mathbf{v}_j\|_2^2 \right),$$

subject to the constraint that $\Theta^T \Theta = \mathbf{I}$. Note that in the above formulation, the first regularization term $\|\mathbf{w}_j\|_2^2$ controls the amount of information specific to each label, while the second regularization term $\|\mathbf{w}_j + \Theta \mathbf{v}_j\|_2^2$ controls the complexity of the models for each label. By setting $\mathbf{u}_j = \mathbf{w}_j + \Theta \mathbf{v}_j$, this problem can be reformulated equivalently as follows:

$$\min_{\{\mathbf{u}_j, \mathbf{v}_j\}, \Theta} \sum_{j=1}^{k} \left(\frac{1}{n} \sum_{i=1}^{n} L(\mathbf{u}_j^T \mathbf{x}_i, \mathbf{y}_i(j)) + \alpha \|\mathbf{u}_j - \Theta \mathbf{v}_j\|_2^2 + \beta \|\mathbf{u}_j\|_2^2 \right)$$

$$\text{s.t.} \quad \Theta^T \Theta = \mathbf{I}. \tag{6.3}$$

In [127], the squared loss, i.e.,

$$L(\mathbf{u}_j^T \mathbf{x}_i, \mathbf{y}_i(j)) = (\mathbf{u}_j^T \mathbf{x}_i - \mathbf{y}_i(j))^2,$$

has been considered. It has been shown [83, 192] that the squared loss function is comparable to other loss functions such as the hinge loss employed in Support Vector Machine (SVM) [207] when appropriate regularization is added. With the squared loss, the optimization problem can be formulated as follows:

$$\min_{\{\mathbf{u}_j, \mathbf{v}_j\}, \Theta} \sum_{j=1}^{k} \left(\frac{1}{n} \left\| \mathbf{u}_j^T \mathbf{X} - \mathbf{Y}^j \right\|_2^2 + \alpha \|\mathbf{u}_j - \Theta \mathbf{v}_j\|_2^2 + \beta \|\mathbf{u}_j\|_2^2 \right)$$

$$\text{s.t.} \quad \Theta^T \Theta = \mathbf{I}, \tag{6.4}$$

where $\mathbf{X} = [\mathbf{x}_1, \ldots, \mathbf{x}_n] \in \mathbb{R}^{d \times n}$ is the data matrix, $\mathbf{Y}^j = [\mathbf{y}_1(j), \ldots, \mathbf{y}_n(j)] \in \mathbb{R}^n$. The formulation in Eq. (6.4) can be expressed compactly as:

$$\min_{\mathbf{U}, \mathbf{V}, \Theta} \frac{1}{n} \left\| \mathbf{U}^T \mathbf{X} - \mathbf{Y} \right\|_F^2 + \alpha \|\mathbf{U} - \Theta \mathbf{V}\|_F^2 + \beta \|\mathbf{U}\|_F^2$$

$$\text{s.t.} \quad \Theta^T \Theta = \mathbf{I}, \tag{6.5}$$

where $\Theta \in \mathbb{R}^{d \times r}$, $\mathbf{U} = [\mathbf{u}_1, \ldots, \mathbf{u}_k] \in \mathbb{R}^{d \times k}$, and $\mathbf{V} = [\mathbf{v}_1, \ldots, \mathbf{v}_k] \in \mathbb{R}^{r \times k}$.

6.1.2 A Trace Ratio Formulation

We show that the formulation in Eq. (6.5) can be transformed to a trace ratio problem. We first show that the optimal $\mathbf{V}^*$ that solves the optimization problem in Eq. (6.5) can be expressed in terms of $\boldsymbol{\Theta}$ and $\mathbf{U}$, as summarized in the following lemma:

Lemma 6.1 *Let* $\mathbf{U}$, $\mathbf{V}$, *and* $\boldsymbol{\Theta}$ *be defined as above. Then the optimal* $\mathbf{V}^*$ *that solves the optimization problem in Eq. (6.5) is given by* $\mathbf{V}^* = \boldsymbol{\Theta}^T \mathbf{U}$.

The full proof of this lemma is given in Appendix A.4.

It follows from Lemma 6.1 that the objective function in Eq. (6.5) can be rewritten as:

$$
\begin{aligned}
& \frac{1}{n} \left\| \mathbf{U}^T \mathbf{X} - \mathbf{Y} \right\|_F^2 + \alpha \| \mathbf{U} - \boldsymbol{\Theta} \mathbf{V} \|_F^2 + \beta \| \mathbf{U} \|_F^2 \\
= \ & \frac{1}{n} \left\| \mathbf{U}^T \mathbf{X} - \mathbf{Y} \right\|_F^2 + \alpha \| \mathbf{U} - \boldsymbol{\Theta} \boldsymbol{\Theta}^T \mathbf{U} \|_F^2 + \beta \| \mathbf{U} \|_F^2 \\
= \ & \frac{1}{n} \left\| \mathbf{U}^T \mathbf{X} - \mathbf{Y} \right\|_F^2 + \mathrm{Tr} \left(\mathbf{U}^T \left((\alpha + \beta)\mathbf{I} - \alpha \boldsymbol{\Theta} \boldsymbol{\Theta}^T \right) \mathbf{U} \right).
\end{aligned} \tag{6.6}
$$

Hence, the optimization problem in Eq. (6.5) can be expressed equivalently as:

$$
\min_{\mathbf{U}, \boldsymbol{\Theta}} \quad \frac{1}{n} \left\| \mathbf{U}^T \mathbf{X} - \mathbf{Y} \right\|_F^2 + \mathrm{Tr} \left(\mathbf{U}^T \left((\alpha + \beta)\mathbf{I} - \alpha \boldsymbol{\Theta} \boldsymbol{\Theta}^T \right) \mathbf{U} \right)
$$
$$
\text{s.t.} \quad \boldsymbol{\Theta}^T \boldsymbol{\Theta} = \mathbf{I}. \tag{6.7}
$$

Next, we show that the optimal $\mathbf{U}^*$ can be expressed in terms of $\boldsymbol{\Theta}$. Taking the derivative of the objective function in Eq. (6.7) with respect to $\mathbf{U}$, and setting it to zero, we obtain

$$
\mathbf{U}^* = \frac{1}{n} \left(\mathbf{M} - \alpha \boldsymbol{\Theta} \boldsymbol{\Theta}^T \right)^{-1} \mathbf{X} \mathbf{Y}^T, \tag{6.8}
$$

where $\mathbf{M}$ is defined as

$$
\mathbf{M} = \frac{1}{n} \mathbf{X} \mathbf{X}^T + (\alpha + \beta)\mathbf{I}. \tag{6.9}
$$

This shows that the optimal $\mathbf{U}^*$ that solves the optimization problem in Eq. (6.7) can be expressed as in Eq. (6.8).

By substituting the expression for $\mathbf{U}^*$ in Eq. (6.8) into Eq. (6.7), we obtain the following optimization problem with respect to $\boldsymbol{\Theta}$:

$$
\max_{\boldsymbol{\Theta}} \quad \frac{1}{n^2} \mathrm{Tr} \left(\mathbf{Y} \mathbf{X}^T \left(\mathbf{M} - \alpha \boldsymbol{\Theta} \boldsymbol{\Theta}^T \right)^{-1} \mathbf{X} \mathbf{Y}^T \right) \tag{6.10}
$$
$$
\text{s.t.} \quad \boldsymbol{\Theta}^T \boldsymbol{\Theta} = \mathbf{I}.
$$

The optimization problem in Eq. (6.10) looks quite complicated. Interestingly, we can show that the optimal $\boldsymbol{\Theta}^*$ can be obtained by solving a generalized eigenvalue problem. The main result is summarized in the following theorem:

Theorem 6.1 *Let* $\mathbf{X}$, $\mathbf{Y}$, *and* Θ *be defined as above. Then the optimal* Θ^* *that solves the optimization problem in Eq. (6.10) can be obtained by solving the following trace maximization problem:*

$$\max_{\Theta} \quad \mathrm{Tr}\left(\left(\Theta^T \mathbf{S}_1 \Theta\right)^{-1} \Theta^T \mathbf{S}_2 \Theta\right) \tag{6.11}$$

$$\text{s. t.} \quad \Theta^T \Theta = \mathbf{I},$$

where $\mathbf{S}_1$ *and* $\mathbf{S}_2$ *are defined as:*

$$\mathbf{S}_1 = \mathbf{I} - \alpha \mathbf{M}^{-1}, \tag{6.12}$$

$$\mathbf{S}_2 = \mathbf{M}^{-1} \mathbf{X} \mathbf{Y}^T \mathbf{Y} \mathbf{X}^T \mathbf{M}^{-1}, \tag{6.13}$$

and $\mathbf{M}$ *is defined in Eq. (6.9).*

Proof The following Sherman–Morrison–Woodbury formula [94] for computing a matrix inverse is needed:

$$(\mathbf{P} + \mathbf{ST})^{-1} = \mathbf{P}^{-1} - \mathbf{P}^{-1}\mathbf{S}\left(\mathbf{I} + \mathbf{TP}^{-1}\mathbf{S}\right)^{-1} \mathbf{TP}^{-1}. \tag{6.14}$$

It follows from Eq. (6.14) that

$$\left(\mathbf{M} - \alpha \Theta \Theta^T\right)^{-1}$$

$$= \mathbf{M}^{-1} + \alpha \mathbf{M}^{-1}\Theta \left(\mathbf{I} - \alpha \Theta^T \mathbf{M}^{-1}\Theta\right)^{-1} \Theta^T \mathbf{M}^{-1}$$

$$= \mathbf{M}^{-1} + \alpha \mathbf{M}^{-1}\Theta \left(\Theta^T \left(\mathbf{I} - \alpha \mathbf{M}^{-1}\right)\Theta\right)^{-1} \Theta^T \mathbf{M}^{-1}, \tag{6.15}$$

where the last equality follows since $\Theta^T \Theta = \mathbf{I}$. By substituting the expression in Eq. (6.15) into the optimization problem in Eq. (6.10), we obtain the following problem:

$$\max_{\Theta} \quad \mathrm{Tr}\left(\mathbf{Y}\mathbf{X}^T \mathbf{M}^{-1}\Theta \left(\Theta^T \left(\mathbf{I} - \alpha \mathbf{M}^{-1}\right)\Theta\right)^{-1} \Theta^T \mathbf{M}^{-1}\mathbf{X}\mathbf{Y}^T\right)$$

$$\text{s. t.} \quad \Theta^T \Theta = \mathbf{I},$$

where the term $\mathbf{Y}\mathbf{X}^T \mathbf{M}^{-1}\mathbf{X}\mathbf{Y}^T$ has been omitted, since it is independent of Θ. Using the definitions of $\mathbf{S}_1$ and $\mathbf{S}_2$ in Eqs. (6.12) and (6.13), respectively, we complete the proof of this theorem. ∎

Let $\mathbf{Z} = [\mathbf{z}_1, \ldots, \mathbf{z}_r]$ be the matrix consisting of the top r eigenvectors corresponding to the largest r nonzero eigenvalues of the generalized eigenvalue problem: $\mathbf{S}_1 \mathbf{z} = \lambda \mathbf{S}_2 \mathbf{z}$. To ensure the constraint $\Theta^T \Theta = \mathbf{I}$, the QR decomposition can be employed. In particular, let $\mathbf{Z} = \mathbf{Z}_q \mathbf{Z}_r$ be the QR decomposition of $\mathbf{Z}$, where $\mathbf{Z}_q$ has orthonormal columns and $\mathbf{Z}_r$ is upper triangular. It is easy to verify [270] that the objective function in Eq. (6.11) is invariant of any nonsingular transformation, that is, $\mathbf{Q}$ and $\mathbf{QN}$ achieve the same objective value for any nonsingular matrix $\mathbf{N} \in \mathbb{R}^{r \times r}$. It follows that the optimal Θ^* solving Eq. (6.11) is given by $\Theta^* = \mathbf{Z}_q$. Note that $\mathbf{S}_1$ is positive definite [see Eq. (6.17) below]; thus $\mathbf{Z}$ can also be obtained by computing the top eigenvectors of $\mathbf{S}_1^{-1}\mathbf{S}_2$.

6.2 An Efficient Implementation

From the discussions in the last section, the optimal Θ^* is given by the eigenvectors of $\mathbf{S}_1^{-1}\mathbf{S}_2 \in \mathbb{R}^{d \times d}$ corresponding to the largest r eigenvalues. When the data dimensionality, i.e., d, is small, the eigenvectors of $\mathbf{S}_1^{-1}\mathbf{S}_2$ can be computed directly. However, when d is large, direct eigendecomposition is computationally expensive. We show how to efficiently compute the eigenvectors for the high-dimensional case.

6.2.1 Reformulation

It follows from the Sherman–Morrison–Woodbury formula in Eq. (6.14) that

$$
\begin{aligned}
\mathbf{M}^{-1} &= \frac{1}{\alpha + \beta}\mathbf{I} - \frac{1}{n(\alpha + \beta)^2}\mathbf{X}\left(\mathbf{I} + \frac{1}{n(\alpha + \beta)}\mathbf{X}^T\mathbf{X}\right)^{-1}\mathbf{X}^T \\
&= \frac{1}{\alpha + \beta}\mathbf{I} - \frac{1}{\alpha + \beta}\mathbf{X}\left(n(\alpha + \beta)\mathbf{I} + \mathbf{X}^T\mathbf{X}\right)^{-1}\mathbf{X}^T.
\end{aligned} \tag{6.16}
$$

Hence,

$$
\mathbf{I} - \alpha\mathbf{M}^{-1} = \frac{\beta}{\alpha + \beta}\mathbf{I} + \frac{\alpha}{\alpha + \beta}\mathbf{X}\left(n(\alpha + \beta)\mathbf{I} + \mathbf{X}^T\mathbf{X}\right)^{-1}\mathbf{X}^T, \tag{6.17}
$$

which is positive definite when $\beta > 0$.

It follows from the definitions of $\mathbf{M}$, $\mathbf{S}_1$, and $\mathbf{S}_2$ in Eqs. (6.9), (6.12), and (6.13) that

$$
\begin{aligned}
&\mathbf{S}_1^{-1}\mathbf{S}_2 \\
&= \left(\mathbf{I} - \alpha\mathbf{M}^{-1}\right)^{-1}\mathbf{M}^{-1}\mathbf{X}\mathbf{Y}^T\mathbf{Y}\mathbf{X}^T\mathbf{M}^{-1} \\
&= (\mathbf{M} - \alpha\mathbf{I})^{-1}\mathbf{X}\mathbf{Y}^T\mathbf{Y}\mathbf{X}^T\mathbf{M}^{-1} \\
&= \left(\frac{1}{n}\mathbf{X}\mathbf{X}^T + \beta\mathbf{I}\right)^{-1}\mathbf{X}\mathbf{Y}^T\mathbf{Y}\mathbf{X}^T\left(\frac{1}{n}\mathbf{X}\mathbf{X}^T + (\alpha + \beta)\mathbf{I}\right)^{-1}.
\end{aligned} \tag{6.18}
$$

Let

$$
\mathbf{X} = \mathbf{U}\mathbf{\Sigma}\mathbf{V}^T = [\mathbf{U}_1, \mathbf{U}_2]\,\mathrm{diag}\,(\mathbf{\Sigma}_1, \mathbf{0})[\mathbf{V}_1, \mathbf{V}_2]^T = \mathbf{U}_1\mathbf{\Sigma}_1\mathbf{V}_1^T
$$

be the Singular Value Decomposition (SVD) of $\mathbf{X}$, where $\mathbf{U} \in \mathbb{R}^{d \times d}$ and $\mathbf{V} \in \mathbb{R}^{n \times n}$ are orthogonal, $\mathbf{\Sigma} \in \mathbb{R}^{d \times n}$ is diagonal, $\mathbf{U}_1\mathbf{\Sigma}_1\mathbf{V}_1^T$ is the compact SVD of $\mathbf{X}$, $\mathbf{U}_1 \in \mathbb{R}^{d \times t}$, $\mathbf{U}_2 \in \mathbb{R}^{d \times (d-t)}$, $\mathbf{V}_1 \in \mathbb{R}^{n \times t}$, $\mathbf{V}_2 \in \mathbb{R}^{n \times (n-t)}$, $\mathbf{\Sigma}_1 \in \mathbb{R}^{t \times t}$ is diagonal, and

$t = \text{rank}(\mathbf{X})$. Then

$$
\begin{aligned}
&\mathbf{S}_1^{-1}\mathbf{S}_2 \\
={}& \mathbf{U}_1\left(\frac{1}{n}\mathbf{\Sigma}_1^2 + \beta\mathbf{I}\right)^{-1}\mathbf{U}_1^T\mathbf{X}\mathbf{Y}^T\mathbf{Y}\mathbf{X}^T\left(\frac{1}{n}\mathbf{X}\mathbf{X}^T + (\alpha+\beta)\mathbf{I}\right)^{-1} \\
&+ \frac{1}{\beta}\mathbf{U}_2\mathbf{I}^{-1}\mathbf{U}_2^T\mathbf{X}\mathbf{Y}^T\mathbf{Y}\mathbf{X}^T\left(\frac{1}{n}\mathbf{X}\mathbf{X}^T + (\alpha+\beta)\mathbf{I}\right)^{-1} \\
={}& \mathbf{U}_1\left(\frac{1}{n}\mathbf{\Sigma}_1^2 + \beta\mathbf{I}\right)^{-1}\mathbf{U}_1^T\mathbf{X}\mathbf{Y}^T\mathbf{Y}\mathbf{X}^T\left(\frac{1}{n}\mathbf{X}^T\mathbf{X} + (\alpha+\beta)\mathbf{I}\right)^{-1} \\
={}& \mathbf{U}_1\left(\frac{1}{n}\mathbf{\Sigma}_1^2 + \beta\mathbf{I}\right)^{-1}\mathbf{U}_1^T\mathbf{X}\mathbf{Y}^T\mathbf{Y}\mathbf{X}^T\mathbf{U}_1\left(\frac{1}{n}\mathbf{\Sigma}_1^2 + (\alpha+\beta)\mathbf{I}\right)^{-1}\mathbf{U}_1^T \\
={}& \mathbf{U}_1\left(\frac{1}{n}\mathbf{\Sigma}_1^2 + \beta\mathbf{I}\right)^{-1}\mathbf{\Sigma}_1\mathbf{V}_1^T\mathbf{Y}^T\mathbf{Y}\mathbf{V}_1\mathbf{\Sigma}_1\left(\frac{1}{n}\mathbf{\Sigma}_1^2 + (\alpha+\beta)\mathbf{I}\right)^{-1}\mathbf{U}_1^T.
\end{aligned}
$$

The second and third equalities follow since the columns of $\mathbf{U}_2$ are in the null space of $\mathbf{X}^T$, that is,

$$\mathbf{X}^T\mathbf{U}_2 = \mathbf{0}.$$

6.2.2   Eigendecomposition

In this section, we show how to obtain the eigendecomposition of $\mathbf{S}_1^{-1}\mathbf{S}_2$ based on the reformulation from the last section. Define three diagonal matrices $\mathbf{D}_1$, $\mathbf{D}_2$, and $\mathbf{D}$ as follows:

$$\mathbf{D}_1 = \left(\frac{1}{n}\mathbf{\Sigma}_1^2 + \beta\mathbf{I}\right)^{-1}\mathbf{\Sigma}_1 \in \mathbb{R}^{t\times t}, \tag{6.19}$$

$$\mathbf{D}_2 = \mathbf{\Sigma}_1\left(\frac{1}{n}\mathbf{\Sigma}_1^2 + (\alpha+\beta)\mathbf{I}\right)^{-1} \in \mathbb{R}^{t\times t}, \tag{6.20}$$

$$\mathbf{D} = \left(\mathbf{D}_1\mathbf{D}_2^{-1}\right)^{\frac{1}{2}} \in \mathbb{R}^{t\times t}. \tag{6.21}$$

Then

$$
\begin{aligned}
\mathbf{S}_1^{-1}\mathbf{S}_2 ={}& \mathbf{U}_1\mathbf{D}_1\mathbf{V}_1^T\mathbf{Y}^T\mathbf{Y}\mathbf{V}_1\mathbf{D}_2\mathbf{U}_1^T \\
={}& \mathbf{U}_1\mathbf{D}(\mathbf{D}^{-1}\mathbf{D}_1)\mathbf{V}_1^T\mathbf{Y}^T\mathbf{Y}\mathbf{V}_1(\mathbf{D}_2\mathbf{D})\mathbf{D}^{-1}\mathbf{U}_1^T \\
={}& \mathbf{U}_1\mathbf{D}\tilde{\mathbf{D}}\mathbf{V}_1^T\mathbf{Y}^T\mathbf{Y}\mathbf{V}_1\tilde{\mathbf{D}}\mathbf{D}^{-1}\mathbf{U}_1^T,
\end{aligned}
$$

where

$$\tilde{\mathbf{D}} = \mathbf{D}^{-1}\mathbf{D}_1 = \mathbf{D}_2\mathbf{D}. \tag{6.22}$$

Denote $\mathbf{C} = \mathbf{Y}\mathbf{V}_1\tilde{\mathbf{D}} \in \mathbb{R}^{k\times t}$ and let

$$\mathbf{C} = \mathbf{P}_1\mathbf{\Lambda}\mathbf{P}_2^T \tag{6.23}$$

be the SVD of $\mathbf{C}$ where $\mathbf{P}_1 \in \mathbb{R}^{k \times k}$ and $\mathbf{P}_2 \in \mathbb{R}^{t \times t}$ are orthogonal, and $\mathbf{\Lambda} \in \mathbb{R}^{k \times t}$ is diagonal. Then the eigendecomposition of $\mathbf{S}_1^{-1}\mathbf{S}_2$ can be derived as follows:

$$
\begin{aligned}
\mathbf{S}_1^{-1}\mathbf{S}_2 &= \mathbf{U}_1\mathbf{D}\mathbf{C}^T\mathbf{C}\mathbf{D}^{-1}\mathbf{U}_1^T \\
&= \mathbf{U}_1\mathbf{D}\mathbf{P}_2\mathbf{\Lambda}^T\mathbf{\Lambda}\mathbf{P}_2^T\mathbf{D}^{-1}\mathbf{U}_1^T \\
&= (\mathbf{U}_1\mathbf{D}\mathbf{P}_2)\,\tilde{\mathbf{\Lambda}}\left(\mathbf{P}_2^T\mathbf{D}^{-1}\mathbf{U}_1^T\right),
\end{aligned}
\tag{6.24}
$$

where $\tilde{\mathbf{\Lambda}} = \mathbf{\Lambda}^T\mathbf{\Lambda} \in \mathbb{R}^{t \times t}$.

6.2.3 The Main Algorithm

It can be observed that Eq. (6.24) gives the eigendecomposition of $\mathbf{S}_1^{-1}\mathbf{S}_2$ corresponding to nonzero eigenvalues. Hence, the eigenvectors of $\mathbf{S}_1^{-1}\mathbf{S}_2$ corresponding to nonzero eigenvalues are given by the columns of $\mathbf{U}_1\mathbf{D}\mathbf{P}_2$. The algorithm for computing the optimal $\mathbf{\Theta}^*$ for high-dimensional data is summarized as follows:

- Compute the SVD of $\mathbf{X}$ as $\mathbf{X} = \mathbf{U}\mathbf{\Sigma}\mathbf{V}^T = \mathbf{U}_1\mathbf{\Sigma}_1\mathbf{V}_1^T$.

- Compute $\mathbf{D}_1$, $\mathbf{D}_2$, $\mathbf{D}$, and $\tilde{\mathbf{D}}$ as in Eqs. (6.19), (6.20), (6.21), and (6.22), respectively.

- Compute the SVD of $\mathbf{C} = \mathbf{Y}\mathbf{V}_1\tilde{\mathbf{D}}$ as $\mathbf{C} = \mathbf{P}_1\mathbf{\Lambda}\mathbf{P}_2^T$.

- Compute the QR decomposition of $\mathbf{U}_1\mathbf{D}\mathbf{P}_2$ as $\mathbf{U}_1\mathbf{D}\mathbf{P}_2 = \mathbf{Q}\mathbf{R}$.

- The columns of the optimal $\mathbf{\Theta}^*$ are given by the first r columns of the matrix $\mathbf{Q}$.

After obtaining $\mathbf{\Theta}^*$, the optimal $\mathbf{U}^*$ given by Eq. (6.8) needs to be computed. Note that the matrix $\mathbf{M} \in \mathbb{R}^{d \times d}$ is involved in Eq. (6.8), and hence it is expensive to compute $\mathbf{U}^*$ directly for high-dimensional data. To this end, the expressions in Eqs. (6.15), (6.16), and (6.17) need to be used so that explicit formations of the matrices $\mathbf{M}$ and $\mathbf{M}^{-1}$ are avoided.

The SVD of $\mathbf{X}$ in the first step takes $O(dn^2)$ time, assuming $d > n$. The size of $\mathbf{C}$ is $k \times t$ where k is the number of labels and $t = \text{rank}(\mathbf{X})$. Hence the SVD of $\mathbf{C}$ in the third step takes $O(tk^2)$ time, assuming $t > k$. The QR decomposition in the fourth step takes $O(dt^2)$ time. Typically, k and t are both small. Thus, the cost for computing $\mathbf{\Theta}^*$ is dominated by the cost for computing the SVD of $\mathbf{X}$. A summary of relevant matrices and their associated computational complexities are listed in Table 6.1.

6.3 Related Work

In [5], a similar formulation has been proposed for multi-task learning. In this formulation, the input data for different tasks can be different, and the following

TABLE 6.1: Summary of relevant matrices
and their associated computational complexities.

Matrix	Size	Computation	Complexity
$\mathbf{X}$	$d \times n$	SVD	$O(dn^2)$
$\mathbf{C}$	$k \times t$	SVD	$O(tk^2)$
$\mathbf{U}_1\mathbf{D}\mathbf{P}_2$	$d \times t$	QR	$O(dt^2)$

optimization problem is involved:

$$
\min_{\{\mathbf{u}_j, \mathbf{v}_j\}, \boldsymbol{\Theta}} \quad \sum_{j=1}^{m} \left(\frac{1}{n_j} \sum_{i=1}^{n_j} L\left(\mathbf{u}_j^T \mathbf{x}_i^j, \mathbf{y}_i(j)\right) + \alpha \|\mathbf{u}_j - \boldsymbol{\Theta}\mathbf{v}_j\|_2^2 \right)
$$
$$
\text{s.\,t.} \quad \boldsymbol{\Theta}^T \boldsymbol{\Theta} = \mathbf{I}, \tag{6.25}
$$

where $\mathbf{x}_i^j$ is the ith instance in the jth task and n_j is the number of instances in the jth task. It has been shown [5] that the resulting optimization problem is nonconvex even for convex loss functions. Hence, an iterative procedure called the *Alternating Structure Optimization* (ASO) algorithm is proposed to compute a locally optimal solution. A similar idea of sharing parts of the model parameters among multiple tasks has been explored in the Bayesian framework [14].

A formulation for extracting shared structures in multi-class classification has been proposed recently [3]. In this formulation, a low-rank transformation is computed to uncover the shared structures in multi-class classification. The final prediction is solely based on the lower-dimensional representations in the dimensionality-reduced space. Moreover, the low-rank constraint is nonconvex, and it is first relaxed to the convex trace norm constraint. The relaxed problem can be formulated as a semidefinite program which is expensive to solve. Hence, the gradient-based optimization technique is employed to solve the relaxed problem.

6.4 Connections with Existing Formulations

The formulation discussed in Section 6.1 includes several existing algorithms as special cases. In particular, by setting the regularization parameters α and β in Eq. (6.5) to different values, several well-known algorithms can be obtained.

- $\alpha = 0$: When the regularization parameter $\alpha = 0$, it can be seen from Eq. (6.5) that this formulation is equivalent to classical ridge regression [114]. In ridge regression, different labels are decoupled, and the solution to each label can be obtained independently by solving a system of linear equations. In this case, no shared information is exploited among different labels.

- $\beta = 0$: When the regularization parameter $\beta = 0$, only the task-specific parameters $\{\mathbf{w}_j\}_{j=1}^{k}$ are regularized. Thus, the formulation discussed in Section

6.1 reduces to the one in [5] in the special case where the input data are the same for all tasks.

- $\alpha = +\infty$: It can be seen from Eq. (6.18) that when α tends to infinity, the following holds:

$$\left(\frac{1}{n}\mathbf{X}\mathbf{X}^T + (\alpha + \beta)\mathbf{I}\right)^{-1} \to \epsilon\mathbf{I},$$

for some small positive ϵ. Hence, the eigenvectors of $\mathbf{S}_1^{-1}\mathbf{S}_2$ approach the eigenvectors of the matrix

$$\left(\frac{1}{n}\mathbf{X}\mathbf{X}^T + \beta\mathbf{I}\right)^{-1}\mathbf{X}\mathbf{Y}^T\mathbf{Y}\mathbf{X}^T. \tag{6.26}$$

This formulation is the same as the problem solved by Orthonormalized Partial Least Squares (OPLS) [265]. In fact, by defining $\mathbf{Y}^T = \mathbf{H}$ as in Section 4.3, different dimensionality reduction algorithms can be obtained, including Canonical Correlation Analysis (CCA), OPLS, Hypergraph Spectral Learning (HSL), and Linear Discriminant Analysis (LDA), which are all discussed in detail in Section 4.3. Thus, the optimal $\mathbf{\Theta}^*$ coincides with the optimal projection matrix computed by different dimensionality reduction algorithms.

- $\beta = +\infty$: When β tends to infinity, the eigenvectors of $\mathbf{S}_1^{-1}\mathbf{S}_2$ are given by the eigenvectors of the matrix $\mathbf{X}\mathbf{Y}^T\mathbf{Y}\mathbf{X}^T$, which is the inter-class scatter matrix used in LDA. In this case, the formulation discussed in Section 6.1 is closely related to the Orthogonal Centroid Method (OCM) [180] in which the optimal transformation is given by the eigenvectors of the inter-class scatter matrix corresponding to the largest eigenvalues.

6.5 A Feature Space Formulation

The formulation discussed in Section 6.1 can be extended to the kernel-induced feature space. Kernel methods will be discussed in detail in Chapter 8. To make the discussion of the shared-subspace learning framework more coherent, we discuss its kernel extension in this section. More details on kernel methods can be found in Chapter 8.

Let $\Phi(X) = [\Phi(\mathbf{x}_1), \ldots, \Phi(\mathbf{x}_n)]$ be the data matrix in the feature space induced by the feature mapping Φ. It follows from the representer theorem [207] that

$$
\begin{aligned}
\mathbf{U} &= \Phi(\mathbf{X})\mathbf{A}, & (6.27) \\
\mathbf{\Theta} &= \Phi(\mathbf{X})\mathbf{B}, & (6.28)
\end{aligned}
$$

for some matrices $\mathbf{A} \in \mathbb{R}^{n \times k}$ and $\mathbf{B} \in \mathbb{R}^{n \times r}$. The feature space formulation of this framework is summarized in the following theorem:

Theorem 6.2 *Let* **A**, **B**, *and* **Y** *be defined as above, and let* $\mathbf{K} = \Phi(\mathbf{X})^T \Phi(\mathbf{X})$ *be the kernel matrix. Then the optimal* **B*** *in Eq. (6.28) can be obtained by solving the following problem:*

$$\max_{\mathbf{B}} \quad \mathrm{Tr}\left(\left(\mathbf{B}^T \hat{\mathbf{S}}_1 \mathbf{B} \right)^{-1} \mathbf{B}^T \hat{\mathbf{S}}_2 \mathbf{B} \right) \tag{6.29}$$

$$\mathrm{s.\,t.} \quad \mathbf{B}^T \mathbf{K} \mathbf{B} = \mathbf{I},$$

where **N**, $\hat{\mathbf{S}}_1$, *and* $\hat{\mathbf{S}}_2$ *are defined as*

$$\mathbf{N} = \frac{1}{n}\mathbf{K}^2 + (\alpha + \beta)\mathbf{K}, \tag{6.30}$$

$$\hat{\mathbf{S}}_1 = \mathbf{K} - \alpha\mathbf{K}\mathbf{N}^{-1}\mathbf{K}, \tag{6.31}$$

$$\hat{\mathbf{S}}_2 = \mathbf{K}\mathbf{N}^{-1}\mathbf{K}\mathbf{Y}^T\mathbf{Y}\mathbf{K}\mathbf{N}^{-1}\mathbf{K}. \tag{6.32}$$

The full proof of this theorem is given in Appendix A.4.

It follows from the Sherman–Morrison–Woodbury formula in Eq. (6.14) that

$$\mathbf{N}^{-1} = \frac{1}{\alpha + \beta}\mathbf{K}^{-1} - \frac{1}{\alpha + \beta}\left(n(\alpha + \beta)\mathbf{I} + \mathbf{K}\right)^{-1}. \tag{6.33}$$

Hence,

$$\mathbf{K} - \alpha\mathbf{K}\mathbf{N}^{-1}\mathbf{K} = \frac{\beta}{\alpha + \beta}\mathbf{K} + \frac{\alpha}{\alpha + \beta}\mathbf{K}(n(\alpha + \beta)\mathbf{I} + \mathbf{K})^{-1}\mathbf{K}.$$

It follows that

$$\hat{\mathbf{S}}_1^{-1}\hat{\mathbf{S}}_2$$
$$= (\mathbf{K} - \alpha\mathbf{K}\mathbf{N}^{-1}\mathbf{K})^{-1}\mathbf{K}\mathbf{N}^{-1}\mathbf{K}\mathbf{Y}^T\mathbf{Y}\mathbf{K}\mathbf{N}^{-1}\mathbf{K}$$
$$= (\mathbf{N} - \alpha\mathbf{K})^{-1}\mathbf{K}\mathbf{Y}^T\mathbf{Y}\mathbf{K}\mathbf{N}^{-1}\mathbf{K}$$
$$= \left(\frac{1}{n}\mathbf{K}^2 + \beta\mathbf{K}\right)^{-1}\mathbf{K}\mathbf{Y}^T\mathbf{Y}\mathbf{K}\left(\frac{1}{n}\mathbf{K} + (\alpha + \beta)\mathbf{I}\right)^{-1}.$$

Similar to the discussion in Section 6.4, the connections between this formulation and related algorithms in the kernel-induced feature space can also be derived.

6.6   Empirical Evaluation

The effectiveness of the shared-subspace learning framework is compared with other state-of-the-art algorithms on multi-topic web page categorization tasks [127].

6.6.1 Empirical Evaluation Setup

The Area Under the receiver operating characteristic Curve, called AUC, and the F1 score are used as the performance measure. To measure the performance across multiple labels using the F1 score, both the macro F1 and the micro F1 scores [155, 269] have been used. The F1 score depends on the threshold values of the classification models. It was shown recently [77] that tuning the threshold based on the F1 score on the training data can significantly improve performance. Hence, the threshold value of each model is tuned based on the training data. Indeed, results show that threshold tuning sometimes outperforms classifiers that are trained to optimize the F1 score directly.

The performance of the shared-subspace learning framework is evaluated by comparing its performance with that of five other relevant methods. Parameters of all the methods are tuned using 5-fold cross-validation based on the F1 score. The setup is summarized as follows:

- **ML_{LS}:** The formulation based on the shared-subspace framework using the the squared loss. The regularization parameters α and β are tuned using 5-fold double cross-validation from the candidate set $[0, 10^{-6}, 10^{-5}, 10^{-4}, 10^{-3}, 10^{-2}, 10^{-1}, 1]$. The performance of the formulation is not sensitive to the dimensionality of the shared subspace r as long as it is not too small. So it is fixed to $5 \times \lfloor (m-1)/5 \rfloor$ in the experiments, where m is the number of labels.

- **CCA+Ridge:** CCA is applied first to reduce the data dimensionality before ridge regression is applied. The regularization parameters for CCA and ridge regression are tuned on the sets $\{10^i | i = -6, -5, \cdots, 1\}$ and $\{10^i | i = -6, -5, \cdots, 0\}$, respectively.

- **CCA+SVM:** CCA is applied first to reduce the data dimensionality before linear SVM is applied. The regularization parameter for CCA is tuned on the set $\{10^i | i = -6, -5, \cdots, 1\}$, and the C value for SVM is tuned on the set $\{10^i | i = -4, -3, \cdots, 4, 5\}$.

- **SVM:** Linear SVM is applied on each label using the one-against-all approach, and the C value for each SVM is tuned on the set $\{10^i | i = -5, -4, \cdots, 4, 5\}$.

- **ASO_{SVM}:** The ASO algorithm proposed in [5] with hinge loss as described in Eq. (6.25). The regularization parameter α is tuned on the set $\{10^i | i = -4, -3, \cdots, 2, 3\}$. The tolerance parameter for testing convergence is set to 10^{-3}, and the maximum number of iterations for ASO is set to 100. This problem is solved using the MOSEK package [4].

- **SVM^{perf}:** The SVM for multivariate performance measures proposed in [129, 130] with $C = 5000$, as it leads to good overall performance.

The SVM problems are solved using the Libsvm [47] software package.

TABLE 6.2:   Statistics of the Yahoo! data sets.

Data set	m	d	n	MaxNPI	MinNPI
Arts	19	17973	7441	1838	104
Business	17	16621	9968	8648	110
Computers	23	25259	12371	6559	108
Education	14	20782	11817	3738	127
Entertainment	14	27435	12691	3687	221
Health	14	18430	9109	4703	114
Recreation	18	25095	12797	2534	169
Reference	15	26397	7929	3782	156
Science	22	24002	6345	1548	102
Social	21	32492	11914	5148	104
Society	21	29189	14507	7193	113

Note: m, d, and n denote the number of labels, the data dimensionality, and the total number of instances, respectively, in the data set after preprocessing. "MaxNPI" and "MinNPI" denote the maximum/minimum number of positive instances for each topic (label).

6.6.2   Web Page Categorization

The multi-topic web page categorization data sets were described in [136, 239, 240], and they were compiled from 11 top-level categories in the "yahoo.com" domain. The web pages collected from each top-level category form a data set. The top-level categories are further divided into a number of second-level subcategories, and those subcategories form the topics to be categorized in each data set. Note that the 11 multi-topic categorization problems are compiled and solved independently as in [240]. In [127], the data are preprocessed by removing topics with less than 100 web pages, words occurring less than 5 times, and web pages without topics. TF-IDF encoding is used to represent web pages, and all web pages are normalized to unit length. The statistics of all data sets are summarized in Table 6.2.

6.6.2.1   Performance Evaluation

We sample 1000 data points from each data set to form the training data (each label is guaranteed to appear in at least one data point), and the remaining data points are used as test data. For ASO algorithm [5], which is computationally expensive, this randomization is performed 10 times to generate 10 random training/test partitions. For all other methods, this random partitioning is repeated 30 times. Table 6.3 reports the averaged performance of the six methods in terms of AUC, macro F1, and micro F1. It can be observed that ML_{LS} achieves the highest AUC on seven data sets, while ASO_{SVM} achieves the highest AUC on the other four data sets. In terms of the macro F1 score, ML_{LS} achieves the highest performance on ten data sets while ASO_{SVM} achieves the highest performance on the remaining one. In terms of the micro F1 score, ML_{LS} outperforms other methods on all data sets. In general, methods that can capture the correlation among different labels, such as ML_{LS} and CCA+SVM, tend to yield higher performance than those that reduce the multi-label problem to a set of independent binary-class problems such as SVM. This shows that incorporation of the correlation information among different labels can improve performance.

TABLE 6.3: Summary of performance for the six compared methods on the Yahoo! data sets in terms of AUC (top section), macro F1 (middle section), and micro F1 (bottom section).

Data set	Arts	Business	Computer	Education	Entertainment	Health
ML_{LS}	0.7611	**0.8313**	**0.7912**	**0.7771**	**0.8282**	0.8539
CCA+Ridge	0.7573	0.8253	0.7893	0.7568	0.8044	0.8557
CCA+SVM	0.7393	0.8003	0.7717	0.7420	0.7749	0.8450
SVM	0.7425	0.7973	0.7641	0.7548	0.8045	0.8439
ASO_{SVM}	**0.7678**	0.8261	0.7847	0.7446	0.8207	**0.8621**
SVM^{perf}	0.7599	0.8185	0.7846	0.7710	0.8234	0.8554
ML_{LS}	**0.3572**	**0.4026**	**0.3093**	**0.4044**	**0.4881**	**0.5971**
CCA+Ridge	0.3176	0.3896	0.2940	0.3640	0.4249	0.5728
CCA+SVM	0.3217	0.3918	0.3006	0.3681	0.4319	0.5689
SVM	0.3374	0.3776	0.2961	0.3819	0.4653	0.5657
ASO_{SVM}	0.3568	0.3736	0.2873	0.3262	0.4344	0.5814
SVM^{perf}	0.3361	0.3211	0.2579	0.3777	0.4656	0.4953
ML_{LS}	**0.4700**	**0.7618**	**0.5529**	**0.4999**	**0.5844**	**0.6816**
CCA+Ridge	0.4530	0.7596	0.5527	0.4498	0.5413	0.6775
CCA+SVM	0.4479	0.7434	0.5392	0.4296	0.5100	0.6646
SVM	0.4134	0.7150	0.4848	0.4560	0.5419	0.6349
ASO_{SVM}	0.4449	0.7384	0.4305	0.4322	0.5605	0.6754
SVM^{perf}	0.4087	0.5892	0.3957	0.4378	0.5336	0.5997

Data set	Recreation	Reference	Science	Social	Society	
ML_{LS}	**0.8126**	0.8223	**0.8287**	**0.8320**	0.7276	
CCA+Ridge	0.8113	0.8200	0.8099	0.8225	0.7216	
CCA+SVM	0.7946	0.7604	0.7790	0.7627	0.7054	
SVM	0.7922	0.8037	0.8025	0.7869	0.7101	
ASO_{SVM}	0.8123	**0.8340**	0.8073	0.7942	**0.7321**	
SVM^{perf}	0.8109	0.8202	0.8236	0.8240	0.7229	
ML_{LS}	**0.4478**	0.4066	**0.4241**	**0.3637**	**0.3256**	
CCA+Ridge	0.4227	0.3483	0.3530	0.3303	0.2992	
CCA+SVM	0.4289	0.3404	0.3660	0.3360	0.3073	
SVM	0.4254	0.3848	0.3976	0.3444	0.3115	
ASO_{SVM}	0.4136	**0.4116**	0.3397	0.3017	0.3023	
SVM^{perf}	0.4184	0.3680	0.3673	0.2978	0.3059	
ML_{LS}	**0.5287**	**0.6016**	**0.5210**	**0.6649**	**0.4853**	
CCA+Ridge	0.5197	0.5535	0.4719	0.6545	0.4813	
CCA+SVM	0.5134	0.4435	0.4478	0.5688	0.4639	
SVM	0.4753	0.5306	0.4565	0.5946	0.3971	
ASO_{SVM}	0.4976	0.5580	0.4564	0.6492	0.4639	
SVM^{perf}	0.4620	0.4733	0.4155	0.4638	0.4034	

Note: All parameters of the six methods are tuned by cross-validation, and the averaged performance over 10 random samplings of training instances for ASO_{SVM} and 30 random samplings for all other methods is reported. The highest performance is highlighted for each data set.

To assess the statistical significance of performance differences between ML_{LS} and other compared methods, the Wilcoxon signed rank test is performed based on the performance on 30 random trials, and the p-values are reported in Table 6.4. A p-value smaller than 0.05 is usually considered an indication of performance difference. It can be observed that most of the performance differences are statistically significant. Note that ASO_{SVM} and SVM^{perf} are computationally expensive, and they require excessive amounts of computational time to obtain results on all 30 random trials, which is necessary for the purpose of the statistical test. Hence, the test results for ASO_{SVM} and SVM^{perf} are omitted. However, it can be observed that the performance of ASO_{SVM} and SVM^{perf} is usually lower than that of other methods, and hence their performance differences with ML_{LS} are expected to be statistically significant.

TABLE 6.4: The p-values obtained by performing Wilcoxon signed rank test to assess the statistical significance of performance differences between ML_{LS} and three other methods in terms of AUC (top section), macro F1 (middle section), and micro F1 (bottom section) on the Yahoo! data sets. A

Data set	Arts	Business	Computer	Education	Entertainment	Health
ML_{LS} vs. CCA+Ridge	2.80e-1	5.31e-3	2.18e-2	9.31e-6	1.79e-5	4.16e-1
ML_{LS} vs. CCA+SVM	7.51e-5	2.35e-6	7.15e-4	2.12e-6	1.73e-6	2.25e-3
ML_{LS} vs. SVM	3.11e-5	1.92e-6	4.86e-5	2.35e-6	1.36e-5	4.44e-5
ML_{LS} vs. CCA+Ridge	1.73e-6	2.22e-4	1.19e-2	1.92e-6	1.73e-6	3.06e-4
ML_{LS} vs. CCA+SVM	1.73e-6	7.71e-4	2.18e-2	2.35e-6	1.73e-6	5.75e-6
ML_{LS} vs. SVM	4.72e-6	1.63e-5	1.47e-2	5.21e-6	3.18e-6	2.60e-6
ML_{LS} vs. CCA+Ridge	2.35e-6	1.71e-1	7.34e-1	1.73e-6	1.73e-6	9.36e-2
ML_{LS} vs. CCA+SVM	4.72e-6	4.86e-5	1.14e-4	1.73e-6	1.92e-6	3.16e-3
ML_{LS} vs. SVM	1.73e-6	1.73e-6	1.73e-6	1.73e-6	1.73e-6	1.73e-6
Data set	Recreation	Reference	Science	Social	Society	
ML_{LS} vs. CCA+Ridge	5.98e-2	5.03e-1	2.22e-4	1.03e-3	3.28e-1	
ML_{LS} vs. CCA+SVM	3.58e-4	1.92e-6	2.35e-6	1.73e-6	3.72e-5	
ML_{LS} vs. SVM	5.79e-5	3.88e-4	3.88e-6	1.92e-6	6.31e-5	
ML_{LS} vs. CCA+Ridge	3.11e-5	1.73e-6	1.73e-6	2.87e-6	1.73e-6	
ML_{LS} vs. CCA+SVM	3.06e-4	1.73e-6	1.73e-6	2.35e-6	3.88e-6	
ML_{LS} vs. SVM	1.47e-4	4.44e-5	3.88e-6	3.06e-4	4.07e-5	
ML_{LS} vs. CCA+Ridge	7.15e-4	1.73e-6	1.73e-6	3.72e-5	4.65e-1	
ML_{LS} vs. CCA+SVM	9.62e-4	1.92e-6	1.73e-6	1.73e-6	3.50e-2	
ML_{LS} vs. SVM	1.73e-6	1.73e-6	1.73e-6	1.73e-6	1.73e-6	

Note: p-value smaller than 0.05 is usually considered an indication of a statistically significant difference.

6.6.2.2   Scalability Evaluation

The scalability of the shared-subspace multi-label formulation is evaluated on all the Yahoo! data sets, and the results for 8 of the 11 data sets are presented in Figures 6.1 and 6.2. A similar trend can be observed from other data sets, and their results are omitted. In particular, the number of training samples on the data sets is increased gradually, and the computation time of ML_{LS}, SVM, and ASO_{SVM} is reported. The training time for a fixed parameter setting and the total time for parameter tuning using cross-validation are plotted in Figures 6.1 and 6.2. It can be observed that SVM is the fastest and ASO_{SVM} is the slowest among the three compared algorithms. Moreover, the difference between ML_{LS} and SVM is small. The computational cost of the shared-subspace formulation is dominated by the cost of the SVD computation on the data matrix $\mathbf{X}$, and it is independent of the number of labels. In contrast, the computational costs of SVM and ASO_{SVM} depend on the number of labels. Hence,

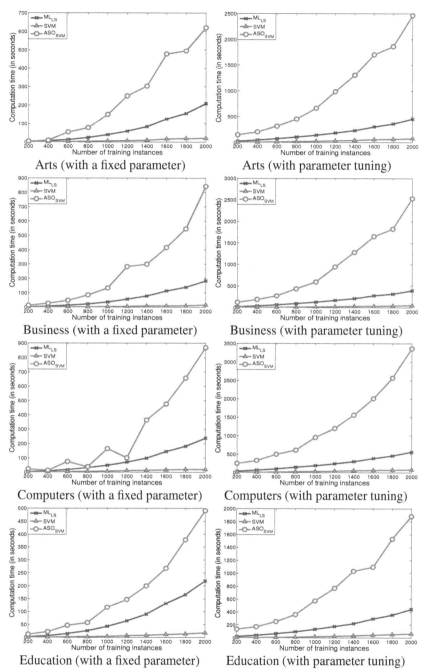

FIGURE 6.1: Comparison of computation time for ML_{LS}, SVM, and ASO_{SVM} on the first four Yahoo! data sets. The computation time for a fixed parameter setting and that for parameter tuning using cross-validation are both depicted for each data set. See the text for more details.

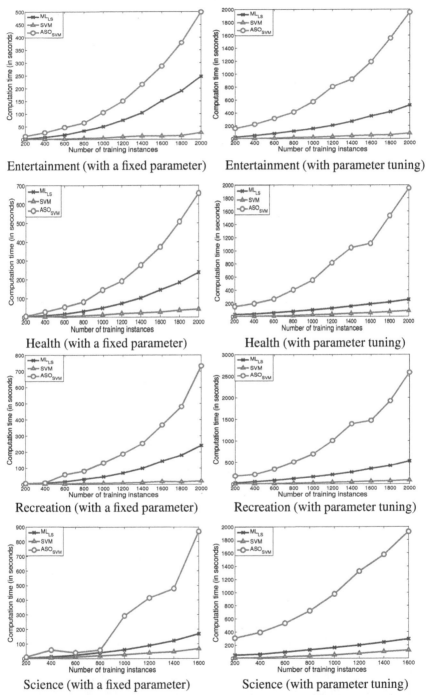

FIGURE 6.2: Comparison of computation time for ML_{LS}, SVM, and ASO_{SVM} on the next four Yahoo! data sets. The computation time for a fixed parameter setting and that for parameter tuning using cross-validation are both depicted for each data set. See the text for more details.

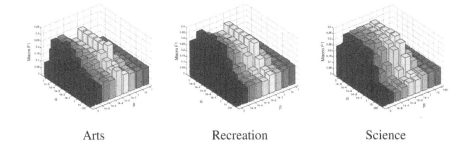

Arts   Recreation   Science

FIGURE 6.3: The change of macro F1 scores as the regularization parameters α and β vary in the range $[0, 10^{-5}, 10^{-4}, 10^{-3}, 10^{-2}, 10^{-1}, 1, 10, 100]$ for the Arts (left panel), Recreation (middle panel), and Science (right panel) data sets.

the difference between SVM and ML_{LS} tends to be smaller on data sets with a larger number of labels. Note that in ML_{LS}, the two regularization parameters α and β are tuned using double cross-validation. However, the SVD on $\mathbf{X}$ needs to be computed only once irrespective of the size of the candidate sets for α and β. This experiment also shows that the running time of ASO_{SVM} may fluctuate as the number of training instances increases. This may be due to the fact that the convergence rate of the ASO_{SVM} algorithm depends on initialization.

6.6.2.3 Sensitivity Analysis

We further conduct a set of experiments to evaluate the sensitivity of the formulation to the values of the regularization parameters α and β. In this experiment, 1000 data points are sampled from each of the three data sets Arts, Recreation, and Science, and the averaged macro F1 scores over 5-fold cross-validation for different values of α and β are depicted in Figure 6.3. It can be observed that the highest performance on all three data sets is achieved at some intermediate values of α and β. Moreover, this experiment shows that the performance of the shared-subspace multi-label formulation is sensitive to the values of the regularization parameters. Note that the parameter tuning time of this formulation does not depend on the size of the candidate sets directly, since the computational cost is dominated by that of the SVD of $\mathbf{X}$, which needs to be performed only once. Hence, a large candidate set for α and β can be employed in practice.

6.6.3 Discussion

It follows from the discussion in Section 6.4 that ridge regression, CCA, and ASO_{SVM} with the same input data are all special cases of the shared-subspace formulation. One appealing feature of this formulation is that it is a general framework that includes several well-known algorithms as special cases. By adjusting the two regularization parameters, the formulation can be adapted to capture the correlation information among labels in various tasks. This effectively avoids the need to apply multiple algorithms, such as ASO_{SVM} and CCA+Ridge, to a given task and choose the one that results in the highest performance.

The experimental results show that the shared-subspace formulation outperforms existing methods in most cases. This may be due to the fact that this formulation is a general framework that includes several traditional algorithms, such as LDA, CCA, and Partial Least Squares (PLS), as special cases. Hence, if the two regularization parameters are tuned properly, the formulation is expected to outperform traditional methods, since it reduces to these methods when the regularization parameters are set to particular values. On the other hand, there are a few cases in the experiments in which the formulation yields low performance. Recall that the shared-subspace formulation assumes that a common subspace is shared among all labels, which may be too restrictive in some cases, and hence leads to low performance. A similar phenomenon has been observed in the contexts of multi-task learning [10,125] and multivariate regression [138]. A commonly used technique to overcome this problem is to cluster the tasks into multiple clusters and impose local constraints onto tasks in the same cluster.

Chapter 7

Joint Dimensionality Reduction and Classification

When the input data lie in a high-dimensional space, dimensionality reduction techniques, such as Principal Component Analysis (PCA), Canonical Correlation Analysis (CCA), Partial Least Squares (PLS), and Linear Discriminant Analysis (LDA), are commonly applied as a separate data preprocessing step before classification algorithms. One limitation of these approaches is the weak connection between dimensionality reduction and classification algorithms. Indeed, dimensionality reduction algorithms such as CCA and PLS and classification algorithms such as SVM optimize different criteria. It is unclear which dimensionality reduction algorithm can best improve a specific classification algorithm such as SVM. In addition, most traditional dimensionality reduction algorithms assume that a common set of samples is involved for all classes. However, in many applications, e.g., when the data is unbalanced, it is desirable to relax this restriction so that the input data associated with each class can be better balanced. This is especially useful when some of the class labels in the data are missing.

In this chapter, we present a joint learning framework in which dimensionality reduction and multi-label classification are performed simultaneously. One appealing feature of these joint learning formulations is that they can be extended naturally to cases where the input data for different labels may differ, overcoming the limitation of traditional dimensionality reduction algorithms.

7.1 Background

In binary-class classification, we are given a data set $\{(\mathbf{x}_i, y_i)\}_{i=1}^n$, where $\mathbf{x}_i \in \mathbb{R}^d$ is the data, $y_i \in \{1, -1\}$ is the associated label, and n is the number of data samples. We consider a linear classifier $f : \mathbf{x} \in \mathbb{R}^d \to f(\mathbf{x}) = \mathbf{w}^T\mathbf{x} + b$ that minimizes the following regularized loss function:

$$L(f) = \sum_{i=1}^n L\left(y_i, f(\mathbf{x}_i)\right) + \mu\Omega(f), \tag{7.1}$$

where $\mathbf{w} \in \mathbb{R}^d$ is the weight vector, $b \in \mathbb{R}$ is the bias, L is a prescribed loss function, Ω is a regularization functional measuring the smoothness of f, and $\mu > 0$ is the reg-

123

ularization parameter. Different loss functions lead to different learning algorithms. Popular loss functions include squared loss and hinge loss used in SVM:

- Squared loss function: $L_2(y, f) = (y - f)^2$;

- Hinge loss function: $L_h(y, f) = \max(0, 1 - yf)$.

In multi-label classification with k labels, each $\mathbf{x}_i$ can be associated with multiple labels. Specifically, we use $\mathbf{y}_i \in \mathbb{R}^k$ to represent the corresponding label information for $\mathbf{x}_i$ in this chapter as follows:

$$\mathbf{y}_i(j) = \begin{cases} 1, & \text{if } \mathbf{x}_i \text{ is associated with } C_j \\ -1, & \text{otherwise.} \end{cases} \tag{7.2}$$

Note that in this chapter we assume that $\mathbf{y}_i(j) = -1$ if $\mathbf{x}_i$ is not associated with the label C_j. Then the model in Eq. (7.1) can be extended to the multi-label case by applying binary relevance, i.e., by constructing one binary classifier for each label independently, in which instances relevant to this label form the positive class, and the rest form the negative class.

7.1.1　Squared Loss

If the squared loss function is applied for multi-label classification, we compute a set of k linear functions, $f_j : \mathbf{x} \rightarrow f_j(\mathbf{x}) = \mathbf{w}_j^T \mathbf{x} + b_j, j = 1, \ldots, k$, that minimize the following objective function:

$$L_2(\{f_j\}) = \sum_{j=1}^{k} \left(\sum_{i=1}^{n} (f_j(\mathbf{x}_i) - \mathbf{y}_i(j))^2 + \mu \|\mathbf{w}_j\|_2^2 \right), \tag{7.3}$$

where $\mathbf{Y} \in \mathbb{R}^{n \times k}$ is the class label indicator matrix. Note that the optimization of the k linear functions f_j $(1 \le j \le k)$ can be decoupled, and the solutions can be obtained by solving k linear systems of equations [26].

7.1.2　Hinge Loss

If hinge loss is applied for multi-label classification, we consider a set of k linear functions $f_j : \mathbf{x} \rightarrow f_j(\mathbf{x}) = \mathbf{w}_j^T \mathbf{x} + b_j, j = 1, \ldots, k$, that minimize the following objective function:

$$L_h(\{f_j\}) = \sum_{j=1}^{k} \left(\sum_{i=1}^{n} (1 - f_j(\mathbf{x}_i)\mathbf{y}_i(j))_+ + \mu \|\mathbf{w}_j\|_2^2 \right), \tag{7.4}$$

where $(z)_+ = \max(0, z)$. The jth linear function can be computed by minimizing the following objective function:

$$\sum_{i=1}^{n} (1 - f_j(\mathbf{x}_i)\mathbf{y}_i(j))_+ + \mu \|\mathbf{w}_j\|_2^2, \tag{7.5}$$

whose dual formulation is given by

$$\max_{\boldsymbol{\alpha}^j \in \mathbb{R}^n} \quad \sum_{i=1}^{n} \alpha_i^j - \frac{1}{2}(\boldsymbol{\alpha}^j)^T \mathbf{D}^j \mathbf{X}^T \mathbf{X} \mathbf{D}^j \boldsymbol{\alpha}^j \tag{7.6}$$

$$\text{s.t.} \quad \sum_{i=1}^{n} \mathbf{y}_i(j)\alpha_i^j = 0, \quad 0 \le \boldsymbol{\alpha}^j \le C,$$

where $\mathbf{X} = [\mathbf{x}_1, \ldots, \mathbf{x}_n] \in \mathbb{R}^{d \times n}$ is the data matrix, $C = \frac{1}{2\mu}$, $\boldsymbol{\alpha}^j = [\alpha_1^j, \ldots, \alpha_n^j]^T \in \mathbb{R}^n$ is the vector of Lagrange dual variables, $\mathbf{D}^j$ is a diagonal matrix with $(\mathbf{D}^j)_{ii} = \mathbf{y}_i(j)$. This is a standard Quadratic Programming (QP) problem [35].

7.2 Joint Dimensionality Reduction and Multi-Label Classification

In this section, we present a joint learning framework in which we perform dimensionality reduction and multi-label classification simultaneously. Formally, in this framework, we learn a set of k linear functions, $f_j : \mathbf{x} \to f_j(\mathbf{x}) = \mathbf{w}_j^T \mathbf{Q}^T \mathbf{x} + b_j$, $j = 1, \ldots, k$, that minimize the following objective function:

$$L_J(\{f_j\}_{j=1}^k, \mathbf{Q}) = \sum_{j=1}^{k} \left(\sum_{i=1}^{n} L\left(f_j(\mathbf{Q}^T \mathbf{x}_i), \mathbf{y}_i(j)\right) + \mu \|\mathbf{w}_j\|_2^2 \right), \tag{7.7}$$

where $\mathbf{Q} \in \mathbb{R}^{d \times r}$ is the projection (transformation) matrix, r is the reduced dimensionality, and $\mathbf{w}_j \in \mathbb{R}^r$ is the weight vector in f_j.

We will show that when squared loss is used, the joint optimization of $\mathbf{Q}$ and $\mathbf{W} = [\mathbf{w}_1, \cdots, \mathbf{w}_k] \in \mathbb{R}^{r \times k}$ results in a closed-form solution. Moreover, the optimal transformation is closely related to existing dimensionality reduction algorithms.

7.2.1 Joint Learning with Squared Loss

We assume both the data $\mathbf{X}$ and the corresponding label $\mathbf{Y}$ are centered. In this case, all bias terms $\{b_j\}_{j=1}^k$ are zero, and the optimization problem in Eq. (7.7) becomes

$$\min_{\mathbf{W},\mathbf{Q}} \quad \left\|\mathbf{W}^T \mathbf{Q}^T \mathbf{X} - \mathbf{Y}\right\|_F^2 + \mu\|\mathbf{W}\|_F^2, \tag{7.8}$$

$$\text{s.t.} \quad \mathbf{Q}^T \mathbf{Q} = \mathbf{I}.$$

where $\mathbf{W} = [\mathbf{w}_1, \ldots, \mathbf{w}_k] \in \mathbb{R}^{r \times k}$. It can be shown that the above formulation admits a closed-form solution. Let $\mathbf{Y} \in \mathbb{R}^{k \times n}$ be the target matrix defined from the labels. Taking the derivative of the objective in Eq. (7.8) with respect to $\mathbf{W}$ and setting it to zero, we have

$$\mathbf{W} = \left(\mathbf{Q}^T \mathbf{X} \mathbf{X}^T \mathbf{Q} + \mu \mathbf{I}\right)^{-1} \mathbf{Q}^T \mathbf{X} \mathbf{Y}^T. \tag{7.9}$$

Substituting $\mathbf{W}$ in Eq. (7.9) into the objective function in Eq. (7.8), we obtain the optimal $\mathbf{Q}$ by solving the following optimization problem:

$$\max_{\mathbf{Q}} \mathrm{Tr} \left(((\mathbf{Q}^T (\mathbf{X}\mathbf{X}^T + \mu \mathbf{I})\mathbf{Q})^{-1} \mathbf{Q}^T \mathbf{X} \mathbf{Y}^T \mathbf{Y} \mathbf{X}^T \mathbf{Q}\right). \tag{7.10}$$

The above result shows that the transformation $\mathbf{Q}$ and the weight matrix $\mathbf{W}$ can be computed in a closed form when squared loss is used. In addition, the joint learning of the transformation matrix $\mathbf{Q}$ and the weight matrix $\mathbf{W}$ can be decoupled into two separate components when the squared loss function is applied, i.e., dimensionality reduction followed by multi-label classification. Therefore, no performance gain can be obtained by optimizing the transformation and the weight matrix jointly when squared loss is applied. This result also justifies the current practice of a separate application of dimensionality reduction for classification.

Note that the optimization problem in Eq. (7.10) is equivalent to the following generalized eigenvalue problem:

$$\mathbf{X}\mathbf{Y}^T\mathbf{Y}\mathbf{X}^T\mathbf{q} = \lambda(\mathbf{X}\mathbf{X}^T + \mu\mathbf{I})\mathbf{q}, \tag{7.11}$$

which is the (regularized) generalized eigenvalue problem in Orthonormalized PLS (OPLS), as discussed in Section 4.3. Thus, the joint learning formulation is closely related to the class of dimensionality reduction algorithms discussed in Chapters 4 and 5.

7.2.2   Joint Learning with Hinge Loss

When hinge loss is employed in the joint learning formulation in Eq. (7.7), we obtain the following optimization problem:

$$\min_{\{\mathbf{w}_j, \xi_i^j\}, \mathbf{Q}} \quad \sum_{j=1}^{k} \left(\frac{1}{2}\|\mathbf{w}_j\|_2^2 + C \sum_{i=1}^{n} \xi_i^j\right) \tag{7.12}$$

$$\text{s.t.} \quad \mathbf{y}_i(j)(\mathbf{w}_j^T \mathbf{Q}^T \mathbf{x}_i + b_j) \geq 1 - \xi_i^j, \ \xi_i^j \geq 0, \ \forall i, j,$$

$$\mathbf{Q}^T \mathbf{Q} = \mathbf{I},$$

where ξ_i^j is the slack variable for $\mathbf{x}_i$ in the jth model f_j. Note that the transformation $\mathbf{Q}$ is the same for all of the models, and it can capture the common structures shared by multiple labels. This extends the formulation proposed in [3] for uncovering the shared structures for multi-class problems. The dual form of the problem in Eq. (7.12) is given by:

$$\min_{\mathbf{Q}} \max_{\{\boldsymbol{\alpha}^j\}} \quad \sum_{j=1}^{k}\left(\sum_{i=1}^{n} \alpha_i^j - \frac{1}{2}\left((\boldsymbol{\alpha}^j)^T \mathbf{D}^j \mathbf{X}^T \mathbf{Q}\mathbf{Q}^T \mathbf{X} \mathbf{D}^j \boldsymbol{\alpha}^j\right)\right)$$

$$\text{s.t.} \quad \sum_{i=1}^{n} \mathbf{y}_i(j)\alpha_i^j = 0, \ 0 \le \boldsymbol{\alpha}^j \le C, \ \forall j, \tag{7.13}$$

$$\mathbf{Q}^T\mathbf{Q} = \mathbf{I}.$$

where $\mathbf{X} = [\mathbf{x}_1, \ldots, \mathbf{x}_n] \in \mathbb{R}^{d \times n}$, $\boldsymbol{\alpha}^j = [\alpha_1^j, \ldots, \alpha_n^j]^T \in \mathbb{R}^n$, and $\mathbf{D}^j$ is a diagonal matrix with $\mathbf{D}_{ii}^j = \mathbf{y}_i(j)$. Note that the formulation in Eq. (7.13) is closely related to the sparse learning algorithm proposed in [266].

7.2.2.1 A Convex-Concave Formulation

The orthonormality constraint on $\mathbf{Q}$ in Eq. (7.13) is nonconvex. We show below how to relax the problem into a convex-concave problem:

Lemma 7.1 *The optimization problem in Eq. (7.13) can be relaxed to the following convex-concave problem:*

$$\max_{\{\boldsymbol{\alpha}^j\}} \min_{\mathbf{Z}} \quad \sum_{j=1}^{k}\left(\sum_{i=1}^{n} \alpha_i^j - \frac{1}{2}\left((\boldsymbol{\alpha}^j)^T \mathbf{D}^j \mathbf{X}^T \mathbf{Z} \mathbf{X} \mathbf{D}^j \boldsymbol{\alpha}^j\right)\right)$$

$$\text{s.t.} \quad \sum_{i=1}^{n} \mathbf{y}_i(j)\alpha_i^j = 0, \ 0 \le \boldsymbol{\alpha}^j \le C, \ \forall j, \tag{7.14}$$

$$\text{Tr}(\mathbf{Z}) = r, \ 0 \preceq \mathbf{Z} \preceq \mathbf{I},$$

where $\mathbf{A} \preceq \mathbf{B}$ *denotes that* $\mathbf{B} - \mathbf{A}$ *is positive semidefinite.*

Proof We first replace $\mathbf{Q}\mathbf{Q}^T$ with $\mathbf{Z}$ in the objective function and add $\mathbf{Q}\mathbf{Q}^T = \mathbf{Z}$ as a new constraint. It follows from the results in [177] that the set $\mathcal{Z} = \{\mathbf{Z} | \text{Tr}(\mathbf{Z}) = r, 0 \preceq \mathbf{Z} \preceq \mathbf{I}\}$ is the convex hull of the nonconvex set $\mathcal{Z}_0 = \{\mathbf{Z} | \mathbf{Z} = \mathbf{Q}\mathbf{Q}^T, \mathbf{Q}^T\mathbf{Q} = \mathbf{I}, \mathbf{Q} \in \mathbb{R}^{d \times r}\}$. Thus, the orthonormality constraint on $\mathbf{Q}$ in Eq. (7.13) can be relaxed to a convex constraint on $\mathbf{Z}$. After this relaxation, the objective is concave in $\{\boldsymbol{\alpha}^j\}_{j=1}^{k}$ and convex in $\mathbf{Z}$. In addition, the maximization problem is strictly feasible in $\{\boldsymbol{\alpha}^j\}_{j=1}^{k}$ and the minimization problem is strictly feasible in $\mathbf{Z}$. Thus, Slater's condition holds [35], and the minimization and maximization can be interchanged. This leads to the convex-concave problem in Eq. (7.14). ∎

Note that all the constraints in the problem in Eq. (7.14) are convex. In addition, the objective is convex in $\mathbf{Z}$ and concave in $\{\boldsymbol{\alpha}^j\}_{j=1}^{k}$. Thus, this optimization problem is a convex-concave problem and the existence of a saddle point is guaranteed by the well-known von Neumann Lemma [172]. Since the objective function is maximized in terms of $\{\boldsymbol{\alpha}^j\}_{j=1}^{k}$ and minimized in terms of $\mathbf{Z}$ at the saddle point, it is also the globally optimal solution to this problem [172].

7.2.2.2 Solving the Min-Max Problem

The prox-method [173] can be employed to solve the min-max formulation in Eq. (7.14), which has a differentiable and convex-concave objective function. The prox-method is a first-order method [22,173] that is specialized for solving the saddle point problem and has a nearly dimension-independent convergence rate of $O(1/N)$, where N is the number of iterations. The key idea of the prox-method is to convert the min-max problem to the associated variational inequality (v.i.) formulation, which is then iteratively solved by a series of v.i. problems. Since each iteration of the prox-method has a low computational cost, it scales to large-size problems.

7.2.2.3 Learning Orthonormal Features

In the above formulations, we require the transformation to be orthonormal, that is, $\mathbf{Q}^T\mathbf{Q} = \mathbf{I}$. We can also require the transformed features to be orthonormal by imposing the following constraint:

$$\mathbf{Q}^T(\mathbf{X}\mathbf{X}^T + \mu\mathbf{I})\mathbf{Q} = \mathbf{I}, \tag{7.15}$$

where a regularization term is added to deal with the singularity problem of the co-variance matrix $\mathbf{X}\mathbf{X}^T$. Similarly, we can relax this constraint into a convex one, resulting in a convex-concave problem.

7.2.2.4 Joint Learning with Squared Hinge Loss

Squared hinge loss is also commonly used in classification, which is defined as $L(y, f) = \max(0, 1 - yf)^2$. With this loss, the optimization problem in Eq. (7.7) becomes:

$$\min_{\{\mathbf{w}_j, \xi_i^j\}, \mathbf{Q}} \quad \sum_{j=1}^{k}\left(\frac{1}{2}\|\mathbf{w}_j\|_2^2 + C\sum_{i=1}^{n}\left(\xi_i^j\right)^2\right) \tag{7.16}$$

$$\text{s. t.} \quad \mathbf{y}_i(j)(\mathbf{w}_j^T\mathbf{Q}^T\mathbf{x}_i + b_j) \geq 1 - \xi_i^j, \; \xi_i^j \geq 0, \; \forall\, i, j,$$

$$\mathbf{Q}^T\mathbf{Q} = \mathbf{I}.$$

The dual form of the problem in Eq. (7.16) is given by:

$$\min_{\mathbf{Q}} \max_{\{\boldsymbol{\alpha}^j\}} \quad \sum_{j=1}^{k}\left(\sum_{i=1}^{n}\alpha_i^j - \frac{1}{2}\left((\boldsymbol{\alpha}^j)^T\left(\mathbf{D}^j\mathbf{X}^T\mathbf{Q}\mathbf{Q}^T\mathbf{X}\mathbf{D}^j + \frac{1}{2C}\mathbf{I}\right)\boldsymbol{\alpha}^j\right)\right)$$

$$\text{s. t.} \quad \sum_{i=1}^{n}\mathbf{y}_i(j)\alpha_i^j = 0, \; 0 \leq \boldsymbol{\alpha}^j \leq C, \; \forall\, j,$$

$$\mathbf{Q}^T\mathbf{Q} = \mathbf{I}. \tag{7.17}$$

Similar techniques can be applied to convert the problem into a convex-concave formulation, which can also be solved using the prox-method [173]. In addition, it can also be extended to learn orthonormal features as discussed above.

7.2.2.5 Related Work

The joint learning formulation in Eq. (7.13) is closely related to the sparse learning algorithm proposed in [266], which works on binary-class problems. The column vectors of $\mathbf{Q}$ are considered as pseudo support vectors in [266], and no orthonormality condition is imposed on $\mathbf{Q}$. In addition, [266] focuses on constructing an approximate SVM by using a small set of support vectors, while we focus on dimensionality reduction embedded in SVM. Joint structure learning and classification for multi-task learning has been studied in [5]. Joint feature extraction and multi-class SVM classification using the low-rank constraint is proposed in [3]. Due to the intractability of this constraint, it is relaxed to the trace norm constraint and the relaxed problem can be solved by gradient descent algorithms. In [9], the authors propose an iterative procedure to learn a common sparse representation for multiple related tasks, and show that the algorithm converges to a global optimum.

7.3 Dimensionality Reduction with Different Input Data

Our discussions above assume that the input data for all labels are the same, i.e., a common data matrix $\mathbf{X}$ is shared for all labels. In many practical applications, especially when the data are unbalanced, it is desirable to relax this restriction so that the input data associated with each label can be better balanced. Traditional dimensionality reduction algorithms such as LDA, CCA, and PLS cannot be applied in such a scenario. Interestingly, the joint formulations from the last section can be extended naturally to deal with this type of data.

Let $\mathbf{X}^j$ be the data matrix of the jth label. We obtain the following optimization problem (in the dual form) under hinge loss:

$$\min_{\mathbf{Q}} \max_{\{\boldsymbol{\alpha}^j\}} \quad \sum_{j=1}^{k}(\sum_{i=1}^{n}\alpha_i^j - \frac{1}{2}((\boldsymbol{\alpha}^j)^T\mathbf{D}^j(\mathbf{X}^j)^T\mathbf{Q}\mathbf{Q}^T\mathbf{X}^j\mathbf{D}^j\boldsymbol{\alpha}^j))$$

$$\text{s.t.} \quad \sum_{i=1}^{n}\mathbf{y}_i(j)\alpha_i^j = 0, \;\; 0 \le \boldsymbol{\alpha}^j \le C, \;\; \forall \, j,$$

$$\mathbf{Q}^T\mathbf{Q} = \mathbf{I}. \tag{7.18}$$

Similar to the discussions from the last section, the optimization problem in Eq. (7.18) can be converted to a convex-concave problem that can be solved efficiently.

7.4　Empirical Evaluation

We evaluate the joint formulations when the input data for different labels are the same or different. Results on data sets with the same input are presented in Section 7.4.1, and those with different inputs are reported in Section 7.4.2.

7.4.1　Evaluation on Multi-Label Data Sets

The two multi-label data sets used are the Arts and Business data sets, and they consist of web pages from the arts and business directories at Yahoo!. Each web page is assigned a variable number of labels indicating its categories. All instances are encoded with TF-IDF and are normalized to have unit length. These data sets are high-dimensional (23,146 and 21,924 dimensions), and we extract 20 labels and 1000 instances from each data set. We report the Area Under the Receiver Operating Characteristic Curve (AUC) of our four formulations in Table 7.1. Hinge loss and squared hinge loss multi-label SVM formulations with orthonormal transformation and orthonormal features are denoted as $\text{MLSVM}^T_{L_h}$, $\text{MLSVM}^F_{L_h}$, $\text{MLSVM}^T_{L_{h2}}$, and $\text{MLSVM}^F_{L_{h2}}$, respectively. The performance of SVM in the original data space and in the dimensionality-reduced space by CCA (CCA+SVM) is also reported.

We observe from the results that the joint learning formulations with orthonormal transformation and orthonormal features achieve the highest performance on the two high-dimensional data sets. The improvement over CCA+SVM is small on the four data sets. This implies that the joint learning of dimensionality reduction and classification is similar to applying them separately in some cases. The experiments also show that formulations based on dimensionality reduction generally outperform

TABLE 7.1:　The mean AUC score achieved by various formulations on the Arts (top) and Business (bottom) data sets.

Ratio	$\text{MLSVM}^T_{L_h}$	$\text{MLSVM}^F_{L_h}$	$\text{MLSVM}^T_{L_{h2}}$	$\text{MLSVM}^F_{L_{h2}}$	CCA+SVM	SVM
20%	63.07±0.92	62.71±0.98	63.07±0.92	62.71±0.99	63.02±1.06	44.07±5.12
30%	64.15±0.60	63.55±0.98	64.15±0.60	63.51±0.96	63.72±0.96	49.61±3.47
40%	65.11±0.76	64.32±0.67	65.11±0.76	64.33±0.66	64.65±0.62	53.94±3.59
50%	65.74±0.67	65.05±1.11	65.74±0.67	65.04±1.13	65.17±1.00	56.92±3.93
60%	66.34±0.76	64.73±1.00	66.34±0.76	64.76±0.99	65.01±0.97	59.01±2.15
20%	68.74±3.56	70.89±1.99	68.74±3.56	70.89±2.00	71.06±2.02	38.39±6.81
30%	74.54±0.69	73.15±1.47	74.54±0.69	73.14±1.48	73.20±1.43	49.07±6.84
40%	75.33±0.91	74.08±1.36	75.33±0.91	74.09±1.37	74.17±1.31	59.82±4.88
50%	76.82±1.34	74.67±1.22	76.82±1.33	74.67±1.22	74.72±1.22	62.11±8.53
60%	77.69±1.47	76.07±1.38	77.69±1.47	76.05±1.37	76.15±1.42	68.59±5.64

Note: The data sets are partitioned into training and test sets with different ratios, and the mean AUC score and standard deviation over ten random trials are reported in each case. Hinge loss and squared hinge loss multi-label SVM formulations with transformation or feature orthonormal are denoted as $\text{MLSVM}^T_{L_h}$, $\text{MLSVM}^F_{L_h}$, $\text{MLSVM}^T_{L_{h2}}$, and $\text{MLSVM}^F_{L_{h2}}$, respectively.

those in the original space, especially when the data dimensionality is high. This justifies the use of dimensionality reduction in multi-label classification.

7.4.2 Evaluation on Data with Different Inputs

The Landmine data set [267] consists of 29 subsets (tasks) that are collected from various landmine fields. Each object in a given task is represented by a 9-dimensional feature vector and a binary label indicating landmine or clutter. The inputs for different tasks are different. We apply $\text{MLSVM}_{L_h}^T$ on the Landmine data to learn a common transformation for all of the tasks, and project them into a lower-dimensional space using this transformation. This common transformation captures the common structures shared by all of these tasks and is expected to improve detection performance. We also apply SVM on each of the tasks independently. The data for each task are partitioned into training and test sets with different proportions, and the mean AUC scores and standard deviations over 50 random partitions in each case are shown in Figure 7.1. We can observe from the figure that the joint learning formulation improves detection performance consistently by capturing the common predictive structures shared among multiple tasks. Note that traditional dimensionality reduction algorithms are not applicable for this problem.

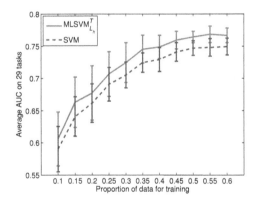

FIGURE 7.1: The mean AUC score for the Landmine detection problem. Different proportions (indicated by the horizontal axis) of the data are used for training, and the mean AUC scores over 50 random partitions are plotted.

Chapter 8

Nonlinear Dimensionality Reduction: Algorithms and Applications

In some applications, it is insufficient to model the data using linear models directly. In this chapter we present nonlinear dimensionality reduction algorithms for multi-label learning using the kernel methods [207]. The basic idea of kernel methods is to map the data instances from the original space to a high-dimensional Hilbert space (feature space) such that linear models in the feature space correspond to nonlinear models in the original input space. We use the *Drosophila* gene expression pattern image annotation problem as an application example for the kernel-based dimensionality reduction methods.

8.1 Background on Kernel Methods

Kernel Methods (KMs) are a class of machine learning algorithms that construct nonlinear models at the computational cost of linear models [207]. Conceptually, kernel machines consist of two parts: a module that performs the mapping into the feature space and a learning algorithm designed to learn linear models in that space [210]. We consider a mapping Φ in this form:

$$\Phi : \mathbf{x} \in \mathcal{X} \rightarrow \Phi(\mathbf{x}) \in \mathcal{F}, \tag{8.1}$$

where $\mathcal{F}$ is the new feature space. In other words, we can select the mapping Φ such that a linear model in $\mathcal{F}$ corresponds to a highly nonlinear model in the original space.

After mapping to the feature space, kernel methods simply compute the inner products between the images of all pairs of data. Formally, we define the kernel as follows:

Definition 8.1 *A kernel is a function κ, such that for all $\mathbf{x}_i, \mathbf{x}_j \in \mathcal{X}$,*

$$\kappa(\mathbf{x}_i, \mathbf{x}_j) = \Phi(\mathbf{x}_i)^T \Phi(\mathbf{x}_j),$$

where Φ is a mapping from $\mathcal{X}$ to a Hilbert space $\mathcal{F}$.

The functional form of the mapping Φ does not need to be known since it is implicitly defined by the choice of kernel $\kappa(\mathbf{x}_i, \mathbf{x}_j) = \Phi(\mathbf{x}_i)^T \Phi(\mathbf{x}_j)$, i.e., the inner product in the kernel-induced feature space. Formally, given n samples $\mathbf{x}_1, \ldots, \mathbf{x}_n \in \mathcal{X}$, the so-called kernel matrix or the Gram matrix $\mathbf{K} \in \mathbb{R}^{n \times n}$, is defined as

$$\mathbf{K}_{ij} = \kappa(\mathbf{x}_i, \mathbf{x}_j). \tag{8.2}$$

A kernel function κ satisfies the finitely positive semidefinite property: for any $\mathbf{x}_1, \ldots, \mathbf{x}_n \in \mathcal{X}$, the Gram matrix $\mathbf{K}$ is symmetric and positive semidefinite, since it defines the inner product between all pairs of points in the feature space [207].

By defining the Gram matrix $\mathbf{K}$, we can define the mapping Φ implicitly. This is the so-called kernel trick [207]. Since the mapping is defined implicitly by the kernel matrix, kernel methods are simple and computationally efficient. In addition, they are flexible, as different kernels can be constructed. Compared with other learning algorithms, one remarkable advantage of kernel methods is that they can accommodate data not in the form of vectors and matrices. For example, different kernels have been proposed to handle different types of data, e.g., graphs [141], strings [70], trees, images [210], etc.

All dimensionality reduction algorithms discussed in this book can be extended to the kernel-induced feature space using the kernel trick. In the following, we will discuss these kernel algorithms, including kernel Canonical Correlation Analysis (CCA), kernel Hypergraph Spectral Learning (HSL), kernel Least Squares, and the relationships among them are also elucidated.

8.2   Kernel Centering and Projection

In this section we discuss kernel centering and projection, since they are basic operations and are widely used in many kernel methods. Assume that we are given a training set and a test set in the feature space mapped by the kernel. Let $\Phi_1 \in \mathbb{R}^{d_f \times n_1}$ and $\Phi_2 \in \mathbb{R}^{d_f \times n_2}$ denote the training set and the test set, respectively, in the feature space, where d_f is the dimension of the feature space, n_1 is the number of samples in the training data set, and n_2 is the number of samples in the test data set. Also, denote the whole data set as $\Phi = [\Phi_1, \Phi_2]$. Prior to centering, the kernel matrix $\mathbf{K}$ can be computed as follows:

$$
\begin{aligned}
\mathbf{K} &= \Phi^T \Phi \\
&= [\Phi_1, \Phi_2]^T [\Phi_1, \Phi_2] \\
&= \begin{bmatrix} \Phi_1^T \Phi_1 & \Phi_1^T \Phi_2 \\ \Phi_2^T \Phi_1 & \Phi_2^T \Phi_2 \end{bmatrix} \\
&= \begin{bmatrix} \mathbf{K}_{11} & \mathbf{K}_{12} \\ \mathbf{K}_{12}^T & \mathbf{K}_{22} \end{bmatrix},
\end{aligned}
$$

where $\mathbf{K}_{11} = \Phi_1^T \Phi_1$, $\mathbf{K}_{12} = \Phi_1^T \Phi_2$ and $\mathbf{K}_{22} = \Phi_2^T \Phi_2$. In the following, we will discuss how to center and project the kernel matrix.

8.2.1 Kernel Centering

In kernel matrix centering, we subtract the mean of the training samples in the feature space, i.e., $\bar{\Phi}_1 = \frac{1}{n_1}\Phi_1 1_{n_1}$, from both the training and the test data sets. The training and test sets after centering can be computed as follows:

$$
\tilde{\Phi}_1 = \Phi_1 - \bar{\Phi}_1 1_{n_1}^T = \Phi_1 - \frac{1}{n_1}\Phi_1 1_{n_1} 1_{n_1}^T = \Phi_1\left(I_{n_1} - \frac{1}{n_1}1_{n_1}1_{n_1}^T\right),
$$

$$
\tilde{\Phi}_2 = \Phi_2 - \bar{\Phi}_1 1_{n_2}^T = \Phi_2 - \frac{1}{n_1}\Phi_1 1_{n_1} 1_{n_2}^T.
$$

Therefore, we can compute $\tilde{\Phi}_1^T \tilde{\Phi}_1$ as

$$
\begin{aligned}
\tilde{K}_{11} &= \tilde{\Phi}_1^T \tilde{\Phi}_1 \\
&= \left(\Phi_1\left(I_{n_1} - \frac{1}{n_1}1_{n_1}1_{n_1}^T\right)\right)^T \Phi_1\left(I_{n_1} - \frac{1}{n_1}1_{n_1}1_{n_1}^T\right) \\
&= \left(I_{n_1} - \frac{1}{n_1}1_{n_1}1_{n_1}^T\right)\Phi_1^T\Phi_1\left(I_{n_1} - \frac{1}{n_1}1_{n_1}1_{n_1}^T\right) \\
&= \left(I_{n_1} - \frac{1}{n_1}1_{n_1}1_{n_1}^T\right)K_{11}\left(I_{n_1} - \frac{1}{n_1}1_{n_1}1_{n_1}^T\right) \\
&= CK_{11}C,
\end{aligned}
$$

where $C = I_{n_1} - \frac{1}{n_1}1_{n_1}1_{n_1}^T$ is the so-called "centering matrix".

Similarly, we can compute $\tilde{\Phi}_1^T \tilde{\Phi}_2$ as

$$
\begin{aligned}
\tilde{K}_{12} &= \tilde{\Phi}_1^T \tilde{\Phi}_2 \\
&= \left(\Phi_1\left(I_{n_1} - \frac{1}{n_1}1_{n_1}1_{n_1}^T\right)\right)^T \left(\Phi_2 - \frac{1}{n_1}\Phi_1 1_{n_1}1_{n_2}^T\right) \\
&= \left(I_{n_1} - \frac{1}{n_1}1_{n_1}1_{n_1}^T\right)\left(\Phi_1^T\Phi_2 - \frac{1}{n_1}\Phi_1^T\Phi_1 1_{n_1}1_{n_2}^T\right) \\
&= \left(I_{n_1} - \frac{1}{n_1}1_{n_1}1_{n_1}^T\right)\left(K_{12} - \frac{1}{n_1}K_{11}1_{n_1}1_{n_2}^T\right) \\
&= C\left(K_{12} - \frac{1}{n_1}K_{11}1_{n_1}1_{n_2}^T\right).
\end{aligned}
$$

Thus, we can center K_{12} using K_{11} and K_{12}.

8.2.2 Kernel Projection

In the following, we discuss how to perform linear projection in the kernel-induced feature space. In particular, we use kernel CCA as an example. Assume that both the training and the test sets are centered as discussed in Section 8.2.1. Suppose we use the training data $\tilde{\Phi}_1$ as one view in CCA (the corresponding kernel $\tilde{K}_{11}$ is used in the computation), and kernel CCA returns the coefficient vector $\alpha \in \mathbb{R}^{n_1}$ for reconstructing the projection vector in the feature space. It follows from the representer theorem that the projection vector $\mathbf{w}$ in the kernel-induced feature space can be expressed as

$$\mathbf{w} = \tilde{\Phi}_1 \alpha. \tag{8.3}$$

Then the data after projection by $\mathbf{w}$ is

$$[\Gamma_1, \Gamma_2] = \mathbf{w}^T[\tilde{\Phi}_1, \tilde{\Phi}_2] = \alpha^T \tilde{\Phi}_1^T [\tilde{\Phi}, \tilde{\Phi}_2] = \alpha^T[\tilde{K}_{11}, \tilde{K}_{12}],$$

where Γ_1 and Γ_2 denote the training and test sets after the projection by $\mathbf{w}$, respectively. Hence, we have

$$\Gamma_1 = \alpha^T \tilde{K}_{11}, \tag{8.4}$$
$$\Gamma_2 = \alpha^T \tilde{K}_{12}. \tag{8.5}$$

Then we can compute the kernel after the linear projection by $\mathbf{w}$ in the feature space as follows:

$$\mathbf{K}_{prj} = \begin{bmatrix} \Gamma_1 & \Gamma_2 \end{bmatrix}^T \begin{bmatrix} \Gamma_1 & \Gamma_2 \end{bmatrix} \tag{8.6}$$

$$= \begin{bmatrix} \Gamma_1^T \Gamma_1 & \Gamma_1^T \Gamma_2 \\ \Gamma_2^T \Gamma_1 & \Gamma_2^T \Gamma_2 \end{bmatrix} \tag{8.7}$$

$$= \begin{bmatrix} \tilde{K}_{11}\alpha\alpha^T\tilde{K}_{11} & \tilde{K}_{11}\alpha\alpha^T\tilde{K}_{12} \\ \tilde{K}_{12}^T\alpha\alpha^T\tilde{K}_{11} & \tilde{K}_{12}^T\alpha\alpha^T\tilde{K}_{12}. \end{bmatrix}. \tag{8.8}$$

8.3 Kernel Canonical Correlation Analysis

When CCA is employed for multi-label dimensionality reduction, $\mathbf{X}$ corresponds to the data and $\mathbf{Y}$ corresponds to the label. Thus, when applying kernel CCA in multi-label learning, only the feature mapping on $\mathbf{X}$ is considered. It follows from the representer theorem [207] that the projection vector $\mathbf{w}_x$ can be represented as:

$$\mathbf{w}_x = \Phi(\mathbf{X})\beta, \tag{8.9}$$

for some vector $\beta \in \mathbb{R}^n$. Consequently, the resulting correlation coefficient ρ in the feature space can be expressed as

$$
\begin{aligned}
\rho &= \frac{\mathbf{w}_x^T \Phi(\mathbf{X}) \mathbf{Y}^T \mathbf{w}_y}{\sqrt{(\mathbf{w}_x^T \Phi(\mathbf{X}) \Phi(\mathbf{X})^T \mathbf{w}_x)(\mathbf{w}_y^T \mathbf{Y}\mathbf{Y}^T \mathbf{w}_y)}} \\
&= \frac{\beta^T \Phi(\mathbf{X})^T \Phi(\mathbf{X}) \mathbf{Y}^T w_y}{\sqrt{\left(\beta^T \Phi(\mathbf{X})^T \Phi(\mathbf{X}) \Phi(\mathbf{X})^T \Phi(\mathbf{X}) \alpha\right)\left(\mathbf{w}_y^T \mathbf{Y}\mathbf{Y}^T \mathbf{w}_y\right)}} \\
&= \frac{\beta^T \mathbf{K} \mathbf{Y}^T \mathbf{w}_y}{\sqrt{\left(\beta^T \mathbf{K}^2 \beta\right)\left(\mathbf{w}_y^T \mathbf{Y}\mathbf{Y}^T \mathbf{w}_y\right)}},
\end{aligned}
$$

where $\mathbf{K} = \Phi(\mathbf{X})^T \Phi(\mathbf{X})$ is the kernel matrix. Similar to the linear case, it can be formulated equivalently as the following optimization problem:

$$
\begin{aligned}
\max_{\beta, \mathbf{w}_y} \quad & \beta^T \mathbf{K} \mathbf{Y}^T \mathbf{w}_y && (8.10) \\
\text{s.t.} \quad & \beta^T \mathbf{K}^2 \beta = 1, \\
& \mathbf{w}_y^T \mathbf{Y}\mathbf{Y}^T \mathbf{w}_y = 1.
\end{aligned}
$$

Assume that $\mathbf{Y}\mathbf{Y}^T$ is nonsingular. It can be shown that β can be obtained by solving the following optimization problem:

$$
\begin{aligned}
\max_{\beta} \quad & \beta^T \mathbf{K} \mathbf{Y}^T \left(\mathbf{Y}\mathbf{Y}^T\right)^{-1} \mathbf{Y}\mathbf{K}\beta && (8.11) \\
\text{s.t.} \quad & \beta^T \mathbf{K}^2 \beta = 1.
\end{aligned}
$$

It can be verified that the optimal β is the eigenvector corresponding to the largest eigenvalue of the following generalized eigenvalue problem:

$$
\mathbf{K}\mathbf{Y}^T \left(\mathbf{Y}\mathbf{Y}^T\right)^{-1} \mathbf{Y}\mathbf{K}\beta = \eta \mathbf{K}^2 \beta. \tag{8.12}
$$

Similar to the discussions in Section 3.1.2, multiple projection vectors under the orthonormality constraints in the feature space can be obtained simultaneously by solving the following optimization problem:

$$
\begin{aligned}
\max_{\mathbf{B}} \quad & \operatorname{Tr}\left(\mathbf{B}^T \mathbf{K}\mathbf{Y}^T \left(\mathbf{Y}\mathbf{Y}^T\right)^{-1} \mathbf{Y}\mathbf{K}\mathbf{B}\right) && (8.13) \\
\text{s.t.} \quad & \mathbf{B}^T \mathbf{K}^2 \mathbf{B} = \mathbf{I}_\ell,
\end{aligned}
$$

where $\mathbf{B} = [\beta_1, \ldots, \beta_\ell] \in \mathbb{R}^{n \times \ell}$ is the coefficient matrix for $\mathbf{X}$ in the feature space, and ℓ is the number of projection vectors. The solution of the optimization problem in Eq. (8.13) consists of the top ℓ eigenvectors of the generalized eigenvalue problem in Eq. (8.12).

To enable nontrivial learning and avoid overfitting, a proper amount of regularization is essential in kernel CCA. This leads to regularized kernel CCA (krCCA), which solves the following optimization problem:

$$\max_{\mathbf{B}} \quad \mathrm{Tr}\left(\mathbf{B}^T\mathbf{K}\mathbf{Y}^T\left(\mathbf{Y}\mathbf{Y}^T\right)^{-1}\mathbf{Y}\mathbf{K}\mathbf{B}\right)$$

$$\text{s.t.} \quad \mathbf{B}^T\left(\mathbf{K}^2+\lambda\mathbf{K}\right)\mathbf{B}=\mathbf{I}_\ell, \tag{8.14}$$

where $\lambda > 0$ is the regularization parameter.

8.4   Kernel Hypergraph Spectral Learning

In this section, we extend hypergraph spectral learning to the kernel-induced feature space. When HSL is applied for multi-label learning, $\mathbf{X}$ corresponds to the data and $\mathbf{Y}$ corresponds to the label. Similar to kernel CCA, we only consider the mapping on the data $\mathbf{X}$. Note that the hypergraph Laplacian $\mathcal{L}$ is constructed from the label $\mathbf{Y}$ only and it remains the same after the mapping of $\mathbf{X}$. It follows from the representer theorem [207] that the projection vectors for the data in the kernel-induced feature space can be written as

$$\mathbf{W} = \Phi(\mathbf{X})\mathbf{B},$$

for some matrix $\mathbf{B} \in \mathbb{R}^{n\times k}$. Thus, the optimization problem in hypergraph spectral learning can be expressed as follows:

$$\min_{\mathbf{B}} \quad \mathrm{Tr}(\mathbf{B}^T\Phi(\mathbf{X})^T\Phi(\mathbf{X})\mathcal{L}\Phi(\mathbf{X})^T\Phi(\mathbf{X})\mathbf{B}) \tag{8.15}$$

$$\text{s.t.} \quad \mathbf{B}^T\Phi(\mathbf{X})^T\Phi(\mathbf{X})\Phi(\mathbf{X})^T\Phi(\mathbf{X})\mathbf{B}=\mathbf{I}_k,$$

where $\mathcal{L}$ is the normalized Laplacian of the hypergraph. Intuitively, data points sharing many common labels tend to be close to each other in the embedded space.

The optimization problem in kernel hypergraph spectral learning can be reformulated into the following optimization problem:

$$\min_{\mathbf{A}} \quad \mathrm{Tr}(\mathbf{B}^T\mathbf{K}\mathcal{L}\mathbf{K}\mathbf{B}) \tag{8.16}$$

$$\text{s.t.} \quad \mathbf{B}^T\mathbf{K}^2\mathbf{B}=\mathbf{I}_k,$$

where $\mathbf{K} = \Phi(\mathbf{X})^T\Phi(\mathbf{X}) \in \mathbb{R}^{n\times n}$ is the kernel matrix.

Note that $\mathbf{S} = \mathbf{I} - \mathcal{L}$, as discussed in Section 4.2, where $\mathbf{S}$ is symmetric and positive semidefinite and it reflects the normalized similarities between different data points. Then the optimization problem in Eq. (8.16) is equivalent to the following form:

$$\max_{\mathbf{B}} \quad \mathrm{Tr}(\mathbf{B}^T\mathbf{K}\mathbf{S}\mathbf{K}\mathbf{B}) \tag{8.17}$$

$$\text{s.t.} \quad \mathbf{B}^T\mathbf{K}^2\mathbf{B}=\mathbf{I}_k.$$

Similarly, the optimal solution $\mathbf{B}$ consists of the eigenvectors corresponding to the largest eigenvalues of the following generalized eigenvalue problem:

$$\mathbf{KSK}\beta = \lambda \mathbf{K}^2 \beta. \tag{8.18}$$

Similar to regularized kernel CCA, regularized kernel hypergraph spectral learning solves the following optimization problem:

$$\max_{\mathbf{B}} \quad \mathrm{Tr}(\mathbf{B}^T \mathbf{KSKB}) \tag{8.19}$$

$$\text{s.\,t.} \quad \mathbf{B}^T (\mathbf{K}^2 + \lambda \mathbf{K})\mathbf{B} = \mathbf{I}_k,$$

where $\lambda > 0$ is the regularization parameter.

8.5 The Generalized Eigenvalue Problem in the Kernel-Induced Feature Space

Recall that CCA, Orthonormalized Partial Least Squares (OPLS), Linear Discriminant Analysis (LDA), and HSL all belong to a class of generalized eigenvalue problem discussed in Chapter 4. In this section we extend this class of generalized eigenvalue problem to the kernel-induced feature space. Similar to previous discussions, we only consider the mapping on the data $\mathbf{X}$. Formally, we consider the generalized eigenvalue problem in the following form:

$$\mathbf{KSK}\alpha = \lambda \mathbf{K}^2 \alpha, \tag{8.20}$$

where $\mathbf{S} \in \mathbb{R}^{n \times n}$ is a symmetric and positive semidefinite matrix. In general, we are interested in the principal eigenvectors corresponding to the nonzero eigenvalues. The generalized eigenvalue problem in Eq. (8.20) is often reformulated as the following eigenvalue problem:

$$(\mathbf{K}^2)^\dagger \mathbf{KSK}\alpha = \lambda \alpha, \tag{8.21}$$

where $(\mathbf{K}^2)^\dagger$ is the Moore–Penrose pseudoinverse of $\mathbf{K}^2$. In addition, the generalized eigenvalue problem in Eq. (8.20) can also be formulated as the following optimization problem:

$$\max_{\mathbf{A}} \quad \mathrm{Tr}(\mathbf{A}^T \mathbf{KSKA}) \tag{8.22}$$

$$\text{s.\,t.} \quad \mathbf{A}^T \mathbf{K}^2 \mathbf{A} = \mathbf{I}.$$

In the following derivation, we generally use the formulation in Eq. (8.21).

Similarly, it can be observed that these kernel dimensionality reduction algorithms, e.g., kernel CCA and kernel HSL, can be considered as special cases of the generalized eigenvalue problem in Eq. (8.20) with different $\mathbf{S}$.

8.6 Kernel Least Squares Regression

Similarly, least squares regression can be formulated in the kernel-induced feature space. Following the representer theorem [207], the weight matrix $\mathbf{W}$ in the feature space can be expressed as

$$\mathbf{W} = \Phi(\mathbf{X})\mathbf{G}, \tag{8.23}$$

for some $\mathbf{G} \in \mathbb{R}^{n \times \ell}$. Substituting Eq. (8.23) into the sum-of-squares error function, we have

$$f = \|\mathbf{W}^T \Phi(\mathbf{X}) - \mathbf{T}\|_F^2 = \|\mathbf{G}^T \mathbf{K} - \mathbf{T}\|_F^2.$$

It follows that the optimal $\mathbf{G}$ is given by

$$\mathbf{G} = \mathbf{K}^\dagger \mathbf{T}^T. \tag{8.24}$$

Similarly, the optimal $\mathbf{G}$ of the kernel ridge regression is given by

$$\mathbf{G} = (\mathbf{K} + \lambda \mathbf{I}_n)^{-1} \mathbf{T}^T.$$

8.7 Dimensionality Reduction and Least Squares Regression in the Feature Space

In this section we extend the equivalence relationship between the class of the generalized eigenvalue problem in Eq. (8.20) and the least squares formulation in the kernel-induced feature space. In particular, we show that under a mild condition[1], the eigenvalue problem in Eq. (8.21) can be formulated as a kernel least squares problem with the same target matrix defined in Theorem 4.2.

In the following discussion, we assume that $\Phi(\mathbf{X})$ is centered in the feature space, that is, $\Phi(\mathbf{X})\mathbf{1} = \mathbf{0}$. We use superscript Φ to denote quantities in the feature space transformed by the mapping Φ.

8.7.1 Matrix Orthonormality Property

To simplify the discussion, we define matrices $\mathbf{C}_X^\Phi$ and $\mathbf{C}_S^\Phi$ as follows:

$$\begin{aligned} \mathbf{C}_X^\Phi &= \mathbf{K}^2 \in \mathbb{R}^{n \times n}, \tag{8.25} \\ \mathbf{C}_S^\Phi &= \mathbf{KSK} \in \mathbb{R}^{n \times n}. \tag{8.26} \end{aligned}$$

---

[1]It states that $\mathrm{rank}(\mathbf{K}) = n - 1$, i.e., $\mathrm{rank}(\Phi(\mathbf{X})) = n - 1$ after the data is centered (of zero mean) in the kernel-induced feature space.

The eigenvalue problem in Eq. (8.21) can then be expressed as

$$\mathbf{C}_X^{\Phi\dagger} \mathbf{C}_S^{\Phi} \boldsymbol{\alpha} = \lambda \boldsymbol{\alpha}. \tag{8.27}$$

Recall that $\mathbf{S}$ is symmetric and positive semidefinite; thus it can be decomposed as

$$\mathbf{S} = \mathbf{H}\mathbf{H}^T, \tag{8.28}$$

where $\mathbf{H} \in \mathbb{R}^{n \times s}$, and $s \leq n$. For all examples discussed in Section 4.3, the closed form of $\mathbf{H}$ can be obtained and $s = k \ll n$.

Since $\mathbf{K}$ is centered, i.e., $\mathbf{K}\mathbf{1} = \mathbf{0}$ and $\mathbf{1}^T\mathbf{K} = \mathbf{0}$, we have $\mathbf{C}\mathbf{K} = \mathbf{K}\mathbf{C} = \mathbf{K}$, where $\mathbf{C} = \mathbf{I} - \frac{1}{n}\mathbf{1}\mathbf{1}^T$ is the centering matrix. It follows that

$$
\begin{aligned}
\mathbf{C}_S^{\Phi} &= \mathbf{K}\mathbf{S}\mathbf{K} \\
&= (\mathbf{K}\mathbf{C})\mathbf{S}(\mathbf{C}\mathbf{K}) \\
&= \mathbf{K}(\mathbf{C}^T\mathbf{S}\mathbf{C})\mathbf{K} \\
&= \mathbf{K}\tilde{\mathbf{S}}\mathbf{K}, \tag{8.29}
\end{aligned}
$$

where $\tilde{\mathbf{S}} = \mathbf{C}^T\mathbf{S}\mathbf{C}$. Note that

$$\mathbf{1}^T\tilde{\mathbf{S}}\mathbf{1} = \mathbf{1}^T\mathbf{C}^T\mathbf{S}\mathbf{C}\mathbf{1} = 0. \tag{8.30}$$

Thus, we can assume that $\mathbf{1}^T\mathbf{S}\mathbf{1} = 0$, that is, both columns and rows of $\mathbf{S}$ are centered.

Let $\mathbf{H}$ be defined in Eq. (4.53). Let $\mathbf{H}\mathbf{P} = \mathbf{Q}\mathbf{R}$ be the QR decomposition of $\mathbf{H}$ with column pivoting, where $\mathbf{Q} \in \mathbb{R}^{n \times r}$ has orthonormal columns, $\mathbf{R} \in \mathbb{R}^{r \times k}$ is upper triangular, $r = \text{rank}(\mathbf{H}) \leq k$, and $\mathbf{P} \in \mathbb{R}^{k \times k}$ is a permutation matrix. It follows from Lemma 4.1 that $\mathbf{Q}^T\mathbf{1} = \mathbf{0}$.

Let $\mathbf{R} = \mathbf{U}_R\boldsymbol{\Sigma}_R\mathbf{V}_R^T$ be the thin Singular Value Decomposition (SVD) of $\mathbf{R} \in \mathbb{R}^{r \times k}$, where $\mathbf{U}_R \in \mathbb{R}^{r \times r}$ is orthogonal, $\mathbf{V}_R \in \mathbb{R}^{k \times r}$ has orthonormal columns, and $\boldsymbol{\Sigma}_R \in \mathbb{R}^{r \times r}$ is diagonal. It follows from Eq. (4.56) that the SVD of $\mathbf{S}$ is

$$\mathbf{S} = (\mathbf{Q}\mathbf{U}_R) \boldsymbol{\Sigma}_R^2 (\mathbf{Q}\mathbf{U}_R)^T.$$

Assume that the kernel $\mathbf{K}$ is centered, and $\text{rank}(\mathbf{K}) = n - 1$ after centering. Let the SVD of $\mathbf{K}$ be

$$
\begin{aligned}
\mathbf{K} &= \mathbf{U}_K\boldsymbol{\Sigma}_K\mathbf{U}_K^T \\
&= [\mathbf{U}_{K1}, \mathbf{U}_{K2}] \, \text{diag}\,(\boldsymbol{\Sigma}_{K1}, 0)\,[\mathbf{U}_{K1}, \mathbf{U}_{K2}]^T \\
&= \mathbf{U}_{K1}\boldsymbol{\Sigma}_{K1}\mathbf{U}_{K1}^T, \tag{8.31}
\end{aligned}
$$

where $\mathbf{U}_K$ is orthogonal, $\boldsymbol{\Sigma}_K \in \mathbb{R}^{n \times n}$, $\mathbf{U}_{K1} \in \mathbb{R}^{n \times (n-1)}$, $\mathbf{U}_{K2} \in \mathbb{R}^{n \times 1}$ and $\boldsymbol{\Sigma}_{K1} \in \mathbb{R}^{(n-1) \times (n-1)}$. Note that $\mathbf{U}_{K2}$ lies in the null space of $\mathbf{K}$, thus $\mathbf{K}\mathbf{U}_{K2} = \mathbf{0}$. Define $\mathbf{M}_1^{\Phi}$ as

$$\mathbf{M}_1^{\Phi} = \mathbf{U}_{K1}^T(\mathbf{Q}\mathbf{U}_R) \in \mathbb{R}^{(n-1) \times r}. \tag{8.32}$$

It can be shown that the columns of $\mathbf{M}_1^{\Phi}$ are orthonormal as summarized in the following lemma:

Lemma 8.1 *Let* $\mathbf{M}_1^{\Phi}$ *be defined as above. Then* $\mathbf{M}_1^{\Phi^T}\mathbf{M}_1^{\Phi} = \mathbf{I}_r$.

Proof Since $\mathbf{K1} = \mathbf{0}$, we have $\mathbf{U}_{K1}^T\mathbf{1} = \mathbf{0}$. Also note that $\mathbf{U}_{K1}^T\mathbf{U}_{K1} = \mathbf{I}_{n-1}$ and $(\mathbf{QU}_R)^T(\mathbf{QU}_R) = \mathbf{I}_r$. It follows from Lemma 4.1 that

$$(\mathbf{QU}_R)^T\mathbf{1} = \mathbf{U}_R^T\mathbf{Q}^T\mathbf{1} = \mathbf{0}.$$

Then we have from Lemma 4.2 that $\mathbf{M}_1^{\Phi^T}\mathbf{M}_1^{\Phi} = \mathbf{I}_r$. ∎

8.7.2 The Equivalence Relationship

We first derive the solution to the eigenvalue problem in Eq. (8.21) in the following theorem:

Theorem 8.1 *Let* $\mathbf{U}_{K1}$, $\mathbf{\Sigma}_{K1}$, $\mathbf{Q}$, $\mathbf{\Sigma}_R$, *and* $\mathbf{U}_R$ *be defined as above. Assume that the kernel is centered, i.e.,* $\mathbf{1}^T\mathbf{K} = \mathbf{0}$ *and* $\mathbf{K1} = \mathbf{0}$, *and* $\mathrm{rank}(\mathbf{K}) = n - 1$. *Then the nonzero eigenvalues of the eigenvalue problem in Eq. (8.21) are* $\mathrm{diag}(\mathbf{\Sigma}_R^2)$, *and the corresponding eigenvectors are* $\mathbf{A}_{eig} = \mathbf{U}_{K1}\mathbf{\Sigma}_{K1}^{-1}\mathbf{U}_{K1}^T\mathbf{QU}_R$.

Proof It follows from Lemma 8.1 that the columns of $\mathbf{M}_1^{\Phi} \in \mathbb{R}^{(n-1)\times r}$ are orthonormal. Hence, there exists $\mathbf{M}_2^{\Phi} \in \mathbb{R}^{(n-1)\times(n-1-r)}$ such that $\mathbf{M}^{\Phi} = [\mathbf{M}_1^{\Phi}, \mathbf{M}_2^{\Phi}] \in \mathbb{R}^{(n-1)\times(n-1)}$ is orthogonal [94]. Then we can derive the eigendecomposition of the matrix $\mathbf{C}_X^{\Phi^{\dagger}}\mathbf{C}_S^{\Phi}$ as follows:

$$
\begin{aligned}
&\mathbf{C}_X^{\Phi^{\dagger}}\mathbf{C}_S^{\Phi} \\
=~& (\mathbf{K}^2)^{\dagger}\mathbf{KSK} \\
=~& (\mathbf{U}_{K1}\mathbf{\Sigma}_{K1}^{-2}\mathbf{U}_{K1}^T)\mathbf{U}_{K1}\mathbf{\Sigma}_{K1}\mathbf{U}_{K1}^T(\mathbf{QU}_R)\mathbf{\Sigma}_R^2(\mathbf{QU}_R)^T\mathbf{U}_{K1}\mathbf{\Sigma}_{K1}\mathbf{U}_{K1}^T \\
=~& \mathbf{U}_{K1}\mathbf{\Sigma}_{K1}^{-1}\mathbf{U}_{K1}^T(\mathbf{QU}_R)\mathbf{\Sigma}_R^2(\mathbf{QU}_R)^T\mathbf{U}_{K1}\mathbf{\Sigma}_{K1}\mathbf{U}_{K1}^T \\
=~& \mathbf{U}_{K1}\mathbf{\Sigma}_{K1}^{-1}\mathbf{M}_1^{\Phi}\mathbf{\Sigma}_R^2\mathbf{M}_1^{\Phi^T}\mathbf{\Sigma}_{K1}\mathbf{U}_{K1}^T \\
=~& \mathbf{U}_K\begin{bmatrix}\mathbf{I}_{n-1}\\\mathbf{0}\end{bmatrix}\mathbf{\Sigma}_{K1}^{-1}\begin{bmatrix}\mathbf{M}_1^{\Phi} & \mathbf{M}_2^{\Phi}\end{bmatrix}\begin{bmatrix}\mathbf{\Sigma}_R^2 & \mathbf{0}\\\mathbf{0} & \mathbf{0}_{n-1-r}\end{bmatrix}\begin{bmatrix}\mathbf{M}_1^{\Phi^T}\\\mathbf{M}_2^{\Phi^T}\end{bmatrix}\mathbf{\Sigma}_{K1}[\mathbf{I}_{n-1},\mathbf{0}]\mathbf{U}_K^T \\
=~& \mathbf{U}_K\begin{bmatrix}\mathbf{I}_{n-1}\\\mathbf{0}\end{bmatrix}\mathbf{\Sigma}_{K1}^{-1}\mathbf{M}^{\Phi}\begin{bmatrix}\mathbf{\Sigma}_R^2 & \mathbf{0}\\\mathbf{0} & \mathbf{0}_{n-1-r}\end{bmatrix}\mathbf{M}^{\Phi^T}\mathbf{\Sigma}_{K1}[\mathbf{I}_{n-1},\mathbf{0}]\mathbf{U}_K^T \\
=~& \mathbf{U}_K\begin{bmatrix}\mathbf{\Sigma}_{K1}^{-1}\mathbf{M}^{\Phi} & \mathbf{0}\\\mathbf{0} & 1\end{bmatrix}\begin{bmatrix}\mathbf{\Sigma}_R^2 & \mathbf{0}\\\mathbf{0} & \mathbf{0}_{n-r}\end{bmatrix}\begin{bmatrix}\mathbf{M}^{\Phi^T}\mathbf{\Sigma}_{K1} & \mathbf{0}\\\mathbf{0} & 1\end{bmatrix}\mathbf{U}_K^T.
\end{aligned} \tag{8.33}
$$

There are r nonzero eigenvalues, which are $\mathrm{diag}(\mathbf{\Sigma}_R^2)$, and the corresponding eigenvectors are

$$\mathbf{A}_{eig} = \mathbf{U}_{K1}\mathbf{\Sigma}_{K1}^{-1}\mathbf{M}_1^{\Phi} = \mathbf{U}_{K1}\mathbf{\Sigma}_{K1}^{-1}\mathbf{U}_{K1}^T\mathbf{QU}_R. \tag{8.34}$$

This completes the proof of the theorem. ∎

Using the same target as in the linear case, the equivalence relationship in the kernel-induced feature space can be established and is summarized in the following theorem:

Theorem 8.2 *Assume that the class indicator matrix* $\mathbf{T}$ *for kernel least squares classification is defined as*

$$\mathbf{T} = \mathbf{U}_R^T \mathbf{Q}^T \in \mathbb{R}^{r \times n}. \tag{8.35}$$

Then the solution to the kernel least squares formulation is given by

$$\mathbf{A}_{ls} = \mathbf{U}_{K1} \mathbf{\Sigma}_{K1}^{-1} \mathbf{U}_{K1}^T \mathbf{Q} \mathbf{U}_R. \tag{8.36}$$

Thus, the eigenvalue problem and the least squares problem are equivalent in the kernel case.

Proof When $\mathbf{T}$ is used as the class indicator matrix, then the solution to the kernel least squares problem is

$$
\begin{aligned}
\mathbf{A}_{ls} &= \mathbf{K}^\dagger \mathbf{T}^T \\
&= \mathbf{K}^\dagger \mathbf{Q} \mathbf{U}_R \\
&= \mathbf{U}_{K1} \mathbf{\Sigma}_{K1}^{-1} \mathbf{U}_{K1}^T \mathbf{Q} \mathbf{U}_R.
\end{aligned}
$$

It follows from Eq. (8.34) that $\mathbf{A}_{ls} = \mathbf{A}_{eig}$. This completes the proof of the theorem. ∎

Note that there are r nonzero eigenvalues of $\mathbf{S}$. In some cases it is common to use the top eigenvectors corresponding to the largest $\ell < r$ eigenvalues as in Principal Component Analysis (PCA). Similar to Corollary 4.1, the equivalence relationship between the generalized eigenvalue problem and the corresponding least squares problem in the kernel-induced feature space still holds if we only keep the top $\ell < r$ eigenvectors of $\mathbf{S}$ as the class indicator matrix.

8.8 Gene Expression Pattern Image Annotation

8.8.1 Problem Description

A detailed knowledge of the expression and interaction of genes is crucial to deciphering the mechanisms underlying cell-fate specification and tissue differentiation. DNA microarrays and RNA *in situ* hybridization are two primary methods for monitoring gene expression levels on a large scale. Microarrays provide a quantitative overview of the relative changes of expression levels of a large number of genes, but they do not often document the spatial information on individual genes. In contrast, RNA *in situ* hybridization uses gene-specific probes and can determine the spatial patterns of gene expression precisely. Recent high-throughput investigations have yielded spatiotemporal information for thousands of genes in organisms such as *Drosophila* [151,231] and mice [46,154]. These data have the potential to provide significant insights into the functions and interactions of genes [144,204].

Drosophila melanogaster is one of the model organisms in developmental biology, and its patterns of gene expression have been studied extensively [6,42,151, 231]. A comprehensive atlas of spatial patterns of gene expression during *Drosophila* embryogenesis has been created by *in situ* hybridization techniques, and the patterns are documented in the form of digital images [101,108,231,242]. Comparative analysis of gene expression pattern images can potentially reveal new genetic interactions and yield insights into the complex regulatory networks governing embryonic development [75,144,183,231].

To facilitate pattern comparison and searching, the images of *Drosophila* gene expression patterns are annotated with anatomical and developmental ontology terms using a controlled vocabulary [101,231]. The basic requirement for annotation is to assign a unique term, not only for each terminally differentiated embryonic structure, but also for the developmental intermediates that correspond to it. Four general classes of terms, called anlage *in statu nascendi*, anlage, primordium, and organ (ordered in terms of developmental time), are used in the annotation. Such an elaborate naming scheme describes a developing "path", starting from the cellular blastoderm stage until organs are formed, that documents the dynamic process of *Drosophila* embryogenesis. Due to the overwhelming complexity of this task, the images are currently annotated manually by human experts. However, the number of available images produced by high-throughput *in situ* hybridization is now rapidly increasing [103,144,183,232,272]. It is therefore tempting to design computational methods for the automated annotation of gene expression patterns.

The automated annotation of *Drosophila* gene expression patterns was originally considered difficult due to the lack of a large reference data set from which to learn. Moreover, the "variation in morphology and incomplete knowledge of the shape and position of various embryonic structures" have made this task more elusive [231]. We attempt to address this problem by resorting to advanced tools developed recently in the computer vision and machine learning research communities and on the large set of annotated data available from the Berkeley *Drosophila* Genome Project (BDGP) [231]. There are several challenging questions that need to be addressed when approaching this problem by computational methods. As has been stated in [231], the first challenge is to deal with the issue that the same embryonic structure can appear in different shapes and positions due to distortions caused by genetic variations and the image acquisition process. Fortunately, recent advances in object recognition research have led to robust methods that can detect regions of interest and extract features that are invariant to a class of local transformations from these regions. These two correlated lines of research have reached some maturity now (see [169] and [168] for an overview).

The second challenge of this task lies in data representation. The embryogenesis of *Drosophila* has been divided into six discrete stage ranges (1–3, 4–6, 7–8, 9–10, 11–12, and 13–16) in the BDGP high-throughput study [231]. Gene expression patterns are documented collectively by a group of images in a specific stage range. Similarly, annotation terms are also associated with a group of patterns sharing a subset of the named structures (Figure 1.4). These attributes of the existing biological data pose challenges, because traditional machine learning tools require that each object in question be represented by a feature vector of fixed length. It is challenging to encode the variable number of images in a group into a fixed-length vector. The existing approach [284] is based on the simplifying assumption that terms are associated with individual images instead of image groups. Kernel methods have been shown to be effective in learning from unconventional data types, since they only require that the similarity between objects be abstracted into the so-called kernel matrix [207]. We extract a number of locally invariant features from each gene expression pattern image, and compute kernels between sets of images based on the pyramid match algorithm [98].

A recent comprehensive study shows that when local features are used to compute kernels between images, a combination of multiple feature types tends to yield better results than even the most discriminative individual feature type [275]. This motivates us to extract multiple feature types from each image and obtain multiple kernel matrices, one for each feature type. Thus, the third challenge for automated gene expression pattern annotation is to develop methods that can combine the multiple kernel matrices effectively. Automated methods for combining multiple kernel matrices, called Multiple Kernel Learning (MKL), have been studied in machine learning recently. In such a framework, the optimal kernel matrix is obtained as a convex combination of a set of pre-defined candidate kernel matrices, and the coefficients for the combination can be computed by optimizing a certain criterion. Methods for MKL have been proposed in the contexts of binary-class [145] and multi-class classification [286], and they have been applied successfully to various biological applications [59, 146]. For the problem of gene expression pattern annotation, a variable number of terms from the controlled vocabulary can be assigned to a group of patterns. Hence, this problem belongs to the more general framework of multi-label learning. Thus, the final challenge for automated gene expression pattern annotation is how to perform multi-label learning effectively and predict all relevant labels for a given image group. In this section, we apply Hypergraph Spectra Learning (HSL) to project and combine the multiple kernel matrices for multi-label data. The overall flowchart of the framework is depicted in Figure 8.1.

8.8.2 Feature Generation and Kernel Construction

There are two primary methods for extracting features. When the images are not well aligned, the covariant region detector is first applied on the images to detect regions of interest. Then, a local descriptor is used to extract features from the detected regions. An alternative approach is to apply a local descriptor on a dense regular grid, instead of regions of interest [99, 148]. Such an approach is motivated from the bag-of-words model from the text-modeling literature, and competitive performance has been achieved on image applications [156]. Since the images in our FlyExpress [242] database are already well-aligned, we take the second approach (Figure 8.1). Instead of tuning the local descriptor and grid size manually, we apply several popular local

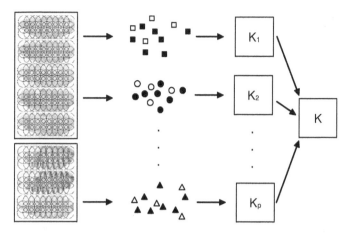

FIGURE 8.1: Illustration of the framework for annotating gene expression patterns. We extract multiple types of features from image groups and construct multiple kernels using the pyramid match algorithm. The multiple kernels are then combined to annotate the image groups. Different shapes represent different types of features, and filled and hollow shapes are used to distinguish features from the two different image groups.

descriptors on regular grids of different sizes, and rely on the MKL framework to select the appropriate local descriptors and grid size. More details on feature generation are described in Section 8.8.4.

The pyramid match algorithm [97–99] computes kernels for variable-sized sets of feature vectors. The main idea of this approach is to convert sets of feature vectors to multi-dimensional, multi-resolution histograms, and then compute the similarity between the corresponding histograms based on histogram intersections. The final similarity between two sets of vectors is computed as a weighted sum of the similarities at the histogram levels. This similarity is an approximation to the similarity of the best partial matching between the feature sets. The resulting similarity matrix based on this measure is provably positive definite, and it can be used in existing kernel-based learning algorithms.

In the pyramid match algorithm, the feature space is partitioned into bins (regions) with increasingly larger granularity. At the finest level, all distinct vectors are guaranteed to be in different bins. The size of the bin increases gradually until a single bin occupies the entire feature space. Each partition of the feature space results in a histogram, and the different partitions lead to a hierarchy (pyramid) of histograms with increasingly coarser resolution. Based on this construction, no vectors share the same bin at the finest level of resolution while all vectors share the same bin at the coarsest level. Hence, any two feature vectors from any two sets begin to share a bin at some level in this histogram pyramid, and they are considered to be matched at this point. The distance between any two vectors can be bounded from above by the size of the bin in which they are matched. Thus the pyramid match algorithm can extract an approximate matching score between two sets of vectors without computing any of the pairwise similarities.

The original pyramid match algorithm proposed in [97] generates uniform bins over the feature space, and the size of the bin is doubled at each of the successive steps in the pyramid. Such a pre-determined construction fails to take advantage of the underlying structure in the feature space, and it suffers from distortion factors that increase linearly with the dimension of the features [98]. [98] proposed the vocabulary-guided pyramid match algorithm in which the positions and sizes of bins in the multi-resolution histograms are determined by applying the hierarchical clustering algorithm on the feature vectors. Each level in the hierarchical clustering corresponds to one level in the histogram pyramid, and the position and size of each bin at a particular level are determined by the clusters at that level. The weight for each match can also be made data-adaptive by estimating the inter-feature distance geometrically. It was shown that this data-dependent hierarchical decomposition scheme can maintain consistent accuracy when the dimension of the feature space increases [98].

The pyramid match algorithms proposed in [97–99] treat the sets of features to be matched as orderless. In some applications, the spatial layout of features within a set may convey critical discriminative information. [148] proposed the spatial pyramid matching algorithm to perform pyramid matching in the two-dimensional image space, thus taking the spatial information into account directly. The main idea of this approach is to quantize the local features in images into a number of discrete types by applying clustering algorithms, and then place a multi-resolution histogram pyramid on the two-dimensional images. It is also possible to integrate geometric information directly into the original pyramid match algorithm by adding the image coordinates as two additional dimensions into each feature vector [148], and we adopt this approach. Note that the original pyramid match algorithms are proposed to match two images; we extend them to match two sets of images.

8.8.3 Multi-Label Multiple Kernel Learning

In [126], a multi-label multiple kernel learning formulation based on a hypergraph for integrating the kernel matrices derived from various local descriptors is presented. The results in Section 8.8.5 show that the integrated kernels yield better performance than the best individual kernel.

We construct a hypergraph (for the collection of the gene expression patterns in question) in which each pattern is represented as a vertex. To document the joint similarity among patterns annotated with a common term, we construct a hyperedge for each term in the vocabulary, and include all patterns annotated with a common term into one hyperedge. Hence, the number of hyperedges in this hypergraph equals the number of terms in the vocabulary. Note that different definitions of the hypergraph Laplacian can be applied in hypergraph spectral learning. To learn from a hypergraph, one can either define the hypergraph Laplacian directly or expand it into a traditional graph for which a Laplacian is constructed. Since it has been shown that the Laplacians defined in both ways are similar [1], we use the expansion-based approaches.

The star and clique expansions are two commonly used schemes for expanding hypergraphs. Following spectral graph embedding theory [54], we project the patterns into a lower-dimensional space in which patterns sharing a common term are close to each other. Formally, we solve the optimization problem in Eq. (8.19).

We show in the following lemma that maximization of the objective function in Eq. (8.19) is equivalent to the minimization of an alternative criterion.

Lemma 8.2 *The kernel matrix that maximizes the objective function in Eq. (8.19) is also the minimizer of the following objective function:*

$$F_1(\mathbf{K}, \mathbf{B}) = \sum_{i=1}^{k} \left(\|\mathbf{K}\boldsymbol{\beta}_i - \mathbf{h}_i\|_2^2 + \lambda \boldsymbol{\beta}_i^T \mathbf{K} \boldsymbol{\beta}_i \right), \tag{8.37}$$

where $\mathbf{B} = (\boldsymbol{\beta}_1, \ldots, \boldsymbol{\beta}_k)$, $\mathbf{h}_i$ *is the ith column of* $\mathbf{H}$ *and* $\mathbf{H}\mathbf{H}^T = \mathbf{S}$.

The full proof of this theorem is given in Appendix A.5.

It follows from the theory of reproducing kernels [207] that the kernel $\mathbf{K}$ in Eq. (8.19) uniquely determines a mapping of the patterns to some feature space. Thus, kernel selection (learning) is one of the central issues in kernel methods. Following the multiple kernel learning framework [145], we obtain an optimal kernel matrix by integrating multiple kernel matrices constructed from various features, that is, $\mathbf{K} = \sum_{j=1}^{p} \theta_j \mathbf{K}_j$ where $\{\mathbf{K}_j\}_{j=1}^{p}$ are the p kernels constructed from various local descriptors and $\{\theta_j\}_{j=1}^{p}$ are the weights satisfying $\sum_{j=1}^{p} \theta_j \operatorname{Tr}(\mathbf{K}_j) = 1$. We show that the optimal weights that maximize the objective function in Eq. (8.19) can be obtained by solving a Semi-Infinite Linear Program (SILP) [112] in which a linear objective is optimized subject to an infinite number of linear constraints. This is summarized in the following theorem:

Theorem 8.3 *Given a set of p kernel matrices* $\mathbf{K}_1, \ldots, \mathbf{K}_p$, *the optimal kernel matrix, in the form of a linear combination of the given p kernel matrices that maximizes the objective function in Eq. (8.19), can be obtained by solving the following SILP problem:*

$$\max_{\boldsymbol{\theta}, \gamma} \quad \gamma \tag{8.38}$$

$$\text{s.t.} \quad \boldsymbol{\theta} \geq 0, \ \boldsymbol{\theta}^T \mathbf{r} = 1,$$

$$\sum_{j=1}^{p} \theta_j S_j(\boldsymbol{\Psi}) \geq \gamma, \quad \text{for all } \boldsymbol{\Psi} \in \mathbb{R}^{n \times k}, \tag{8.39}$$

where $S_j(\boldsymbol{\Psi})$, *for* $j = 1, \cdots, p$, *is defined as*

$$S_j(\boldsymbol{\Psi}) = \sum_{i=1}^{k} \left(\frac{r_j}{4} \boldsymbol{\psi}_i^T \boldsymbol{\psi}_i + \frac{1}{4\lambda} \boldsymbol{\psi}_i^T \mathbf{K}_j \boldsymbol{\psi}_i - r_j \boldsymbol{\psi}_i^T h_i \right), \tag{8.40}$$

$\boldsymbol{\Psi} = [\boldsymbol{\psi}_1, \ldots, \boldsymbol{\psi}_k]$, $\mathbf{r} = (r_1, \cdots, r_p)^T$, *and* $r_j = \operatorname{Tr}(\mathbf{K}_j)$.

The full proof of this theorem is given in Appendix A.5. Note that the matrix $\mathbf{S}$ obtained from standard clique and star expansions is symmetric and positive semidefinite, and the definitions of the matrix $\mathbf{H}$ for clique and star expansions are given in Section 4.3.3.

8.8.4   Empirical Evaluation Setup

We apply the framework discussed above for annotating gene expression patterns. We use a collection of images obtained from the FlyExpress database [242], which contains standardized and aligned images. All the images used are taken from the lateral view with the anterior to the left. The size of each raw image is 128×320 pixel.

We apply nine local descriptors on regular grids of two different sizes on each image. The nine local descriptors are SIFT, shape context, PCA-SIFT, spin image, steerable filters, differential invariants, complex filters, moment invariants, and cross correlation. These local descriptors are commonly used in objection recognition problems (more details can be found in [168]). The sizes of the grids we used are 16 and 32 pixels in radius and spacing (Figure 8.1), and 133 and 27 local features are produced for each image, respectively.

It is known that local textures are important discriminative features of gene expression pattern images, and features constructed from filter banks and raw pixel intensities are effective in capturing such information [243]. We therefore apply Gabor filters with different wavelet scales and filter orientations on each image to obtain global features of 384 and 2592 dimensions. We also sample the pixel values of each image using a bilinear technique, and obtain features of 10240, 2560, and 640 dimensions. The resulting features are called "global features".

After generating the features, we apply the vocabulary-guided pyramid match algorithm [98] to construct kernels between image sets. A total of 23 kernel matrices (2 grid sizes $\times$ 9 local descriptors + 2 Gabor + 3 pixel) are obtained. Then, the MKL formulation is employed to obtain the optimal integrated kernel matrix. The performance of kernel matrices (either single or integrated) is evaluated by applying the support vector machines for each term and treating image sets annotated with this term as positive, and all other image sets as negative. We extract different numbers of terms from the FlyExpress database and use various numbers of image sets annotated with the selected terms for the experiments.

Precision and recall are two commonly used criteria for evaluating the performance of multi-label classification systems [57]. For each term, let Π and Λ denote the indices of patterns that are annotated with this term by the framework discussed above and by human curators in BDGP, respectively. Then, precision P and recall R for this term are defined as

$$P = |\Pi \cap \Lambda|/|\Pi|$$
$$R = |\Pi \cap \Lambda|/|\Lambda|,$$

where $|\cdot|$ denotes the set cardinality. The F1 score is the harmonic mean of precision and recall as

$$F1 = \frac{2PR}{P+R}.$$

To measure performance across multiple terms, we use both the macro F1 (average of F1 across all terms) and the micro F1 (F1 computed from the sum of per-term contingency tables) scores, which are commonly used in text and image applications [57].

In each case, the entire data set is randomly partitioned into training and test sets with ratio 1:1. This process is repeated ten times, and the averaged performance is reported.

8.8.5   Annotation Results

We apply the formulations discussed above (star, clique, and kCCA) to combine various kernel matrices derived from different local descriptors. The performance of multiple kernel learning based on the soft margin 1-norm Support Vector Machine (SVM1) criterion proposed in [145] is also reported. Since the SVM1 formulation is only applicable to binary-class problems, we apply the formulation for each term by treating image sets annotated with this term as positive, and all other image sets as negative. To demonstrate the effectiveness of the multiple kernel learning formulation for integrating kernels, we also report results obtained by combining the candidate kernels with uniform weights, along with the performance of the best individual kernel (among the 23 kernels) for each data set. To compare with the existing method proposed in [284], we extract wavelet features from images and apply the min-redundancy max-relevance feature selection algorithm to select a subset of features. As was done in [284], we assign terms to individual images and apply linear discriminant analysis to annotate each image. Note that this setup does not consider image group information and is the same as the one proposed in [284]. The annotation results measured by F1 score, precision, and recall are summarized in Tables 8.1–8.4.

TABLE 8.1:   Performance of integrated kernels on gene expression pattern annotation in terms of macro F1 score.

# of terms	10			20			30		
# of sets	1000	1500	2000	1000	1500	2000	1000	1500	2000
Star	**0.5661**	**0.5741**	**0.5434**	0.4396	0.4903	0.4575	0.3852	0.4437	0.4162
Clique	0.5251	0.5220	0.4876	**0.4536**	**0.5125**	**0.4926**	**0.4065**	**0.4747**	**0.4563**
kCCA	0.5487	0.5608	0.5323	0.3987	0.4635	0.4477	0.3497	0.4240	0.4063
SVM1	0.4924	0.5413	0.5353	0.3780	0.4640	0.4356	0.3523	0.4352	0.4200
Uniform	0.4947	0.5498	0.5418	0.3727	0.4703	0.4480	0.3513	0.4410	0.4191
BIK	0.5418	0.5430	0.5185	0.4241	0.4515	0.4344	0.3782	0.4312	0.3996
Z&P	0.3756	0.3810	0.3775	0.2695	0.2759	0.2804	0.2086	0.2470	0.2379
# of terms	40			50			60		
# of sets	1000	1500	2000	1000	1500	2000	1000	1500	2000
Star	0.3768	0.4019	0.3927	0.3522	0.3850	0.3862	0.3219	0.3364	0.3426
Clique	**0.4145**	**0.4346**	**0.4283**	**0.3872**	**0.4106**	**0.4198**	**0.3594**	**0.3631**	**0.3639**
kCCA	0.3538	0.3872	0.3759	0.3303	0.3642	0.3666	0.2996	0.3137	0.3263
SVM1	0.3741	0.4048	0.3955	0.3481	0.3869	0.3991	0.3316	0.3462	0.3570
Uniform	0.3719	0.4111	0.3986	0.3436	0.3920	0.4023	0.3298	0.3548	0.3586
BIK	0.3914	0.3954	0.3827	0.3701	0.3849	0.3763	0.3456	0.3448	0.3419
Z&P	0.2117	0.2171	0.2310	0.1926	0.2284	0.2167	0.1764	0.1827	0.1679

TABLE 8.2: Performance of integrated kernels on gene expression pattern annotation in terms of micro F1 score.

# of terms	10			20			30		
# of sets	1000	1500	2000	1000	1500	2000	1000	1500	2000
Star	**0.5841**	**0.6011**	0.5728	0.4861	0.5199	0.4847	0.4472	0.4837	0.4473
Clique	0.5424	0.5429	0.5079	**0.5039**	**0.5422**	**0.5247**	**0.4682**	**0.5127**	**0.4894**
kCCA	0.5727	0.5922	0.5643	0.4581	0.4994	0.4887	0.4209	0.4737	0.4532
SVM1	0.5290	0.5781	0.5786	0.4361	0.5024	0.4844	0.4239	0.4844	0.4632
Uniform	0.5341	0.5870	**0.5837**	0.4390	0.5096	0.4975	0.4242	0.4939	0.4683
BIK	0.5585	0.5650	0.5637	0.4614	0.4735	0.4562	0.4189	0.4484	0.4178
Z&P	0.4031	0.4032	0.3796	0.3034	0.2985	0.2827	0.2612	0.2441	0.2125
# of terms	40			50			60		
# of sets	1000	1500	2000	1000	1500	2000	1000	1500	2000
Star	0.4277	0.4470	0.4305	0.4168	0.4347	0.4212	0.4000	0.4171	0.3999
Clique	**0.4610**	**0.4796**	**0.4660**	**0.4454**	**0.4546**	**0.4580**	**0.4314**	**0.4420**	**0.4251**
kCCA	0.4095	0.4420	0.4271	0.4000	0.4241	0.4086	0.3778	0.4042	0.3920
SVM1	0.4248	0.4570	0.4415	0.4095	0.4420	0.4429	0.3947	0.4234	0.4188
Uniform	0.4268	0.4673	0.4492	0.4092	0.4518	0.4482	0.3999	0.4358	0.4226
BIK	0.4100	0.4196	0.4009	0.3914	0.4051	0.3957	0.3869	0.3905	0.3781
Z&P	0.2406	0.2310	0.2203	0.2203	0.2174	0.2114	0.1977	0.1826	0.1586

TABLE 8.3: Performance of integrated kernels on gene expression pattern annotation in terms of precision.

# of terms	10			20			30		
# of sets	1000	1500	2000	1000	1500	2000	1000	1500	2000
Star	0.5246	0.5141	0.4861	0.4629	0.5349	0.4842	0.4674	0.5533	0.5089
Clique	0.4586	0.4375	0.3968	0.4531	0.5244	0.5053	0.4674	0.5510	0.5379
kCCA	0.5448	0.5443	0.5230	0.4917	0.5737	0.5585	0.5056	0.6120	0.6102
SVM1	0.5973	0.6163	0.5985	0.5387	0.6121	0.6211	0.5124	0.6323	0.6227
Uniform	**0.6258**	**0.6462**	**0.6155**	**0.5691**	**0.6417**	**0.6495**	**0.5379**	**0.6576**	**0.6450**
BIK	0.4956	0.4830	0.4687	0.4247	0.4994	0.4814	0.4265	0.5089	0.4779
Z&P	0.3298	0.3244	0.3182	0.2311	0.2455	0.2453	0.1897	0.2164	0.2106
# of terms	40			50			60		
# of sets	1000	1500	2000	1000	1500	2000	1000	1500	2000
Star	0.5122	0.5559	0.5510	0.4968	0.5611	0.5509	0.5256	0.5439	0.5614
Clique	0.5219	0.5502	0.5660	0.5078	0.5433	0.5831	0.5240	0.5501	0.5665
kCCA	0.5235	0.6116	0.6421	0.5124	0.6154	0.6139	0.5373	0.5894	0.6642
SVM1	0.5253	0.6151	0.6476	0.5196	0.6126	0.6429	0.5176	0.5628	0.6427
Uniform	**0.5596**	**0.6511**	**0.6766**	**0.5349**	**0.6504**	**0.6782**	**0.5625**	**0.5986**	**0.6717**
BIK	0.4626	0.5200	0.5299	0.4470	0.5093	0.5519	0.4744	0.5125	0.573
Z&P	0.1877	0.1958	0.2127	0.1765	0.2037	0.1976	0.1570	0.1627	0.1515

TABLE 8.4: Performance of integrated kernels on gene expression pattern annotation in terms of recall.

# of terms	10			20			30		
# of sets	1000	1500	2000	1000	1500	2000	1000	1500	2000
Star	0.6482	0.6892	0.6694	0.5019	0.5303	0.5117	0.4033	0.4535	0.4338
Clique	0.6331	0.6654	0.6527	0.5238	0.5649	0.5479	0.4284	0.4820	0.4636
kCCA	0.5952	0.6285	0.5966	0.4111	0.4483	0.4259	0.3292	0.3854	0.3603
SVM1	0.4890	0.5383	0.5211	0.3494	0.4237	0.3890	0.3178	0.3898	0.3665
Uniform	0.4830	0.5378	0.5198	0.3403	0.4219	0.3948	0.3098	0.3919	0.3626
BIK	**0.6625**	**0.6991**	**0.6954**	**0.5507**	0.5726	**0.5613**	**0.4648**	**0.5156**	**0.4983**
Z&P	0.4990	0.5504	0.5881	0.4242	0.3990	0.4460	0.2599	0.3869	0.3990

# of terms	40			50			60		
# of sets	1000	1500	2000	1000	1500	2000	1000	1500	2000
Star	0.3675	0.3901	0.3811	0.3346	0.3573	0.3606	0.2961	0.3124	0.3143
Clique	0.4075	0.4210	0.4063	0.3701	0.3808	0.3834	0.3336	0.3323	0.3244
kCCA	0.3171	0.3366	0.3174	0.2905	0.3075	0.3008	0.2575	0.2603	0.2597
SVM1	0.3322	0.3528	0.3300	0.3035	0.3300	0.3298	0.2844	0.2945	0.2878
Uniform	0.3218	0.3569	0.3285	0.2963	0.3325	0.3280	0.2789	0.3014	0.2873
BIK	**0.4555**	**0.4764**	**0.4767**	**0.4337**	0.4638	**0.4678**	**0.4158**	**0.4335**	**0.4374**
Z&P	0.3271	0.2985	0.3327	0.2783	0.3427	0.3107	0.2757	0.3023	0.3069

In this experiment, we first select a number of terms and then extract a certain number of image sets annotated with at least one of the selected terms. The numbers of terms used are 10, 20, 30, 40, 50, and 60, and the numbers of image sets used are 1000, 1500, and 2000 in each case. Tables 8.1–8.4 report the performance obtained by kernels combined with star expansion, clique expansion, and CCA. We also report the performance achieved by kernels combined with SVM1 in which an optimal kernel is learned for each term separately. To provide a baseline, we report the performance achieved by kernels combined from the candidate kernels with uniform weights. The performance of the Best Individual Kernel (BIK) over all local descriptors and grid sizes on the same data set is also reported. In addition, the results obtained by the method proposed in [284] are reported, and is denoted as Z&P in Tables 8.1–8.4. The performance shown in Tables 8.1–8.4 is the averaged scores over ten random partitions of the entire data set into training and test sets with ratio 1:1.

It can be observed from the results that in terms of both macro and micro F1 scores, the kernels integrated by either the star or clique expansion achieve the highest performance on all but one of the data sets. This shows that the kernel learning formulation is effective in combining multiple kernels and potentially exploiting the complementary information contained in different kernels. For all data sets, integrated kernels outperform the best individual kernel. In terms of precision and recall, our results indicate that SVM1 and Uniform achieve higher precision than the kernel learning formulations, while they both yield significantly lower recall. On the other hand, the best individual kernel produces slightly higher recall than the formulations, while it yields significantly lower precision. Note that precision and recall are two competing criteria, and one can always achieve a perfect score on one of them at the price of the other. Hence, the kernel learning formulation achieves a harmonic balance between precision and recall, as indicated by the F1 scores. Note that BIK can have both higher precision and higher recall than the formulation, since we report the highest precision and the highest recall among all of the candidate kernels separately. Hence, the BIK for precision and recall may not correspond to the same kernel. For all the four measures, the kernel learning formulations outperform the method proposed in [284] significantly. This shows that the annotation performance can be improved by considering the image group information.

Stage range		BDGP terms	Predicted terms
1–3		maternal	maternal
4–6		cellular blastoderm	cellular blastoderm
7–8		trunk mesoderm anlage anterior endoderm anlage posterior endoderm anlage head mesoderm anlage	trunk mesoderm anlage anterior endoderm anlage posterior endoderm anlage
9–10		trunk mesoderm primordium anterior endoderm primordium posterior endoderm primordium inclusive hindgut primordium	trunk mesoderm primordium anterior endoderm primordium posterior endoderm primordium
11–12		embryonic central brain glia lateral cord glia neuroblasts of ventral nervous system procephalic neuroblasts	embryonic central brain glia lateral cord glia neuroblasts of ventral nervous system procephalic neuroblasts embryonic central brain neuron lateral cord neuron
13–16		embryonic central nervous system ventral nerve cord embryonic central brain neuron lateral cord neuron ventral midline lateral cord glia embryonic central brain glia	embryonic central nervous system ventral nerve cord embryonic central brain neuron lateral cord neuron lateral cord glia embryonic central brain glia embryonic central brain

FIGURE 8.2: Annotation results for sample patterns in the six stage ranges. BDGP terms denote terms that are assigned by human curators in the Berkeley *Drosophila* Genome Project [231], and predicted terms denote terms predicted by the computational framework. These patterns are randomly sampled from each stage range, and hence they may not correspond to the same gene.

Figure 8.2 shows some annotation results obtained by clique expansion for sample patterns in each stage range. Note that the pyramid match algorithm can compute kernels between variable-sized sets of images. Thus, terms can be predicted for image sets of an arbitrary size. Overall, the computational framework achieves promising performance on annotating gene expression patterns. Meanwhile, we realize that the

FIGURE 8.3: The original five images in stage range 13-16 from BDGP. The first and the third images are taken from the lateral view; the second and the fourth images are taken from the ventral view; the fifth image is taken from the dorsal view. Only the first and the third images are used in our experiments shown in the bottom of Figure 8.2.

current framework suffers from some potential limitations. By comparing the BDGP terms and the predicted terms for patterns in stage ranges 7–8 and 9–10, we can see that the structures related to endoderm are predicted correctly while some of those related to mesoderm are prone to error. This may be due to the fact that, when viewed laterally, structures related to mesoderm are more prone to be hidden than those related to endoderm. This phenomenon becomes clearer when we examine the results for stage range 13–16 in Figures 8.2 and 8.3. As shown in Figure 8.3, there are a total of five images in this set in the original BDGP database. Among these five images, only two of them (the first and third) are taken from the lateral view and hence are used in our experiments. The second and the fourth images are taken from the ventral view, and the fifth image is taken from the dorsal view. The structure *ventral midline* can only be documented by digital images taken from the ventral view, as can be seen from the second and the fourth images in Figure 8.3. Since we only use images from the lateral view, it can be seen from Figure 8.2 that our framework cannot predict this term correctly. This problem can potentially be solved by using images taken from other views such as ventral and dorsal. However, incorporation of images with multiple views may complicate the computational procedure and so requires a special care.

To evaluate the scalability of the kernel learning formulations, we vary the number of terms and the number of image sets, and compare the computation time. When the number of terms is increased from 20 to 60 on a data set of 500 image sets, the computation time increases from approximately 4 seconds to 11 seconds. In terms of the number of image sets, data sets of 1500 and 2000 image sets with 60 terms take around 3 and 4 minutes, respectively.

Proofs

A.1 Proofs for Chapter 2

Proof of Theorem 2.1

Proof We use the superscript i to denote the variables at the ith iteration. For example, the data matrices $\mathbf{X}$ and $\mathbf{Y}$ at the ith iteration are denoted as $\mathbf{X}^{(i)}$ and $\mathbf{Y}^{(i)}$, respectively. It follows from Algorithm 2.2 that

$$
\begin{aligned}
\mathbf{X}^{(i+1)} &= \mathbf{X}^{(i)} - \mathbf{p}^{(i)} \mathbf{t}^{(i)T} \\
&= \mathbf{X}^{(i)} - \mathbf{X}^{(i)} \frac{\mathbf{t}^{(i)} \mathbf{t}^{(i)T}}{\mathbf{t}^{(i)T} \mathbf{t}^{(i)}} \\
&= \mathbf{X}^{(i)} - \mathbf{X}^{(i)} \frac{\mathbf{t}^{(i)} \mathbf{w}^{(i)T} \mathbf{X}^{(i)}}{\mathbf{t}^{(i)T} \mathbf{t}^{(i)}} \\
&= \left(\mathbf{I} - \mathbf{X}^{(i)} \frac{\mathbf{t}^{(i)} \mathbf{w}^{(i)T}}{\mathbf{t}^{(i)T} \mathbf{t}^{(i)}} \right) \mathbf{X}^{(i)} \\
&= \mathbf{B}^{(i)} \mathbf{X}^{(i)},
\end{aligned}
$$

where $\mathbf{B}^{(i)} = \mathbf{I} - \mathbf{X}^{(i)} \frac{\mathbf{t}^{(i)} \mathbf{w}^{(i)T}}{\mathbf{t}^{(i)T} \mathbf{t}^{(i)}}$. Without loss of generality, we assume that $i < j$. Thus, we have

$$
\begin{aligned}
\mathbf{X}^{(j)} &= \mathbf{B}^{(j-1)} \mathbf{X}^{(j-1)} \\
&= \mathbf{B}^{(j-1)} \mathbf{B}^{(j-2)} \mathbf{X}^{(j-2)} \\
&= \cdots \\
&= \mathbf{B}^{(j-1)} \cdots \mathbf{B}^{(i+1)} \mathbf{X}^{(i+1)} \\
&= \mathbf{Z} \mathbf{X}^{(i+1)},
\end{aligned}
$$

where $\mathbf{Z} = \mathbf{B}^{(j-1)} \cdots \mathbf{B}^{(i+1)}$. Then the inner product between $\mathbf{t}^{(i)}$ and $\mathbf{t}^{(j)}$ for $i \neq j$

can be computed as follows:

$$
\begin{aligned}
\mathbf{t}^{(i)^T}\mathbf{t}^{(j)} &= \mathbf{t}^{(i)^T}\mathbf{X}^{(j)^T}\mathbf{w}^{(j)} \\
&= \mathbf{t}^{(i)^T}\mathbf{X}^{(i+1)^T}\mathbf{Z}^T\mathbf{w}^{(j)} \\
&= \mathbf{t}^{(i)^T}\left(\mathbf{X}^{(i)} - \mathbf{p}^{(i)}\mathbf{t}^{(i)^T}\right)^T\mathbf{Z}^T\mathbf{w}^{(j)} \\
&= \mathbf{t}^{(i)^T}\left(\mathbf{X}^{(i)} - \mathbf{X}^{(i)}\frac{\mathbf{t}^{(i)}\mathbf{t}^{(i)^T}}{\mathbf{t}^{(i)^T}\mathbf{t}^{(i)}}\right)^T\mathbf{Z}^T\mathbf{w}^{(j)} \\
&= \mathbf{t}^{(i)^T}\left(\mathbf{I} - \frac{\mathbf{t}^{(i)}\mathbf{t}^{(i)^T}}{\mathbf{t}^{(i)^T}\mathbf{t}^{(i)}}\right)\mathbf{X}^{(i)^T}\mathbf{Z}^T\mathbf{w}^{(j)} \\
&= \left(\mathbf{t}^{(i)^T} - \mathbf{t}^{(i)^T}\frac{\mathbf{t}^{(i)}\mathbf{t}^{(i)^T}}{\mathbf{t}^{(i)^T}\mathbf{t}^{(i)}}\right)\mathbf{X}^{(i)^T}\mathbf{Z}^T\mathbf{w}^{(j)} \\
&= 0.
\end{aligned}
$$

Similarly, we can show that $\mathbf{u}^{(i)^T}\mathbf{u}^{(j)} = 0$ for $i \neq j$. ∎

Proof of Theorem 2.2

Proof Based on the matrix representation of $\mathbf{S}_s$ in Eq. (2.31), we can simplify $\mathrm{Tr}(\mathbf{S}_s\mathbf{S}_s^T)$ as

$$
\begin{aligned}
\mathrm{Tr}(\mathbf{S}_s\mathbf{S}_s^T) &= \mathrm{Tr}(\mathbf{U}_1\mathbf{\Sigma}^{-1}\mathbf{G}\mathbf{V}_1^T\mathbf{V}_1\mathbf{G}\mathbf{\Sigma}^{-1}\mathbf{U}_1^T) \\
&= \mathrm{Tr}(\mathbf{U}_1\mathbf{\Sigma}^{-2}\mathbf{G}^2\mathbf{U}_1^T) \\
&= \mathrm{Tr}(\mathbf{\Sigma}^{-2}\mathbf{G}^2) \\
&= \sum_{i=1}^{r}\frac{f(\sigma_i)^2}{\sigma_i^2}.
\end{aligned}
$$

Following Eq. (2.25), the variance of $\hat{\boldsymbol{\beta}}_s$ is

$$
\begin{aligned}
\mathrm{Tr}(\mathrm{var}(\hat{\boldsymbol{\beta}}_s)) &= \sigma^2\,\mathrm{Tr}(\mathbf{S}_s\mathbf{S}_s^T) \\
&= \sigma^2\sum_{i=1}^{r}\frac{f(\sigma_i)^2}{\sigma_i^2}.
\end{aligned}
$$

Next we analyze the squared bias of the estimator $\hat{\boldsymbol{\beta}}_s$:

$$
\begin{aligned}
\text{bias}^2(\hat{\boldsymbol{\beta}}_s) &= (\mathbb{E}[\hat{\boldsymbol{\beta}}_s] - \boldsymbol{\beta})^T(\mathbb{E}[\hat{\boldsymbol{\beta}}_s] - \boldsymbol{\beta}) \\
&= (\mathbf{S}_s\mathbf{X}^T\boldsymbol{\beta} - \boldsymbol{\beta})^T(\mathbf{S}_s\mathbf{X}^T\boldsymbol{\beta} - \boldsymbol{\beta}) \\
&= (\mathbf{U}_1\mathbf{G}\mathbf{U}_1^T\boldsymbol{\beta} - \boldsymbol{\beta})^T(\mathbf{U}_1\mathbf{G}\mathbf{U}_1^T\boldsymbol{\beta} - \boldsymbol{\beta}) \\
&= \boldsymbol{\beta}^T\mathbf{U}_1\mathbf{G}\mathbf{U}_1^T\mathbf{U}_1\mathbf{G}\mathbf{U}_1^T\boldsymbol{\beta} - 2\boldsymbol{\beta}^T\mathbf{U}_1\mathbf{G}\mathbf{U}_1^T\boldsymbol{\beta} + \boldsymbol{\beta}^T\boldsymbol{\beta} \\
&= \boldsymbol{\beta}^T\mathbf{U}_1\mathbf{G}^2\mathbf{U}_1^T\boldsymbol{\beta} - 2\boldsymbol{\beta}^T\mathbf{U}_1\mathbf{G}\mathbf{U}_1^T\boldsymbol{\beta} + \boldsymbol{\beta}^T[\mathbf{U}_1, \mathbf{U}_1^\perp][\mathbf{U}_1, \mathbf{U}_1^\perp]^T\boldsymbol{\beta} \\
&= \boldsymbol{\beta}^T\mathbf{U}_1\mathbf{G}^2\mathbf{U}_1^T\boldsymbol{\beta} - 2\boldsymbol{\beta}^T\mathbf{U}_1\mathbf{G}\mathbf{U}_1^T\boldsymbol{\beta} + \boldsymbol{\beta}^T\mathbf{U}_1\mathbf{U}_1^T\boldsymbol{\beta} + \boldsymbol{\beta}^T\mathbf{U}_1^\perp\mathbf{U}_1^{\perp^T}\boldsymbol{\beta} \\
&= \boldsymbol{\beta}^T\mathbf{U}_1(\mathbf{G}^2 - 2\mathbf{G} + \mathbf{I})\mathbf{U}_1^T\boldsymbol{\beta} + \boldsymbol{\beta}^T\mathbf{U}_1^\perp\mathbf{U}_1^{\perp^T}\boldsymbol{\beta} \\
&= \boldsymbol{\beta}^T\mathbf{U}_1(\mathbf{G} - \mathbf{I})^2\mathbf{U}_1^T\boldsymbol{\beta} + \boldsymbol{\beta}^T\mathbf{U}_1^\perp\mathbf{U}_1^{\perp^T}\boldsymbol{\beta} \\
&= \sum_{i=1}^{r}(f(\sigma_i) - 1)^2(\mathbf{u}_i^T\boldsymbol{\beta})^2 + \sum_{i=r+1}^{d}(\mathbf{u}_i^T\boldsymbol{\beta})^2.
\end{aligned}
$$

To summarize, the Mean Squared Error (MSE) of $\hat{\boldsymbol{\beta}}_s$ is

$$
\text{MSE}(\hat{\boldsymbol{\beta}}_s) = \sigma^2\sum_{i=1}^{r}\frac{f(\sigma_i)^2}{\sigma_i^2} + \sum_{i=1}^{r}(f(\sigma_i) - 1)^2(\mathbf{u}_i^T\boldsymbol{\beta})^2 + \sum_{i=r+1}^{d}(\mathbf{u}_i^T\boldsymbol{\beta})^2.
$$

Similarly, we can compute the variance and squared bias for the estimator $\hat{\mathbf{Y}}_s = \hat{\boldsymbol{\beta}}_s^T\mathbf{X} = \mathbf{Y}\mathbf{S}_s^T\mathbf{X}$. Note that $\text{Tr}(\mathbf{X}^T\mathbf{S}_s\mathbf{S}_s^T\mathbf{X})$ can be simplified as follows:

$$
\begin{aligned}
\text{Tr}(\mathbf{X}^T\mathbf{S}_s\mathbf{S}_s^T\mathbf{X}) &= \text{Tr}(\mathbf{V}_1\boldsymbol{\Sigma}\mathbf{U}_1^T\mathbf{U}_1\boldsymbol{\Sigma}^{-1}\mathbf{G}\mathbf{V}_1^T\mathbf{V}_1\mathbf{G}\boldsymbol{\Sigma}^{-1}\mathbf{U}_1^T\mathbf{U}_1\boldsymbol{\Sigma}\mathbf{V}_1^T) \\
&= \text{Tr}(\mathbf{V}_1\mathbf{G}^2\mathbf{V}_1^T) \\
&= \text{Tr}(\mathbf{G}^2\mathbf{V}_1^T\mathbf{V}_1) \\
&= \text{Tr}(\mathbf{G}^2) \\
&= \sum_{i=1}^{r}f(\sigma_i)^2.
\end{aligned}
$$

Thus, we can derive the variance of $\hat{\mathbf{Y}}_s$ using Eq. (2.25):

$$
\text{Tr}(\text{var}(\hat{\mathbf{Y}}_s)) = \sigma^2\,\text{Tr}(\mathbf{X}^T\mathbf{S}_s\mathbf{S}_s^T\mathbf{X}) = \sigma^2\sum_{i=1}^{r}f(\sigma_i)^2.
$$

The squared bias of $\hat{\mathbf{Y}}_s$ can be computed as follows:

$$
\begin{aligned}
\text{bias}^2(\hat{\mathbf{Y}}_s) &= (\boldsymbol{\beta}^T\mathbf{U}_1\mathbf{G}\boldsymbol{\Sigma}\mathbf{V}_1^T - \boldsymbol{\beta}^T\mathbf{X})(\boldsymbol{\beta}^T\mathbf{U}_1\mathbf{G}\boldsymbol{\Sigma}\mathbf{V}_1^T - \boldsymbol{\beta}^T\mathbf{X})^T \\
&= \boldsymbol{\beta}^T\mathbf{U}_1\mathbf{G}\boldsymbol{\Sigma}\mathbf{V}_1^T\mathbf{V}_1\boldsymbol{\Sigma}\mathbf{G}\mathbf{U}_1^T\boldsymbol{\beta} - 2\boldsymbol{\beta}^T\mathbf{U}_1\mathbf{G}\boldsymbol{\Sigma}\mathbf{V}_1^T\mathbf{X}^T\boldsymbol{\beta} + \boldsymbol{\beta}^T\mathbf{X}\mathbf{X}^T\boldsymbol{\beta} \\
&= \boldsymbol{\beta}^T\mathbf{U}_1\mathbf{G}^2\boldsymbol{\Sigma}^2\mathbf{U}_1^T\boldsymbol{\beta} - 2\boldsymbol{\beta}^T\mathbf{U}_1\mathbf{G}\boldsymbol{\Sigma}^2\mathbf{U}_1^T\boldsymbol{\beta} + \boldsymbol{\beta}^T\mathbf{U}_1\boldsymbol{\Sigma}^2\mathbf{U}_1^T\boldsymbol{\beta} \\
&= \boldsymbol{\beta}^T\mathbf{U}_1(\mathbf{G}^2\boldsymbol{\Sigma}^2 - 2\mathbf{G}\boldsymbol{\Sigma}^2 + \boldsymbol{\Sigma}^2)\mathbf{U}_1^T\boldsymbol{\beta} \\
&= \boldsymbol{\beta}^T\mathbf{U}_1\boldsymbol{\Sigma}^2(\mathbf{G} - \mathbf{I})^2\mathbf{U}_1^T\boldsymbol{\beta} \\
&= \sum_{i=1}^{r}\sigma_i^2(f(\sigma_i) - 1)^2(\mathbf{u}_i^T\boldsymbol{\beta})^2.
\end{aligned}
$$

Thus, the MSE of $\hat{\mathbf{Y}}_s$ is:

$$
\begin{aligned}
\mathrm{MSE}(\hat{\mathbf{Y}}_s) &= \mathrm{Tr}(\mathrm{var}(\hat{\mathbf{Y}}_s)) + \mathrm{bias}^2(\hat{\mathbf{Y}}_s) \\
&= \sigma^2 \sum_{i=1}^{r} f(\sigma_i)^2 + \sum_{i=1}^{r} \sigma_i^2 (f(\sigma_i) - 1)^2 (\mathbf{u}_i^T \boldsymbol{\beta})^2.
\end{aligned}
$$

This completes the proof of this theorem.   ∎

Proof of Theorem 2.6

Proof Denote $\mathbf{S}_Z = \mathbf{Z}\mathbf{Z}^T$. Then we can simplify $\mathbf{S}_Z$ as follows:

$$
\begin{aligned}
\mathbf{S}_Z &= \mathbf{Z}\mathbf{Z}^T \\
&= \mathbf{Z}_0 \mathbf{C}\mathbf{C}^T \mathbf{Z}_0^T \\
&= \mathbf{Z}_0 \mathbf{C}\mathbf{Z}_0 \\
&= \mathbf{Z}_0 \left(\mathbf{I} - \frac{1}{n}\mathbf{1}_n\mathbf{1}_n^T \right) \mathbf{Z}_0^T \\
&= \mathbf{Z}_0 \mathbf{Z}_0^T - \frac{1}{n}\mathbf{Z}_0 \mathbf{1}_n \mathbf{1}_n^T \mathbf{Z}_0^T \\
&= \begin{bmatrix} n_1 & 0 & \cdots & 0 \\ 0 & n_2 & \cdots & 0 \\ \vdots & \vdots & \ddots & \vdots \\ 0 & 0 & \cdots & n_{k-1} \end{bmatrix} - \frac{1}{n} \begin{bmatrix} n_1 \\ n_2 \\ \vdots \\ n_{k-1} \end{bmatrix} \begin{bmatrix} n_1 & n_2 & \cdots & n_{k-1} \end{bmatrix} \\
&= \mathbf{D} - \frac{1}{n}\mathbf{v}\mathbf{v}^T,
\end{aligned}
$$

where $\mathbf{D} = \mathrm{diag}\,(n_1, n_2, \ldots, n_{k-1}) \in \mathbb{R}^{(k-1)\times(k-1)}$ and $\mathbf{v} = [n_1, n_2, \ldots, n_{k-1}]^T \in \mathbb{R}^{k-1}$. Using the Sherman–Morrison–Woodbury formula [94], we can compute the inverse of $\mathbf{S}_Z$ as

$$
\begin{aligned}
\mathbf{S}_Z^{-1} &= \left(\mathbf{D} - \frac{1}{n}\mathbf{v}\mathbf{v}^T \right)^{-1} \\
&= \mathbf{D}^{-1} + \frac{1}{n - \mathbf{v}^T\mathbf{D}^{-1}\mathbf{v}} \left(\mathbf{D}^{-1}\mathbf{v}\mathbf{v}^T\mathbf{D}^{-1} \right) \\
&= \mathbf{D}^{-1} + \frac{1}{n - \sum_{i=1}^{k-1} n_i} \left(\mathbf{1}_{k-1}\mathbf{1}_{k-1}^T \right) \\
&= \mathbf{D}^{-1} + \frac{1}{n_k} \left(\mathbf{1}_{k-1}\mathbf{1}_{k-1}^T \right).
\end{aligned}
$$

It follows that

$$
\begin{aligned}
\mathbf{X}\mathbf{Z}_0^T &= [\mathbf{X}_1, \mathbf{X}_2, \ldots, \mathbf{X}_k]\,\mathbf{Z}_0 \\
&= \left[\mathbf{X}_1 \mathbf{1}_{n_1}, \mathbf{X}_2 \mathbf{1}_{n_2}, \ldots, \mathbf{X}_{k-1}\mathbf{1}_{n_{k-1}} \right] \\
&= [n_1\bar{\mathbf{x}}_1, n_2\bar{\mathbf{x}}_2, \ldots, n_{k-1}\bar{\mathbf{x}}_{k-1}].
\end{aligned}
$$

Therefore, we can rewrite $\mathbf{XZ}(\mathbf{ZZ}^T)^{-1}\mathbf{ZX}^T$ as follows:

$$
\begin{aligned}
\mathbf{XZ}^T(\mathbf{ZZ}^T)^{-1}\mathbf{ZX}^T &= \mathbf{XC}^T\mathbf{Z}_0^T\left(\mathbf{D}^{-1} + \frac{1}{n_k}\left(\mathbf{1}_{k-1}\mathbf{1}_{k-1}^T\right)\right)\mathbf{Z}_0\mathbf{CX}^T \\
&= \mathbf{XZ}_0^T\left(\mathbf{D}^{-1} + \frac{1}{n_k}\left(\mathbf{1}_{k-1}\mathbf{1}_{k-1}^T\right)\right)\mathbf{Z}_0\mathbf{X}^T \\
&= \mathbf{XZ}_0^T\mathbf{D}^{-1}\mathbf{Z}_0\mathbf{X}^T + \frac{1}{n_k}\mathbf{XZ}_0^T\mathbf{1}_{k-1}\mathbf{1}_{k-1}^T\mathbf{Z}_0\mathbf{X}^T \\
&= \sum_{i=1}^{k-1} n_i\bar{\mathbf{x}}_i\bar{\mathbf{x}}_i^T + \frac{1}{n_k}\sum_{i=1}^{k-1}n_i\bar{\mathbf{x}}_i\left(\sum_{i=1}^{k-1}n_i\bar{\mathbf{x}}_i\right)^T \\
&= \sum_{i=1}^{k-1} n_i\bar{\mathbf{x}}_i\bar{\mathbf{x}}_i^T + \frac{1}{n_k}(-n_k\bar{\mathbf{x}}_k)\left(-n_k\bar{\mathbf{x}}_k\right)^T \\
&= \sum_{i=1}^{k} n_i\bar{\mathbf{x}}_i\bar{\mathbf{x}}_i^T \\
&= \sum_{i=1}^{k} n_i(\bar{\mathbf{x}}_i - \bar{\mathbf{x}})(\bar{\mathbf{x}}_i - \bar{\mathbf{x}})^T \\
&= \mathbf{S}_b.
\end{aligned}
$$

In the above derivation we use the fact that $\sum_{i=1}^{k} n_i\bar{\mathbf{x}}_i = \sum_{i=1}^{n}\mathbf{x}_i = \mathbf{0}$, which implies that $\sum_{i=1}^{k-1} n_i\bar{\mathbf{x}}_i = -n_k\bar{\mathbf{x}}_k$. This completes the proof of this theorem. ∎

A.2 Proofs for Chapter 3

Proof of Lemma 3.1

Proof We can decompose $(\mathbf{XX}^T)^\dagger(\mathbf{XHH}^T\mathbf{X}^T)$ as follows:

$$
\begin{aligned}
(\mathbf{XX}^T)^\dagger(\mathbf{XHH}^T\mathbf{X}^T) &= \mathbf{U}_1\mathbf{\Sigma}_1^{-2}\mathbf{U}_1^T\mathbf{XHH}^T\mathbf{X}^T \\
&= \mathbf{U}_1\mathbf{\Sigma}_1^{-1}\mathbf{AH}^T\mathbf{V}_1\mathbf{\Sigma}_1\mathbf{U}_1^T \\
&= \mathbf{U}\begin{bmatrix}\mathbf{I}_r \\ \mathbf{0}\end{bmatrix}\mathbf{\Sigma}_1^{-1}\mathbf{AA}^T\mathbf{\Sigma}_1\begin{bmatrix}\mathbf{I}_r & \mathbf{0}\end{bmatrix}\mathbf{U}^T \\
&= \mathbf{U}\begin{bmatrix}\mathbf{\Sigma}_1^{-1}\mathbf{AA}^T\mathbf{\Sigma}_1 & \mathbf{0} \\ \mathbf{0} & \mathbf{0}\end{bmatrix}\mathbf{U}^T \\
&= \mathbf{U}\begin{bmatrix}\mathbf{\Sigma}_1^{-1}\mathbf{P} & \mathbf{0} \\ \mathbf{0} & \mathbf{I}\end{bmatrix}\begin{bmatrix}\mathbf{\Sigma}_A\mathbf{\Sigma}_A^T & \mathbf{0} \\ \mathbf{0} & \mathbf{0}\end{bmatrix}\begin{bmatrix}\mathbf{P}^T\mathbf{\Sigma}_1 & \mathbf{0} \\ \mathbf{0} & \mathbf{I}\end{bmatrix}\mathbf{U}^T,
\end{aligned}
$$

where the last equality follows from Eq. (3.32). Thus, the eigenvectors corresponding to the top ℓ eigenvalues of $(\mathbf{X}\mathbf{X}^T)^\dagger(\mathbf{X}\mathbf{H}\mathbf{H}^T\mathbf{X}^T)$ are given by

$$\mathbf{W} = \mathbf{U}_1\mathbf{\Sigma}_1^{-1}\mathbf{P}_\ell.$$

This completes the proof of the lemma.   ∎

Proof of Lemma 3.2

Proof Let the Singular Value Decomposition (SVD) of $\mathbf{Y}$ be

$$\mathbf{Y} = \mathbf{U}_y\mathbf{\Sigma}_y\mathbf{V}_y^T, \tag{A.41}$$

where $\mathbf{U}_y \in \mathbb{R}^{k\times k}$, $\mathbf{V}_y \in \mathbb{R}^{n\times k}$, and $\mathbf{\Sigma}_y \in \mathbb{R}^{k\times k}$ is diagonal. Since $\mathbf{Y}$ is assumed to have full column rank, all the diagonal elements of $\mathbf{\Sigma}_y$ are positive. Thus,

$$\begin{aligned}
\mathbf{A}_{cca} &= \mathbf{V}_1^T\mathbf{H}_{cca} = \mathbf{V}_1^T\mathbf{V}_y\mathbf{U}_y^T \\
\mathbf{A}_{pls} &= \mathbf{V}_1^T\mathbf{H}_{pls} = \mathbf{V}_1^T\mathbf{V}_y\mathbf{\Sigma}_y\mathbf{U}_y^T.
\end{aligned}$$

It follows that $\mathbf{A}_{cca} = \mathbf{A}_{pls}\mathbf{U}_y\mathbf{\Sigma}_y^{-1}\mathbf{U}_y^T$ and $\mathbf{A}_{pls} = \mathbf{A}_{cca}\mathbf{U}_y\mathbf{\Sigma}_y\mathbf{U}_y^T$. Thus, the range spaces of $\mathbf{A}_{cca}$ and $\mathbf{A}_{pls}$ are the same.   ∎

Proof of Lemma 3.3

Proof We can decompose $(\mathbf{X}\mathbf{X}^T + \gamma\mathbf{I})^{-1}(\mathbf{X}\mathbf{H}\mathbf{H}^T\mathbf{X}^T)$ as follows:

$$\begin{aligned}
&(\mathbf{X}\mathbf{X}^T + \gamma\mathbf{I})^{-1}(\mathbf{X}\mathbf{H}\mathbf{H}^T\mathbf{X}^T) \\
=\;& \mathbf{U}_1(\mathbf{\Sigma}_1^2 + \gamma\mathbf{I})^{-1}\mathbf{\Sigma}_1\mathbf{V}_1^T\mathbf{H}\mathbf{H}^T\mathbf{V}_1\mathbf{\Sigma}_1\mathbf{U}_1^T \\
=\;& \mathbf{U}_1(\mathbf{\Sigma}_1^2 + \gamma\mathbf{I})^{-1/2}(\mathbf{\Sigma}_1^2 + \gamma\mathbf{I})^{-1/2}\mathbf{\Sigma}_1\mathbf{V}_1^T\mathbf{H}\mathbf{H}^T \\
&\mathbf{V}_1\mathbf{\Sigma}_1(\mathbf{\Sigma}_1^2 + \gamma\mathbf{I})^{-1/2}(\mathbf{\Sigma}_1^2 + \gamma\mathbf{I})^{1/2}\mathbf{U}_1^T \\
=\;& \mathbf{U}_1(\mathbf{\Sigma}_1^2 + \gamma\mathbf{I})^{-1/2}\mathbf{B}\mathbf{B}^T(\mathbf{\Sigma}_1^2 + \gamma\mathbf{I})^{1/2}\mathbf{U}_1^T \\
=\;& \mathbf{U}\begin{bmatrix}\mathbf{I}_r \\ 0\end{bmatrix}(\mathbf{\Sigma}_1^2 + \gamma\mathbf{I})^{-1/2}\mathbf{B}\mathbf{B}^T(\mathbf{\Sigma}_1^2 + \gamma\mathbf{I})^{1/2}\begin{bmatrix}\mathbf{I}_r & 0\end{bmatrix}\mathbf{U}^T \\
=\;& \mathbf{U}\begin{bmatrix}(\mathbf{\Sigma}_1^2 + \gamma\mathbf{I})^{-1/2}\mathbf{B}\mathbf{B}^T(\mathbf{\Sigma}_1^2 + \gamma\mathbf{I})^{1/2} & 0 \\ 0 & 0\end{bmatrix}\mathbf{U}^T \\
=\;& \mathbf{U}\begin{bmatrix}(\mathbf{\Sigma}_1^2 + \gamma\mathbf{I})^{-1/2}\mathbf{P}_B & 0 \\ 0 & \mathbf{I}\end{bmatrix}\begin{bmatrix}\mathbf{\Sigma}_B\mathbf{\Sigma}_B^T & 0 \\ 0 & 0\end{bmatrix}\begin{bmatrix}\mathbf{P}_B^T(\mathbf{\Sigma}_1^2 + \gamma\mathbf{I})^{1/2} & 0 \\ 0 & \mathbf{I}\end{bmatrix}\mathbf{U}^T.
\end{aligned}$$

Thus, the eigenvectors corresponding to the top ℓ eigenvalues of $(\mathbf{X}\mathbf{X}^T + \gamma\mathbf{I})^{-1}(\mathbf{X}\mathbf{H}\mathbf{H}^T\mathbf{X}^T)$ are given by $\mathbf{U}_1(\mathbf{\Sigma}_1^2 + \gamma\mathbf{I})^{-1/2}\mathbf{P}_{B\ell}$.   ∎

Proof of Theorem 3.4

Proof First, we show that $\mathbf{A} = \mathbf{B}\mathbf{B}^\dagger\mathbf{A}$. Let the compact SVD of $\mathbf{B}$ be $\mathbf{B} = \mathbf{U}_B\mathbf{\Sigma}_B\mathbf{V}_B^T$, where $\mathbf{U}_B \in \mathbb{R}^{d\times r_B}$, $\mathbf{V}_B \in \mathbb{R}^{d\times r_B}$, $\mathbf{\Sigma}_B \in \mathbb{R}^{r_B\times r_B}$ is diagonal and $r_B = \mathrm{rank}(\mathbf{B})$. Thus, we have $\mathcal{R}(\mathbf{B}) = \mathcal{R}(\mathbf{U}_B)$. Since $\mathcal{R}(\mathbf{A}) \subseteq \mathcal{R}(\mathbf{B}) = \mathcal{R}(\mathbf{U}_B)$, there exists a matrix $\mathbf{R} \in \mathbb{R}^{r_B \times d}$ such that $\mathbf{A} = \mathbf{U}_B \mathbf{R}$. Thus, we have

$$
\begin{aligned}
\mathbf{BB}^\dagger \mathbf{A} &= \mathbf{BB}^\dagger \mathbf{U}_B \mathbf{R} \\
&= \mathbf{U}_B \mathbf{\Sigma}_B \mathbf{V}_B^T \mathbf{V}_B \mathbf{\Sigma}_B^{-1} \mathbf{U}_B^T \mathbf{U}_B \mathbf{R} \\
&= \mathbf{U}_B \mathbf{R} \\
&= \mathbf{A}.
\end{aligned}
$$

Note that we assume that $\mathbf{A}$ and $\mathbf{B}$ are symmetric. Thus, we have $\mathbf{A} = \mathbf{BB}^\dagger \mathbf{A} = \mathbf{AB}^\dagger \mathbf{B}$.

Suppose $(\lambda, \mathbf{w})(\lambda \neq 0)$ is an eigenpair of the eigenvalue problem $\mathbf{B}^\dagger \mathbf{Aw} = \lambda \mathbf{w}$; then we have

$$
\begin{aligned}
& \mathbf{B}^\dagger \mathbf{Aw} = \lambda \mathbf{w} \\
\Leftrightarrow\ & \mathbf{V}_B \mathbf{\Sigma}_B^{-1} \mathbf{U}_B^T \mathbf{U}_B \mathbf{Rw} = \lambda \mathbf{w} \\
\Rightarrow\ & \mathbf{Rw} = \lambda \mathbf{\Sigma}_B \mathbf{V}_B^T \mathbf{w} \\
\Rightarrow\ & \mathbf{U}_B \mathbf{Rw} = \lambda \mathbf{U}_B \mathbf{\Sigma}_B \mathbf{V}_B^T \mathbf{w} \\
\Leftrightarrow\ & \mathbf{Aw} = \lambda \mathbf{Bw},
\end{aligned}
$$

which implies that $(\lambda, \mathbf{w})$ is also an eigenpair of the generalized eigenvalue problem $\mathbf{Aw} = \lambda \mathbf{Bw}$.

Next we prove the second part of this theorem. Suppose $(\lambda, \mathbf{w})(\lambda \neq 0)$ is an eigenpair of the generalized eigenvalue problem $\mathbf{Aw} = \lambda \mathbf{Bw}$. Then we have

$$
\begin{aligned}
& \mathbf{Aw} = \lambda \mathbf{Bw} \\
\Rightarrow\ & \mathbf{AB}^\dagger \mathbf{Bw} = \lambda \mathbf{Bw} \\
\Rightarrow\ & \mathbf{B}^\dagger \mathbf{A} \left(\mathbf{B}^\dagger \mathbf{Bw} \right) = \lambda \mathbf{B}^\dagger \mathbf{Bw},
\end{aligned}
$$

which implies that $(\lambda, \mathbf{BB}^\dagger \mathbf{w})$ is also an eigenpair of the eigenvalue problem $\mathbf{B}^\dagger \mathbf{Aw} = \lambda \mathbf{w}$. Note that in the derivation we use the fact that $\mathbf{A} = \mathbf{AB}^\dagger \mathbf{B}$. This completes the proof of this theorem. ∎

A.3 Proofs for Chapter 4

Proof of Lemma 4.1

Proof Since $\mathbf{P}$ is a permutation matrix, we have $\mathbf{P}^T \mathbf{P} = \mathbf{PP}^T = \mathbf{I}_k$. Then $\mathbf{H}$ can be reformulated as follows:

$$
\begin{aligned}
\mathbf{H} &= \mathbf{H}(\mathbf{PP}^T) \\
&= \mathbf{QRP}^T.
\end{aligned}
$$

Hence, we have

$$
\begin{aligned}
\mathbf{1}^T \mathbf{S} \mathbf{1} &= \mathbf{1}^T \mathbf{H} \mathbf{H}^T \mathbf{1} \\
&= \mathbf{1}^T \mathbf{Q} \mathbf{R} \mathbf{P}^T \mathbf{P} \mathbf{R}^T \mathbf{Q}^T \mathbf{1} \\
&= \mathbf{1}^T \mathbf{Q} \mathbf{R} \mathbf{R}^T \mathbf{Q}^T \mathbf{1} \\
&= 0.
\end{aligned}
$$

Note that $\mathbf{R}\mathbf{R}^T$ is positive definite; therefore, we can conclude that $\mathbf{Q}^T \mathbf{1} = \mathbf{0}$. This completes the proof of this lemma. ∎

Proof of Lemma 4.2

Proof Since $\mathbf{A}^T \mathbf{1} = \mathbf{0}$ and $\mathbf{A}^T \mathbf{A} = \mathbf{I}_{m-1}$, we can construct the orthogonal matrix $\mathbf{A}_x$ as follows:

$$
\mathbf{A}_x = \left[\mathbf{A}, \frac{1}{\sqrt{m}} \mathbf{1} \right] \in \mathbb{R}^{m \times m}. \tag{A.42}
$$

Then we have

$$
\mathbf{I}_m = \mathbf{A}_x \mathbf{A}_x^T = \mathbf{A} \mathbf{A}^T + \frac{1}{m} \mathbf{1} \mathbf{1}^T \Leftrightarrow \mathbf{A} \mathbf{A}^T = \mathbf{I}_m - \frac{1}{m} \mathbf{1} \mathbf{1}^T.
$$

Since $\mathbf{B}^T \mathbf{1} = \mathbf{0}$ and $\mathbf{B}^T \mathbf{B} = \mathbf{I}_p$, we obtain that

$$
\begin{aligned}
\mathbf{F}^T \mathbf{F} &= \mathbf{B}^T \mathbf{A} \mathbf{A}^T \mathbf{B} \\
&= \mathbf{B}^T \left(\mathbf{I}_m - \frac{1}{m} \mathbf{1} \mathbf{1}^T \right) \mathbf{B} \\
&= \mathbf{B}^T \mathbf{B} - \frac{1}{m} (\mathbf{B}^T \mathbf{1})(\mathbf{B}^T \mathbf{1})^T \\
&= \mathbf{I}_p.
\end{aligned}
$$

This completes the proof of this lemma. ∎

A.4 Proofs for Chapter 6

Proof of Lemma 6.1

Proof The only term in Eq. (6.5) that depends on $\mathbf{V}$ is $\| \mathbf{U} - \mathbf{\Theta} \mathbf{V} \|_F^2$, which can be expressed equivalently as:

$$
\begin{aligned}
\| \mathbf{U} - \mathbf{\Theta} \mathbf{V} \|_F^2 &= \mathrm{Tr} \left((\mathbf{U}^T - \mathbf{V}^T \mathbf{\Theta}^T)(\mathbf{U} - \mathbf{\Theta} \mathbf{V}) \right) \tag{A.43} \\
&= \mathrm{Tr}(\mathbf{U}^T \mathbf{U} + \mathbf{V}^T \mathbf{\Theta}^T \mathbf{\Theta} \mathbf{V} - 2 \mathbf{U}^T \mathbf{\Theta} \mathbf{V}),
\end{aligned}
$$

where the property that $\| \mathbf{A} \|_F^2 = \mathrm{Tr}(\mathbf{A}^T \mathbf{A})$ for any matrix $\mathbf{A}$ has been used. The following equality can be obtained by taking the derivative of the expression in Eq. (A.43) with respect to $\mathbf{V}$, and setting it to zero:

$$2\mathbf{\Theta}^T\mathbf{\Theta}\mathbf{V}^* - 2\mathbf{\Theta}^T\mathbf{U} = 0 \quad \Rightarrow \quad \mathbf{V}^* = \mathbf{\Theta}^T\mathbf{U},$$

where $\mathbf{\Theta}^T\mathbf{\Theta} = \mathbf{I}$. This completes the proof of the lemma. ∎

Proof of Theorem 6.2

Proof Consider the term $\|\mathbf{U} - \mathbf{\Theta}\mathbf{V}\|_F^2$ in Eq. (6.5), which can be expressed in the feature space as

$$\mathrm{Tr}(\mathbf{A}^T\mathbf{K}\mathbf{A} + \mathbf{V}^T\mathbf{B}^T\mathbf{K}\mathbf{B}\mathbf{V} - 2\mathbf{A}^T\mathbf{K}\mathbf{B}\mathbf{V}). \tag{A.44}$$

Taking the derivative of the expression in Eq. (A.44) with respect to $\mathbf{V}$, and setting it to zero, we obtain

$$\mathbf{V} = \mathbf{B}^T\mathbf{K}\mathbf{A}, \tag{A.45}$$

where the property that $\mathbf{B}^T\mathbf{K}\mathbf{B} = \mathbf{I}$ has been used. Substituting this expression for $\mathbf{V}$ into Eq. (6.5), and expressing all terms in the feature space, the following optimization problem with respect to $\mathbf{A}$ and $\mathbf{B}$ can be obtained:

$$\min_{\mathbf{A},\mathbf{B}} \quad \frac{1}{n}\left\|\mathbf{A}^T\mathbf{K} - \mathbf{Y}\right\|_F^2 + \mathrm{Tr}\left(\mathbf{A}^T\left((\alpha + \beta)\mathbf{K} - \alpha\mathbf{K}\mathbf{B}\mathbf{B}^T\mathbf{K}\right)\mathbf{A}\right)$$
$$\text{s.t.} \quad \mathbf{B}^T\mathbf{K}\mathbf{B} = \mathbf{I}. \tag{A.46}$$

Taking the derivative of the objective function in Eq. (A.46) with respect to $\mathbf{A}$, and setting it to zero, the following expression for $\mathbf{A}$ can be obtained:

$$\mathbf{A} = \frac{1}{n}(\mathbf{N} - \alpha\mathbf{K}\mathbf{B}\mathbf{B}^T\mathbf{L})^{-1}\mathbf{K}\mathbf{Y}^T, \tag{A.47}$$

where $\mathbf{N}$ is defined in Eq. (6.30). Substituting this expression for $\mathbf{A}$ into the objective function in Eq. (A.46), the following optimization problem with respect to $\mathbf{B}$ is obtained:

$$\max_{\mathbf{B}} \quad \frac{1}{n^2}\mathrm{Tr}\left(\mathbf{Y}\mathbf{K}\left(\mathbf{N} - \alpha\mathbf{K}\mathbf{B}\mathbf{B}^T\mathbf{K}\right)^{-1}\mathbf{K}\mathbf{Y}^T\right)$$
$$\text{s.t.} \quad \mathbf{B}^T\mathbf{K}\mathbf{B} = \mathbf{I}. \tag{A.48}$$

It follows from the Sherman–Morrison–Woodbury formula in Eq. (6.14) that

$$\left(\mathbf{N} - \alpha\mathbf{K}\mathbf{B}\mathbf{B}^T\mathbf{K}\right)^{-1}$$
$$= \mathbf{N}^{-1} + \alpha\mathbf{N}^{-1}\mathbf{K}\mathbf{B}\left(\mathbf{B}^T(\mathbf{K} - \alpha\mathbf{K}\mathbf{N}^{-1}\mathbf{K})\mathbf{B}\right)^{-1}\mathbf{B}^T\mathbf{K}\mathbf{N}^{-1}.$$

This theorem can be proved by noticing the definitions of $\tilde{\mathbf{S}}_1$ and $\tilde{\mathbf{S}}_2$ in Eqs. (6.31) and (6.32), respectively. ∎

A.5   Proofs for Chapter 8

Proof of Lemma 8.2

Proof Since the null space of $\mathbf{K}^2 + \lambda\mathbf{K}$ lies in the null space of $\mathbf{KSK}$, the optimal value achieved by the optimization problem in Eq. (8.19) is given by $\mathrm{Tr}\left((\mathbf{K}^2 + \lambda\mathbf{K})^+\mathbf{KSK}\right)$. Consider the maximization of the following objective function with respect to $\mathbf{B}$:

$$F_2(\mathbf{K}, \mathbf{B}) = \sum_{i=1}^{k} \frac{\left(\boldsymbol{\beta}_i^T \mathbf{K}\mathbf{h}_i\right)^2}{\boldsymbol{\beta}_i^T \left(\mathbf{K}^2 + \lambda\mathbf{K}\right)\boldsymbol{\beta}_i}. \tag{A.49}$$

The optimal $\boldsymbol{\beta}_i$ is given by $\boldsymbol{\beta}_i^* = (\mathbf{K}^2 + \lambda\mathbf{K})^\dagger\mathbf{K}\mathbf{h}_i$. Thus the maximum value of $F_2(\mathbf{B}, \mathbf{K})$ achieved by $\mathbf{B}^* = [\boldsymbol{\beta}_1^*, \dots, \boldsymbol{\beta}_k^*]$ is given by $F_2^*(\mathbf{K}) = \mathrm{Tr}\left((\mathbf{K}^2 + \lambda\mathbf{K})^+\mathbf{KSK}\right)$. This shows that, when optimized with respect to $\mathbf{B}$, the objective functions in Eqs. (8.19) and (A.49) achieve the same value.

We next show the equivalence between the objective functions in Eqs. (8.37) and (A.49). The objective function $F_1(\mathbf{K}, \mathbf{B})$ in Eq. (8.37) is the sum-of-squares error function in the kernel-induced feature space, and its optimal value is

$$F_1^*(\mathbf{K}) = -\sum_{i=1}^{k} (\mathbf{K}\mathbf{h}_i)^T(\mathbf{K}^2 + \lambda\mathbf{K})^+\mathbf{K}\mathbf{h}_i + \mathbf{h}_i^T\mathbf{h}_i. \tag{A.50}$$

Thus maximizing $\sum_{i=1}^{k} (\mathbf{K}\mathbf{h}_i)^T(\mathbf{K}^2 + \lambda\mathbf{K})^+\mathbf{K}\mathbf{h}_i$ with respect to $\mathbf{K}$ is equivalent to minimizing $F_1^*(\mathbf{K})$. This completes the proof. ∎

Proof of Theorem 8.3

Proof Let $\boldsymbol{\xi}_i = \mathbf{K}\boldsymbol{\beta}_i - \mathbf{h}_i$. Define the Lagrangian function for the optimization problem in Eq. (8.37) as follows:

$$L = \sum_{i=1}^{k} \|\boldsymbol{\xi}_i\|_2^2 + \lambda \sum_{i=1}^{k} \boldsymbol{\beta}_i^T \mathbf{K}\boldsymbol{\beta}_i - \sum_{i=1}^{k} \boldsymbol{\psi}_i^T (\mathbf{K}\boldsymbol{\beta}_i - h_i - \boldsymbol{\xi}_i), \tag{A.51}$$

where the $\boldsymbol{\psi}_i$'s are the vectors of Lagrangian dual variables. By following the standard Lagrangian technique, we get the Lagrangian dual function as

$$g(\boldsymbol{\psi}_1, \dots, \boldsymbol{\psi}_k) = \sum_{i=1}^{k} \left(-\frac{1}{4}\boldsymbol{\psi}_i^T\left(\mathbf{I} + \frac{1}{\lambda}\mathbf{K}\right)\boldsymbol{\psi}_i + \boldsymbol{\Psi}^T\mathbf{h}_i\right). \tag{A.52}$$

The optimal $\boldsymbol{\psi}_1^*, \dots, \boldsymbol{\psi}_k^*$ can be obtained by maximizing the dual function. Since strong duality holds, the primal and dual objectives coincide and the optimal $\mathbf{K}$ can be computed by solving the following optimization problem:

$$\min_{\boldsymbol{\theta}: \boldsymbol{\theta} \geq 0, \boldsymbol{\theta}^T r=1} \quad \max_{\boldsymbol{\psi}_1, \dots, \boldsymbol{\psi}_k} \left\{ \sum_{i=1}^{k} \left(-\frac{1}{4}\boldsymbol{\psi}_i^T\left(\mathbf{I} + \frac{1}{\lambda}\sum_{j=1}^{p} \theta_j\mathbf{K}_j\right)\boldsymbol{\psi}_i + \boldsymbol{\psi}_i^T\mathbf{h}_i\right)\right\}.$$

Since $\sum_{j=1}^{p} \theta_j r_j = 1$, the above objective function can be expressed as

$$\sum_{j=1}^{p} \theta_j \sum_{i=1}^{k} \left(-\frac{r_j}{4} \psi_i^T \psi_i - \frac{1}{4\lambda} \psi_i^T \mathbf{K}_j \psi_i + r_j \psi_i^T \mathbf{h}_i \right).$$

Thus it follows from the definition of $S_j(\mathbf{\Psi})$ in Eq. (8.40) that the optimization problem in Eq. (A.5) can be expressed equivalently as

$$\max_{\boldsymbol{\theta}:\boldsymbol{\theta}\geq 0, \boldsymbol{\theta}^T \mathbf{r}=1} \quad \min_{\mathbf{\Psi}} \sum_{j=1}^{p} \theta_j S_j(\mathbf{\Psi}). \qquad (A.53)$$

Assume $\mathbf{\Psi}^*$ is the optimal solution to the problem in Eq. (A.53), and define $\gamma^* = \sum_{j=1}^{p} \theta_j S_j(\mathbf{\Psi}^*)$ as the minimum value. We have $\sum_{j=1}^{p} \theta_j S_j(\mathbf{\Psi}) \geq \gamma^*$ for all $\mathbf{\Psi}$. By defining $\gamma = \min_{\mathbf{\Psi}} \sum_{j=1}^{p} \theta_j S_j(\mathbf{\Psi})$ and substituting γ into the objective function, we prove this theorem. ∎

References

[1] S. Agarwal, K. Branson, and S. Belongie. Higher order learning with graphs. In *Proceedings of the 23rd International Conference on Machine Learning (ICML)*, pages 17–24, 2006.

[2] G.E. Alexander and E.M. Reiman. *The Dementias: Diagnosis, Treatment and Research*, chapter Neuroimaging. American Psychiatric Pub, Washington, DC, 3rd edition, 2003.

[3] Y. Amit, M. Fink, N. Srebro, and S. Ullman. Uncovering shared structures in multiclass classification. In *Proceedings of the 24th International Conference on Machine Learning (ICML)*, pages 17–24, 2007.

[4] E.D. Andersen and K.D. Andersen. The Mosek interior point optimizer for linear programming: An implementation of the homogeneous algorithm. In H. Frenk, K. Roos, T. Terlaky, and S. Zhang, editors, *High Performance Optimization*, volume 33 of *Applied Optimization*, pages 197–232. Springer, 2000.

[5] R.K. Ando and T. Zhang. A framework for learning predictive structures from multiple tasks and unlabeled data. *Journal of Machine Learning Research*, 6:1817–1853, 2005.

[6] M.N. Arbeitman, E.E. Furlong, F. Imam, E. Johnson, B.H. Null, B.S. Baker, M.A. Krasnow, M.P. Scott, R.W. Davis, and K.P. White. Gene expression during the life cycle of *Drosophila melanogaster*. *Science*, 297(5590):2270–2275, 2002.

[7] J. Arenas-García and G. Camps-Valls. Efficient kernel orthonormalized PLS for remote sensing applications. *IEEE Transactions on Geoscience and Remote Sensing*, 46(10):2872–2881, 2008.

[8] J. Arenas-García, K.B. Petersen, and L.K. Hansen. Sparse kernel orthonormalized PLS for feature extraction in large data sets. In *Advances in Neural Information Processing Systems 19 (NIPS)*, pages 33–40. 2007.

[9] A. Argyriou, T. Evgeniou, and M. Pontil. Convex multi-task feature learning. *Machine Learning*, 73(3):243–272, 2008.

[10] A. Argyriou, A. Maurer, and M. Pontil. An algorithm for transfer learning in a heterogeneous environment. In W. Daelemans, B. Goethals, and K. Morik, editors, *Machine Learning and Knowledge Discovery in Databases*, volume 5211, pages 71–85. Springer, 2008.

[11] F.R. Bach and M. Jordan. Kernel independent component analysis. *Journal of Machine Learning Research*, 3:1–48, 2003.

[12] F.R. Bach and M. Jordan. A probabilistic interpretation of canonical correlation analysis. Technical report, University of California, Berkeley, 2005.

[13] K. Bache and M. Lichman. UCI machine learning repository, 2013.

[14] B. Bakker and T. Heskes. Task clustering and gating for Bayesian multitask learning. *Journal of Machine Learning Research*, 4:83–99, 2003.

[15] M. Balasubramanian, E.L. Schwartz, J.B. Tenenbaum, V. de Silva, and J.C. Langford. The Isomap algorithm and topological stability. *Science*, 295(5552):7a, 2002.

[16] M. Barker and W. Rayens. Partial least squares for discrimination. *Journal of Chemometrics*, 17(3):166–173, 2003.

[17] C. Bartenhagen, H.-U. Klein, C. Ruckert, X. Jiang, and M. Dugas. Comparative study of unsupervised dimension reduction techniques for the visualization of microarray gene expression data. *BMC Bioinformatics*, 11(1):567, 2010.

[18] M.S. Bartlett. Further aspects of the theory of multiple regression. *Mathematical Proceedings of the Cambridge Philosophical Society*, 34(1):33–40, 1938.

[19] M. Belkin and P. Niyogi. Laplacian eigenmaps and spectral techniques for embedding and clustering. In *Advances in Neural Information Processing Systems 13 (NIPS)*, pages 585–591, 2001.

[20] M. Belkin and P. Niyogi. Laplacian eigenmaps for dimensionality reduction and data representation. *Neural Computation*, 15(6):1373–1396, 2003.

[21] R.E. Bellman. *Adaptive Control Processes: A Guided Tour*. Princeton Universsity Press, Princeton, NJ, 1961.

[22] A. Ben-Tal and A. Nemirovski. Non-Euclidean restricted memory level method for large-scale convex optimization. *Mathematical Programming*, 102(3):407–56, 2005.

[23] C. Berge. *Graphs and Hypergraphs*. Elsevier, New York, 1973.

[24] C. Berge. *Hypergraphs: The Theory of Finite Sets*. North-Holland, Amsterdam, 1989.

[25] P. Berntsson and S. Wold. Comparison between X-ray crystallographic data and physicochemical parameters with respect to their information about the calcium channel antagonist activity of 4-phenyl-1,4-dihydropyridines. *Quantitative Structure-Activity Relationships*, 5(2):45–50, 1986.

[26] C.M. Bishop. *Pattern Recognition and Machine Learning.* Springer, New York, 2006.

[27] D.M. Blei, A. Ng, and M. Jordan. Latent Dirichlet allocation. *Journal of Machine Learning Research*, 3:993–1022, 2003.

[28] H. Blockeel, L. Schietgat, J. Struyf, S. Dzeroski, and A. Clare. Decision trees for hierarchical multilabel classification: A case study in functional genomics. In J. Frnkranz, T. Scheffer, and M. Spiliopoulou, editors, *Knowledge Discovery in Databases*, volume 4213, pages 18–29. Springer, 2006.

[29] M. Bolla. Spectra, Euclidean representations and clusterings of hypergraphs. *Discrete Mathematics*, 117(1-3):19–39, 1993.

[30] M. Borga, T. Landelius, and H. Knutsson. A unified approach to PCA, PLS, MLR and CCA. Technical report, Computer Vision Laboratory, Linköping University, Linköping, Sweden, 1997.

[31] A.-L. Boulesteix. PLS dimension reduction for classification with microarray data. *Statistical Applications in Genetics and Molecular Biology*, 3(1):33, 2004.

[32] A.-L. Boulesteix and K. Strimmer. Predicting transcription factor activities from combined analysis of microarray and chip data: A partial least squares approach. *Theoretical Biology and Medical Modelling*, 2(1):23, 2005.

[33] A.-L. Boulesteix and K. Strimmer. Partial least squares: A versatile tool for the analysis of high-dimensional genomic data. *Briefings in Bioinformatics*, 8(1):32–44, 2007.

[34] M.R. Boutell, J. Luo, X. Shen, and C.M. Brown. Learning multi-label scene classification. *Pattern Recognition*, 37(9):1757–1771, 2004.

[35] S. Boyd and L. Vandenberghe. *Convex Optimization.* Cambridge University Press, Cambridge, UK, 2004.

[36] R. Briandet, E.K. Kemsley, and R.H. Wilson. Discrimination of arabica and robusta in instant coffee by Fourier transform infrared spectroscopy and chemometrics. *Journal of Agricultural and Food Chemistry*, 44(1):170–174, 1996.

[37] K. Brinker, J. Fürnkranz, and E. Hüllermeier. A unified model for multilabel classification and ranking. In *Proceedings of the 17th European Conference on Artificial Intelligence (ECAI)*, pages 489–493, 2006.

[38] M.P.S. Brown, W.N. Grundy, D. Lin, N. Cristianini, C.W. Sugnet, T.S. Furey, M. Ares, and D. Haussler. Knowledge-based analysis of microarray gene expression data by using support vector machines. *Proceedings of the National Academy of Sciences*, 97(1):262–267, 2000.

[39] C. Burges. Geometric methods for feature extraction and dimensional reduction–A guided tour. In *Data Mining and Knowledge Discovery Handbook*, pages 59–92. Springer, New York, 2005.

[40] N.A. Butler and M.C. Denham. The peculiar shrinkage properties of partial least squares regression. *Journal of the Royal Statistical Society: Series B*, 62(3):585–593, 2000.

[41] D. Cai, X. He, and J. Han. SRDA: An efficient algorithm for large-scale discriminant analysis. *IEEE Transactions on Knowledge and Data Engineering*, 20(1):1–12, 2008.

[42] J.A. Campos-Ortega and V. Hartenstein. *The Embryonic Development of Drosophila melanogaster*. Springer, New York, 2nd edition, 1997.

[43] E. Candès. Compressive sampling. In *International Congress of Mathematics*, number 3, pages 1433–1452, Madrid, Spain, 2006.

[44] K. Cao, D. Rossouw, C. Robert-Grani, and P. Besse. A sparse PLS for variable selection when integrating omics data. *Statistical Applications in Genetics and Molecular Biology*, 7(1):35, 2008.

[45] M.A. Carreira-Perpinan. *Continuous latent variable models for dimensionality reduction and sequential data reconstruction*. PhD thesis, University of Sheffield, Sheffield, UK, 2001.

[46] J.P. Carson, T. Ju, H.C. Lu, C. Thaller, M. Xu, S.L. Pallas, M.C. Crair, J. Warren, W. Chiu, and G. Eichele. A digital atlas to characterize the mouse brain transcriptome. *PLoS Computational Biology*, 1(4):e41, 2005.

[47] C.-C. Chang and C.-J. Lin. LIBSVM: A library for support vector machines. *ACM Transactions on Intelligent Systems and Technology*, 2(3):27:1–27:27, 2011.

[48] O. Chapelle, B. Schölkopf, and A. Zien. *Semi-Supervised Learning*. The MIT Press, Cambridge, MA, 2006.

[49] Y. Chen and J.Z. Wang. Image categorization by learning and reasoning with regions. *Journal of Machine Learning Research*, 5:913–939, 2004.

[50] W. Cheng and E. Hüllermeier. Combining instance-based learning and logistic regression for multilabel classification. *Machine Learning*, 76(2-3):211–225, 2009.

[51] H. Chun and S. Keles. Expression quantitative trait loci mapping with multivariate sparse partial least squares regression. *Genetics*, 182(1):79–90, 2009.

[52] H. Chun and S. Keles. Sparse partial least squares regression for simultaneous dimension reduction and variable selection. *Journal of the Royal Statistical Society: Series B*, 72(1):3–25, 2010.

[53] F. Chung. *Expanding Graphs*, volume 10, chapter The Laplacian of a hypergraph, pages 21–36. American Mathematical Society, Providence, RI, 1993.

[54] F. Chung. *Spectral Graph Theory*. American Mathematical Society, Providence, RI, 1997.

[55] A. Clare and R.D. King. Knowledge discovery in multi-label phenotype data. In L. Raedt and A. Siebes, editors, *Principles of Data Mining and Knowledge Discovery*, volume 2168, pages 42–53. Springer, 2001.

[56] T.F. Cox and M.A.A. Cox. *Multidimensional Scaling*. Chapman and Hall/CRC, Boca Raton, FL, 2nd edition, 2000.

[57] R. Datta, D. Joshi, J. Li, and J.Z. Wang. Image retrieval: Ideas, influences, and trends of the new age. *ACM Computing Surveys*, 40:5:1–5:60, 2008.

[58] T. De Bie, N. Cristianini, and R. Rosipal. *Handbook of Computational Geometry for Pattern Recognition, Computer Vision, Neurocomputing and Robotics*, chapter Eigenproblems in Pattern Recognition. Springer-Verlag, New York, 2005.

[59] T. De Bie, L.-C. Tranchevent, L.M.M. van Oeffelen, and Y. Moreau. Kernel-based data fusion for gene prioritization. *Bioinformatics*, 23(13):i125–132, 2007.

[60] S. De Jong. SIMPLS: An alternative approach to partial least squares regression. *Chemometrics and Intelligent Laboratory Systems*, 18(3):251–263, 1993.

[61] S. De Jong. PLS shrinks. *Journal of Chemometrics*, 9(4):323–326, 1995.

[62] S.C. Deerwester, S.T. Dumais, T.K. Landauer, G.W. Furnas, and R.A. Harshman. Indexing by latent semantic analysis. *Journal of the American Society of Information Science*, 41:391–407, 1990.

[63] S.R. Delwiche, Y. Chen, and W.R. Hruschka. Differentiation of hard red wheat by near-infrared analysis of bulk samples. *Cereal Chemistry*, 72(3):243–247, 1995.

[64] K. Dembczynski, W. Cheng, and E. Hüllermeier. Bayes optimal multilabel classification via probabilistic classifier chains. In *Proceedings of the 27th International Conference on Machine Learning (ICML)*, pages 279–286, 2010.

[65] T.G. Dietterich, R.H. Lathrop, and T. Lozano-Pérez. Solving the multiple instance problem with axis-parallel rectangles. *Artificial Intellegence*, 89(1-2):31–71, 1997.

[66] D.L. Donoho. High-dimensional data analysis: the curses and blessings of dimensionality. In *American Mathematical Society Conference on Mathematical Challenges of the 21st Century*. 2000.

[67] D.L. Donoho. Compressed sensing. *IEEE Transactions on Information Theory*, 52(4):1289–1306, 2006.

[68] D.L. Donoho. For most large underdetermined systems of linear equations, the minimal 11-norm near-solution approximates the sparsest near-solution. *Communications on Pure and Applied Mathematics*, 59(7):907–934, 2006.

[69] D.L. Donoho and C. Grimes. Hessian eigenmaps: Locally linear embedding techniques for high-dimensional data. *Proceedings of the National Academy of Sciences*, 100(10):5591–5596, 2003.

[70] R. Durbin, S.R. Eddy, A. Krogh, and G. Mitchison. *Biological Sequence Analysis: Probabilistic Models of Proteins and Nucleic Acids*. Cambridge University Press, Cambridge, UK, 1999.

[71] B. Efron, T. Hastie, I. Johnstone, and R. Tibshirani. Least angle regression. *Annals of Statistics*, 32:407, 2004.

[72] A. Efros, V. Isler, J. Shi, and M. Visontai. Seeing through water. In *Advances in Neural Information Processing Systems 17 (NIPS)*, pages 393–400, 2004.

[73] A. Elgammal and C.-S. Lee. Separating style and content on a nonlinear manifold. In *Proceedings of the 2004 IEEE Computer Society Conference on Computer Vision and Pattern Recognition (CVPR)*, volume 1, pages 478–485, 2004.

[74] A. Elisseeff and J. Weston. A kernel method for multi-labeled classification. In *Advances in Neural Information Processing Systems 14 (NIPS)*, pages 681–687, 2001.

[75] B. Estrada, S.E. Choe, S.S. Gisselbrecht, S. Michaud, L. Raj, B.W. Busser, M.S. Halfon, G.M. Church, and A.M. Michelson. An integrated strategy for analyzing the unique developmental programs of different myoblast subtypes. *PLoS Genetics*, 2(2):e16, 2006.

[76] A. Esuli, T. Fagni, and F. Sebastiani. Boosting multi-label hierarchical text categorization. *Information Retrieval*, 11:287–313, 2008.

[77] R.-E. Fan and C.-J. Lin. A study on threshold selection for multi-label classification. Technical report, Department of Computer Science and Information Engineering, National Taiwan University, 2007.

[78] R.A. Fisher. The use of multiple measurements in taxonomic problems. *Annals of Eugenics*, 7:179–188, 1936.

[79] I.E. Frank and J.H. Friedman. A statistical view of some chemometrics regression tools. *Technometrics*, 35(2):109–135, 1993.

[80] Y. Freund and R.E. Schapire. A decision-theoretic generalization of on-line learning and an application to boosting. *Journal of Computer and System Sciences*, 55(1):119–139, 1997.

[81] J. Friedman, T. Hastie, H. Höfling, and R. Tibshirani. Pathwise coordinate optimization. *The Annals of Applied Statistics*, 1(2):302–332, 2007.

[82] K. Fukunaga. *Introduction to Statistical Pattern Recognition*. Academic Press, New York, 1990.

[83] G.M. Fung and O.L. Mangasarian. Multicategory proximal support vector machine classifiers. *Machine Learning*, 59(1-2):77–97, 2005.

[84] J. Fürnkranz, E. Hüllermeier, E. Loza Mencía, and K. Brinker. Multilabel classification via calibrated label ranking. *Machine Learning*, 73(2):133–153, 2008.

[85] G. Fyfe and G. Leen. Two methods for sparsifying probabilistic canonical correlation analysis. In *Neural Information Processing*, pages 361–370, 2006.

[86] S. Gao, W. Wu, C.-H. Lee, and T.-S. Chua. A maximal figure-of-merit learning approach to text categorization. In *Proceedings of the 26th Annual International ACM SIGIR Conference on Research and Development in Information Retrieval (SIGIR)*, pages 174–181, 2003.

[87] S. Gao, W. Wu, C.-H. Lee, and T.-S. Chua. A MFoM learning approach to robust multiclass multi-label text categorization. In *Proceedings of the 21st International Conference on Machine Learning (ICML)*, pages 329–336, 2004.

[88] P. Geladi. Notes on the history and nature of partial least squares (PLS) modelling. *Journal of Chemometrics*, 2(4):231–246, 1988.

[89] C.R. Genovese, N.A. Lazar, and T. Nichols. Thresholding of statistical maps in functional neuroimaging using the false discovery rate. *NeuroImage*, 15(4):870–878, 2002.

[90] Z. Ghahramani, T.L. Griffiths, and P. Sollich. *Bayesian Nonparametric Latent Feature Models*, pages 201–225. Oxford University Press, Oxford, UK, 2007.

[91] N. Ghamrawi and A. McCallum. Collective multi-label classification. In *Proceedings of the 14th ACM International Conference on Information and Knowledge Management (CIKM)*, pages 195–200, 2005.

[92] A. Gifi. *Nonlinear Multivariate Analysis*. Wiley Series in Probability & Statistics. John Wiley & Sons, Inc., New York, 1990.

[93] S. Godbole and S. Sarawagi. Discriminative methods for multi-labeled classification. In H. Dai, R. Srikant, and C. Zhang, editors, *Advances in Knowledge Discovery and Data Mining*, volume 3056, pages 22–30. Springer, 2004.

[94] G.H. Golub and C.F. Van Loan. *Matrix Computations*. Johns Hopkins Press, Baltimore, MD, 3rd edition, 1996.

[95] T.R. Golub, D.K. Slonim, P. Tamayo, C. Huard, M. Gaasenbeek, J.P. Mesirov, H. Coller, M.L. Loh, J.R. Downing, M.A. Caligiuri, C.D. Bloomfield, and E.S. Lander. Molecular classification of cancer: Class discovery and class prediction by gene expression monitoring. *Science*, 286(5439):531–537, 1999.

[96] J. Gottfries, K. Blennow, A. Wallin, and C.G. Gottfries. Diagnosis of dementias using partial least squares discriminant analysis. *Dementia*, 6:83–88, 1995.

[97] K. Grauman and T. Darrell. The pyramid match kernel: Discriminative classification with sets of image features. In *Proceedings of the 10th IEEE International Conference on Computer Vision (ICCV)*, pages 1458–1465, 2005.

[98] K. Grauman and T. Darrell. Approximate correspondences in high dimensions. In *Advances in Neural Information Processing Systems 19 (NIPS)*, pages 505–512. 2007.

[99] K. Grauman and T. Darrell. The pyramid match kernel: Efficient learning with sets of features. *Journal of Machine Learning Research*, 8:725–760, 2007.

[100] A. Gretton, O. Bousquet, A.J. Smola, and B. Schölkopf. Measuring statistical dependence with Hilbert-Schmidt norms. In S. Jain, H. Simon, and E. Tomita, editors, *Algorithmic Learning Theory*, volume 3734, pages 63–77. Springer, 2005.

[101] G. Grumbling, V. Strelets, and The FlyBase Consortium. FlyBase: anatomical data, images and queries. *Nucleic Acids Research*, 34:D484–488, 2006.

[102] H. Gu, Z. Pan, B. Xi, V. Asiago, B. Musselman, and D. Raftery. Principal component directed partial least squares analysis for combining nuclear magnetic resonance and mass spectrometry data in metabolomics: Application to the detection of breast cancer. *Analytica Chimica Acta*, 686(1-2):57–63, 2011.

[103] R. Gurunathan, B. Van Emden, S. Panchanathan, and S. Kumar. Identifying spatially similar gene expression patterns in early stage fruit fly embryo images: binary feature versus invariant moment digital representations. *BMC Bioinformatics*, 5(202):13, 2004.

[104] E. Hale, W. Yin, and Y. Zhang. Fixed-point continuation for ℓ_1-minimization: Methodology and convergence. *SIAM Journal on Optimization*, 19(3):1107–1130, 2008.

[105] D.R. Hardoon and J. Shawe-Taylor. KCCA for different level precision in content-based image retrieval. In *Proceedings of the 3rd International Workshop on Content-Based Multimedia Indexing*, 2003.

[106] D.R. Hardoon and J. Shawe-Taylor. Sparse canonical correlation analysis. In *Sparsity and Inverse Problems in Statistical Theory and Econometrics Workshop*, 2008.

[107] D.R. Hardoon, S. Szedmak, and J. Shawe-taylor. Canonical correlation analysis: An overview with application to learning methods. *Neural Computation*, 16(12):2639–2664, 2004.

[108] C. Harmon, P. Ahammad, A. Hammonds, R. Weiszmann, S. Celniker, S. Sastry, and G. Rubin. Comparative analysis of spatial patterns of gene expression in *Drosophila melanogaster* imaginal discs. In *Proceedings of the 11th Annual International Conference on Research in Computational Molecular Biology (RECOMB)*, pages 533–547, 2007.

[109] T. Hastie, R. Tibshirani, and J. Friedman. *The Elements of Statistical Learning: Data Mining, Inference, and Prediction*. Springer, New York, 2nd edition, 2009.

[110] J. He, H. Gu, and Z. Wang. Bayesian multi-instance multi-label learning using Gaussian process prior. *Machine Learning*, pages 1–23, 2012.

[111] I. Helland. On the structure of partial least squares regression. *Communications in Statistics–Simulation and Computation*, 17(2):581–607, 1988.

[112] R. Hettich and K.O. Kortanek. Semi-infinite programming: Theory, methods, and applications. *SIAM Review*, 35(3):380–429, 1993.

[113] G.E. Hinton and R.R. Salakhutdinov. Reducing the dimensionality of data with neural networks. *Science*, 313(5786):504–507, 2006.

[114] A.E. Hoerl and R.W. Kennard. Ridge regression: Biased estimation for nonorthogonal problems. *Technometrics*, 12(1):55–67, 1970.

[115] R. Horn and C. Johnson. *Matrix Analysis*. Cambridge University Press, Cambridge, UK, 1985.

[116] A. Höskuldsson. PLS regression methods. *Journal of Chemometrics*, 2(3):211–228, 1988.

[117] H. Hotelling. Relations between two sets of variables. *Biometrika*, 28:312–377, 1936.

[118] D. Hsu, K. Sham, J. Langford, and T. Zhang. Multi-label prediction via compressed sensing. In *Advances in Neural Information Processing Systems 22 (NIPS)*, pages 772–780. 2009.

[119] S. Huang, M.O. Ward, and E.A. Rundensteiner. Exploration of dimensionality reduction for text visualization. In *Proceedings of the 3rd International Conference on Coordinated and Multiple Views in Exploratory Visualization (CMV)*, pages 63–74, 2005.

[120] X. Huang, W. Pan, S. Park, X. Han, L.W. Miller, and J. Hall. Modeling the relationship between LVAD support time and gene expression changes in the human heart by penalized partial least squares. *Bioinformatics*, 20(6):888–894, 2004.

[121] J.J. Hull. A database for handwritten text recognition research. *IEEE Transactions on Pattern Analysis and Machine Intelligence*, 16(5):550–554, 1994.

[122] E. Hüllermeier, J. Fürnkranz, W. Cheng, and K. Brinker. Label ranking by learning pairwise preferences. *Artificial Intelligence*, 172(16-17):1897–1916, 2008.

[123] T.R. Hvidsten, J. Komorowski, A.K. Sandvik, and A. Laegreid. Predicting gene function from gene expressions and ontologies. In R. Altman, K. Dunker, L. Hunter, K. Lauderdale, and Klein T., editors, *Pacific Symposium on Biocomputing*. World Scientific, 2001.

[124] K. Iizuka and T. Aishima. Soy sauce classification by geographic region based on NIR spectra and chemometrics pattern recognition. *Journal of Food Science*, 62(1):101–104, 1997.

[125] L. Jacob, F.R. Bach, and J.-P. Vert. Clustered multi-task learning: A convex formulation. In *Advances in Neural Information Processing Systems 21 (NIPS)*, pages 745–752. 2009.

[126] S. Ji, L. Sun, R. Jin, S. Kumar, and J. Ye. Automated annotation of *Drosophila* gene expression patterns using a controlled vocabulary. *Bioinformatics*, 24(17):1881–1888, 2008.

[127] S. Ji, L. Tang, S. Yu, and J. Ye. A shared-subspace learning framework for multi-label classification. *ACM Transactions on Knowledge Discovery from Data*, 4(2):1–29, 2010.

[128] B. Jin, B. Muller, C. Zhai, and X. Lu. Multi-label literature classification based on the gene ontology graph. *BMC Bioinformatics*, 9(1):525, 2008.

[129] T. Joachims. A support vector method for multivariate performance measures. In *Proceedings of the 22nd International Conference on Machine Learning (ICML)*, pages 377–384, 2005.

[130] T. Joachims. Training linear SVMs in linear time. In *Proceedings of the 12th ACM SIGKDD International Conference on Knowledge Discovery and Data Mining (KDD)*, pages 217–226, 2006.

[131] T. Joachims and F. Sebastiani. Guest editors' introduction to the special issue on automated text categorization. *Journal of Intelligent Information Systems*, 18(2-3):103–105, 2002.

[132] R.A. Johnson. *Applied Multivariate Statistical Analysis*. Prentice Hall, Upper Saddle River, NJ, 4th edition, 1998.

[133] I.T. Jolliffe. *Principal Component Analysis*. Springer, New York, 2nd edition, 2002.

[134] F. Kang, R. Jin, and R. Sukthankar. Correlated label propagation with application to multi-label learning. In *Proceedings of the 2006 IEEE Computer Society Conference on Computer Vision and Pattern Recognition (CVPR)*, volume 2, pages 1719–1726, 2006.

[135] S. Kaski and J. Peltonen. Dimensionality reduction for data visualization. *IEEE Signal Processing Magazine*, 28(2):100–104, 2011.

[136] H. Kazawa, T. Izumitani, H. Taira, and E. Maeda. Maximal margin labeling for multi-topic text categorization. In *Advances in Neural Information Processing Systems 17 (NIPS)*, pages 649–656. 2004.

[137] J.R. Kettenring. Canonical analysis of several sets of variables. *Biometrika*, 58(3):433–451, 1971.

[138] S. Kim, K.-A. Sohn, and E.P. Xing. A multivariate regression approach to association analysis of a quantitative trait network. *Bioinformatics*, 25:i204–i212, 2009.

[139] P. Koehn. Europarl: A parallel corpus for statistical machine translation. In *Conference Proceedings: the Tenth Machine Translation Summit*, pages 79–86. AAMT, 2005.

[140] D. Koller and M. Sahami. Hierarchically classifying documents using very few words. In *Proceedings of the 14th International Conference on Machine Learning (ICML)*, pages 170–178, 1997.

[141] R.I. Kondor and J. Lafferty. Diffusion kernels on graphs and other discrete structures. In *Proceedings of the 19th International Conference on Machine Learning (ICML)*, pages 315–322, 2002.

[142] N. Krämer. An overview on the shrinkage properties of partial least squares regression. *Computational Statistics*, 22(2):249–273, 2007.

[143] N. Krämer, M. Sugiyama, and M. Braun. Lanczos approximations for the speedup of kernel partial least squares regression. In *Proceedings of the 12th International Conference on Artificial Intelligence and Statistics (AISTATS)*, volume 5, pages 288–295, 2009.

[144] S. Kumar, K. Jayaraman, S. Panchanathan, R. Gurunathan, A. Marti-Subirana, and S.J. Newfeld. BEST: A novel computational approach for comparing gene expression patterns from early stages of *Drosophlia melanogaster* develeopment. *Genetics*, 169:2037–2047, 2002.

[145] G.R.G. Lanckriet, N. Cristianini, P. Bartlett, L.E. Ghaoui, and M. Jordan. Learning the kernel matrix with semidefinite programming. *Journal of Machine Learning Research*, 5:27–72, 2004.

[146] G.R.G. Lanckriet, T. De Bie, N. Cristianini, M. Jordan, and W.S. Noble. A statistical framework for genomic data fusion. *Bioinformatics*, 20(16):2626–2635, 2004.

[147] K. Lang. Newsweeder: Learning to filter netnews. In *Proceedings of the 12th International Conference on Machine Learning (ICML)*, pages 331–339, 1995.

[148] S. Lazebnik, C. Schmid, and J. Ponce. Beyond bags of features: Spatial pyramid matching for recognizing natural scene categories. In *Proceedings of the 2006 IEEE Computer Society Conference on Computer Vision and Pattern Recognition (CVPR)*, pages 2169–2178, 2006.

[149] K. Le Cao, P. Martin, C. Robert-Granie, and P. Besse. Sparse canonical methods for biological data integration: application to a cross-platform study. *BMC Bioinformatics*, 10(1):34, 2009.

[150] E.G. Learned-Miller and J.W. Fisher III. ICA using spacings estimates of entropy. *Journal of Machine Learning Research*, 4:1271–1295, 2003.

[151] E. Lécuyer, H. Yoshida, N. Parthasarathy, C. Alm, T. Babak, T. Cerovina, T.R. Hughes, P. Tomancak, and H.M. Krause. Global analysis of mRNA localization reveals a prominent role in organizing cellular architecture and function. *Cell*, 131:174–187, 2007.

[152] D.D. Lee and H.S. Seung. Learning the parts of objects by non-negative matrix factorization. *Nature*, 401(6755):788–791, 1999.

[153] J.A. Lee and M. Verleysen. *Nonlinear Dimensionality Reduction*. Springer, New York, 2007.

[154] E.S. Lein, M.J. Hawrylycz, N. Ao, M. Ayres, and A. Bensinger et al. Genome-wide atlas of gene expression in the adult mouse brain. *Nature*, 445:168–176, 2006.

[155] D. Lewis, Y. Yang, T. Rose, and F. Li. RCV1: A new benchmark collection for text categorization research. *Journal of Machine Learning Research*, 5:361–397, 2004.

[156] F.-F. Li and P. Perona. A Bayesian hierarchical model for learning natural scene categories. In *Proceedings of the 2005 IEEE Computer Society Conference on Computer Vision and Pattern Recognition (CVPR)*, pages 524–531, 2005.

[157] Y. Li and J. Shawe-Taylor. Using KCCA for Japanese–English cross-language information retrieval and document classification. *Journal of Intelligent Information Systems*, 27(2):117–133, 2006.

[158] O.C. Lingjaerde. Shrinkage structure of partial least squares. *Scandinavian Journal of Statistics*, 27(3):459–473, 2000.

[159] C. Lippert, Z. Ghahramani, and K.M. Borgwardt. Gene function prediction from synthetic lethality networks via ranking on demand. *Bioinformatics*, 26(7):912–918, 2010.

[160] J. Liu, S. Ji, and J. Ye. *SLEP: Sparse Learning with Efficient Projections*. Arizona State University, Tempe, AZ, 2009.

[161] Y. Liu. Yeast gene function prediction from different data sources: An empirical comparison. *The Open Bioinformatics Journal*, (5):69–76, 2011.

[162] Y. Liu and W. Rayens. PLS and dimension reduction for classification. *Computational Statistics*, 22(2):189–208, 2007.

[163] E. Loza Mencía and J. Fürnkranz. Pairwise learning of multilabel classifications with perceptrons. In *Proceedings of the 2008 IEEE International Joint Conference on Neural Networks (IJCNN)*, pages 2900–2907, 2008.

[164] C.D. Manning, P. Raghavan, and H. Schze. *Introduction to Information Retrieval*. Cambridge University Press, Cambridge, UK, 2008.

[165] O. Maron and A.L. Ratan. Multiple-instance learning for natural scene classification. In *Proceedings of the 15th International Conference on Machine Learning (ICML)*, pages 341–349, 1998.

[166] M.J. Marton, J.L. DeRisi, H.A. Bennett, V.R. Iyer, M.R. Meyer, C.J. Roberts, R. Stoughton, J. Burchard, D. Slade, H. Dai, D.E. Bassett Jr, L.H. Hartwell, P.O. Brown, and S.H. Friend. Drug target validation and identification of secondary drug target effects using DNA microarrays. *Nature Medicine*, 11(4):1293–1301, 1998.

[167] A.K. McCallum. Multi-label text classification with a mixture model trained by EM. In *AAAI 99 Workshop on Text Learning*, 1999.

[168] K. Mikolajczyk and C. Schmid. A performance evaluation of local descriptors. *IEEE Transactions on Pattern Analysis and Machine Intelligence*, 27(10):1615–1630, 2005.

[169] K. Mikolajczyk, T. Tuytelaars, C. Schmid, A. Zisserman, J. Matas, F. Schaffalitzky, T. Kadir, and L. Van Gool. A comparison of affine region detectors. *International Journal of Computer Vision*, 65(1-2):43–72, 2005.

[170] M. Momma and K.P. Bennett. Sparse kernel partial least squares regression. In *Proceedings of the 16th Annual Conference on Computational Learning Theory (COLT)*, pages 216–230, 2003.

[171] Da.W. Mount. *Bioinformatics: Sequence and Genome Analysis*. Cold Spring Harbor Laboratory Press, Cold Spring Harbor, NY, 2nd edition, 2004.

[172] A. Nemirovski. Efficient methods in convex programming, 1994. Lecture Notes.

[173] A. Nemirovski. Prox-method with rate of convergence $o(1/t)$ for variational inequalities with Lipschitz continuous monotone operators and smooth convex-concave saddle point problems. *SIAM Journal on Optimization*, 15(1):229–251, 2005.

[174] A. Ng, M. Jordan, and Y. Weiss. On spectral clustering: Analysis and an algorithm. In *Advances in Neural Information Processing Systems 14 (NIPS)*, pages 849–856, 2001.

[175] D.V. Nguyen and D.M. Rocke. Tumor classification by partial least squares using microarray gene expression data. *Bioinformatics*, 18(1):39–50, 2002.

[176] M.C. Ortiz, L.A. Sarabia, C. Symington, F. Santamaria, and M. Inigueze. Analysis of ageing and typification of vintage ports by partial least squares and soft independent modelling class analogy. *Analyst*, 121(8):1009–1013, 1996.

[177] M.L. Overton. Optimality conditions and duality theory for minimizing sums of the largest eigenvalues of symmetric matrices. *Mathematical Programming*, 62(1):321–357, 1993.

[178] C.C. Paige and M.A. Saunders. LSQR: An algorithm for sparse linear equations and sparse least squares. *ACM Transactions on Mathematical Software*, 8(1):43–71, 1982.

[179] C.H. Park and M. Lee. On applying linear discriminant analysis for multi-labeled problems. *Pattern Recognition Letters*, 29:878–887, 2008.

[180] H. Park, M. Jeon, and J.B. Rosen. Lower dimensional representation of text data based on centroids and least squares. *BIT Numerical Mathematics*, 43(2):427–448, 2003.

[181] E. Parkhomenko, D. Tritchler, and J. Beyene. Sparse canonical correlation analysis with application to genomic data integration. *Statistical Applications in Genetics and Molecular Biology*, 8(1):1, 2009.

[182] B.N. Parlett. *The Symmetric Eigenvalue Problem*. SIAM, Philadelphia, 1998.

[183] H. Peng and E.W. Myers. Comparing *in situ* mRNA expression patterns of *Drosophila* embryos. In *Proceedings of the 8th Annual International Conference on Research in Computational Molecular Biology (RECOMB)*, pages 157–166, 2004.

[184] A. Phatak and F. de Hoog. Exploiting the connection between PLS, Lanczos methods and conjugate gradients: alternative proofs of some properties of PLS. *Journal of Chemometrics*, 16(7):361–367, 2002.

[185] V. Pihur, S. Datta, and S. Datta. Reconstruction of genetic association networks from microarray data: a partial least squares approach. *Bioinformatics*, 24(4):561–568, 2008.

[186] M. Pintore, H. van de Waterbeemd, N. Piclin, and J.R. Chrétien. Prediction of oral bioavailability by adaptive fuzzy partitioning. *European Journal of Medicinal Chemistry*, 38(4):427–431, 2003.

[187] R. Pless. Image spaces and video trajectories: using Isomap to explore video sequences. In *Proceedings of the 9th IEEE International Conference on Computer Vision (ICCV)*, pages 1433–1440, 2003.

[188] P. Rai and H. Daume. Multi-label prediction via sparse infinite CCA. In *Advances in Neural Information Processing Systems 22 (NIPS)*, pages 1518–1526. 2009.

[189] S. Rännar, F. Lindgren, P. Geladi, and S. Wold. A PLS kernel algorithm for data sets with many variables and fewer objects. Part 1: Theory and algorithm. *Journal of Chemometrics*, 8(2):111–125, 1994.

[190] J. Read. *Scalable Multi-label Classification*. PhD thesis, University of Waikato, Hamilton, New Zealand, 2010.

[191] J. Read, B. Pfahringer, G. Holmes, and E. Frank. Classifier chains for multi-label classification. In W. Buntine, M. Grobelnik, D. Mladenic, and J. Shawe-Taylor, editors, *Machine Learning and Knowledge Discovery in Databases*, volume 5782, pages 254–269. Springer, 2009.

[192] R. Rifkin and A. Klautau. In defense of one-vs-all classification. *Journal of Machine Learning Research*, 5:101–141, 2004.

[193] J.A. Rodriguez. On the Laplacian eigenvalues and metric parameters of hypergraphs. *Linear and Multilinear Algebra*, 50(1):1–14, 2002.

[194] J.A. Rodriguez. On the Laplacian spectrum and walk-regular hypergraphs. *Linear and Multilinear Algebra*, 51(3):285–297, 2003.

[195] S. Rosenberg. *The Laplacian on a Riemannian Manifold: An Introduction to Analysis on Manifolds*. Cambridge University Press, Cambridge, UK, 1997.

[196] R. Rosipal and N. Krämer. Overview and recent advances in partial least squares. In C. Saunders, M. Grobelnik, S. Gunn, and J. Shawe-Taylor, editors, *Subspace, Latent Structure and Feature Selection*, volume 3940, pages 34–51. Springer, 2006.

[197] R. Rosipal and L.J. Trejo. Kernel partial least squares regression in reproducing kernel Hilbert space. *Journal of Machine Learning Research*, 2:97–123, 2002.

[198] R. Rosipal, L.J. Trejo, and B. Matthews. Kernel PLS-SVC for linear and nonlinear classification. In *Proceedings of the 20th International Conference on Machine Learning (ICML)*, pages 640–647, 2003.

[199] S.T. Roweis and S. Lawrence. Nonlinear dimensionality reduction by locally linear embedding. *Science*, 290(5500):2323–2326, 2000.

[200] D.E. Rumelhart, G.E. Hinton, and R.J. Williams. Learning internal representations by error propagation. In *Symposium on Parallel and Distributed Processing*, pages 318–362, 1986.

[201] Y. Saad. *Numerical Methods for Large Eigenvalue Problems*. Halsted Press, New York, 1992.

[202] H. Saigo, N. Krämer, and K. Tsuda. Partial least squares regression for graph mining. In *Proceedings of the 14th ACM SIGKDD International Conference on Knowledge Discovery and Data Mining (KDD)*, pages 578–586, 2008.

[203] P.D. Sampson, A.P. Streissguth, H.M. Barr, and F.L. Bookstein. Neurobehavioral effects of prenatal alcohol: Part II. Partial least squares analysis. *Neurotoxicology and Teratology*, 11(5):477–491, 1989.

[204] A.A. Samsonova, M. Niranjan, S. Russell, and A. Brazma. Prediction of gene expression in embryonic structures of *Drosophila melanogaster*. *PLoS Computational Biology*, 3(7):1360–1372, 2007.

[205] L.K. Saul, K.Q. Weinberger, J.H. Ham, F. Sha, and D.D. Lee. *Semi-Supervised Learning*, chapter Spectral methods for dimensionality reduction, pages 293–308. MIT Press, Cambridage, MA, 2006.

[206] R.E. Schapire and Y. Singer. Boostexter: A boosting-based system for text categorization. *Machine Learning*, 39:135–168, 2000.

[207] B. Schölkopf and A. J. Smola. *Learning with Kernels: Support Vector Machines, Regularization, Optimization, and Beyond*. MIT Press, Cambridge, MA, 2002.

[208] F. Sebastiani. Machine learning in automated text categorization. *ACM Computing Surveys*, 34:1–47, 2002.

[209] A. Shashua and A. Levin. Linear image coding for regression and classification using the tensor-rank principle. In *Proceedings of the 2001 IEEE Computer Society Conference on Computer Vision and Pattern Recognition (CVPR)*, pages 42–49, 2001.

[210] J. Shawe-Taylor and N. Cristianini. *Kernel Methods for Pattern Analysis*. Cambridge University Press, Cambridge, UK, 2004.

[211] J. Shi and J. Malik. Normalized cuts and image segmentation. *IEEE Transactions on Pattern Analysis and Machine Intelligence*, 22(8):888–905, 2000.

[212] C. Sigg, B. Fischer, B. Ommer, V. Roth, and J.M. Buhmann. Nonnegative CCA for audiovisual source separation. In *IEEE Workshop on Machine Learning for Signal Processing*, pages 253–258, 2007.

[213] C. Silla and A. Freitas. A survey of hierarchical classification across different application domains. *Data Mining and Knowledge Discovery*, 22:31–72, 2011.

[214] E. Sksjvi, M. Khalighi, and P. Minkkinen. Waste water pollution modelling in the southern area of Lake Saimaa, Finland, by the simca pattern recognition method. *Chemometrics and Intelligent Laboratory Systems*, 7(1-2):171–180, 1989.

[215] S. Sra and I.S. Dhillon. Nonnegative matrix approximation: Algorithms and applications. Technical report, Computer Sciences, University of Texas at Austin, 2006.

[216] B. Stenger, A. Thayananthan, P.H.S. Torr, and R. Cipolla. Estimating 3D hand pose using hierarchical multi-label classification. *Image Vision Computing*, 25:1885–1894, 2007.

[217] J. Sun, S. Boyd, L. Xiao, and P. Diaconis. The fastest mixing Markov process on a graph and a connection to a maximum variance unfolding problem. *SIAM Review*, 48(4):681–699, 2006.

[218] L. Sun, B. Ceran, and J. Ye. A scalable two-stage approach for a class of dimensionality reduction techniques. In *Proceedings of the 16th ACM SIGKDD International Conference on Knowledge Discovery and Data Mining (KDD)*, pages 313–322, 2010.

[219] L. Sun, S. Ji, and J. Ye. Hypergraph spectral learning for multi-label classification. In *Proceedings of the 14th ACM SIGKDD International Conference on Knowledge Discovery and Data Mining (KDD)*, pages 668–676, 2008.

[220] L. Sun, S. Ji, and J. Ye. A least squares formulation for canonical correlation analysis. In *Proceedings of the 25th International Conference on Machine Learning (ICML)*, pages 1024–1031, 2008.

[221] L. Sun, S. Ji, and J. Ye. A least squares formulation for a class of generalized eigenvalue problems in machine learning. In *Proceedings of the 26th International Conference on Machine Learning (ICML)*, pages 977–984, 2009.

[222] L. Sun, S. Ji, and J. Ye. Canonical correlation analysis for multilabel classification: A least-squares formulation, extensions, and analysis. *IEEE Transactions on Pattern Analysis and Machine Intelligence*, 33(1):194–200, 2011.

[223] L. Sun, S. Ji, S. Yu, and J. Ye. On the equivalence between canonical correlation analysis and orthonormalized partial least squares. In *Proceedings of the 21st International Joint Conference on Artifical Intelligence (IJCAI)*, 2009.

[224] Y.-Y. Sun, Y. Zhang, and Z.-Z. Zhou. Multi-label learning with weak label. In *Proceedings of the 24th AAAI Conference on Artificial Intelligence (AAAI)*, pages 593–598, 2010.

[225] E. Sundbom, O. Bodlund, and T. Hjerback. Object relation and defensive operations in transsexuals and borderline patients as measured by the defense mechanism test. *Nordic Journal of Psychiatry*, 49(5):379–388, 1995.

[226] F. Tai and H.-T. Lin. Multi-label classification with principle label space transformation. In *Proceedings of the 2nd International Workshop on Learning from Multi-Label Data*, pages 45–52, 2010.

[227] L. Tenenboim-Chekina, L. Rokach, and B. Shapira. Identification of label dependencies for multi-label classification. In *Proceedings of the 2nd International Workshop on Learning from Multi-Label Data*, pages 53–60, 2010.

[228] A. Tenenhaus, A. Giron, E. Viennet, M. Bera, G. Saporta, and B. Fertil. Kernel logistic PLS: A tool for supervised nonlinear dimensionality reduction and binary classification. *Computational Statistics & Data Analysis*, 51(9):4083–4100, 2007.

[229] C.J.F. Ter Braak and S. De Jong. The objective function of partial least squares regression. *Journal of Chemometrics*, 12(1):41–54, 1998.

[230] R. Tibshirani. Regression shrinkage and selection via the lasso. *Journal of the Royal Statistical Society: Series B*, 58(1):267–288, 1996.

[231] P. Tomancak, A. Beaton, R. Weiszmann, E. Kwan, S. Shu, S. Lewis, S. Richards, M. Ashburner, V. Hartenstein, S. Celniker, and G. Rubin. Systematic determination of patterns of gene expression during *Drosophila* embryogenesis. *Genome Biology*, 3(12):research0088.1–0088.14, 2002.

[232] P. Tomancak, B. Berman, A. Beaton, R. Weiszmann, E. Kwan, V. Hartenstein, S. Celniker, and G. Rubin. Global analysis of patterns of gene expression during *Drosophila* embryogenesis. *Genome Biology*, 8(7):R145, 2007.

[233] A.B. Torralba and A. Oliva. Semantic organization of scenes using discriminant structural templates. In *Proceedings of the 7th IEEE International Conference on Computer Vision (ICCV)*, pages 1253–1258, 1999.

[234] K. Trohidis, G. Tsoumakas, G. Kalliris, and I. Vlahavas. Multilabel classification of music into emotions. In *Proceedings of the 9th International Conference on Music Information Retrieval (ISMIR)*, pages 325–330, 2008.

[235] G. Tsoumakas and I. Katakis. Multi label classification: An overview. *International Journal of Data Warehousing and Mining*, 3(3):1–13, 2007.

[236] G. Tsoumakas, I. Katakis, and I. Vlahavas. Effective and efficient multilabel classification in domains with large number of labels. In *Proceedings of ECML/PKDD 2008 Workshop on Mining Multidimensional Data (MMD)*, 2008.

[237] G. Tsoumakas, I. Katakis, and I. Vlahavas. *Data Mining and Knowledge Discovery Handbook*, chapter Mining Multi-label Data, pages 667–686. Springer, New York, 2nd edition, 2010.

[238] G. Tsoumakas and I. Vlahavas. Random k-labelsets: An ensemble method for multilabel classification. In *Machine Learning: ECML 2007*, volume 4701, pages 406–417, 2007.

[239] N. Ueda and K. Saito. Single-shot detection of multiple categories of text using parametric mixture models. In *Proceedings of the 8th ACM SIGKDD International Conference on Knowledge Discovery and Data Mining (KDD)*, pages 626–631, 2002.

[240] N. Ueda and K. Saito. Parametric mixture models for multi-labeled text. In *Advances in Neural Information Processing Systems 16 (NIPS)*, pages 721–728. 2003.

[241] L.J.P. van der Maaten, E.O. Postma, and H.J. van den Herik. Dimensionality reduction: A comparative review. Technical report, Maastricht University, 2007.

[242] B. van Emden, H. Ramos, S. Panchanathan, S. Newfeld, and S. Kumar. Fly-Express: An image-matching web-tool for finding genes with overlapping patterns of expression in *Drosophila* embryos. Technical report, Arizona State University, Tempe, AZ, 2006.

[243] M. Varma and A. Zisserman. Texture classification: Are filter banks necessary? In *Proceedings of the 2003 IEEE Computer Society Conference on Computer Vision and Pattern Recognition (CVPR)*, pages 691–698, 2003.

[244] M.A.O. Vasilescu and D. Terzopoulos. Multilinear subspace analysis of image ensembles. In *Proceedings of the 2003 IEEE Computer Society Conference on Computer Vision and Pattern Recognition (CVPR)*, volume 2, pages 93–99, 2003.

[245] J. Venna and S. Kaski. Comparison of visualization methods for an atlas of gene expression data sets. *Information Visualization*, 6:139–154, 2007.

[246] J. Venna, J. Peltonen, K. Nybo, H. Aidos, and S. Kaski. Information retrieval perspective to nonlinear dimensionality reduction for data visualization. *Journal of Machine Learning Research*, 11:451–490, 2010.

[247] J.-P. Vert and M. Kanehisa. Graph-driven feature extraction from microarray data using diffusion kernels and kernel CCA. In *Advances in Neural Information Processing Systems 15 (NIPS)*, pages 1425–1432, 2003.

[248] H.D. Vinod. Canonical ridge and econometrics of joint production. *Journal of Econometrics*, 4(2):147–166, 1976.

[249] S. Vogrincic and Z. Bosnic. Ontology-based multi-label classification of economic articles. *Computer Science and Information Systems*, 8(1):101–119, 2011.

[250] R. Vong, P. Geladi, S. Wold, and K. Esbensen. Source contributions to ambient aerosol calculated by discriminant partial least squares regression (PLS). *Journal of Chemometrics*, 2(4):281–296, 1988.

[251] S. Waaijenborg, P.C. Verselewel, and A.H. Zwinderman. Quantifying the association between gene expressions and DNA-markers by penalized canonical correlation analysis. *Statistical Applications in Genetics and Molecular Biology*, 7(1), 2008.

[252] S. Waaijenborg and A. Zwinderman. Penalized canonical correlation analysis to quantify the association between gene expression and DNA markers. *BMC Proceedings*, 1(Suppl 1):S122, 2007.

[253] H. Wang, C. Ding, and H. Huang. Multi-label classification: Inconsistency and class balanced k-nearest neighbor. In *Proceedings of the 24th AAAI Conference on Artificial Intelligence (AAAI)*, 2010.

[254] D.S. Watkins. *Fundamentals of Matrix Computations*. John Wiley & Sons, Inc., New York, 1991.

[255] J.A. Wegelin. A survey of partial least squares (PLS) methods, with emphasis on the two-block case. Technical report, University of Washington, 2000.

[256] K.Q. Weinberger and L.K. Saul. Unsupervised learning of image manifolds by semidefinite programming. In *Proceedings of the 2004 IEEE Computer Society Conference on Computer Vision and Pattern Recognition (CVPR)*, volume 2, pages 988–995, 2004.

[257] S.M. Weiss, N. Indurkhya, and T. Zhang. *Text Mining: Predictive Methods for Analyzing Unstructured Information*. Springer, Berlin, 2004.

[258] A. Wiesel, M. Kliger, and A. Hero. A greedy approach to sparse canonical correlation analysis. *arXiv:0801.2748*, 2008.

[259] D.M. Witten, R. Tibshirani, and T. Hastie. A penalized matrix decomposition, with applications to sparse principal components and canonical correlation analysis. *Biostatistics*, 10(3):515–534, 2009.

[260] D.M. Witten and R.J. Tibshirani. Extensions of sparse canonical correlation analysis with applications to genomic data. *Statistical Applications in Genetics and Molecular Biology*, 8(1):28, 2009.

[261] H. Wold. Estimation of principal components and related models by iterative least squares. In P.R. Krishnaiaah, editor, *Multivariate Analysis*, pages 391–420. Academic Press, New York, 1966.

[262] H. Wold. Path models with latent variables: The NIPALS approach. In Blalock et al., editor, *Quantitative Sociology: International Perspectives on Mathematical and Statistical Model Building*, pages 307–357. Academic Press, New York, 1975.

[263] H. Wold. *Encyclopedia of Statistical Sciences*, volume 6, chapter Partial least squares, pages 581–591. John Wiley & Sons, Inc., New York, 1985.

[264] S. Wold. *Chemometrics, Mathematics and Statistics in Chemistry*. Reidel Publishing Company, Dordrecht, Holland, 1984.

[265] K. Worsley, J.-B. Poline, K. J. Friston, and A.C. Evans. Characterizing the response of PET and fMRI data using multivariate linear models. *Neuroimage*, 6(4):305–319, 1997.

[266] M. Wu, B. Schölkopf, and G. Bakir. A direct method for building sparse kernel learning algorithms. *Journal of Machine Learning Research*, 7:603–624, 2006.

[267] Y. Xue, X. Liao, L. Carin, and B. Krishnapuram. Multi-task learning for classification with Dirichlet process priors. *Journal of Machine Learning Research*, 8:35–63, 2007.

[268] R. Yan, J. Tesic, and J.R. Smith. Model-shared subspace boosting for multi-label classification. In *Proceedings of the 13th ACM SIGKDD International Conference on Knowledge Discovery and Data Mining (KDD)*, pages 834–843, 2007.

[269] Y. Yang and J.O. Pedersen. A comparative study on feature selection in text categorization. In *Proceedings of the 14th International Conference on Machine Learning (ICML)*, pages 412–420, 1997.

[270] J. Ye. Characterization of a family of algorithms for generalized discriminant analysis on undersampled problems. *Journal of Machine Learning Research*, 6:483–502, 2005.

[271] J. Ye. Least squares linear discriminant analysis. In *Proceedings of the 24th International Conference on Machine Learning (ICML)*, pages 1087–1094, 2007.

[272] J. Ye, J. Chen, Q. Li, and S. Kumar. Classification of *Drosophila* embryonic developmental stage range based on gene expression pattern images. In *Proceedings of the 4th Annual International Conference on Computational Systems Bioinformatics (CSB)*, pages 293–298, 2006.

[273] K. Yu, S. Yu, and V. Tresp. Multi-label informed latent semantic indexing. In *Proceedings of the 28th International ACM SIGIR Conference on Research and Development in Information Retrieval (SIGIR)*, pages 258–265, 2005.

[274] D. Zhang, A.F. Frangi, and J. Yang. Two-dimensional PCA: A new approach to appearance-based face representation and recognition. *IEEE Transactions on Pattern Analysis and Machine Intelligence*, 26(1):131–137, 2004.

[275] J. Zhang, M. Marszalek, S. Lazebnik, and C. Schmid. Local features and kernels for classification of texture and object categories: A comprehensive study. *International Journal of Computer Vision*, 73(2):213–238, 2007.

[276] M. Zhang and Z. Zhou. ML-KNN: A lazy learning approach to multi-label learning. *Pattern Recognition*, 40(7):2038–2048, 2007.

[277] M.-L. Zhang and Z.-J. Wang. MIMLRBF: RBF neural networks for multi-instance multi-label learning. *Neurocomputing*, 72(16-18):3951–3956, 2009.

[278] M.-L. Zhang and K. Zhang. Multi-label learning by exploiting label dependency. In *Proceedings of the 16th ACM SIGKDD International Conference on Knowledge Discovery and Data Mining (KDD)*, pages 999–1008, 2010.

[279] M.-L. Zhang and Z.-Z. Zhou. Multilabel neural networks with applications to functional genomics and text categorization. *IEEE Transactions on Knowledge and Data Engineering*, 18(10):1338–1351, 2006.

[280] Y. Zhang and Z. Zhou. Multi-label dimensionality reduction via dependence maximization. *ACM Transactions on Knowledge Discovery from Data*, 4(3):1–21, 2010.

[281] Z. Zhang and H. Zha. Principal manifolds and nonlinear dimensionality reduction via tangent space alignment. *SIAM Journal on Scientific Computing*, 26:313–338, 2005.

[282] D. Zhou, J. Huang, and B. Schölkopf. Beyond pairwise classification and clustering using hypergraphs. Technical Report 143, Max Plank Institute for Biological Cybernetics, Tubingen, Germany, 2005.

[283] D. Zhou, J. Huang, and B. Schölkopf. Learning with hypergraphs: Clustering, classification, and embedding. In *Advances in Neural Information Processing Systems 19 (NIPS)*, pages 1601–1608, 2007.

[284] J. Zhou and H. Peng. Automatic recognition and annotation of gene expression patterns of fly embryos. *Bioinformatics*, 23(5):589–596, 2007.

[285] Z.-H. Zhou and M.-L. Zhang. Multi-instance multi-label learning with application to scene classification. In *Advances in Neural Information Processing Systems 20 (NIPS)*, pages 1609–1616. 2007.

[286] A. Zien and C.S. Ong. Multiclass multiple kernel learning. In *Proceedings of the 24th International Conference on Machine Learning (ICML)*, pages 1191–1198, 2007.

[287] J.Y. Zien, M.D.F. Schlag, and P.K. Chan. Multilevel spectral hypergraph partitioning with arbitrary vertex sizes. *IEEE Transactions on Computer-Aided Design of Integrated Circuits and Systems*, 18(9):1389–1399, 1999.

[288] H. Zou and T. Hastie. Regularization and variable selection via the elastic net. *Journal of the Royal Statistical Society: Series B*, 67(2):301–320, 2005.

[289] H. Zou, T. Hastie, and R. Tibshirani. Sparse principal component analysis. *Journal of Computational and Graphical Statistics*, 15(2):265–286, 2006.

Index